Khrushchev
and the First Russian Spring

KHRUSHCHEV
and the First Russian Spring

The Era of Khrushchev Through the Eyes
of His Advisor

Fedor Burlatsky

Translated from the Russian
by Daphne Skillen

A ROBERT STEWART BOOK

CHARLES SCRIBNER'S SONS
New York

MAXWELL MACMILLAN INTERNATIONAL
New York Oxford Singapore Sydney

Charles Scribner's Sons
Macmillan Publishing Company
866 Third Avenue
New York, NY 10022

Macmillan Publishing Company is part of the Maxwell Communication
Group of Companies.

Library of Congress Cataloging-in-Publication Data

Burlachuk, Foka Fedorovich.
    Khrushchev and the first Russian spring: the era of Khrushchev
through the eyes of his advisor/Fedor Burlatsky; translated from the
Russian by Daphne Skillen.
      p. cm.
    "A Robert Stewart book."
    Includes bibliographical references and index.
    ISBN 0-684-19419-8
    1. Soviet Union—Politics and government—1953–1985.
2. Khrushchev, Nikita Sergeevich, 1894–1971. 3. Heads of state—
Soviet Union—Biography. 4. Communists—Soviet Union—
Biography. 5. Burlachuk, Foka Fedorovich. I. Title.
DK274.B86   1992   91–37776   CIP
947.085′2′092—dc20

Macmillan Books are available at special discounts for bulk purchases for
sales promotions, premiums, fund-raising, or educational use. For details,
contact:

Special Sales Director
Macmillan Publishing Company
866 Third Avenue
New York, NY 10022

10 9 8 7 6 5 4 3 2 1

Printed in the United States of America

Contents

Boris, Boris! All tremble before you,
None dares even remind you
Of the fate of that unfortunate child;
Meanwhile, here in a dark cell a hermit
Writes the terrible testimony against you:
You will not escape the judgement of this world,
As you will not escape God's judgement.

Pushkin, Boris Godunov

Translator's Note

The transliteration system of the *Slavonic and East European Review* is followed, except in certain cases where the form more familiar to the Western reader is used, such as 'Khrushchev', 'Gorbachev'. The author prefers his name to be translated as Fedor Burlatsky.

Khrushchev
and the First Russian Spring

Introduction

The purpose of this book is to reconstruct an image of Khrushchev; one that will reveal political and more importantly psychological aspects of the man and his world, which I observed over the course of many years.

As a speech-writer and frequently an adviser to Khrushchev and Andropov, as well as to Brezhnev, Kosygin and other Soviet leaders, I have had the opportunity of witnessing political life from the inside. Therefore I am concerned less with actual events, which have been described often enough, but rather with the political manners and mores of people who were carried to the heights of Mount Olympus by either chance or cunning, by fair means or foul.

For almost five years, from 1960 to 1965, I was close to Khrushchev. I listened to his speeches, I watched him perform, I heard his private conversations with Soviet and foreign political leaders. I accompanied him abroad six times.

If I were to seek a parallel I would say that my work most of all resembled what Ted Sorensen did for John Kennedy. Ted and I met many times at conferences on the Cuban Missile Crisis and it came as a pleasant surprise to me to learn that on different sides of the ocean we were doing roughly the same sort of work and, strange as it may seem, experiencing very similar feelings. We were both, perhaps, among the most liberal advisers to these two major leaders, who found the wisdom and courage to prevent a slide into nuclear war.

Khrushchev is interesting in his own right. It is impressive that this man, the son of a simple peasant, who had worked as a miner and metalworker and had only a minimal education – up to the very end he had not learned to write without mistakes – was carried to the pinnacle of power. Stalin showed a liking for him, yet with the audacity of a great leader he smashed Stalin's cult. Later, when he had attained power, he held in his hands the fate of all humanity during the Cuban Missile Crisis.

In the eyes of our forebears only God had the right to announce the Day of Judgement and the Apocalypse. But history is a great joker: it entrusted that power to a simple peasant from the village of Kalinovka in Kursk region, a son of poor unfortunate Russia, forgotten by God and tormented by the Mongolian yoke, the cruel tsars and, in our own times, by Stalinism.

It is difficult for the Western reader to comprehend what the name and the era of Khrushchev meant for our generation of Russians and Soviets, people who in their youth had endured the horrors of the Second World War and the even more frightening Stalinist terror. Imagine for a moment many thousands and millions of people on their knees or sprawled on the ground in front of an idol. Suddenly someone appears and says: 'Look, this is only a copper statue which you've made yourselves and placed on a pedestal.' And having spoken, he throws a metal loop around its neck and with the help of bulldozers and tanks brings it crashing down. The idol fell in this way not only in Moscow but in many Eastern European capitals.

No less interesting is the Khrushchev era, which the writer Ilya Erenburg so aptly named the Thaw. It was one of the most important and perhaps complex periods in the history of the Soviet Union and, for that matter, of the world. Its importance lies in the features it shared with *perestroika* and the first steps towards democratization now taking place in our country. Its complexity is illustrated by the words used to describe it: after a 'glorious' start, the decade ended up with the label of 'voluntaristic and subjectivist'.

It was a time of acute political battles and broken destinies. Khrushchev had dealt a crushing blow to the cult of Stalin, but his hand somehow stopped before the awesome immensity of the Stalinist system. The transition from the Cold War to peaceful coexistence began, and once again a window was opened on the world. But no door opened, and the Soviet people remained cut off from modern civilization. At that abrupt turning point society took deep breaths of the air of renewal and choked, from either too much or too little oxygen.

For a long time talk of these tumultuous years in the Soviet Union has not been acceptable. It is as if some hand had torn out a whole chapter of our history. For almost twenty years Khrushchev's name was taboo. But life will find its own course. I think I was the first person to write the truth about Khrushchev, almost twenty years after his fall. Since then a flood of writings and reminiscences has poured forth.

This book is not simply a memoir. I have filled out my own personal observations with information taken from historical documents of the Thaw period, and have paid much attention to the relationships between Khrushchev and other leaders such as Tito, Kadar, Mao Tse-tung, Eisenhower and Kennedy.

I have long been interested in the question of political leadership in our heroic yet tragic world. I have written about Lenin and Stalin, Mao

Tse-tung and Deng Xiao-ping, Hitler and Franco, Kennedy and other leaders. Yet Khrushchev is part of the life of my generation and of my own political life, and I keep returning to him.

Khrushchev is relevant to a special interest of mine: the phenomenon I call authoritarian-patriarchal political culture. This culture gave birth to our revolution and our political system, and was consolidated by them. Each leader in his own way – Lenin, Stalin, Khrushchev and Brezhnev – embodied this phenomenon. But Khrushchev, a strong personality with hardly any cultural background, perhaps exemplified it most precisely.

I have found Khrushchev's memoirs especially valuable as a source from which to reflect on the fate of our country after Stalinism. In the first place, they were written by a man who was himself a part of that era but had the courage to renounce it. Secondly, they were written by a man with an austere and penetrating political mind, whose judgements retain their value today. Thirdly, they were written by a leader who longed with all his soul that the Soviet people and the peoples of the world might live in peace and prosperity.

Finally, a word about the style of memoirs. By comparison with the reminiscences of Winston Churchill – another major figure of the twentieth century – who continued to argue the rightness of his case and settle accounts with his opponents, Khrushchev's memoirs are moving in their sincerity, simplicity and confessional nature. To all appearances, towards the end of his life this unusual man wanted to understand and interpret the past and to hand on his honest opinions to posterity. There is no hint of vanity or coquetry, no sign that he is inflating his personal role, no attempt to lay the blame on others.

We see a person deeply immersed in himself and the events in which he participated, weighing every step of his life on the scales of an old man's wisdom. Gone is the self-confidence which had so hindered Khrushchev in the final stages of his political career. The passions of the struggle have been extinguished, the thunder of applause can no longer be heard. What remains is the common sense of a simple Russian peasant.

The memoirs cover different aspects of the history of our country and of Khrushchev's multi-faceted career: the Twentieth Party Congress and the preparation of the secret speech about Stalin; the Twenty-Second Party Congress which resulted in the removal of the tyrant's body from the Lenin Mausoleum; the murder of Kirov and the extermination of two-thirds of the delegates to the Seventeenth Party Congress; the repressions of the military and the Kuznetsov and Voznesensky 'affair'; the war with Finland, the treaty with Hitler, the Warsaw Uprising, the Korean War, the death of Stalin and the arrest of Beria; the Berlin Wall and the Cuban Missile Crisis; reminiscences of

3

different leaders from different countries; meetings with scientists and the intelligentsia – in short, all or almost all the most important events from the mid-thirties to the mid-sixties, a period of three decades. There is still a great deal of research to be done by historians on the events described in the memoirs.

But this book is not only about Khrushchev and his colleagues; it is also about the generation of the Twentieth Party Congress. It is a description of people of that generation; their struggles, doubts, contradictions and political culture, which are of particular interest today. They are the key to understanding how *perestroika* has been achieved, what its aims are and what its consequences might be. For it is precisely the children of the Twentieth Party Congress who are the leadership now.

Not a single episode and not a single character in this book is fictitious. In almost all cases I have used real names; I have changed a few so as not to offend anyone with my subjective comments. I have endeavoured to be absolutely sincere and truthful in relation to myself as well, and I hope that this feature of my book, as well as the events I describe, will be appreciated by my readers.

1 The Thaw

In the manner of my favourite English novelists I shall begin this story with myself, not only so as to describe the author of this book but to give the reader a clearer picture of a political adviser's role.

Not everyone is aware that the Thaw under Khrushchev did not begin in 1956 during the Twentieth Party Congress. It began immediately after Stalin's death. His death shook everyone in the Soviet Union to the core, even if the emotions it aroused were varied. Something that had seemed unshakeable, eternal and immortal was gone. The simple thought that a man had died and his body had to be consigned to the earth hardly entered anyone's head. The institution of power, which lay at the very foundation of our society, had crumbled and collapsed. What would life be like now, what would happen to us and to the country?

I remember the memorial ceremony in the marble hall of the presidium of the USSR Academy of Sciences on Lenin Avenue. At the time I was working as secretary of the social sciences section of the publishing board, which was headed by Aleksandr Nesmeyanov, the president of the Academy. Nesmeyanov opened the ceremony. In a voice totally devoid of emotion, as if distanced from worldly things, he announced the death of that great man, leader of the party and the state and an outstanding scholar. Then he used an expression which was immediately imprinted on my mind – 'continuity' in the leadership of the party and the country would be ensured by G. M. Malenkov, a faithful follower of Lenin and comrade-in-arms of Stalin. The word 'continuity' meant that up there too they sensed that an essential prop of the state was missing.

Of the other speakers I remember Academician N. V. Tsitsin, a supporter of the biologist Lysenko, who was a close friend of Khrushchev's. Tsitsin sobbed on the rostrum. In fact virtually everyone cried. My eyes were also moist due to the solemnity of the occasion and, for the first time, a feeling of anticipation that important changes lay ahead.

I also remember that when I left the gathering I made a strange comment to whoever was beside me. I don't know whether I was being serious or ironic but I said: 'Only one living classic remains now – Mao Tse-tung. I must get his works immediately.' I didn't know that twenty years later I would write his biography.

I happened to be in Trubnaya Square at the time of Stalin's funeral, which many writers have described. But I was there before the crush and the bloodshed. My wife and I were renting a room in Pechatnikov Lane which was not far from the square. Our son had been born a few weeks before Stalin's death and had caught a cold in the maternity home. They had let him leave after a week, concealing from us that he was suffering from severe pneumonia. We had great difficulty in getting him into the Filatov Hospital. I was going across Trubnaya Square early in the morning not for Stalin's funeral but on my way to the hospital to save my son's life. I managed to get through between the cars at the very moment when someone had the bright idea of cutting off all the exits. In the crush that followed dozens of people died in that square alone. The tyrant was still extracting his bloody tribute from the people.

I must point out that I have disliked Stalin since my teens. I think that to a great extent I owe this to my mother. She worked in a textile factory in Kiev and even before the October Revolution she was involved in the political struggle. After the Revolution she joined a partisan detachment and used to go out on reconnaissance dressed as a gypsy. Later she served in the 6th Army where she met my father. His life had been quite different. Coming from a lower-middle-class family, he had managed to graduate from a classics-based grammar school and took two courses at the conservatoire in Petrograd before the Revolution. Then he threw himself enthusiastically into political activity and joined the 6th Army, which moved from Petrograd to defend the Ukraine.

My mother was very proud of the fact that Lenin's wife, Nadezhda Krupskaya, had described her and others at a meeting in Kiev as the first 'swallows' heralding the revolution. At the end of the 1920s, however, my mother and father abandoned party work and took up their professions – my mother became a doctor and my father worked in finance departments. This is probably what saved them from the repressions of the thirties. My mother was fanatically dedicated to the Revolution and could not comprehend or accept what happened under Stalin, although to the end of her days she retained her faith that all obstacles would be overcome, that all revolutions had their twists and turns and backward steps and that one simply had to remain patient and never lose hope. In time everything would come out right.

I was not called Fedor by chance, but in honour of Friedrich Engels. Perhaps that is why I have always been drawn to him more than to our other classical figure. The first songs I heard from my mother in my youth were 'Hostile Winds Blow Over Us' and 'Our Steam Train, Rush Forward . . .' I later included verses from the last song in Khrushchev's speech at the Twenty-Second Party Congress. He liked them very much – my mother and he were revolutionaries of the same generation.

My parents were constantly moving from one place to another and I now realize that this was because my father feared the repressions. They didn't tell me this when I was young. My father wrote about these undoubtedly dramatic events in poems dedicated to my mother: 'You struggled for the light of the Commune, but inadvertently left the serried ranks. Still in your heart the old chords sing, like the fiery call of unrequited yearning.' My mother never imposed her views on me, but brought me up to admire the heroism of the civil war and the whole Leninist period of our history and to be critical of everything that took place in the thirties.

My political maturity, however, came later. I arrived in Moscow in 1950 to enrole as a postgraduate student. I had to get into the university at any price, especially as I hadn't a single rouble left to pay for a return ticket. Being a confident young man, I arrived at my interview with V. P. Peshkov, secretary of the USSR Academy of Sciences and a physicist by profession, and put forward this proposal to him: 'I graduated from my institute in two years. I only need one year to complete the postgraduate course. I promise to finish my dissertation in that time. You're a physicist – take me on as an experiment.' Peshkov laughed and I obtained permission to do the course in one year. And I kept my word, except that I was one day late.

During my postgraduate days I got to know a man with the strange Cossack name of Gerus. Longin Gerus had been chairman of either the Stavropol or Rostov soviet way back at the time of the first revolution of 1905. After the revolution had failed he emigrated to the United States and learned English. When he returned to Russia after the October coup he did not take part in political life, but taught English at a school. However, as always, he had a keen interest in everything that was taking place in the party and in the country.

Gerus lived in a tiny room in a communal flat near the Krasnyye Vorota, where he found enough space to put up a camp bed for me. Three times a day he fed me and himself on buckwheat porridge with milk, which was all we could afford. But this was not my main nourishment.

In my landlord's wretchedly furnished room there was an enormous bookcase stacked with political literature. On the shelves lay the proceedings of all the party congresses, which had been banned from every library in the country. He had the first edition of Lenin's works with detailed commentaries, and the works of Bukharin, Trotsky,

Zinoviev, Kamenev, Rykov and Tomsky – in short, all the members of Lenin's Old Guard.

I read them at night by candlelight, making myself comfortable in a corner on the floor. In particular I pored over the proceedings of the congresses at the end of the twenties and was staggered by the intensity of feeling, the variety of opinions and the prescient forecasts of the future. To this day I remember one of Kamenev's speeches, in which he openly talks of the formation of a personality cult around Stalin, of an authoritarian Stalinist regime, and of imminent bloody repressions within the party itself.

After these nocturnal reading sessions I began to reread the records of the trials against the opposition in 1936–8 with different eyes. I was staggered that others could not see that it was all a monstrous lie from start to finish. I was surprised that even such a shrewd person as Lion Feuchtwanger, who had been present at one of the trials, could not see the truth, which was as transparent as water. In fact Feuchtwanger points out how strange it was that Bukharin calmly stirred his cup of tea with a spoon while revealing the most terrible crimes about himself – that he had served in the tsarist security police and that he had been preparing to assassinate Lenin. Despite this, Feuchtwanger allowed himself to be deceived.

There is no doubt that a great master indeed was stage-managing this bloody political spectacle if a man such as Feuchtwanger, who had lived through Fascism, could not detect with his finely tuned ear the false notes in the orchestra. I tried to imagine even then at what price such staggering results had been achieved. Why did such major political figures, who had gone through tsarist prisons and penal servitude, submit like lambs to the slaughter, covering themselves and others with the filth of denunciation? Did no one at the trials have enough courage to say at least one word that would indicate to those present that it was all a crude and cruel farce? How could it have happened? Were they tortured? Were they promised that they would not be killed and that their families would not be hurt? Were they persuaded of the historical necessity of such a cruel purge? Even then it occurred to me that these were simply performances in which the speeches and even the heckling had been thoroughly rehearsed. They were performances that had been repeated several times so that the accused no longer knew whether he was in a real court or at just another rehearsal.

I am writing about this because subsequently I often read and heard many of our scholars and writers, such as Konstantin Simonov, people who were older and more experienced than me, justify themselves by maintaining one and the same thing – that they blindly believed in the leader. Not only did they believe in him but they were sincere when they worshipped him in their poems and books. One never knows, but I

8

find this unconvincing. It was very much to their advantage to be known as Stalinists. As far back as I remember, even in my youth, I felt profound loathing for the idea that one man could determine everything: how we should live, what we should do and even what we should think. I was disgusted by the genuflectory psalms of praise and the rituals of false populism.

The reader will not believe me when I say that after reading long into the night I would often dream that I was arguing with Stalin. It would all be very clear, like a good film. I would accuse him of his crimes and talk about the national calamity, that all thought had been suppressed and that people were being brought up into slavish submissiveness. He would reply in his characteristic accent, refuting all this authoritatively. I think now that I had caught the political disease, which entered my conscious and subconscious mind. In later years I repeatedly dreamed of discussions with Khrushchev, Andropov and other figures. Strange, but nonetheless true. Perhaps that is how a political animal is formed: different impressions, experiences and knowledge, all intertwined, become the very essence of his being.

I must say that in our postgraduate years my close friends and I chatted about Stalin in an extremely imprudent way. One day S. Pokrovsky, who worked in the department at the Institute of the State and Law of the USSR Academy of Sciences where I was doing my postgraduate course, invited me and my friend G. Shakhnazarov, who is now an aide to President Mikhail Gorbachev, to a restaurant at the House of Journalists. He began a conversation about Stalin. In my customary rash manner I was just about to take a dive off the deep end when my friend kicked me under the table and said jokingly: 'Why talk about this, Serafim Aleksandrovich? We have wonderful shashliks, wine. Let's talk about women.' Pokrovsky tried to resume the conversation and I nearly took the bait once more, but again my friend kicked me. So Pokrovsky did not hook us as he had expected to. Many years later, when it was revealed that Pokrovsky had sent several postgraduates to prison (one of them was shot), I realized that my friend had saved my life.

Pokrovsky's own life reveals a great deal about events in the twenties and thirties. He was a well-spoken man, obviously from the intelligentsia, and had a strange passion for provoking scandalous public debates. He would get his claws into some academic and in a well-informed and caustic way would bandy his name, works and words about from every available rostrum. One of his constant targets was G. Yushkov, a professor of the old, pre-revolutionary school, well known as an historian of the state and law. This baggy, already middle-aged and probably sickly man literally could not bear being in the presence of Pokrovsky, who accused the esteemed professor of anti-Marxism at every opportunity.

All his life Yushkov had sincerely tried to base his works on the firm ground of Marxism and Stalinism, but his honesty and objectivity meant he kept slipping from this position. I invited Yushkov to act as my examiner when I had to defend my dissertation. This was on the advice of my supervisor, S. Kechekyan, who incidentally had been an untenured lecturer at Petersburg University in the past. Yushkov agreed on condition that there would be no sign of Serafim Pokrovsky at the examination. Kechekyan approached Pokrovsky, who promised not to come and speak. But, as always, he lied. He turned up and as usual spent a long time settling scores with Yushkov, who could not stand it any more and left the meeting.

According to Yushkov, who in his turn had kept a close eye on this 'rogue', Pokrovsky had started his career as a member of the 'Trotskyist opposition'. While still a second-year student at Leningrad University Pokrovsky became a lecturer on the faculty, presumably because of his outstanding abilities. During discussions in the late twenties he spoke in defence of Trotsky and later, probably, of Zinoviev, for which he was exiled to Voronezh, although such exiles were not typical then. It was there that his change of personality took place. At that time his friend, Professor Levin, was publishing Pokrovsky's articles in Leningrad under his own name, and dutifully sending the money earned from them to the impoverished Pokrovsky.

In the early thirties Pokrovsky wrote his first denunciation to the security organs. And on whom did he inform, if not his own benefactor! According to people familiar with the incident the denunciation read like this: 'I request that you prosecute Professor Levin, who is publishing articles written by the not unknown Trotskyist, Pokrovsky.' A truly Dostoyevskian character! Only someone with a perverted mind could have thought up such a denunciation.

As a result Pokrovsky began to work regularly for agencies of the NKVD. He was brought back to Moscow, successfully defended his dissertation and began work as a senior research assistant in the sector and institute where I was studying.

Later something even more incredible happened. When the complete works of Stalin came out, one of the last volumes contained replies from the 'supreme leader' to two letters written by Pokrovsky at the end of the twenties. At that time Pokrovsky had been disputing many Stalinist directives and ideas. In the first letter Stalin's reply was quite detailed, but in the second Stalin limited himself to a short explanation and the remark: 'I am ending this correspondence as you are an egocentric upstart.' You can imagine how alarmed the heads of the Institute of the State and Law were when this letter was published. Pokrovsky was immediately sacked. He appealed to the court and was reinstated, not without the prompting, no doubt, of the security organs where Pokrovsky continued to serve as an agent. Later his life took an even stranger turn.

After the Twentieth Party Congress in 1956 Pokrovsky was reinstated as a party member. At our party gathering he beat his breast and said, 'We are old Communists,' as he turned out to be one of the oldest party members. However, the mother of one of the postgraduates who had been shot because of Pokrovsky's denunciation, managed to acquire documents from the security organs and appealed to the Institute to expel Pokrovsky from the party. The meeting of the party organization was unanimous in its decision; justice triumphed and Pokrovsky was once again – this time for good – expelled from the party. On leaving the party meeting he bumped into me in the corridor and, in quite a jolly mood, his eyes sparkling, said: 'Well, so what? They've taken away one ticket, but I've got two left,' and showed me two tickets to the theatre.

Many years later when I was working as deputy director of the Institute of Empirical Sociological Research at the USSR Academy of Sciences, Pokrovsky's son – Pokrovsky himself was no longer alive – asked me to enrol him as an assistant. I was faced with a dilemma. Although a son should not have to answer for his father, it would still have been unpleasant to see regularly the offspring of a man who had tried to put me behind bars. Fortunately Pokrovsky's son changed his mind and saved me from this difficult decision.

Incidentally it was Pokrovsky, together with the head of our sector, who persistently advised me to include at least one quotation from Stalin in my dissertation. I was stubborn, however, and argued that Stalin had written nothing about N. A. Dobrolyubov, the famous Russian critic of the 1860s who was the subject of my thesis. Thus, we can see that in Stalin's times people's lives and feelings were not at all straightforward: some spent their time putting people in prison, others spent their time in prison; some played the role of the hammer, others that of the anvil; some were informers, others were victims of denunciation.

The problem of choice and the moral imperative remain a matter of conscience for each person, even in times of the cruellest tyranny. That has always been and will always be the case in all periods for any nation under any regime. Giordano Bruno went to the stake, Galileo preferred to renounce his views so that he could continue to fight for the truth, Copernicus' main works were published only after his death. The dilemma which faces the great figures in this world is in essence no different from that which every person, even the most insignificant, has to face. Often the choice is just as difficult, although it may not be as important or noticeable.

The postgraduate students clearly divided into two unequal groups.

The larger group was made up of members of 'aristocratic' families, who joined us as a rule by virtue of a telephone call from a relative or benefactor. Among the postgraduates at our and neighbouring institutes at the time were Stalin's and Malenkov's sons-in-law and the sons of such ministers as Ginzburg, Abakumov and many others of lesser rank. Strictly speaking, Stalin's son-in-law was by then no longer regarded as a relative. There was an amusing story about this. He lived with Svetlana Stalin in the Kremlin. One day when he was returning home a security guard took away his special pass without so much as an explanation. This was how he learned that he had been expelled from the leader's family. At that time the struggle against 'cosmopolitanism' was underway and Stalin considered it inconvenient for his daughter to have a Jewish husband. On his insistence, Svetlana married Zhdanov's son, whom she also threw over after a while.

There was one girl among the postgraduates who was tall and plump with large buttocks. An interesting story went round about her. She was walking along the Arbat, which was very close to our institute, when suddenly a black car stopped beside her. A man in the uniform of a colonel stepped out and asked her to follow him into the car. Afterwards it emerged that she had been taken to Lavrenty Beria's residence, which was at the end of the Arbat. Beria was at that time the all-powerful head of the security organs. It is not known how long she spent with him, but afterwards she was given a flat on one of Moscow's main streets. She was a nervous person and it was said that she was a bit odd. She would sit on a chair and fidget all the time. Pokrovsky took a fancy to her and because of this it was said that he liked second-hand goods.

I was in the poor but proud democratic group. We felt contempt for the life-style of the offspring of the bureaucracy with their drinking sessions, group sex, dances and constant chatter about football. But then we worked ten to fourteen hours a day. Maybe this was that 'simple peasant truth' dreamt of by Vasisualy Lokhankin, that unforgettable Russian intellectual from Ilf and Petrov's book *The Golden Calf*.

At this time my friendship with the extremely kind Longin Gerus came to a sorry end. One day I found a note next to my plate of buckwheat porridge and milk. The handwriting was unsteady and it said: 'Petr Mikhaylovich [he had forgotten my name!], Unfortunately we must part. I have difficulty in sleeping and your reading every night doesn't help. Please forgive me and find yourself another flat.' I searched doggedly and eventually found a place in a hostel for postgraduates on Malaya Bronnaya. It was a single room which I shared with G. Marchuk, who is now president of the USSR Academy of Sciences.

My academic life ended suddenly. I had been asked to write a review of some book on Herzen for *Kommunist*, the theoretical journal of the Central Committee of the Communist Party. I am not certain which caught the editor's attention more, my review or the fact that it was written by a young twenty-five-year-old Candidate of Sciences, hungry for active work. Not many people remember now that very soon after Stalin's death a search began for young people who would get things moving in cultural and political life. That's how I found myself on the journal *Kommunist*. More than a dozen other people like me from academic and journalistic circles were taken on at the same time. Later I saw the same thing happen in the apparatus of the Central Committee. New names began to appear in print, people like Vladimir Dudintsev, V. Pomerantsev, Bulat Okudzhava and Yevgeny Yevtushenko, who personified the Thaw.

It is only natural that these changes occurred more slowly in the political sphere. Many of my peers got stuck at the level of adviser, but at this level there was a vigorous intake of new blood. I am not certain whether this was the result of instructions from above or whether it happened spontaneously, but the older generation at that time tended to lean on young people for support. It was young people who personified the Thaw. The names we see on the surface of *perestroika* today are almost without exception people of my generation. The most crucial period will arrive with a new wave of young enthusiasts and reformers, who will have the same passionate faith in the need for change and be as fanatical in implementing it as the children of the Twentieth Party Congress.

*

The first few months after Stalin's death were full of trepidation. Beria's pronouncement from the Mausoleum at the memorial ceremony, and his repetition of the words 'He who isn't blind can see' sounded ominous. But the first speeches by Khrushchev, Malenkov and other leaders already sounded different. They spoke about the people and their needs, about food, the problem of housing and a pardon for those who had been prisoners of war. They said that the aim of socialism could not lie only in industrial growth. In short, the winds of change were blowing.

For a while our journal was housed in the building of the Central Committee of the Communist Party of the Soviet Union, and we were in the same party organization as those who worked there. I remember most of all a conference of party and state workers in which the then leadership of the party took part. Malenkov gave the main report. Its main thrust was the struggle against bureaucracy 'all the way to its total elimination'. To a considerable extent he repeated the points in his speech at the Nineteenth Party Congress. His talk was interspersed with such scathing remarks as 'the degeneration of certain links in the state apparatus', 'the passing of certain state organs beyond party control', 'the total neglect of people's needs', 'bribery and the degeneration of the moral character of Communism' and so on. You should have seen the faces of those present, who represented that very apparatus he was proposing to smash. Bewilderment was mingled with dismay, dismay with fright and fright with indignation.

A deathly silence followed the speech. It was broken by the lively and apparently cheerful voice of Khrushchev, who said, 'All this is true, of course, Georgy Maksimilianovich, but the apparatus is our buttress.' Only after that did the friendly, stormy and prolonged applause break out. The First had achieved in one phrase what all the verbose and passionate speeches of the Chairman of the Council of Ministers could not. Incidentally, Khrushchev himself later quarrelled with the apparatus and tested its strength.

Within the editorial board of the journal surprising moves were also afoot. About three months after Stalin's death we were instructed to write an article on the role of the masses in history. The bulk of the work was to be done by the philosopher M. Kammari, who was known for his works on the role of personality in history, with help from his deputy and myself. I reread the article recently. It speaks so sharply against the cult of personality and of the need to struggle against bureaucracy and develop democracy that I wondered where all these ideas had come from.

The editorial board supported my proposal to conduct concrete social research into prisons and camps, the privileged supply of food and medical services, and the sources of non-labour income. Discussing this plan with me A. Sobolev, the deputy editor, walking with large measured strides around his room, said, 'We must raise our voices and show how indignant we are at the bureaucracy and the degeneration of our apparatus.'

For this work I took on an amazing man, Nefedov, a living relic of Lenin's times and a former member of the Workers' and Peasants' Inspectorate, who with youthful passion seized the chance to clear out the Augean stables of Stalin's regime. Together we visited many prisons and camps in the Ryazan region. We sent off a large group of students to compare canteens and buffets in factories and in the ministries. From the statistics directorate we received information about the unequal distribution of income. All in all, we gathered five fat volumes of material which, alas, never saw the light of day.

The facts were so incriminating that the editorial board did not even send a memorandum about the research to the party organs. I remember that at that time more murders were committed in the

Ryazan region than in the whole of England. How could a journal publicize such facts when it had asserted for decades that the 'relics of capitalism' in people's consciousness had become almost totally obliterated?

I distinctly remember a speech given at a closed meeting by V. Malyshev, a prominent economist of the time. He spoke of how backward we were by comparison with the West in the fields of science, technology and labour productivity, of the tendency towards technical stagnation and the lack of an inner mechanism which would lead to a self-developing economy; of how the peasant's interest in his labour had been destroyed and workers had no incentive to work; of the wretched standard of living, particularly in the countryside, and the ineffectiveness of administrative methods of economic management. This was more than thirty years ago. It is strange how we have gone over and over the same set of problems, and it is only now that we are beginning to discover solutions.

It is true that even then there were experienced people in the editorial board who responded sceptically to all these verbal fireworks. One of them was Sergey Pavlovich Mezentsev, my immediate boss. He told me that as an eighteen-year-old lad he had left his village during the period of collectivization, carrying his belongings in a bundle on a stick and limping, as his foot had been injured in the harvest. He could not read or write. Later he went to classes at the workers' faculty and the party school and finally he became a member of the editorial board running the party journal. We were in charge of the criticism and bibliography section. You should have seen the difficulty with which he read reviews of thick scholarly books on, say, the history of Kievan Rus or modern capitalism or philosophical trends in the nineteenth century.

When he received reviews from venerable academicians and professors he usually handed them over to me with short comments such as 'Is this so?' or 'Is this correct?' delicately marked in the margin with his sharp pencil. Once out of sheer mischief, without really wanting to hurt him, I wrote an answer next to each one of his comments: 'Do you think so?' – 'I do', 'Is this right?' – 'Right', 'Not really?' – 'Really' and so on. I sealed the article in an envelope and gave it to someone to take into the next room. Half an hour later Mezentev limped in, sat opposite me and said sadly: 'You're young, Fedor. Oh, how young and hot-headed you are. You'd better watch out or you'll come to a sticky end.' I was so ashamed I could have died on the spot.

It is interesting now to see which of the two of us turned out to be the wiser. I must admit that this simple peasant, five times less educated than me, proved to be right in many of our arguments. At that time I had written an article on the development of Soviet democracy, which I got past the editorial board with colossal difficulty. I wrote that the soviets of working people's deputies should receive full powers and become a permanently working organization, not one which simply acted as a rubber stamp for resolutions already prepared by the apparatus. I said that not one but several candidates should be proposed at elections to the soviets if we wanted proper voting. I pointed out that to prevent repressions we had to have a courtroom with a people's jury comprising ten people who would decide, without the judge's presence, whether a defendant was guilty or not guilty.

I took great pains to convince him that soon, very soon, our Soviet parliament, like parliaments in other civilized countries, would discuss each law, argue and disagree, scrutinize different proposals, vote on the majority principle and not unanimously, criticize ministers and pick holes in the government, monitoring the effectiveness of its expenditure.

'You're naive, Fedor. That's never going to happen,' Mezentsev would say. 'Believe me, this won't happen in our lifetime. There's no point in putting so much effort and nervous energy into it. All our laws and decrees will be drawn up as always by the party apparatus and the soviets will do no more than endorse them. That's the way it's always been and always will be. And you shouldn't have bothered to write against Lysenko. Of course, he's probably not very educated but he's a home-grown product. Mark my words, he'll be back, he'll definitely be back, because he's our very own and we understand him.'

Mezentsev was right after all. Lysenko returned under Khrushchev.

Truly, Erasmus was unsurpassed in his knowledge of human psychology. Stupidity, which relies on the experience of simple common sense, is valued more highly than the intellect, nourished by the fruit of imagination. If I could only see Mezentsev again I would admit sincerely that bookish wisdom meant little and that the hunger for change that I felt did me no good.

In general, despite their negative qualities, those who had become party workers in the Stalinist period showed a certain reliability and solidity. I cannot remember a single case of someone in the central party apparatus at that time openly lying to one's face. Of course, he might conceal something or simply not tell you anything, he might refuse to comment with an 'excuse me' and 'please' – but he would not lie outright. Later on I had many opportunities to witness the high-fliers from the Komsomol. They would greet you with open, charming smiles and say: 'You know how much I think of you. Yes, I'll see to this matter instantly, I'll speak to the man who can help. Consider the matter settled.' And as soon as you went out the door, they would be on the phone saying, 'Tell him to go to hell. What a smart arse! Thinks he's more progressive than anyone else.'

I soon moved to the international department of the journal. Having invited me to be his deputy, the head of the department said: 'You'd better leave domestic subjects alone or you'll soon come a cropper . . .' My first pieces on international problems attracted the attention of prominent party heads. True, in the beginning, not quite in the way I would have liked.

Together with a party worker named Belyakov I wrote an article on revolutionary theory. We tried to prove that in civilized capitalist countries it would be impossible to have a violent revolution of the type that had taken place in backward Russia. Some other democratic version of socialism would become firmly established through exclusively peaceful parliamentary means and the people themselves would repulse any party or group that tried to bring down the traditional democratic structure.

After this publication the head of our department called me in and said that Mikhail Andreyevich Suslov had personally rung up to express his dissatisfaction with the article. According to Suslov, the article was strongly biased in favour of a transition to socialism by peaceful parliamentary politics. He maintained that one should not exclude the possibility of a swift violent seizure of power, like that which had presented itself to our party.

The head of the department was very nervous. He was bustling around his desk and repeating over and over again: 'What a calamity! What's going to happen now? What do you think, Fedor Mikhaylovich?' I said that I expected nothing would happen, at least not immediately, because I did not think that any party in the capitalist countries had any real chance of gaining power either by parliamentary or non-parliamentary means. 'That's not the point,' the man said irritably. 'That's not our problem. I'm talking about Mikhail Andreyevich. Now he's going to watch every article, especially yours. That's the problem.' 'He'll forget about it tomorrow,' I tried to console him. 'No, you're totally wrong. He never forgets anything.' I was later to realize that he was right. Suslov had a tenacious memory for faces and speeches, especially when there was any disagreement with his own view.

The editor-in-chief of *Kommunist*, S. Abalin, had had a tragic life. All the political struggles from the thirties to the fifties had passed in waves over his soft, fragile soul. When he was a young man, as an ordinary soldier in the Red Army, he had married a revolutionary activist. In 1939 his wife (he had parted from her by then) was arrested.

In the meantime, his career advanced and finally, against his will, he was made editor-in-chief of *Kommunist*. I know for a fact that he repeatedly asked the leadership to release him from this job as he did not understand theoretical matters. He received the usual answer for those times: 'You are a soldier of the party and must fulfil its tasks.' The unfortunate man suffered endlessly at his post.

Eventually Abalin's wishes were met half-way, but in a rather odd manner. After the Nineteenth Party Congress a large Presidium of the Central Committee of the All-Union Communist Party (Bolsheviks) was formed in place of the narrower Politburo.* We know now that Stalin was once again intending to renew the composition of the top leadership and to dismiss or, as in the past, 'liquidate' his comrades-in-arms who had outstayed their welcome. One unexpected promotion to the Presidium was D. Chesnokov, a man from the world of science.

He was appointed editor-in-chief of the journal *Kommunist*, although the previous editor had not been removed from his post, so that for a time two editors were equally in charge. As a rule, Chesnokov would arrive at our meetings a bit late, when the editorial board was already seated around the long table. He would walk slowly and self-importantly to the chairman's seat, limply shaking hands with only one of the members of the board, his colleague the philosopher Kammari, and sit down in the armchair. In fact Chesnokov did not reign long: immediately after Stalin's death he was stripped of his post not only on the Presidium but in the journal as well. Abalin continued to sweat it out.

Everything was simpler before Stalin's death. All you had to do was check any statement in your article against *The Short Course of the History of the All-Union Communist Party (Bolsheviks)* and correct it accordingly. After 1953, when new, unexpected and contradictory ideas poured forth, when every day something happened and the ideological edifice constructed over decades began to crack and disintegrate, Abalin became totally confused. He would rush to and fro, uncertain where he should be or how he should respond to the controversial and uncompromising clashes which took place at almost every session of the journal's editorial board. Basically he wanted everything to be settled quietly and as a matter of course. 'Must you carry on like this?' he would say. 'Well, work it out . . . fix it up . . . what's the point of arguing and quarrelling?' But the arguments would not cease.

After the rehabilitations began, Abalin's first wife returned from the back of beyond. He visited her in hospital and spent several hours talking to her in private. Soon afterwards he was found dead in his flat. He was sitting in an armchair in the kitchen, all the gas plates on the cooker had been turned on and the windows and doors were closed. He

---

* The Presidium was the top policy-making body between 1952 and 1966, when the Politburo was reintroduced.

was buried quietly as if it had been an accident. This honest, weak man could not bear the burden the Thaw had placed on his conscience.

*

One clear frosty morning in January 1958 Nikolay Vasilyevich Matkovsky, an aide to O. Kuusinen, picked me up at the newspaper office in a Zil car. It was the first time I had travelled in a Zil and I felt uncomfortable sitting next to my companion with quite a large space separating us from the chauffeur in front. Obviously this was what it was like in a hearse, I thought, only there you would be in a different pose.

'Of course, in such weather seamen prefer to sit in the cabin rather than on deck,' Matkovsky joked, obviously trying to help me get over my embarrassment. 'I hope my sailor's jargon doesn't offend you. I'm an old salt who can't get used to diplomatic ways and always goes straight to the point. You don't mind if I address you by your first name? After all, I'm ten years older than you.'

'Of course not. That, incidentally, is not only a seaman's privilege. My boss at the newspaper does the same, though I, of course, address him formally.'

'Well, I could address you formally, but you'll gain little from that,' Matkovsky said with a toothy grin, his grey eyes under their thick white lashes sparkling. It seemed that my reply had put him on his guard and he wondered how to interpret it: was this swarthy fellow giving himself airs or was he simply waffling?

'No, Nikolay Vasilyevich, I simply wanted to ask permission to address you formally. I would feel awkward otherwise, it wouldn't be right . . .'

'As you wish. You scholars and journalists are better versed at social rituals. It's up to you.'

Later I realized that I had made a big blunder in distancing myself from this man with his 'open seafaring nature', as Matkovsky described himself. Georgy Arbatov, who had presumably given my name to Kuusinen, behaved differently. He willingly switched to first-name terms with this ex-sailor and profited a great deal from it!

I imagine that Otto Vilgelmovich Kuusinen knew Arbatov from their joint work on the journal *Novoye Vremya*, where he had long been a member of the editorial board. When Kuusinen was instructed to prepare a textbook, on the fundamentals of Marxism-Leninism he brought in Arbatov, who helped him to organize a new authors' collective consisting of young scholars and journalists. I say 'new' because Kuusinen had been offered another authors' collective with which he had quickly become disenchanted. They were not people capable of thinking independently or tackling in a fresh and original way the problems of contemporary international developments that worried him so deeply.

Matkovsky informed me of this while we were driving through Moscow along the Volokolamsky highway towards the village of Snigiri, where Kuusinen lived in his dacha.

'He's a wonderful old man, you'll see,' Matkovsky said, flashing his smile. 'Well, I lie, he's hardly an old man. He's younger than you and me in spirit, that's for sure. An innovator, a real innovator. He delves to the bottom of our ideas, which are as stagnant as stinking puddles on the deck. And not only in spirit. You'll see how he skis and skates and exercises on the cross-bars. And he's over seventy!'

Somewhat paralysed by this sailor's stormy temperament and shivering in the badly-heated car, I sat huddled in a corner, feeling like a bride who is being taken to an unknown and cantankerous bridegroom. Of course nothing awful would happen if the bridegroom rejected her and it was far from certain that she would like him, but still it was unpleasant to have to go through this inspection.

'Don't be shy, lad' – my talkative companion had detected my discomfiture. 'The old man isn't impatient. He doesn't accept anything on faith and never makes a decision immediately. He liked your article about the need to develop Soviet democracy. He will give you a chance to write a section on the state in the book before deciding whether to include you or not in the authors' collective. So you'll have time . . .'

Wanting to entertain me during the long trip, Matkovsky began to recount stories about Kuusinen when he had been in the Comintern. He said that Kuusinen had always been renowned for his extraordinary capacity for work. At that time it was customary in the Comintern (and not only there) for sessions to last well into the early hours of the morning.

'They were making plans for the world revolution,' Matkovsky said. 'They were discussing which country would erupt first and when. During these all-night vigils each person had his own characteristic activity.

'One of the members of the Comintern, Harry Pollitt, had a weakness for Armenian brandy and would sip glass after glass, with no snacks in between, washing down the brandy with mineral water. On the other hand Kuusinen had exercising rings attached to his study ceiling and would use every break to pull himself up and perform various figures. Dimitrov once observed, "Comrade Kuusinen, this is where you learned your flexible tactics." Kuusinen replied, "Well, we've never been flexible enough in tactics, but I never forget our long-term strategy." '

I listened open-mouthed to Matkovsky's stories, not knowing whether to believe him or not.

However, it is likely that this was the normal mode of behaviour among members of the Comintern: both their passionate theoretical arguments and their competitive lively humour. Listening to Matkovsky I was reminded of the time that Harry Pollitt visited our journal. He did not give any grand official speeches, but spoke simply and entertainingly about the not very entertaining Communist Party of Great Britain. Several Comintern jokes, which I gathered later were fairly typical ones, stuck in my memory for a long time.

'The worst thing is that we believed Comrade Yevgeny Varga [a well-known international economist of that period] every time he predicted there would be a profound economic crisis in the West,' Harry Pollitt said. 'We believed that any minute now there would be a crisis and Little Red Riding Hood (that's our party) would grow big and strong and eat up the capitalist wolf. Crises came and went, but we remained Little Red Riding Hood.'

I remember that this joke shocked the older members of our journal. One of Harry Pollitt's toasts really did seem quite indecent. It happened during a luncheon in response to our well-prepared and considered toasts in honour of the Communist Party of Great Britain, all the fraternal parties and the victorious Revolution. Before making his toast, Harry Pollitt picked up a large glass – not the usual small brandy glass – and filling it up to the brim with Armenian brandy pronounced: 'I warmly support everything that has been said here. And now, let's drink a non-party toast. I want to drink to our wives and mistresses and hope they never bump into each other around the same table!'

Our old boys nearly fell off their chairs, while the young ones were amazed at his audacity in violating the rituals of toasting.

When Harry Pollitt began making caustic remarks about the way we wrote our articles in 'Chinese party slang', the executive secretary of the editorial board could stand it no longer and in a whisper which could be heard by everyone around the table said: 'No wonder there's never been a revolution in Britain.' For this he received a stern frown from the official in charge of Pollitt who later, when he got the chance, remarked to the executive secretary: 'Harry Pollitt was an outstanding figure in the world Communist movement when you were still sitting as an accountant in your collective farm.'

I remembered this while listening to Matkovsky's entertaining stories, looking out of the window of the limousine during his short pauses.

The car sped between snow-covered fields, forests and copses. I loved this white blanket of snow and the bluish grey smoke from which the sun seemed to have been torn out and forced onto the horizon. The white snow always calms me and reconciles me with what is immense and unbounded around us, and from which we constantly turn away, fixing our gaze on trivial everyday tasks as invisible as the snowflakes lost in the endless blanket of snow.

But I could not concentrate on these thoughts any longer. The car went through the gates softly, almost timidly, and stopped next to a not very large wooden two-storey house. While we shook off the snow in the small hall a large woman in an apron told us in a sing-song voice that Otto Vilgelmovich was expecting us in his study on the first floor. We climbed up the narrow creaking staircase onto a mezzanine, where in the corner facing the window stood a small table heaped with books and manuscripts.

There was so much paper on the table that I could barely see the armchair behind it, in which a small, frail and rather old man sat, wrapped in a checked rug and some furs. His small bald head and face, all skin and bone, added to the impression of senility. But this first impression was completely demolished when one looked at his eyes and his expression. His eyes were blocks of ice, blue and not very large, drawing in and absorbing into their depths everything that came within their field of vision; eyes that seemed to exist independently of his facial expression, living their own life, directly in contact with some centre of intellectual activity hidden in the depths of his cranium. His head reminded me somewhat of Picasso's at the same age. Maybe it just seemed like that to me when I first saw him, but afterwards I could not rid myself of this association.

This thin, small, old man seemed extremely important to me and I felt an unaccustomed timidity and a desire to make a good impression on him. But he remained silent, resting his calm, cold, blue-eyed gaze blankly on me, although I soon came to realize that this blank look hid a mind that worked continuously, tirelessly and almost mechanically.

'Well, Otto Vilgelmovich, here he is,' Matkovsky began noisily. 'I think he's a good lad, but he's got a swollen head and doesn't want to speak on first-name terms with me. Of course, I'm only joking,' said Matkovsky and turned to me. 'Otto Vilgelmovich will tell you of his plans for a chapter in our textbook on the state. This chapter must be original and perhaps the central one in the book. Well, I've completed my mission and will now remain silent.'

'Yes, quite, quite,' the old gentleman squeaked. 'I've invited you to try . . . to try and approach this subject in a new way. You said correctly in your article that it's necessary to develop Soviet democracy. But what does that mean? What do you think?'

I began to list the main arguments in my article, but Kuusinen stopped me with his gaze.

'Yes, quite . . . but do you think we have to retain the dictatorship of the proletariat when we have built a socialist society, or should we proceed to a new stage of state development?'

I must say this question confused me, not that I had not thought of it before but because an answer to such a question was, as we used to say at the newspaper, fraught with unpredictable consequences. One could say out loud that the dictatorship of the proletariat was not needed; that it had fulfilled its purpose in the civil war, in the unprecedented effort of the pre-war period and in the Patriotic War when the severest discipline and mobilization at the front and rear were essential. I knew very well that the dictatorship of the proletariat had been used as a slogan in the thirties to justify mass repressions. But could one say this to a man who represented the top echelons of the country's leadership? True, the very way he put the question hinted that his approach was different. I never, however, completed these thoughts under his attentive searching gaze, which was demanding the most sincere answer from me and not a formal one.

'To speak honestly, Otto Vilgelmovich, I think that the dictatorship of the proletariat has fulfilled its role in our country. It must be transformed. Strictly speaking, this process is already taking place and our task should be to accelerate it consciously.'

'Quite.' The rug stirred, which as I later understood meant that Kuusinen had become extremely agitated. 'But the question is, what will this dictatorship be transformed into?'

'I think into a state of the people and not of one class; into a socialist democracy.'

'Yes, quite, quite, perhaps to an all-people's state? Marx criticized the slogan "the people's state", but that was a long time ago and besides he was referring to a quite different state. Lassalle hoped to replace Junker bourgeois power with a people's state. This was an illusion, a deception. The situation here is quite different now that the dictatorship of the proletariat has completed its historical task.'

Here he paused for quite a long time and I was not certain if I was meant to add something more to what he had said. He seemed to be reflecting on the conversation as if each word, having detached itself from him, had acquired its own independent meaning and form and needed reappraising.

I could not restrain myself and said: 'Then should the chapter for the textbook be written in this spirit?'

'Yes, quite, quite, in this spirit. It has to be substantiated theoretically. One must look at Lenin to see why and for what reason the dictatorship of the proletariat was necessary and prove that it is no longer necessary today.'

'Are we talking only about theory, or practice?' I asked. 'Is the point to make major changes to the political system?'

'Yes, quite,' Kuusinen answered. 'At first theoretically and then . . .' he made a gesture with his hands somewhere into the distance, 'and then in practice . . .'

I understood that 'then' would not be very soon and that for the moment we would have to get theoretical recognition that state institutions had to be transformed in important ways.

'Maybe we should include Fedor Mikhaylovich in our memorandum?' Matkovsky put in his word.

'Yes, yes, include him in the memorandum as well, but the main thing is to peruse all Lenin's works and restore the truth, so that we can substantiate an all-people's state.'

The invitation to me and other young theoreticians to join the authors' collective was not achieved without a difficult struggle on Kuusinen's part. I could see this from the first session, which was attended by both the old and the new authors. We sat around the table and discussed how the work would be redistributed. Those sections which had already been written and had not turned out successfully were handed out to the new writers. One of the 'old' writers who had been rejected and wanted to offend Kuusinen said, 'Did you know, Otto Vilgelmovich, that the Western press has commented on your election to the Central Committee Presidium?'

'And what do they write?' Otto Vilgelmovich asked calmly.

'They write the following, I quote: "The Presidium of the Central Committee of the Communist Party of the Soviet Union has elected an old party member, Kuusinen, who is known for his unorthodox views and his struggle against dogmatism." '

The speaker looked up triumphantly, seeking support from those around him, but found it only in two or three of the outsiders.

'Yes, quite,' Kuusinen drawled in his usual manner. 'They write about my struggle against dogmatism, but I don't understand how they managed to find out about my arguments with you?'

Friendly laughter was the response to this subtle, 'typically Comintern' joke.

It was customary at that time to release writers of party textbooks from their normal duties so that they could gather at a dacha and concentrate fully on the task. We were housed in a dacha in Nagornoye on the Kurkinskoye highway, a branch of the main road to Leningrad.

It was a small two-storey wooden house in which we all had our own room with a writing table, a bed, a bedside table and our own toilet. Three times a day we were herded into a nearby building for meals, where we sat at a common table with members of another authors' collective who were working on a textbook of the history of the Communist Party of the Soviet Union. When our bosses were not there, this social gathering often turned into a sharp slanging match between the two groups of writers.

Kuusinen seldom came, and in his absence two people were virtually in charge: Georgy Arbatov and Aleksey Belyakov. The former, as I have already mentioned, was a journalist; the latter worked in the inter-national department of the Communist Party Central Committee and subsequently became Kuusinen's aide. These two men complemented each other well. Arbatov was blessed with a quite unique talent: he wrote quickly, like a machine, throwing out page after page directly onto the floor. He had no trouble dashing off fifteen or twenty pages in a couple of hours. He found it very easy to put Kuusinen's ideas and the ideas of other members of the collective into literary form.

As for Belyakov, he wrote virtually nothing at all. He even gave the impression that he felt contempt for this occupation. But he was an unusually good speaker. His views were always original and the novelty and depth of his approach were often striking. He was a grand master at drafting outlines. The subject did not matter to him; he composed and rearranged with equal pleasure the outlines of the whole textbook, separate chapters, the presentation of issues, the method of research – in a word, everything.

Arbatov was an imposing and distinguished man: large, with a grave and what we called brooding face, an enormous nose and a sloping but impressive forehead. At that time he was keen on yoga and we often found him standing on his head in his room. His thinning hair would spill out on the floor in spikes, which invariably provoked mirth, though this did not worry him in the least. He had an instinctive and deeply-ingrained sense of his own worth and importance.

Belyakov, on the other hand, had a surly look. He found it difficult to socialize, but once he had got close to someone he was capable of pouring out his philosophical thoughts for hours, not concerned in the least if one agreed with him or not. He was slender, strong, dark-haired and, on the whole, rather handsome. He was invariably a great success with our typists and chatted endlessly with them in their room, no matter how urgent the work was.

I was helplessly infatuated with Belyakov, so much so that I even named my second son after him. He liked me too and tolerated my adoration, finding me a good listener, ready to imbibe his outpourings for hours on end.

I remember that the memorandum Kuusinen prepared with our assistance, which was sent to the top echelons of the leadership, had the somewhat provocative title, 'The Abolition of the Dictatorship of the Proletariat and the Transition to an All-People's State'. Its impact was like a bomb going off. The overwhelming majority of the leadership not only rejected it but were terribly indignant. Only Kuusinen's eyes showed his amusement. Experienced in the ways of the apparatus, he had submitted it beforehand for Khrushchev's approval and had received his firm support.

We were in Kuusinen's study when he was listening on the internal phone to some of the top officials' comments on the memorandum. He held the receiver in such a way that we could hear what was being said.

'Otto Vilgelmovich!' the receiver screeched. 'What does this mean? What have you written! Why do you distort everything! For Lenin the dictatorship of the proletariat was the cornerstone of Marxism. And you shove in some new quotations by Lenin that no one has ever heard of . . .'

'Yes, quite, no one has . . . no one has heard of them because these very important utterances by Lenin were kept under lock and key. I suppose you know that even today many of Lenin's works have not been published . . .'

'I know nothing, I've never heard of it. We were taught a different kind of Marxism,' the receiver growled and was laid down.

'Yes, quite correct,' Kuusinen noted, turning to us. 'He was taught differently. I'm afraid that even the lecturers at the trade technical college where he graduated might not have heard of these words of Lenin.'

Again the internal phone rang.

'Hello,' Kuusinen said politely, as usual.

The receiver was silent for a while and then a piercing woman's voice burst forth. Later we realized it was Furtseva, Central Committee secretary and later to become Minister of Culture.

'Otto Vilgelmovich, how could you encroach upon the holy of holies – the dictatorship of the proletariat! What will happen to our state and our ideology if we ourselves shake their foundations?'

'I think our state and our ideology will become stronger,' the old man answered cheerfully. 'In fact, if the state embraced the whole people and also preserved the leadership of the working class it would, of course, only gain and lose nothing. And at the same time no one could justify reprisals against you or any of us with a quotation about the dictatorship of the proletariat.'

'You know, you're going too far. What are you hinting at? We now have a collective leadership and no one is planning to put anyone in prison!'

'Yes, quite, quite,' Kuusinen was delighted. 'A collective leadership means a direct transition to socialist democracy.'

'Not at all, Otto Vilgelmovich. You don't convince me. And you won't convince anyone. My advice to you is to take back your memorandum before it's too late, before it is discussed.'

'It's not too late,' Kuusinen mumbled, slightly mockingly. 'It's never too late to restore the truth. As for the discussion, I can't help feeling that by then you will have reconsidered your position . . .'

'Never! Not for anything! You could say I imbibed the dictatorship with my mother's milk and I'll fight to the death for it!'

'Why to the death? It's a theoretical question. We'll see, we'll discuss it and reach a collective decision.'

Kuusinen turned out to be right. Not one of his opponents even risked coming out against the memorandum when the discussion was held. By this time everyone knew that the 'First' supported it and had recommended that the idea of an all-people's state be included in the Party Programme, a task which was subsequently entrusted to me.

On the whole Khrushchev listened to Kuusinen, who provided him with a vital link to Lenin. He once said, 'Don't lay your hands on Kuusinen. He's the only person left who continues to think.'

I talked to Otto Vilgelmovich about many things: how the new views of the state would change our political system and how it would be based on principles of democracy; how firm guarantees against a regime of personal power would be created; how new political institutions of public self-government would appear.

After all, the foundations of our political system had not essentially changed since the revolution. They had been preserved in the same form in which they had existed under Lenin. They had not hindered the radical political and ideological changes that had taken place under Stalin. Why not? How could we protect our country from an authoritarian regime in the future? This was the object of our discussions and our tormented thoughts. Later on I wrote a book called *The State and Communism*, which was inspired by these discussions with Kuusinen.

My period in the authors' collective came to an end, although not quite in the manner that I would have liked. I had not done my work badly and all the sections on the state were included in the textbook as I wrote them. But I had carelessly made several ironic comments about our leaders and perhaps for this reason, even before the editing had been completed, Kuusinen's permission was sought to send some members of the collective home. I was one of them.

'It's a shame this has happened,' Arbatov said as he saw me off. 'I thought you would remain in the main collective, but the old man has decided to narrow down the group radically so that we don't get in each other's way. But you can be assured that all the sections you have written will remain as they are. We won't touch them.'

Well, at least I had that to be grateful for. Arbatov had brought me into the collective in the first place; maybe I really was no longer needed for the final stages of the work, and in any case there was no point in being sarcastic about good people.

My work in Kuusinen's authors' collective did not pass unnoticed. Apparently Kuusinen was a close acquaintance of Yu. V. Andropov from the time they had worked together in the Karelian republic.

2 Andropov

My meeting with this man changed the course of my life. It was a meeting that was so unexpected and unforeseen that it could be regarded as pure accident or, if you like, the hand of fate.

Here's what happened. I was cycling with my son on Kurkinskoye highway near Moscow. If you have been there you will probably know the famous and incredibly beautiful cycle track, which is often used for national and international cycling competitions. This place is known as the Soviet Switzerland.

Between the holiday house called Verkhneye Nargornoye and the holiday village called Nizhneye Nagornoye – both belonging to the same department – there is a very steep, winding road. An ordinary cyclist will not usually take the risk of going down it. But my seven-year-old son and I were daring fellows and we used to whistle down together on one semi-racing bike. The most exciting part, having got down the slope, was to try and get as high as possible up the equally steep slope on the other side. We practically never made it to the top and would leap off half-way.

On that sunny summer's day we did not manage to get very high. We got off the bike and, pushing it, slowly walked up the steep hill. My thoughts were not even remotely connected with work. The intense heat, my usual proclivity for abstract thought and the constant family cares that surrounded me had caused me to feel a sense of mild protest tinged with irony. What am I doing, I thought, what am I dedicating the best years of my life to? After all, there is no greater slavery than domestic slavery. I was amazed that this simple thought had never entered anyone's head. 'Man is born free but is everywhere in chains.' I remember how stirred I had been by these words from Rousseau's *Social Contract* as a student of the history of political science. He was writing about social slavery, but there was nothing you could do about that form of slavery: you did not determine the time and place of your birth or your social condition. But there was another form of slavery that was far more burdensome, and it was voluntary. A man is born free and submits to the absolute power of a woman. You fall under the total control of another person, alien to you in culture, habits and life-style.

Of course, domestic slavery also had its other side. Nothing could compare with that inexpressible joy of seeing, feeling and absorbing this tiny copy of yourself, this strange bundle of existence, which gradually begins to acquire your appearance and in its funny way repeats all your gestures, movements and habits. If not for this marital thrall I would never have experienced that feeling of something inner, deep and subconscious totally engulfing one's whole being.

Meanwhile this small embodiment of myself, my little Sergey, was walking next to me with fast, slightly tottering yet lively and energetic steps, his sparkling dark hazel eyes filled with deep thoughts, mischief and a kind of magnetic force . . . My God! How long ago it all was!

We had not yet reached the top when a Chayka car drew up beside us and a man with a slight limp leaped out. It was Lev Nikolayevich Tolkunov, whom I had known for a long time.

'Fedor, fancy seeing you here on your bike. Haven't you got anything better to do at a time like this?' he asked, with his wide, slightly Japanese-like smile. 'Come and work for us in our department. I've been appointed deputy and my position as consultant is vacant. I will recommend you.'

'I know how to ride a bike, but I haven't the foggiest notion about working in a department,' I said, somewhat taken aback by his persistence, although I had long ago made it a rule never to show surprise at anything.

'What are you going on about bikes for? If you like, you can ride your bike in your spare time, if you have any of course.' Tolkunov continued to smile inscrutably. 'Come tomorrow morning to Entrance No. 3. I will order a pass for you.'

I did not have time to reply, nor did he wait for one. The magnificent Chayka disappeared around the bend. Tolkunov and I worked together – at least, our offices were in the same corridor. *Kommunist* had moved to the third floor of the building which belonged to *Pravda*, where he was working at the time. We were not exactly great friends, but we often played table tennis together in a room on our floor. Once or twice, strolling outside in the courtyard, we had talked about serious matters.

'Who is he, Dad?' my son asked. He had always been curious and poked his nose into everything. 'Where has he invited you to work? What is a department?'

I did not answer. What could I say when I myself only had the vaguest idea of what it meant to work in a department? How could I work there when I found it difficult enough to put up with the minimal discipline required on a journal? In a department you had to arrive on the stroke of nine and sit there until six every day, maybe seven or eight.

Was I capable of doing that? Anyway, what did I know about departmental matters? I had never managed anyone or anything and had no particular desire to do so. By that time I had written two books and my articles were being published in almost every issue of the journal. More than anything else I wanted to write and, if possible, to try my hand at literature. Even at the journal, where I had enough time to do my own work, I felt oppressed, chained to my desk, forced to publish something in every issue. How could I even contemplate working in a department where one probably did not have a minute to oneself?

Despite the modest position I held at the journal I felt that I was actively participating in the tumultuous political events of the late fifties. Every article I wrote (and I had several dozen articles published in the journal) had provoked lively discussions among our collective and beyond it.

'You like walking the tightrope, Fedor Mikhaylovich,' a very experienced and resourceful colleague on the newspaper once said to me. 'Take care you don't fall off!'

But that worried me least of all. I was often told that I had a genetic shortcoming – an underdeveloped instinct for self-preservation. It was true: I had broken my hand three times, my leg once and had even managed to damage my spine. But that, of course, was not the point. Having become involved in political life after 1953 I profoundly believed that I was a part of the most progressive tendencies in our country. Perhaps it meant being somewhat ahead of the times, but some rash person had to take on this dangerous mission, even if it was against his own interests.

Many people in the post-Stalin generation felt that way. The political pendulum had swung so far in the direction of an authoritarian regime and total control that it must inevitably have gathered enormous momentum to swing in the opposite direction. I was meeting more and more people in political life who were infected with a messianic desire to reform our ideology and the whole of our society. It was a struggle against tyranny which was all the more embittered as it clashed sharply with the mood of the majority, who continued by force of inertia to think and live by the old rules.

There was something else that worried me as well; a sense of guilt towards those who had been slightly older than me at school, the majority of whom had died at the front. My brother had gone to the war and had fought at Stalingrad. He returned an invalid and died soon after. We were the first generation to escape death at the front, although we had prepared ourselves for it. As Vladimir Vysotsky later sang, 'We lads wanted to fight the tanks.' For us, Stalinism was just such a tank. We felt an inexorable urge to take the risk and fight the heirs of Stalin.

The episode with Tolkunov had so little effect on me that I did not even tell my wife about it when we returned to our small room on the second floor of the two-storey manor house in Nagornoye. I say 'manor house', although that is not quite correct. Strictly speaking, the house had been built about twenty years before on the model of an old manor house of mediocre design.

I am describing these everyday details to let the reader see that I was in no way prepared to meet the man who was to become a political legend in our country and who for many years and in many ways determined my fate.

There was nothing usual about my first meeting with Yuri Vladimirovich Andropov, or Yu.V., as everyone called him in his absence. He was then head of the Liaison with Communist and Workers' Parties of Socialist Countries Department of the Central Committee of the CPSU. I had hardly heard anything about him before we met, though I had been in the building where his department was situated. Literally a few days earlier I had gone to that same Entrance No. 3 and up to the second floor, where I had been invited by a man who had a room next to Yu.V.'s and whose work concerned the international Communist movement. I had edited his article and he had asked to see me immediately because, as I was told, my suggestions and comments had made a good impression on him. Later I found out that the head of the Central Committee International Department also had his eye on me and wanted to size me up for the same reason as did Yu.V. – to see if I would go for the job of consultant in his department.

So I entered Yu.V.'s office not feeling unduly nervous although, of course, not without some curiosity. The journalistic and academic circles in which I moved at the time had little respect for rank, not to mention the fact that from my earliest days I had responded critically to all figures of authority, trying to make my own independent judgement of a person's worth and resisting outside pressure. Moreover, it was very natural for me to respond to every situation as if it were a game. It was as if everything taking place around me was not real, as if some unspoken agreement had been made beforehand and everyone was playing a role, treating it as a matter of indifference and of little importance, while what was important remained unarticulated and took place somewhere in a mysterious consciousness, or even in the subconscious.

This often saved me in difficult situations. People without this sense of theatre would often freeze up, fearing for their fate or for the work they were doing, and this would hinder them from actively discussing a problem or getting something done. It seemed to me better to maintain a slightly aloof and ironic approach to any situation. Of course, this characteristic had its negative side. I was often careless and rash in my remarks and, as Yu.V. used to say later, 'exposed my flanks'.

31

I remember I was not overawed when Yu. V., after the usual handshake, returned to his seat behind the desk. Tolkunov had accompanied me to the study and we sat down on little chairs on opposite sides of the room in a line with Yu.V.'s desk. Casting a quick glance around the room, I saw two enormous windows, covering almost the entire wall and looking out on the entrance side, a portrait of Lenin over Yu.V.'s head and an extended table on his left, around which there were no less than ten or twelve massive chairs and the chairman's armchair. I did not know then that I would sit around that table hundreds of times for hours on end, usually in the same place on Yu.V.'s left, and participate with him in the joint collective work of composing, editing and rewriting the documents and speeches of our country's leaders; work which was difficult, frequently stormy, endlessly tiring but very inspiring. But all this was still to come.

In the meantime I sat smiling cheerfully for some reason in response to Yu.V.'s soft smile. At that time he was already wearing glasses, but they did not hide his large, radiant blue eyes and his penetrating and firm gaze. He had an enormous forehead, which looked as if it had been specially shaven clean on both sides of his temples, a large impressive nose, thick lips and a cleft chin, and he liked to keep his hands on the table, interlocking his fingers then separating them again time after time. In short, from the first glance this large massive figure inspired confidence and good will. I felt well disposed to him before he had uttered a single word.

'I've been told you work in the international department of the journal,' he said in a resonant voice.

'Yes, I'm deputy head of the department.'

'And how would you feel about working here with us?' he asked unexpectedly.

I remember he put this question to me at the very beginning of our conversation, so that it took me by surprise. I would have expected such a question closer to the end, after he had got to know me. I only realized later that this question did not commit Yu.V. to anything. He had not yet made an offer. It was his way of getting to know a candidate. I did not feel this to be a well-rehearsed social gambit, or a desire to make a person uncomfortable and then watch his reaction. It simply reflected one of Yu.V.'s characteristic qualities, an uncommonly well-developed intuition which seldom let him down.

'I haven't thought about it,' I said quite sincerely, amazed at the turn of events and forgetting to come out with the accepted formula of how highly I appreciated the confidence placed in me. I added: 'To be honest, I'm not at all certain how useful I would be in your department. I like to write, but I don't know that I'm particularly suited for work in the apparatus.'

'Whatever else there might be, you'll have more than enough opportunity to write. As a matter of fact, we were interested in you because we don't have enough people who can write well and think theoretically. We have enough organizers. Pure administrative work will be the least of your worries. Our consultants are assigned to work on important political documents. Your work at the journal and your qualifications – you're working for a doctorate in jurisprudence, aren't you? – could be very useful to us for party work.'

'I have never worked on the problems of socialist countries . . .'

'But you have written about Soviet political experience, about our state, about the development of democracy . . .' Tolkunov put his word in. 'That's just the background you need to understand the experience of other socialist countries.'

'Well, what do you think?' Yu.V. smiled politely. 'I think we get along with each other, don't you?'

'As far as I'm concerned, there's no doubt about it.'

'Good, then,' Yu.V. said and shook my hand in a friendly way.

I don't remember how I found myself in the corridor, hurrying after Tolkunov, who despite his limp was walking with quick athletic strides towards his room on the third floor.

'You'll find it interesting here, Fedor,' Tolkunov said. 'You'll see, we'll work well together.'

I did not know what to say and so continued smiling that stupid smile which had been my reaction to meeting the head of this important department, a man who seemed to be both so eminent and at the same time so charming. Tolkunov said goodbye on the landing and I walked down the stairs from the second floor. Handing in my pass to the man in charge, who went by the title of lieutenant, I walked out into the street where a couple of dozen black and white Volga cars, which had only recently appeared on the streets of Moscow, were standing by the entrance.

I was still relishing the pleasant feeling I had experienced at the meeting, but quite frankly it did not enter my head that anything would come of it and that it would change my life and set me on a different course. I saw myself as a person with a talent for quite different things – for literature and academic work, but certainly not for politics. Future events showed how wrong I had been in evaluating myself and my vocation. But who knows? Perhaps I was right then, and mistaken when I thought I could become a political animal.

*

Ten days passed. I had not forgotten the meeting – that would have been impossible – but I had put it out of my mind, although deep down a feeling of satisfaction remained which I could not quite comprehend. I thought I was simply pleased at having made a good impression on such an important person. Suddenly I got a phone call in the middle of the day at the office. It was Tolkunov.

'Fedor! Come to work tomorrow morning. A pass has been ordered for you. A decision has been reached.'

'A decision? What decision?'

'What do you mean? You've been appointed a consultant at the department. The First signed it personally. So don't dawdle and be here tomorrow. We're up to our ears in work. So, see you later. [I heard another phone ringing in the background, and so loudly!] Yu.V. has sent for me.'

I put the receiver down with such an odd expression on my face that my colleague, sitting across the table from me, asked: 'Has something happened? Did you make a blunder in your article?'

'No, nothing terrible has happened, only I'll probably have to hand over all my work to you today.'

'You don't say! Is it that bad?'

'I'm being moved to the department,' I said, still a bit confused.

'Well, why are you moping, old man? We'll have to drink to that and see you off.'

'Instead of throwing a farewell party, I'll leave you my small library. It consists of thirteen volumes of the works of Stalin on glossy paper and extravagantly bound.'

The next morning I was already sitting at my desk by a window looking out at the enclosed courtyard. I did not like the room: it was as narrow as a pencil box and reminded me of my first room in a three-roomed apartment, which I had been allocated when working on the journal. It was sausage-like and always draughty because the window faced the door. Moreover, the room was associated with painful memories. Four of us had lived there – me, my wife, our son and the nanny – and it became five when my mother arrived after she had retired.

For about three days I languished in my 'pencil box', not knowing what to do with myself. It was 1960 and the whole department was busy at a conference of representatives of the Communist and workers' parties and no one had any time for me. On the third day, towards evening, I heard the familiar and by now dear tones of Tolkunov: 'Fedor, are you very busy at the moment? I want to drag you off somewhere. You'll find it interesting. I'm on my way out now.'

Overjoyed, I quickly walked down the stairs from the second floor and ran to the entrance just as the limping Tolkunov appeared. We got into a car and in three minutes we were entering the Kremlin. Showing his pass, Tolkunov imperiously said, 'He's with me,' and I was let through, but not before they had thoroughly compared my physiognomy with the photograph on my pass.

My heart was pounding joyfully: it was the first time I had been inside the Kremlin. I walked proudly by Tolkunov's side, having time to glance around me and try to memorize everything – the majestic old towers, the church cupolas and the whitish roadway with its parking lot for the black cars, which looked out of place against the background of these majestic antiquities.

We went up to the top floor and, passing a wide indoor stairway, found ourselves in an enormous hall with numerous tables on which there were drinks and a variety of snacks. There were at least two hundred people crowding around the tables, clinking glasses, making toasts, moving from place to place and making such a din that it was difficult to hear anything.

My attention was distracted by loud conversation at the very end of the hall where our leaders and those of other parties had gathered. I began to push my way closer to hear what Nikita Sergeyevich Khrushchev was saying. Standing about ten feet from him, I was able to observe him at close quarters for the first time.

The older generation, of course, remembers this distinctive figure, but the younger generation has probably never even seen his portrait. By then he had turned sixty, but he looked very strong, agile and mischievously cheerful. At the slightest provocation he would burst out laughing, opening his enormous mouth with its badly arranged and protruding teeth, some of which were his own and some metallic.

His wide face with its two warts and his enormous bald head, large upturned nose and very protruding ears could well have belonged to a peasant from a village in central Russia or a worker living near Moscow – the kind you can see moving along the queue to the wine counter. The impression of a man from the common folk was especially accentuated by his thick figure and what appeared to be, due to his continuous gesticulations, inordinately long arms. Only his eyes – hazel eyes, either brimming with humour or anger, either radiating kindness or authority – only his eyes, I repeat, betrayed that he was a purely political animal, who had gone through thick and thin and was capable of the most abrupt turnabouts either in conversation, at official appearances or in deciding matters of state.

When I first saw him he was standing with a glass in his hand and everyone else, Soviet and foreign guests, was sitting around several tables that had been pushed close together. He held a glass of brandy which hindered his gesticulations, but he waved the glass about in the air, spilling brandy on the white tablecloth and frightening those next to him without being aware of it himself. Only later, his passions aroused, his eyes no longer narrowed but wide with the horror of his reminiscences, did he carefully place the glass on the table, thus releasing his right hand which was absolutely essential to add conviction to his words. Here I heard for the first time a story which he later repeated twice in my presence in circumstances which were more private and involved only a few people. The amazing thing was that he repeated the story almost word for word.

'When Stalin died, we, the members of the Presidium, went to the Blizhnyaya dacha in Kuntsevo. He was lying on the sofa and there were no doctors about. In the last months of his life Stalin seldom turned to doctors. He was scared of them. Perhaps Beria had frightened him or he himself believed that the doctors were hatching plots against him and other leaders. He was being treated at the time by a major in the security police, who had once been an assistant veterinarian. He trusted him. It was he who had rung and told us of Stalin's death and had called the doctors. There we were, standing by the dead body, hardly saying a word to each other, each thinking his own thoughts. Later we began to disperse. Two people got into each car. The first to leave were Malenkov and Beria, followed by Molotov and Kaganovich. At that moment Mikoyan said to me, "Beria has gone to Moscow to seize power." I answered, "While this bastard is around none of us can feel safe." It was then that the thought became firmly lodged in my mind that the first thing to do was to remove Beria. But how could one even begin to talk about this with the other leaders? At that time anyone could be spying on you or inform on you if you said something. Several months later I began to visit all the members of the Presidium one by one. The most dangerous visit was to Malenkov; after all he and Lavrenty were friends. Well, I came to see him and said, "This is the way it is. We must remove Beria. As long as he is among us, free to move about and with the security organs in his hands, our own hands are tied. Nor is it certain that he won't play a trick on us at any moment. Look," I said, "for some reason special divisions are being moved to Moscow." One must give Georgy Malenkov his due – he supported me on this at the expense of his personal friendship. Apparently, he was scared of his own friend. Malenkov was then chairman of the Council of Ministers and chaired the sessions of the Presidium of the Central Committee. In short, he had something to lose. Then I went to see Molotov. He thought for a long time, was silent and listened, but in the end he said, "Yes, you're right, it can't be avoided. Only it has to be done in such a way that things don't turn out worse." I told him about my plan, which went as follows: to replace the guard at the entrance, where the session of the Presidium took place, with reliable officers and there and then at the session to arrest this viper. After that I went to see Voroshilov. Klim Yefremovich is sitting here now, he remembers. I had to talk to him a long time. He was very worried that everything might come unstuck. Am I right, Klim?'

'Yes, you're right,' Kliment Yefremovich confirmed loudly and blushed, either because of the story or the drink. 'Anything to prevent a war,' he added rather irrelevantly.

'Well, as for war, that's a separate subject,' the First continued. 'So, after that I went to see Kaganovich and told him everything. He said, "What side is the majority on? Who is supporting whom? Will someone support him?" But when I told him about the others he also agreed. And so I came to the session. We all sat down, but Beria wasn't there. So, I thought, he's probably found out. Our heads will roll. Who knows where we'll find ourselves tomorrow. But in he came, with a briefcase in his hands. I guessed right away what he had in that briefcase! I had also come prepared for the occasion . . .' and here the speaker patted the right-hand pocket of his baggy suit. 'Beria sat down, sprawled in his chair and asked, "So, what's the issue on the agenda? Why have we gathered here so unexpectedly?" I kicked Malenkov under the table and whispered, "Open the meeting. Let me speak." I noticed he went white and couldn't open his mouth. I jumped up myself and said, "There is one issue on the agenda. The anti-party, divisive activities of the agent of imperialism, Beria. The proposal," I said, "is to remove Beria from the Presidium and from the Central Committee, to expel him from the party and to hand him over to a military tribunal. Who is for the proposal?" And I was the first to raise my hand. Then everyone else raised their hands. Beria turned green and went for his briefcase. But I snatched his briefcase – and held it! "You must be joking," I said, "stop that!" At the same time I was pressing the buzzer. Here officers from Moskalenko's military garrison ran in. I had coordinated it with them earlier. I gave them the order: "Remove this viper, this traitor to the motherland and put him where he belongs." Beria began to mumble something, he was all green and had shat his pants. He was so brave when he grabbed others and stood them up against the wall. Well, you know the rest. He was judged and sentenced to be shot. That's how it was. And now let's drink to' – and once again he picked up his glass – 'let's drink to this never happening again anywhere. We ourselves have washed out this stinking, dirty spot and have done everything to guarantee that nothing like this ever happens in the future. I want to assure you, comrades, that we will create guarantees against this and together we will go forward towards the heights of Communism! To the health of the leaders of all the fraternal parties!'

At that moment I finally tore my eyes away from the storyteller and glancing to one side saw Yu.V. He was sitting silently, his head bowed, staring blankly. I found out afterwards that he did not as a rule like drinking and was unable to himself, as he suffered from high blood pressure. But at the time it seemed to me he felt embarrassed for Khrushchev, that he considered it out of place to speak about such matters with a crowd around. Maybe I was mistaken, but his face was very expressive and you could always tell what mood he was in. (Hardly anyone, of course, could guess what his thoughts were.)

As for me, I was astounded by everything I had seen and heard, and particularly by the ease with which I had been admitted to the hidden mysteries of the state.

Subsequently, Khrushchev returned to his story of Beria's arrest many times, introducing new details. The most important ones were to do with the reactions of the different leaders to his proposal to remove this butcher. Voroshilov was not the only one who vacillated; Kaganovich wavered for a long time, asking persistently who was for and who against, and even Mikoyan, with whom Khrushchev had first raised the question, thought at first that Beria was perhaps not entirely beyond salvation and might still be able to work in the collective. The description of the arrest also changed somewhat.

In 1960 Khrushchev failed to mention the part played by Marshal Zhukov, as not long before he had succeeded in dismissing him from his posts in the leadership. Later, honesty triumphed over opportunism and Khrushchev acknowledged that Zhukov had played the leading part in the arrest, together with Moskalenko and other military personnel. Incidentally, I was told by an interesting person, V. Lesnichy, a party worker from one of the research centres near Moscow, about a speech Zhukov gave to their collective. Zhukov spoke about Beria, whom he loathed with all the strength of his indomitable spirit.

According to Zhukov, at eleven o'clock on the day they were to seize Beria 'the phone rang. 'Khrushchev said, "Georgy Konstantinovich, please come and see me. It is very important." I got into the car and arrived. When I entered the office he stood up, approached me and taking my hand, said, "Georgy Konstantinovich, we have to arrest that bastard Beria today. Don't ask me any questions; I'll explain everything later." I took a deep breath, closed my eyes and said, "Nikita Sergeyevich, I have never been a policeman, but this is a policeman's mission that I will fulfil with great pleasure. What do I have to do?" Khrushchev said, "Take the generals with you, accompany them through the Borovitsky Gate, enter the reception room where the session of the Presidium will take place, wait for me to buzz, enter, seize him and stay there until three in the morning, when the guard changes. Then the major will come, he will give the password and you will hand over Beria. That's all." ' Zhukov continued, 'Then I told Batitsky and Moskalenko to get in the back of the car, covered them with a horse-rug as they didn't have passes, drove through the Borovitsky Gate into the Kremlin and entered the reception room. Nobody except me knew why we were there. We waited. There was no buzz at 1 pm, nor at five minutes past one. I imagined that Beria had arrested everyone and was looking for me. The situation was very alarming. At fifteen minutes past one the buzzer went. We got out our pistols: one man stood by the entrance and Moskalenko and I walked in. Beria was sitting on the left-hand side. I went towards him and saw a briefcase lying in front of him. The thought flashed through my mind that perhaps he had a weapon in there. I pushed aside the briefcase, grabbed Beria by the hands and cried out, "Beria is under arrest!" He leaped up and cried out, "Georgy Konstantinovich, what's going on?" In reply I cried out again, "Silence!" I turned around – and marched out with him. It seemed to me that not all the members of the Presidium knew about the arrest and suspected that this was a military coup. We led Beria away, took off his pince-nez, smashed it, cut the buttons off his trousers and sat there until three o'clock in the morning. Then we took him away.'

That was Zhukov's story. Someone in the audience at the collective asked him: 'What would you say was the most important thing in your life?' Without hesitation the Marshal had answered, 'The arrest of Beria!' So there you have it . . .

The episode with the briefcase, mentioned by both Khrushchev and Zhukov, was a pure piece of Freudianism. It appears that one of them had pushed the briefcase aside; the other had grabbed it, assuming there was a weapon in it. But there was no weapon, as they both acknowledged later. However, they repeated the episode of the briefcase over and over again because in their minds it symbolized the horror of what might have happened if they had failed.

But let us return to the hall, where Khrushchev had not yet finished with his outspoken reminiscences. He raised his brandy glass:

'I have often been asked why I suddenly decided to give that speech at the Twentieth Congress. We believed in that man for so many years. We had elevated him. We created his cult. There was an enormous risk. What would be the reaction from party leaders, from leaders abroad, from our whole country? Well, I want to tell you a story, which I remember from my youth when I was still learning to read and write. There used to be a book called *How to Read and Recite*, which included many interesting things. I read a story in that book, but I don't remember who the author was. There were these political prisoners in jail under tsarism – Socialist Revolutionaries, Mensheviks and Bolsheviks. Amongst them was an old shoemaker named Pinya, who was in prison by mistake. They decided to elect a headman of their cell. Each party proposed its own candidate and a great argument broke out. What were they to do? Then someone proposed the shoemaker Pinya, an inoffensive fellow who didn't belong to any of the parties. Everyone laughed, but they later agreed. And Pinya became the headman. Then one day they decided to escape from prison. They began to dig an underground tunnel. How long they dug, we don't know, but they reached the outside. Then the question arose of who should be the first to go down the tunnel. Maybe the prison authorities already knew about the tunnel and were waiting for them guns in hand. The first one to crawl out would be the first to die. Some said the Socialist Revolutionary fighters should go, while the Socialist Revolutionaries said it should be the Bolsheviks. At that moment the old shoemaker Pinya rose up from the corner and said, "As you chose me to be headman, I will have to be the first." And that's what I did at the Twentieth Congress. As I was chosen to be First, I had to – like the shoemaker Pinya, I was obliged to be the first to tell the truth about the past, whatever the consequences and the risks to me. Lenin taught us that if the party is not scared of telling the truth it will never perish. We have learned all the lessons of the past and we would like our brother parties to learn these lessons. Then our common victory will be ensured. I would like to drink to our unity and loyalty to the legacy of the great Lenin.'

Everyone began to clap, although I noticed that the representatives of two or three parties abstained. The reader will easily guess who I mean: the Chinese and Albanian representatives. Everyone remembers the sharp debate which broke out after the 1960 conference, although despite the very difficult struggle that ensued a joint statement had been agreed upon.

Meanwhile one toast followed another and it was around midnight before the noisy evening came to an end. I had been introduced to many prominent people, but I felt awkward for almost the whole evening. It seemed to me that I had penetrated this high-level gathering by some unlawful means and had heard things that I should not have heard. Everyone had arrived dressed in either black or navy blue suits, which was the custom at the time. At work you wore a navy blue suit in winter and a grey one in summer. I did not have either a black or a navy blue suit. I was wearing a light brown suit, defiantly flaunting spangles and shoulder pads which had been sewn on by a tailor who wanted to turn me into a 'trendy'. I stood out like a sore thumb in these odd clothes at such a high-level meeting. (This timidity and other such hang-ups soon passed. For that matter, I began to have my suits made properly at a special tailor's – a navy blue and a grey suit and even the diplomatic black one.)

Obviously Tolkunov knew what he was doing. He carried me to Olympus right away and gave me the opportunity to meet our main 'clients'; that is, those for whom we had to write speeches and provide information and documents.

I was staggered by the rapid changes that had taken place in my life. I was particularly surprised at how quickly the head of the department had made up his mind about me, although he had only seen me for a few minutes. I only learned later that he had inquired about me from a person he trusted completely. This was Otto Vilgelmovich Kuusinen, who had not long previously entered the top ranks of our party and state.

3 A Populist

Does history make personalities or do personalities make history? I have often pondered on this question when writing about the political figures of the twentieth century and I still have no clear answer.

Mikhail Bulgakov, whose name was rehabilitated in Khrushchev's time, asks in his novel *The Master and Margarita*, in the words of the devil Woland: can people accept the idea of freedom of will if their lives are so limited that they are in no condition to plan at least a thousand years ahead? There's another problem: a brick doesn't fall on somebody's head accidentally. Everything is predestined. The belief in predestination was also inculcated in us in our youth although, it's true, it was called determinism. Perhaps this came from Hegel, that the real is rational. This means that what was, had to be. It is only with age and experience that we have come to understand the multiple possibilities of history. History has many options and different figures take part in the game.

A pawn reaches the final row and is transformed into a queen. Or the queen falls into a trap and becomes the pawn's victim. I don't want to be drawn into a discussion of the problem of 'the people' versus 'the outstanding individual' as, in the final analysis, the social and moral impulses which determine the nature of an epoch always emerge out of the people. But in a specific period a major historical personality makes an enormous imprint on history. At any rate one thing is obvious – that a political figure, especially the ruler of a country, acts not only as the instrument of history, but influences events and destinies in the most direct way.

How was it possible for someone like Khrushchev to come to power after Stalin? One would have thought that Stalin had thoroughly purged the party of opponents, whether genuine or imaginary, rightists or leftists. In the 1950s one of his aphorisms made the rounds: 'Where there's a person, there's a problem. Remove the person and you've removed the problem.' As a result it would seem that only the most faithful and reliable would have remained alive. How did he miss seeing in Khrushchev the man who would bury his cult?

In his last years Stalin turned against Molotov and Mikoyan, no doubt preparing the same fate for them as had befallen other leaders, who had been destroyed with their connivance and support. At the Nineteenth Party Congress in October 1952 a move was also made to get rid of another batch of comrades-in-arms. Strangely enough Khrushchev was not among them.

Was it the blindness of old age? I doubt it. Niccolò Machiavelli, a brilliant debunker of tyrants, once said: 'If Brutus had pretended to be a fool he would have become Caesar.' I think Khrushchev somehow managed to give the impression that he was quite tame, a man of no special ambitions. It is said that during the long sessions lasting well into the morning at the Blizhnyaya dacha in Kuntsevo, where the leader lived during his last thirty years, Khrushchev used to dance the hopak. At this time he went around in a Ukrainian peasant shirt, giving the impression of being a 'jolly Cossack' far from any claims to power, just a reliable executor of another's will. It appears, however, that Khrushchev already nursed a deep sense of protest, even if he himself did not fully realize how strong it was. This began to emerge the day after Stalin's death.

What sort of a person was Khrushchev, the man who became the third leader of the Soviet Union after the Revolution? What was his life like before his swift rise to power? These questions were on everyone's mind, including mine, as we observed the first steps he took and later watched him in action during the course of that 'glorious decade'. We knew little about Khrushchev, as he had spent the greater part of his career in the Ukraine. The first time we became aware of him was after his report on the Party Rules at the Nineteenth Party Congress. No one then regarded him as a possible successor to Stalin. This modest figure was pushed into the background by the more famous names of Molotov, Malenkov, Mikoyan, Beria, Bulganin and Voroshilov.

It was, therefore, with all the more interest that we began to search for information about Khrushchev's early career. The one short biography that came out during his lifetime was of unique importance. Strictly it wasn't even a biography, more a sketch about his life and work in the Ukraine. It was called *The Story of an Eminent Miner (N. S. Khrushchev in the Donbas)*. Few copies were printed, and they were distributed chiefly in the Ukraine. Khrushchev was not interested, at least at that time, in having a biography of himself disseminated. Everyone still vividly remembered how sharply he had criticized *A Short Biography of Stalin*, published in 1949, to mark Stalin's seventieth birthday, which depicted the 'supreme leader of all the peoples' as the wisest, greatest, most brilliant leader in the history of mankind.

★

Nikita Sergeyevich Khrushchev was born on the 4th (according to the Old Style calendar) or the 17th of April (New Style) 1894, in Kursk province, in the village of Kalinovka. His parents – his father Sergey Nikanorovich and his mother Ksenia Ivanovna – were simple peasants. As well as Nikita they had a daughter, Irina.

This is how Khrushchev himself described his life at a luncheon given in his honour at the Twentieth Century Fox film studios in the United States on 19 September 1959: 'You want to know who I am? I began to work as soon as I learned to walk. Until I was fifteen I tended calves and sheep, later I tended cows for a landowner. After that I worked in a factory owned by Germans, then I worked in the mines owned by the French. I worked in chemical factories, which were owned by the Belgians, but now – I am the Prime Minister of the great Soviet state.'[1]

At another time in another place, he again recalled his early life. 'I remember how I used to tend sheep, only I wasn't a shepherd but one rank lower. Sometimes the shepherd would send me off, saying, "Well, Nikita, run and make sure the sheep don't stray." And I would run off and bring them back. In the village I also looked after the calves. Later on I worked in factories and in the damp mines. I often came out of the mines wet and had to walk three kilometres home. The capitalists didn't build washrooms or changing-rooms for us. If Gorky went through the "universities of the people", I was brought up in the miners' "university". This was the working man's Cambridge, a "university" for the unfortunate people of Russia.'[2]

Nikita was an inquisitive boy. In the winter he went to school and fairly quickly learned to read and write. When he was fourteen – this was in 1908 – he moved with his family to the Uspensky mine in the Donbas.

At first Nikita worked at his previous job and tended cows, but soon he became a metal-fitter after a period as an apprentice. Khrushchev loved his work and was proud of it. Subsequently, when discussing the standard of living of workers then and under Soviet power, he relied on his own experience to make an honest assessment:

'I got married in 1914 when I was twenty,' he said. 'Because I had a very good profession I was able to rent an apartment right away. My apartment consisted of a drawing room, kitchen, bedroom and dining room. The years of the revolution came and went; it is painful to think that I, a worker, had lived in far better conditions under capitalism than the workers enjoyed under Soviet power. We have overthrown the monarchy and the bourgeoisie, we have won our freedom, but people live worse than they used to. It's not surprising that some people say, 'What sort of freedom is this? You promised us paradise. Perhaps we'll turn up in paradise after we die, but we would like to live better on earth. After all we're not making any special demands. Just give us a corner we can call our own.

'As a metal worker in the Donbas before the revolution I earned forty to forty-five roubles a month. Black bread cost two kopeks a pound, white bread, five kopeks. Lard went for twenty-two kopeks a pound, an egg cost a kopek. Good quality boots, like these that I'm wearing now, cost six roubles, at the most seven roubles. But after the Revolution wages declined sharply, while prices soared.'

It is interesting to note that psychologically Khrushchev did not leave his profession behind even when he held high posts in the 1930s. He was delighted at his promotions – he had become first secretary of the Moscow party *obkom*,★ first secretary of the Moscow city party committee and a candidate member of the Politburo as well – but he constantly feared a reversal in his fortunes. He acknowledged that his enormous responsibilities left him with a greater sense of fear than triumph. For many years he kept and carried around with him his metal-working kit: a ruler, set squares and other tools of the trade. Throughout the whole Stalinist period the feeling never left him that at any moment he might be thrown out and would have to return to his original occupation.[3]

In spite of his relative prosperity and a good profession the young metal-worker was dissatisfied. It wasn't just the heavy labour; he was outraged by the way the bosses treated the workers. The local police officer Yanovsky made this report to his superior: 'In my settlement, as well as at the Vetka mine at the Yuzovka station, there are 54,171 men and women; the settlement has one church, one Orthodox chapel, one mosque and one Gregorian prayer house. There are sixteen state wine shops and seventeen bars . . .'[4] We must assume that Nikita Sergeyevich used to drop in at these bars and wine shops together with his friends as, throughout his life, he had a weakness for good drink.

In Yuzovka Khrushchev received his first lessons in revolutionary struggle. The worker Yemelyan Kosenko held gatherings in his wattle and daub cottage in the evenings: girls were invited, Nikita played his accordion and everyone participated in sing-songs. Ideas began to form in his mind about ways of struggling against the bosses at the mines.

Nikita became friendly with a young miner, Panteley Makhinya, who introduced him to Russian literature and then to revolutionary books. Later, in his mature years, when he was the leader of the country, Khrushchev used to remember poems he had read in those youthful days: 'Over a truthful book I love to stoke the fires of emotion; So as to burn and burn and not burn out in our bustling life.'

The lines 'to burn and burn and not burn out' cut especially deeply

★ Regional party committee.

into the young miner's consciousness. He had a bold, even headstrong character and appropriately made these lines the *modus vivendi* of his entire life. His energy, vigour and daring could have been the envy of any record-breaking athlete or war hero.[5]

In Panteley Makhinya's tiny room Khrushchev first heard the words of the *Communist Manifesto*, which remained etched in his mind for life: 'A spectre is haunting Europe – the spectre of Communism . . .'

Those who took part in these meetings remember Nikita's words: 'This is what I think, lads. There will come a time when the working people will organize themselves, crush the tsar and all those bourgeois bastards and become lords of the earth themselves. What a life we will lead then!'[6]

At that time Nikita Sergeyevich had already come under suspicion. A curious document, a secret police agent's denunciation dated 25 May 1915, has been preserved which describes the strikes and represents the young Khrushchev as one of the leading organizers. He was put under secret police surveillance.

Due to police pressure Khrushchev and other workers who had taken part in the strike were fired. His friends, however, helped him to find work at another mine. Khrushchev used to joke about this: 'Well, lads, I changed my citizenship. I used to bow down to the Germans, now I will serve the French.'

Did Khrushchev's touchiness about any form of dependence on foreign capital originate here? Such touchiness was generally a characteristic of Soviet Communists, including Stalin, Bukharin and many others. Perhaps it explains why foreign concessions were such a controversial issue during the NEP period. Despite Lenin's stubborn insistence, the majority of party functionaries treated this idea with great apprehension. This attitude might also explain why Soviet leaders after the Second World War indignantly rejected the Marshall Plan, which offered economic aid to the ravaged country. Perhaps this explains why Khrushchev himself felt so ambivalent about the technological progress he saw abroad. On the one hand, he wanted to utilize the best achievements of the West; he admired the American farmer Hart's corn harvest and promoted the cultivation of this crop in the USSR very forcefully. On the other hand he feared any kind of intrusion from foreign business. This defensiveness, formed in his youth, made it difficult for him to grasp such new economic facts as the mutual dependence of national economies and the need to participate in the international division of labour.

Of course there were political reasons for Khrushchev's stance, but these basic attitudes, which took shape even before the Revolution, cannot be underestimated.

*

In March 1914 the paper *The Miners' Leaflet* began to circulate in the Donbas. Khrushchev was one of those who distributed it, as well as Lenin's *Pravda* and other underground literature, among the workers.

At a press conference held in Moscow on 12 June 1960 for Soviet and foreign journalists Khrushchev explained that his class approach to the exploitative nature of Western countries took shape in his youth: 'I would like to compare this exploitation with the situation in many enterprises in pre-revolutionary Russia. I am reminded of my youth when I used to work in the mines in Donbas where some capitalists would not pay the workers in money but in "vouchers", their own paper money. A trader by the name of Karakozov used to sell his goods in exchange for these orders. When the workers borrowed money from each other they used to say, "Lend me some karakozis." A rouble's worth of these "karakozis" often went for ten kopeks. You couldn't use this money anywhere except at Karakozov's and he sold rotten, lousy things, robbing the working people.'[7]

In March 1915 we see Khrushchev taking part in a major strike in the settlement of Rudchenkovka. He gave a fiery speech at the meeting and the police tried to arrest him, but the workers defended Nikita and chased them out of the workshops.

From 1916 these mines, and indeed the whole of the Donbas, became the forum for mass strikes and demonstrations by the workers. During one of the strikes in which Khrushchev took part the police opened fire on unarmed workers. Four men were killed and two injured. Mass arrests followed, but they could not prevent the approaching revolution.

Khrushchev describes how he and other Donbas workers greeted the news of the February Revolution. His article on this subject, 'Memoirs of a Rudchenkovka Worker', was published in 1922 on the fifth anniversary of the Revolution.

'On the day that the chains of autocracy were broken one couldn't help remembering the difficult years of the war – the high prices, the low wages and the people humiliated by those who did not work or who possessed some modicum of power. Then suddenly the day came. One evening we received telegrams with the news that the revolution had broken out in Petersburg. I remember with what joy we read this telegram hiding behind the lathe in the workshop. We were all confident that there would be no return to the past. I was overwhelmed by emotion, I wanted to laugh and cry. We felt certain of victory and the police standing nearby did not frighten us.'

A workers' meeting elected a provisional executive committee, which was charged with organizing elections to a soviet of workers' deputies. Khrushchev was elected to the committee and soon after became a member of the workers' soviet. The first thing the soviet did was to arrest the police officials, disband the police force and replace it with a workers' militia detachment. A few months later in August 1917 the Rudchenkovka miners set up their own military-revolutionary committee and Khrushchev was elected to it. Even at that time he supported the Bolshevik party line. At a meeting organized by the miners Khrushchev held the red flag high and proclaimed, 'Out with the rotten Kerensky government! Long live the Bolsheviks!'

After the October Revolution Khrushchev headed the soviet of mineworks committees, representing the trade unions of metal-workers in the mining industry. The soviet brought together the trade union organizations of eight major mines and other enterprises in Yuzovka. Here Khrushchev was educated in trade-union struggle, fighting for the interests of the workers.

In the civil war that was soon to follow we see Khrushchev in the ranks of the fighting Red Guard. He joined the First Donetsk Proletarian Regiment, which fought against the White Army of General Kaledin. However, when Rudchenkovka was taken by the Germans and the troops of the Central Rada (the nationalist Ukrainian government), Khrushchev had to flee. He was hidden underground in the mines and from there escaped into the steppe, passing through the enemy's occupying forces.

Khrushchev joined the Red Army and soon became a commissar. He fought in many areas of the country and at the heroic defence of Tsaritsyn, which was subsequently renamed Stalingrad. Of course, the young army commissar could not have imagined that more than twenty years later he would again be fighting in this region in the great battle for Stalingrad, this time as a member of the Military Council.

In his speech at the Twentieth Century Fox studios in Los Angeles, Khrushchev described his life during the civil war:

'I recall several episodes during the civil war and my meetings and conversations with the intelligentsia of former tsarist Russia. When we defeated the White Guards and pushed them into the Black Sea I was serving in the ranks of the Red Army. Our unit was in the Kuban and I stayed in a house which belonged to a family of the intelligentsia. The mistress of the house had once studied at the institute for girls of the nobility in St Petersburg, while I, it seems, when I lived in her house, still smelled of coal. Other members of the intelligentsia also lived there – a lawyer, an engineer, a teacher and a musician.

'We Red Army soldiers used to talk to them. When they got to know me, a Communist, they saw not only that I didn't eat human flesh but that I was simply starving. Sometimes I didn't even have any bread, but I didn't take any away from them, and I didn't ask for anything.

'Members of the old intelligentsia began to realize that Communists were honest people, who were not out for personal gain but were committed to the common welfare. I remember the mistress of the house asking me what I knew about ballet: "After all you are a simple miner!" I knew nothing about ballet; not only had I never seen a ballet but I'd never met a ballerina. I didn't have the foggiest. But I said, just wait, we will have everything and ballet too. To tell you the truth if someone had asked me what the future held in store I probably wouldn't have known how to answer, but I firmly believed that a wonderful life awaited us.'

This story was typical of a whole generation of young revolutionary activists. Their 'elders', as Lenin and many of his colleagues were called, were erudite and educated, skilled professional publicists and men of letters, who had accomplished enormous feats educating themselves in works of theory. By contrast, the Khrushchev generation came to the revolution with the simple baggage of 'class instinct'.

This instinct shaped political consciousness according to a simple formula: we are the workers, they are the bourgeoisie and landowners. The intelligentsia, of course, is closer to the rich than the poor. Our job is to take power from the oppressors of the working class, crush their resistance, subordinate them to our will and then . . . we shall, of course, build a new life never before envisaged on this earth. As we sang in the 'Internationale': 'We will destroy the world by force down to its foundations, and then we will build a new, new world. He who was nothing will become all.'

For Khrushchev and his generation of more simple folk, one thing was clear: the pyramid had to be turned over and those at the bottom brought up to the top. What sort of society would emerge? Well, that would come later. It is strange that even after Khrushchev had been through the great school of political life and had visited many countries in the world, including France, England and the United States, he never freed himself, as we will see later, from this black and white formula acquired during his revolutionary youth. The capitalists stood on one side, the Communists on the other. There were the workers and the exploiters. There was the socialist camp and the capitalist camp and struggle between them was inevitable. One would bury the other.

I would go further and say that Khrushchev was typical of a certain section of the working class. These were first-generation workers who had only recently come from the countryside. One could name dozens of descendants of skilled workers who had been schooled in politics and theory even before the revolution and the first years of Soviet power. Men like Khrushchev had been shepherds before they became industrial workers. They hated the landowner and the capitalist equally, but they only had a vague idea of how they would topple the previous system or what they would put in its place.

At the end of the civil war Khrushchev returned to his native

Rudchenkovka. In his grey uniform he once again became a miner and the young leader of a party cell. He became the head of the Rudchenkovka group of the party organization. The so-called epoch of War Communism had not yet come to an end and the devastation was awful. Inflation had reached such a scale that half a loaf of bread cost a million roubles. Labour conscription was compulsory for the whole male population – men from eighteen to forty-six years of age, skilled workers up to the age of fifty, technical specialists up to the age of sixty-five. Those who evaded these duties were often shot or sent to prison. The local paper, under the characteristic heading 'The Dictatorship of Labour' wrote in June 1920: 'Our latest task is to conduct resolutely labour conscription. This is one of the complex tasks whose completion will bring us yet another step closer to Communism. We call for the general mobilization of all non-working elements under the slogan: "In the workers' republic there is no place for parasites and idlers. They will either be shot or reprocessed on the great millstone of labour." '

These were cruel times. As historians now testify, 14–18 million people died during the civil war. Of them, only 900,000 were killed at the front. The rest fell victim to typhus and other diseases, as well as to the White and Red terror. War Communism was partly the result of the horrors of the civil war and partly the result of the errors of a whole generation of revolutionaries. It meant the direct appropriation of foodstuffs from the peasants wihout compensation, rations for workers of from a pound to a quarter of a pound of black bread, compulsory labour, execution and prison for market dealings, an enormous army of orphans who had lost their parents, famine, people turning into savages in many areas of the country – such was the dreadful cost of the most radical revolution ever to have shaken the world.

In 1921 the period of the New Economic Policy (NEP) began. Grain requisitioning was ended and a system of ordinary taxation introduced. Peasant life began to form again within the framework of the family unit. The first steps were taken to revive industry. It was at this moment that the appeal known as 'Lenin's call-up' rang out to young workers, who had only recently left the ranks of the Red Army, to 'Learn, Learn, Learn!' – so that they would be able to run the state. Lenin wrote, 'NEP fully ensures the creation of the economic and political foundation of socialism.' It all depended on the 'cultural capacities of the proletariat and its vanguard'. Khrushchev was among the first of these young people to respond to the call.

In May 1921 he became a student at the Don Technical College. At the same time he studied in the workers' faculty. His energy and boldness and his irrepressible character got him elected secretary of the technical college's party cell. This was the first step in his ascent to the political leadership of the country.

In 1926 the technical college was turned into the Industrial Institute and Khrushchev continued his studies there. After some time he became secretary of the *raykom** in the Petrovo–Marinsky area, which he knew well.

*

Khrushchev made his first appearance at a nationwide political forum in 1925 when he was elected a delegate to the Fourteenth Party Congress. This was the famous occasion when Stalin clashed with the 'new opposition', led by Zinovyev and Kamenev. Khrushchev resolutely took Stalin's side. When he returned home he said in his report to the plenum of the district party committee: 'Our line is the line of the majority, that is, of the Party Congress and the Central Committee.'[8]

Let each person state what his position is, declared the young party organizer. As we can see, his position was clear from the very start. He went along with the majority and Stalin directed the majority. It is not that easy now to imagine how political forces were demarcated at that time. Many people think that Stalin's success was achieved through the struggle he waged against other members of Lenin's Politburo and his exceptional mastery of intrigue and behind-the-scenes machinations. But it was much more complicated than that.

More than a million people were recruited into the party as a result of 'Lenin's call-up' campaign. For the most part they were young people, Red Army soldiers or workers from lower Komsomol cells. As distinct from the Old Guard which consisted of the intelligentsia or quasi-intelligentsia, the new generation of Communists was of working and partly peasant origins. They knew little or nothing about the complicated theoretical questions discussed at the Thirteenth, Fourteenth and subsequent Party Congresses.

People like Trotsky, Kamenev and Zinovyev – or even Bukharin – made little impression on them. They were an alien breed to these young workers and peasants, who regarded them as 'idle debaters', obfuscating questions that were clear enough. The clearest question of all was the need to work and mobilize the workers, peasants and specialists. Moreover, the majority of these new young Communists had grown up in the cruel period of the civil war when everything had been simple: there were Whites and Reds – one side would win, the other would be ranged against the wall.

Stalin was a great deal less educated and cultured than Trotsky, Zinovyev or Bukharin, and his personal qualities were more attractive to the masses. He never complicated matters, but put forward simple,

* District party committee.

comprehensible slogans. Build socialism in one country. Mobilize forces and speed up industrialization. Use the countryside – where else could resources come from? Crush the opposition which interfered with work. Oppose world imperialism and its attempts to strangle the first workers' state.

I am, therefore, inclined to think that Khrushchev took Stalin's side sincerely. Of course, it was probably also important to him that he was supporting the majority. It was instinctive for the working man to be an integral part of the collective and not to break with the common ranks or stand out as a loner, appearing superior to the rest. This can be called the 'herd instinct', but to put it this way would be inaccurate, not to say insulting. It was a feeling more like the camaraderie of soldiers in battle, where victory can only be achieved through communal effort. The 'smart Alec' must submit to the general will! Of course the young Khrushchev was staggered by the transformations that had taken place in his life. He had been elected to the Fourteenth Congress of the All-Union Communist Party (Bolsheviks) and was a member of the Ukrainian delegation with the right to a consultative vote. This was his first visit to Moscow.

Perhaps Khrushchev would have remained a middle-ranking leader all his life were it not for a series of fortunate coincidences. S. V. Kosior, who ten years later was shot on Stalin's orders, had been elected general secretary of the Ukrainian Communist Party. It was customary for each new leader to begin his work by overhauling the party apparatus and Khrushchev was among the new people invited to work for him. Khrushchev was appointed deputy head of the organization department of the Central Committee of the Ukrainian Communist Party. A year later, when the Industrial Academy opened in Moscow in 1929, Khrushchev became one of its first students. At the academy he was actively involved in the struggle against Bukharin's supporters and as a result of his resolute stance he was made head of the academy's party bureau.

Did Khrushchev understand the essential differences which separated Bukharin and Stalin in the struggle between the so-called 'right opposition' and the advocates of the 'general line'? He himself said he did not. Khrushchev had not advanced far enough in political consciousness to concern himself with the theoretical issues of the day: whether the policies of NEP should be continued or curtailed, whether industrialization directed at peasant consumer demands was preferable to industrialization which would involve plundering the countryside, whether full-scale collectivization should be enforced or a variety of forms of ownership and voluntary cooperatives developed in the villages, whether the new party democracy should be preserved or a cult of personality created.

What he did understand well was the struggle for power. He observed the way Bukharin's supporters at the Industrial Academy tried to wangle their representatives onto the Bauman area party conference, pushing him and other leaders of the party bureau aside. This had nothing to do with theoretical disagreements. It was a head-on clash and only one side could win. Of course, he could count on powerful support in this battle as he was putting forward the official Stalinist line, which was the line of the overwhelming majority, while the opposition had very few supporters. The cultural dimension which I have mentioned was by no means a peripheral matter. The opposition consisted of the intelligentsia, while Stalin's supporters consisted of rank and file workers. In the event, Khrushchev's choice was determined by class instinct in its primitive form.

It was not only a fortunate coincidence for Khrushchev that he entered the Industrial Academy, where he was immediately promoted to being a party leader; it was fortunate for him that a fellow student at the academy was Nadezhda Sergeyevna Alliluyeva, Stalin's wife. She had been elected party organizer of one of the groups and they frequently saw each other. Khrushchev believed that he was indebted to her for the fact that he caught Stalin's eye.

Khrushchev was to say later: 'When I became secretary of the Moscow and regional committees I often met Stalin and used to go to Stalin's for family dinners when Nadezhda Sergeyevna was alive, and I understood that being at the Industrial Academy and fighting for the general line at the Academy had been of crucial importance. She apparently spoke a great deal about me to Stalin and Stalin often reminded me of this in our conversations . . . At first I didn't even understand, as I'd already forgotten the incidents concerned, but afterwards I would remember . . . ah, obviously Nadezhda Sergeyevna had told him . . . I think this determined my position. Most importantly, it determined Stalin's attitude toward me. I call it my lottery ticket – I drew a lucky lottery ticket. That's why I remained alive when my contemporaries, schoolfellows, friends and acquaintances with whom I had worked in party organizations laid down their lives as "enemies of the people".'[9]

It is hardly likely that anyone but Khrushchev could afford the luxury of being so sincere and self-disparaging. It is more usual to attribute success to one's personal merits, astute actions and precise feel for the situation, so essential when swimming in political waters and in particular in such stormy waters as the 1930s. Khrushchev did not overrate his abilities. He felt that meeting Nadezhda Alliluyeva predestined his fate. There is also no doubt that Khrushchev himself was not idle but energetically fighting his way up the political ladder.

It is more likely that the first step in Khrushchev's political career was due to M. Mekhlis, editor-in-chief of *Pravda*, who had apparently heard of Khrushchev's active campaign against the 'right opposition' at the Industrial Academy. He suggested that Khrushchev come out with a provocative article in *Pravda*, which would launch an attack on Bukharin's supporters.

This took place before the Sixteenth Party Congress in the summer of 1930. From his own account, as I have already mentioned, the 'right opposition' was trying to send its supporters to the Bauman area party conference. They despatched Khrushchev on official business to a collective farm under the patronage of the Academy so that he would not interfere with their designs. By the time Khrushchev returned the party conference was in session, largely attended by the 'rightists'. During the session he was suddenly called to the telephone, and a voice said, 'This is Mekhlis, editor of *Pravda*, speaking. Could you come right away. I'll send a car to pick you up. I have an urgent matter to discuss with you.'

A little while later Khrushchev found himself in the *Pravda* offices with Mekhlis. Mekhlis read him a letter which had allegedly been received from the Industrial Academy. This letter exposed 'machinations' in the party cell bureau which had enabled the 'right oppositionists' to be selected to the Bauman area party conference by illegal means.

'Do you agree with the contents of this letter?' Mekhlis asked Khrushchev.

'Yes, absolutely,' Khrushchev replied.

'Would you agree to sign this letter?' Mekhlis asked.

'How can I sign it?' Khrushchev was amazed. 'I didn't write this letter. I don't even know who did.'

'That's not important,' Mekhlis answered. 'I'm asking you to sign this letter because I trust you. I've heard a great deal about you and the role you've been playing at the Industrial Academy. Your signature will assure me that this letter genuinely reflects the situation in the Academy.'

'All right, I'll sign it,' Khrushchev agreed.

He signed the letter, returned to the car and was driven back to his hostel. The next day, 26 May 1930, the letter appeared in *Pravda*. It was like a thunderbolt from the blue. Classes at the Academy were suspended and a meeting was called which demanded the recall of all delegates to the Bauman area party conference. Among those on the Industrial Academy's list were Stalin and Bukharin. Of course, no one dreamed of recalling Stalin. Nor was Bukharin recalled, but that was because of a decree from above which said that Bukharin was not to be touched for the present. Those who were recalled were Rykov, Uglanov and others known as the 'right deviationists'. Khrushchev, of course, chaired the meeting and was elected a delegate to the party conference. These changes had occurred so rapidly that there was no time to print new credentials. The newly-fledged delegates were simply given the credentials of the old delegates. Khrushchev even had trouble getting into the party conference as his credentials bore somebody else's name. But he got through in the end.[10]

We can assume that this event and probably many others of a similar nature played a decisive role in Khrushchev's rapid progress to the top, but they hardly show the ambitious young man in a good light.

He comes off even worse in his treatment of Lenin's wife, N. K. Krupskaya and Lenin's sister, M. I. Ulyanova, who were at the same party conference in the Bauman area in Moscow. He met Krupskaya, who seemed a broken old woman.

'We all opposed Nadezhda Konstantinovna at the conference,' Khrushchev writes with some pain in his memoirs. 'People avoided her like the plague. On Stalin's orders she was under surveillance, as it was considered that she had strayed from the party line. Later on, when I worked in the Moscow city party committee, Nadezhda Konstantinovna worked in the complaints bureau of the Moscow city soviet and she often forwarded complaints to me at the city party committee. I always used to let her know what could and could not be done about these complaints. We sometimes met and she realized that I was a supporter of the general line and that I was a product of Stalin's times, and she treated me accordingly.'[11]

No small part in Khrushchev's career was played by L. M. Kaganovich, who was at the time a Politburo member as well as secretary of the Central Committee and first secretary of the Moscow *obkom*. He had known Khrushchev in the Ukraine. It was on Kaganovich's initiative that Khrushchev received his first major appointments. Khrushchev, who never finished his studies at the Industrial Academy, was elected in 1931 on Kaganovich's recommendation as first secretary of the Bauman party *raykom*. He did not remain long in this post and several months later became secretary of the Krasnopresensky *raykom* and in 1932 second secretary of the Moscow city party committee.

The Seventeenth Party Congress, which was such a tragedy for the two-thirds of the delegates whom Stalin destroyed or left to rot in prison, served as a springboard for Khrushchev to move higher up the ladder of power. Immediately after the congress he became secretary of the city party committee and second secretary of the Moscow regional party committee, of which Kaganovich was first secretary.

In 1935, just after Khrushchev had reached the age of forty, he held the post of first secretary of the Moscow party *obkom*. This was an important post as it took in the present-day districts of Tula, Kaluga, Ryazan and Kalinin.

The gloomiest and most obscure chapter of Khrushchev's career, and one which has not been fully revealed to this day, is the extent to which he participated in the mass repressions in the mid-1930s. There is no doubt that he was in the position of the hammer and not the anvil, although he did not play the same role as higher-ranking leaders such as Molotov, Mikoyan, Kaganovich, Andreyev or Voroshilov. Nevertheless, he had on his conscience thousands of innocent lives from both the Ukraine and Moscow. As the archives open today to reveal the monstrous slaughter of the 1930s, we see, alas, Khrushchev's signature side by side with Stalin's on many of the documents sentencing people to be 'liquidated'.

Stalin had the habit of binding all members of the leadership in collective guilt, making sure that they shared responsibility with him for the destruction of their former friends and comrades. Khrushchev recalls: 'When the investigation of a case had ended and Stalin had decided that others should sign the document, he would sign it himself there and then at the session and immediately pass it around and those who were present would sign without looking, relying on Stalin's information and his assessment of the crime. In this way it became rather like a collective verdict.'

The archives will reveal all or almost all the documents, and it will then be possible to establish precisely which of them bear Khrushchev's signature. The number will probably not be great, but Khrushchev cannot avoid collective responsibility for the mass killings.

The following story related by Khrushchev is fairly characteristic of the times: 'All candidate members of the Moscow city party committee and the Moscow *raykom* could be elected only with the approval of the NKVD. The NKVD had the last word in deciding whether or not a person could be elected. We thought that was the way it had to be, otherwise enemies would worm their way into the Party organs. This is what happened at the Moscow party conference in 1937. A military commissar whom we in the area regarded as a good comrade worked at the Frunze Military Academy and we put him up as candidate for the city committee elections. When his name was called for the ballot sheet the whole conference broke out into prolonged enthusiastic applause. Suddenly, at that very moment, a note was handed to me from the NKVD which said: "Make sure you stop this person from getting onto the city party committee. He cannot be trusted. He is connected with enemies of the people and will be arrested." We obediently spoke out against him. This made a gloomy impression on the delegates at the conference. The next night this man was arrested.'[12]

Although, on the whole, Khrushchev was honest and sincere, he often had to suppress these qualities. At that time it was the custom for party leaders who worked closely with the NKVD to inspect prisons. Khrushchev writes about one such visit to a prison where he found the old Bolshevik Treyvas, a man whose name had been widely known in the 1920s as a Komsomol leader.

'Now, after so many years have passed, I must say that Treyvas was a good, faithful and active worker. He was a clever man and I was very pleased with him. Treyvas' life ended tragically. He had been elected secretary of the Kaluga city party committee and did his work very well. You might say that the city committee made something of a name for itself. But he didn't manage to escape the meat-grinder when it started to work in 1937.'

Khrushchev, of course, did nothing to save Treyvas; even if he had wanted to, it would have been impossible. The choice was simple: either send people to prison or end up there yourself. It is also true that many of those who carried out the terrible slaughter themselves became victims of the repressions. The meat-grinder, as Khrushchev put it, worked unceasingly.

One must assume that because of Khrushchev's obedient behaviour he was made a deputy to the USSR Supreme Soviet and a member of its Presidium. At the same time he also became candidate member of the Politburo of the Central Committee of the All-Union Communist Party (Bolsheviks), replacing Postyshev, an old Communist and former leader of the Ukrainian party organization.

A year before, during the terrible days of 1937, almost all the members of the Central Committee of the Ukrainian party organization had been wiped out. In that year alone 150,000 Communists had been arrested in the republic.[13] Khrushchev was sent to the Ukraine to head the republic's party organization on 20 January 1938. It was fortunate for him that the main wave of repressions in the Ukraine had subsided by the time he arrived. Nevertheless, he probably had a hand in the later stages of the purges.

It is hard to tell whether he had a say in the arrest of the Ukrainian party leaders P. Postyshev and S. V. Kosior which took place outside the republic in 1938. However, in his speech at the Eighteenth Party Congress in 1939 Khrushchev deemed it necessary to state that 'the Ukrainian people' felt nothing but hatred for bourgeois nationalists and all base spies – men like Lyubchinko, Khvyl, Zatonsky and other vermin. These were all former Ukrainian leaders executed by Stalin.

At the time Khrushchev was a 100-percent Stalinist. In many passages of his memoirs he acknowledges with disarming honesty that during Stalin's lifetime he was completely under his influence. It is strange to hear him say in the twilight of his days that he had been captivated by Stalin's 'charm'. Speaking about the dramatic

Seventeenth Party Congress, Khrushchev notes that during his time in the Moscow city party committee he quite frequently had the opportunity to meet and listen to Stalin and sometimes even received direct instructions from him on certain matters. He was 'literally fascinated by Stalin', by his 'attentiveness and concern'; everything Stalin said and did produced an 'enchanting impression' on him.

This fascination with Stalin did not waver even after Kirov's murder. Khrushchev describes this tragic event in detail, as at the time he was leader of the Moscow city party organization and was directly involved in the matter. On the evening of 1 December 1934, the day Kirov was killed, Khrushchev received a telephone call from Kaganovich who asked him to come over urgently. He ordered a car and was driven to the Kremlin. The first person he saw was Kaganovich, who had apparently been waiting for him. Khrushchev says, 'I saw from his appearance that he was frightened; it made me apprehensive. I was literally taken aback and wondered what had happened. He said, you know something awful has happened. Kirov has been murdered in Leningrad.'

Kaganovich informed him that arrangements were being made to send a delegation to Leningrad, that Stalin, Voroshilov and Molotov would be going and that it was up to Khrushchev to put together a delegation from the Moscow party organization and Moscow workers. Khrushchev gathered together a delegation and left on the same train as Stalin, Voroshilov and Molotov. They had separate carriages and Khrushchev did not see them on the journey. Describing his impressions after the meeting in Leningrad, Khrushchev says that he had not doubted the version put forward at the time that the murderer was Nikolayev, who had been expelled from the party for taking part in the Trotskyist opposition. Consequently he saw the hand of the Trotskyists in this affair – 'they were apparently behind the murder' which aroused 'sincere outrage and indignation in us all'.

Most of all Khrushchev was astonished at Kaganovich's reaction to Kirov's murder; in his words, he was 'very scared'. As for Stalin, he only saw him when he was standing in the guard of honour at Kirov's lying-in-state in Leningrad. 'Stalin knew how to conduct himself; his face was impenetrable.'

Khrushchev describes how Kirov's murder was followed by a purge in Moscow directed mainly at criminal elements who 'really littered the streets of Moscow'. Lists were drawn up and suspicious elements deported. Khrushchev took part in organizing this. In his words, this was the first stage of the purge after Kirov's murder. In fact, of course, it was not only 'criminals' but mainly political victims who were deported. Khrushchev claimed not to know who they were and what fate awaited them.[14] Like Pontius Pilate, he washed his hands of any connection with the purge which took place in Moscow in the period between Kirov's murder and the trials of 1936–8.

He saw it as his duty to carry out instructions concerning the purges, and one must assume that the lists were drawn up in consultation with him. If this is not so, then it seems he didn't exhibit any 'unhealthy interest' in who these people were, why they were deported, and where to.

In his memoirs Khrushchev gives detailed information about the repressions against the military, describing each of the figures whom he knew personally: mainly Yakir, Tukhachevsky, Blyukher and Uborevich. He remembers their tragic fate with pain but feels no personal responsibility. At this time Khrushchev was in the Ukraine and did not directly take part in the repressions against the higher and middle ranks of the army. We know from the documents of the Twenty-Second Party Congress that these lists were drawn up by Stalin along with Molotov, Kaganovich and Mikoyan. In the same way Khrushchev describes how Kuznetsov and Voznesensky were shot in the post-war period. Khrushchev was not involved but in the depths of his soul he was distressed and frightened by these events, driving thoughts of them from his mind and, at any rate, not permitting himself to doubt the correctness of Stalin's policy. The only option was to turn inwards and concentrate on day-to-day problems; drive away any doubts and suspicions and share them with no one. Otherwise a person like Khrushchev could not have hidden his feelings, and would not have survived these cruel years.

★

The role Khrushchev played in the mass repressions and Stalinist purges was in no way comparable to the role played by Stalin's closest colleagues. This was partly because Khrushchev lived outside Moscow for almost twelve years. As a rule Stalin did not keep either Khrushchev or other republican leaders informed about Politburo matters or decisions, let alone behind-the-scenes secret information about the repressions or the persecution of specific figures. Nevertheless, this is not the only factor that impelled Khrushchev to expose Stalin after his death. The main explanation lies in Khrushchev's personal qualities: the humanity, kindness and sincerity which were not erased despite his involvement in many of the terrible affairs of that time.

It was Stalin who first noticed these aspects of Khrushchev's character.

Khrushchev's well-known English biographer, Edward Crankshaw, correctly notes: 'At some stage in this terrible war Khrushchev, who was first among the Soviet leaders to feel the direct impact of it, and who was never to be far from the front line and the desolation of the threatened areas, underwent a change of heart. It is impossible to tell just when and how; it was a thing he never mentioned. But the Khrushchev who emerged from the war in 1945 was not at all the same man as the Khrushchev who was all but overwhelmed and swept away by it in the summer of 1941. Russia, much later, was to profit from this change.'[15]

A typical incident occurred in 1946. The harvest in the Ukraine had failed and the republic was experiencing a terrible famine. Meanwhile a directive had come from Moscow to send 400 million pounds of grain to the state, much more than could possibly have been harvested from the Ukraine. In other words, the Ukrainians would have been left without any grain, and still not fulfilled the quota. Khrushchev possessed accurate information about the situation in the Ukraine; he had received reports that many people were dying of hunger and that there had even been cases of cannibalism. Khrushchev had received a report that a human head and the soles of feet had been found under a bridge in Vasilkovo, a small town near Kiev. The corpse had been eaten.

There were other similar cases. A. Kirichenko, secretary of the Odessa party *obkom*, told Khrushchev of a terrible visit he had made to one of the villages in the region. He had been told to go to a collective farm to see a woman who worked there. The woman had the corpse of her child on the table and was cutting it up. It could have been a boy or a girl. She kept chattering away: 'We've already eaten Manechka and now we'll pickle Vanechka. That should keep us going for a while.' The woman had gone mad. There were many cases of cannibalism among normal people as well. These facts shook Khrushchev, and despite the directive from Moscow he decided to write a memorandum to Stalin, reporting that the Ukraine would not be able to fulfil any demands for grain and that in fact it was in need of aid from state reserves. Stalin exploded with rage when he received the memorandum. He sent Khrushchev an insulting telegram in which he called him a 'dubious character' and ordered him to Moscow.

Stalin had just returned from a holiday in Sochi. Khrushchev left for Moscow immediately. He was prepared for the worst; they might even declare him an 'enemy of the people' and send him forthwith to the Lubyanka. Nonetheless, he had decided to tell Stalin that his report accurately reflected what was happening in the Ukraine. Khrushchev insisted on economic aid. This only fanned Stalin's anger all the more.

'You're soft-bellied,' Stalin told Khrushchev. 'They're deceiving you. They're playing on your sentimentality. They want us to squander our state reserves.'

There were many who led Stalin on, inflaming his distrust of Khrushchev. The Cheka was spreading rumours that he had submitted to local pressure and had become a Ukrainian nationalist. That same year, in 1946, Khrushchev visited Stalin again and told him about another episode which he had witnessed himself.

Khrushchev had gone to visit his cousin, a woman who lived in a village, where she had several apple trees. These trees had disappeared.

'Where are the apple trees?'

'I've chopped them down.'

'What do you mean, you've chopped them down! Whatever for?'

'Well, you have to pay a tax on every apple tree . . .'

When Khrushchev had told Stalin this story, Stalin accused him of wanting to abolish the tax and shouted: 'You're a *narodnik*! That's what you are! A *narodnik*!'[16]

Many Western historians think that ideologically Khrushchev had *narodnik* tendencies and that this explains why he suddenly changed his estimation of Stalin at the Twentieth Party Congress. I can't agree with this. The concept of *narodnichestvo* is not the same as what in the West is known as 'populism'. Traditionally the *narodnik* movement, which existed in Russia from 1860 to 1889, did not always demonstrate a genuine attempt to understand or safeguard the interests of the people. It is well known that the *narodniks* assassinated the 'liberator tsar' Alexander II. They were not averse to using terrorist methods and were the direct precursors of today's Red Brigades. Their idealization of 'the people as a whole', 'the soul of the people' and 'the people's superiority' over the 'spineless, weak, liberal intelligentsia' played a very ugly role in preparing the frame of mind that existed in the revolutionary period of February and October 1917. Their hatred of landowners and capitalists often combined with a rejection of Western culture and all civilized values. Their methods of struggle were no better than those of the police. Their only reply to state terror was terror from below.

I don't think that when Stalin accused Khrushchev of being a *narodnik* he had in mind any commitment to this historical movement with its well-defined characteristics. He was more likely referring in a crude and vulgar way to Khrushchev's commitment to defending ordinary people. It's no accident that Stalin placed Khrushchev's *narodnichestvo* at the same level as his soft-bellied approach and his sentimentality.

It seems to me that Khrushchev's innate humanism, which he never lost despite the ordeals of this bleak epoch, was the main reason that he became a great fighter against tyranny, shattering the cult of Stalin and his regime. A very normal fear held him back from defending those who were unjustly condemned in the Stalinist period, but a feeling of pain, repentance, guilt and responsibility for everything that had happened accumulated in him all the more.

This psychological interpretation of the motivation behind Khrushchev's secret speech at the Twentieth Party Congress is reinforced by the style of his speech. He offers few arguments, appraisals or even figures about the mass repressions. What stands out most of all and makes the strongest impression is the way Khrushchev describes the fate of individuals, particularly of people he knew personally and with whom he felt an inner bond, even after they had been denounced as 'enemies of the people' and were stood up against the wall. Khrushchev's emotional responses were rooted in his humanity, and it was primarily this that impelled him to undertake his heroic feat.

Khrushchev's rise to power, therefore, was both inevitable and accidental. Stalin himself promoted him step by step, thus unwittingly preparing the ground for his elevation. He did not realize that Khrushchev represented a tendency within the party expressed by such dissimilar figures as Dzerzhinsky, Bukharin, Rykov, Rudzutak and Kirov, who had advocated the development of NEP and democratization and had opposed the use of force in industry and agriculture, let alone culture. Despite the cruel Stalinist repressions this tendency never died out. In this sense Khrushchev's emergence was inevitable.

Of course there was also a large element of chance. If Malenkov had struck a deal with Beria or if the Stalinist Guard had joined forces in 1953 and not in June 1957, Khrushchev would not have become leader. History would have taken a different course. It is hard to believe this, but in fact everything hung by a thread.

History made the correct decision after all by responding to the real problems in Soviet life. New policies and radical changes were needed to deal with the critical situation: the half-ruined countryside which was becoming more and more impoverished, industry which lagged behind technologically, an acute housing shortage, the low standard of living among the population, millions confined in prisons and camps, the country's isolation from the outside world. And so Khrushchev arrived, as the hope of the people and a precursor of new times.

4 Stalin

Everything about the Twentieth Party Congress was profoundly exciting. What made Khrushchev decide to give his speech about Stalin* knowing that the overwhelming majority of delegates would be against such revelations? Where did he find the courage and certainty that it would be successful? It was one of those rare cases in history when a political leader risked his own personal power and even his life in the name of a higher public cause. Not one other figure in the post-Stalin leadership would have given such a speech on the cult of personality. Only Khrushchev could have done it so bravely, with so much feeling and, in many ways, so little forethought. One had to have Khrushchev's character – a desperation to the point of adventurism – and to have lived through the suffering, fear and time-serving to risk such a step.

I was not at the congress when Khrushchev gave his speech about Stalin. It is known that the speech was given after the elections to the Central Committee of the Communist Party, when Khrushchev had already been elected First Secretary of the Party. He probably considered it imprudent to give the speech before the elections, and not without reason. From my talks with many party workers at the time I was convinced that Khrushchev's action had been very risky.

I first felt the full drama of these events from Sergey Pavlovich Mezentsev, editor of our section at *Kommunist*, who was a delegate in the editorial group at the congress. He returned to the office right after the session and sat down in his armchair without saying a word. He was as white as snow – or more grey than white, like the colour of salt-marshes.

'Well, what was it like, Sergey Pavlovich?' I asked. He did not reply; his lips did not even move, as if his tongue had got stuck between his teeth. I sat with him for a while and poured him a glass of water. He took a sip, then another. He remained sitting. Still, not a sound.

* This speech was first published in full in the Soviet Union in 1989 – in the journal *Izvestiya TsK KPSS*, no. 3, 1989. It was published earlier in 1988 but not in full.

'Come on, Sergey Pavlovich, tell me. Did they kick someone out or elect someone they shouldn't have? Or have they decided to close down our journal?' I quipped, inappropriately.

'The journal? . . . It's not the journal . . . The things that were said . . . God knows what we're supposed to think . . . what will happen next . . . what should we do?'

'Go home, probably, it's time to go home. It's almost eight. As it is, I stayed behind to hear what you had to say.'

'I can't tell you. They made a special stipulation that there should be no leaks. Otherwise our enemies will use it to chop us down at the roots!'

'How, Sergey Pavlovich? We have the most powerful state and an army that even America fears. It's not all that long ago that we exploded the bomb, not the atomic bomb, but the thermonuclear one.'

'I'm not talking about that.' Sergey frowned. 'There are different kinds of bombs. This is a bomb as well, only a time-bomb. We don't know when it will explode, and what will remain of our ideology when it does.'

'Sergey Pavlovich, you're talking in riddles. Why don't you just say what it's all about?'

'I can't. You must understand, I can't. I don't have the right to. You'll have to wait. Maybe after a while everyone will be informed officially, because the press should know . . . and party workers as well. There will be thousands of questions . . .'

I did not find out that evening. True, several days later we all – at least all of us at the journal – already knew what had been said in the secret speech. Not long afterwards the whole world knew. Through various channels the speech had got into the hands of the foreign media. It was a sensation, and was widely used by our opponents and ill-wishers to review critically the whole of Soviet history after Lenin.

I remember when the secret speech was read out to us at the office of *Kommunist*. Three people took turns to read it out and each put something of his own emotions into the words he uttered. A young editor of one department, a man of my generation who had graduated from the prestigious Institute of International Relations, even seemed cheerful, either because the truth had been revealed or because representatives of the old generation had been exposed. One of the older men, reading the text in his turn, kept stumbling over every phrase, testing it for size as if weighing up the accuracy of the information and shaking his head, showing in every gesture his distrust and disapproval of what was happening.

The facts about the Stalinist repressions staggered us the most. None of us – decidedly none of us at all – could have imagined the scale of the crime, although even then we were not told the whole truth about the victims. What we did learn shocked us to the core.

It was clear the country had to reject its old methods. It was unclear what the new methods would be and how quickly the new decisions would produce results. Everyone wanted to go further and faster, but many were apprehensive that the search for new methods and the break-up of traditions would destabilize the situation and rock the boat. Mezentsev, of course, was one of them. In fact, his attitude reflected the way many party workers thought in the 1950s. They were against the secret speech and against the bitter struggle that would ensue over the legacy of the past and, especially, over the new decisions to be taken in the future.

As I have already mentioned, I often heard Khrushchev reminisce about Stalin. These were long monologues, reflections often lasting many hours, in which he seemed to be deliberating with himself and his own conscience. He had been deeply wounded by Stalinism. Different emotions intermingled: a mystical fear of Stalin, who was capable of destroying anybody for a single false move, gesture or look, and horror over the innocent blood that had been shed. He felt personally responsible for the destruction of lives and a sense of protest that had been pent up in him for decades was straining to break loose like steam from a boiler.

Khrushchev notes in his memoirs that from Stalin's death right up until Beria's arrest Stalinist principles of governing the country continued to operate. Everything remained as it had been. Nobody had even thought of rehabilitating the people who had perished and been branded 'enemies of the people' or of freeing prisoners from the camps.

'For three years,' Khrushchev recalls, 'we proved to be unable to break with the past and find the courage and resoluteness to raise the curtain and see what had been hidden behind it – the arrests, the trials, the lawlessness, the shootings and all the other things that had been taking place in our country under Stalin's dictatorship. It seemed as if our actions under Stalin had chained us down and we could not free ourselves from his control even after his death.

'Right up to 1956 we were not able psychologically to rid ourselves of the concept of "enemies of the people". We stubbornly continued to believe in Stalin's idea that we were surrounded by enemies with whom we had to fight, using methods that had been justified theoretically and employed in Stalin's lifetime. We had waged a cruel class struggle and strengthened the foundations of our revolution. We could not imagine that all these executions and trials were themselves criminal from the legal point of view. Nevertheless, that was how it was. Deeds committed by Stalin would have been considered criminal in any country, with the exception of the Fascist states of Hitler and Mussolini.'

When did Khrushchev begin to doubt Stalin's 'genius'?

The first psychological turning point for Khrushchev came after the arrest and exposure of Beria. As an emotional person, Khrushchev was always moved by the fate of individuals. But even those details which emerged during Beria's trial did not produce a crucial change in Khrushchev's consciousness. He continued to blame Beria personally for everything. 'We did everything possible to shield Stalin, not realizing fully that we were protecting a criminal and a murderer guilty of mass extermination. I repeat that only in 1956 did we free ourselves from our devotion to Stalin.'

This is not quite accurate. Konstantin Simonov, in his reminiscences of Stalin, writes about his clash with Khrushchev. A few days after Stalin's death Simonov published an article in *Literaturnaya gazeta*, in which he declared that the main task of a writer was to reflect the great historical role of the greatest genius – Stalin. Khrushchev was extremely irritated by this article. He rang up the Union of Writers and demanded that Simonov be dismissed from his post as editor. He did not succeed, but he had obviously already changed his attitude to Stalin.

*

Let us turn to Khrushchev's speech at the closed session of the Twentiety Party Congress on 24–5 February 1956. The text of that speech is available virtually everywhere in the world, but in the Soviet Union it was published only in 1988. I will not relate the contents of this speech in detail, as I am more interested in Khrushchev's evaluation of Stalin – what he criticized him for, and what he omitted to criticize him for and even continued to praise.[1]

The crux of the speech was its description of the monstrous slaughter of human beings that had occurred under Stalin. It was this that most of all staggered those at the congress, as well as all Communists at the time. As Khrushchev said, out of the 139 members and candidate members of the Party Central Committee elected at the Seventeenth Congress, ninety-eight people, or 70 per cent, were arrested and shot (the majority in 1937–8). Out of the 1,966 delegates to this congress with voting or advisory rights, 1,108 people were arrested on charges of counter-revolutionary crimes. The number of arrests and charges of counter-revolutionary crimes increased more than tenfold from 1936 to 1937.

Quoting other figures on these monstrous mass repressions, Khrushchev dwelt in detail on the suspicious circumstances surrounding Kirov's murder. In particular, he reported that after the murder top functionaries of the Leningrad NKVD were given very light sentences, but in 1937 they were shot. One could assume that they had been shot to cover up the traces of the truth. He described in detail the tragic fate of

Postyshev, Eykhe, Rudzutak and many other prominent figures. Rudzutak, candidate member of the Politburo and a party member since 1905, who had spent ten years in a tsarist penal camp, categorically retracted in court the confession which had been forced – 'beaten' – out of him during interrogation.

The minutes of the session of the Military Collegium of the Supreme Court contains the following statement by Rudzutak:

'. . . The only plea he addresses to the court is to inform the Central Committee of the All-Union Communist Party (Bolsheviks) that the NKVD still has centres which have not been eliminated, where cases are craftily fabricated and innocent people are forced to admit to crimes which they did not commit . . . The methods are such that they force people to lie and slander entirely innocent people, as well as those who have already been accused.' Sentence was pronounced on him in twenty minutes and Rudzutak was shot.

When the wave of mass arrests began to recede in 1939 and the leaders of regional party organizations began to accuse NKVD workers of employing methods of physical pressure against those arrested, Stalin sent a coded telegram on 20 January 1939 to secretaries of regional and area committees, to the central committees of Communist Parties in the republics, to the People's Commissars of Internal Affairs and to the heads of the NKVD organs. This telegram stated: 'The Central Committee of the All-Union Communist Party (Bolsheviks) explains that the use of methods of physical pressure in NKVD practice has been permitted since 1937 by the Central Committee of the All-Union Communist Party (Bolsheviks).' These were 'permissible and correct methods'.

Of course, Khrushchev did not and could not tell the whole truth about the Stalinist repressions. Today the figure of forty million victims is quoted, including alleged 'kulaks' in the thirties and repressed ethnic peoples during the Second World War. But even then Khrushchev poured out his pent-up feelings of indignation and protest, renouncing the barbaric methods of interrogation, the beatings and the destruction of honest and innocent people.

A question arose in our minds: who of those still alive would bear responsibility for these crimes, and what guarantees would there be to prevent this happening again? Khrushchev raised the first question, but did not touch on the second. In his speech he said: 'We have to consider this matter seriously and analyse it so that we can preclude any possibility of a repetition in any form of that which existed under Stalin, who absolutely refused to tolerate a collective attitude to leadership and work, and who used crude violence not only against everything that contradicted his views, but also against everything that seemed to his capricious and despotic character contrary to his ideas.'

In analysing the causes of the mass repressions Khrushchev blamed Stalin for having elevated himself so far above the party and the people that he stopped taking the Central Committee and the party into consideration.

If before the Seventeenth Congress Stalin took the views of the collective into consideration, after full unanimity had been achieved in the party as a result of the complete political annihilation of the Trotskyists, Zinovyevists and Bukharinists, Stalin began increasingly to disregard the views of the Central Committee and even the Politburo. Stalin thought he could decide everything alone, while the colleagues he still needed were given merely walk-on parts. He treated everyone in such a way that it only remained for them to obey and praise him.

Thus, for Khrushchev the main cause of the repressions lay in the excessive and unprecedented way Stalin had propagated his cult of personality. Khrushchev refers to *The Short Biography of Stalin* and *The Short Course of the History of the All-Union Communist Party (Bolsheviks)*, written by a group of authors, but in which Stalin added his own comments. This is how he wrote about himself: 'Masterfully fulfilling the tasks of the supreme leader of the party and the people and enjoying the full support of the whole Soviet people, Stalin did not, however, permit any element of self-importance, conceit or vanity to colour his actions.' The initial text of the biography contained the following words: 'Stalin is the Lenin of today.' This sentence seemed to Stalin to be too feeble and he changed it to: 'Stalin is the worthy successor of Lenin's work or, as it is said in our party, Stalin is the Lenin of today.' Yet another example: 'Stalin's military mastership was displayed in defence and offence. With the perspicacity of genius, Comrade Stalin divined the enemy's plans and repulsed them.'

Khrushchev explains that although *The Short Course of the History of the All-Union Communist Party (Bolsheviks)* had been written by a group of authors, Stalin removed any reference to them, writing in *The Short Biography*: 'The book *The Short Course of the History of the All-Union Communist Party (Bolsheviks)*, written by Comrade Stalin and approved by a commission of the Central Committee of the All-Union Communist Party (Bolsheviks), appeared in 1938.' Finally, even the tsars, according to Khrushchev, did not create prizes which they named after themselves. The apotheosis of the worship of Stalin could be seen in the words of the Soviet national anthem, approved by Stalin himself: 'Stalin brought us up on loyalty to the people, He inspired us to great toil and heroic deeds.'

I should also point out that it was at the secret speech that Lenin's 'testament' was mentioned for the first time. In it Lenin suggests that Stalin should be removed from his post of General Secretary; Khrushchev remarks on Stalin's complete disregard of the principles of collective leadership established by Lenin.

There was a gap of thirteen years between the Eighteenth and Nineteenth Party Congresses; plenary sessions of the Central Committee were hardly held at all. Not one Central Committee plenum took place during the war. True, as Khrushchev noted, there was an attempt to call a Central Committee plenum in October 1941, and members of the Central Committee arrived in Moscow from all parts of the country. They waited for two days for the plenum to open, but in vain. Stalin got frightened and did not even want to meet or talk to members of the Central Committee.

In connection with this, Khrushchev contrasts Lenin's attitude towards opposition with Stalin's. As an example he refers to Kamenev's and Zinovyev's article arguing against Lenin's plan for an armed uprising, which was published on the eve of the October Revolution. Lenin put the question of their expulsion from the party to the Central Committee, which rejected the idea; after the revolution Zinovyev and Kamenev were given leading posts. The same was true for Trotsky.

Khrushchev notes that Lenin had no doubts about the rightness of the Red Terror and used the most severe measures to crush the enemy; but he did this only in exceptional cases. He quotes Lenin's speech at the session of the All-Russian Central Executive Committee on 2 February 1920, when he announced the abolition of the death penalty: 'Terror was imposed on us by the terrorism of the Entente . . . As soon as we gained a decisive victory, even before the end of the war, immediately after taking Rostov, we abandoned the use of the death penalty and thus showed that we are abiding by the promises of our own programme. We say that the use of violence issues from the task of defeating the exploiters and crushing the landowners and capitalists, and when this is accomplished we will give up all extreme measures. We have proved this in practice.'[2]

In contrast to this, Stalin exercised methods of administrative violence, repression and terror. The mass arrests, the deportations of many thousands of people, the shootings without trial or normal investigation, had created an atmosphere in which there was no security, and terror and even horror prevailed. Condemning this, Khrushchev emphasized that extreme measures should have been taken only against those who had committed a crime against the Soviet system.

I remember that even then Khrushchev's explanation of the causes of the Stalinist mass terror seemed to me inadequate and even naive. He sought an explanation principally in Stalin's character. Even much later, in his memoirs, he once again returned to this same explanation as, in essence, the most important cause of the irrational mass slaughter. In one place he talks of Stalin's 'despotism'; in another he writes that Stalin was 'a very distrustful person – he was morbidly suspicious'.[3]

Khrushchev goes on: 'He could look at someone and say, "Why are you so shifty today?" or "Why are you turning away today and avoiding looking me straight in the eyes?" Such morbid suspicion created in him a general distrust toward prominent Party members whom he had known for years. Everywhere and in everything he saw "enemies", "hypocrites" and "spies".'

Describing the 'Leningrad affair' after the war, Khrushchev again emphasizes this characteristic.

'We must say that after the war the situation became even more complicated. Stalin became even more capricious, irritable and cruel; in particular his suspicions intensified. His persecution mania began to take on incredible proportions. Many people were becoming enemies in his eyes.' The same thing, the same reason lies behind the so-called 'doctors' plot'. According to Khrushchev, Stalin sent for Ignatyev, former minister of state security, and told him: 'If you don't obtain a confession from the doctors we will shorten you by a head.' And having called for the investigator, he gave him these instructions: 'Beat, beat and once again, beat them.' This suspicion, compounded by his arbitrary behaviour, gave rise to his sense of unlimited autocratic power.

Khrushchev described how at one meeting Stalin told him about the conflict with Tito in Yugoslavia. Pointing to a letter lately sent to Tito, Stalin asked him, 'Have you read this?' and without waiting for a reply, said, 'All I have to do is wag my little finger and there will be no Tito. He will fall . . .' Khrushchev notes: 'This statement expressed Stalin's megalomania, but he always behaved like that: "All I have to do is wag my little finger and there will be no Führer" or "All I have to do is wag my little finger once more and Voznesenky, Kuznetsov and many others will vanish." '⁴

It cannot be said that Khrushchev put Stalin's despotic rule entirely down to his character, but it is important to note that he only partially moved from criticizing Stalin personally to criticizing Stalinism as a regime, let alone to criticizing the system as a whole. This can be seen from the concluding remarks of his speech at the Twentieth Party Congress.

Khrushchev notes – not only, I imagine, to please the functionaries, but quite sincerely – that there is no doubt that Stalin performed services to the party, the working class and the international workers' movement. In his opinion, Stalin had been convinced that everything he did was necessary to protect the interests of working people against plots by enemies and an attack from the imperialist camp. He assumes that Stalin saw all this from the point of view of the interests of the working class and working people and as necessary in securing the victory of socialism and Communism.

'We cannot say,' Khrushchev continues, 'that his acts were the acts of an insane despot. He considered that this had to be done in the interests of the party and the toiling masses, in the name of protecting revolutionary gains. This is where the tragedy lies!'

Khrushchev went on to say that everything should be done to end the cult of personality forever as it was alien to Marxism-Leninism, to return to the painstaking implementation of Leninist principles of party leadership and, finally, to restore socialist democracy fully as expressed in the constitution of the USSR, and to combat abuses of power.

It is not hard, however, to see the limitations of Khrushchev's critique of Stalin. He still shared Stalin's general line on collectivization and industrialization and on the struggle against the opposition.

And not only Khrushchev! We should remember that the majority of people destroyed by Stalin continued to believe in Stalinism. Many of them before they were shot cried out: 'Long live Comrade Stalin!' That was the cry of Yagoda, Stalin's executioner, who was destroyed by his own ruthless machine. Even those who were deported to hard labour in Solovki or Vorkuta continued their embittered arguments with the Bukharinists, Trotskyists, Zinovyevists, not to mention the Socialist Revolutionaries and Mensheviks.

Khrushchev himself in his speech at the Twentieth Congress said: 'We must affirm that the party had to conduct a serious fight against the Trotskyists, the right deviationists and the nationalists, as a result of which it ideologically disarmed all the enemies of Leninism. This ideological fight was carried out successfully, as a result of which the party was strengthened and hardened. Stalin played a positive role . . . Let us consider for a moment what would have happened if in 1928–9 the political line of the right deviation had won or if we had taken the road of "cotton-dress industrialization" or of the kulaks, etc. We would not now have a powerful heavy industry, we would not have collective farms, we would be weak and unarmed in the capitalist encirclement.'

According to Khrushchev, it was thanks to the struggle waged by Stalin that the overwhelming majority supported the general line and the party could organize the toiling masses to carry out the Leninist policy of building socialism. For Khrushchev Stalin's mistake lay in the fact that he distorted Lenin's policy; the mistake was not in his approach to Lenin's policy, but only in the methods, particularly the use of severe repressive measures, which were intolerable when socialism had essentially been constructed and the exploiting classes had been liquidated. The aims were correct; but the methods were false, harmful and barbaric. Strangely enough, we hear to this day the same arguments from those who oppose the radical restructuring of the existing system.

It would be ahistorical to speak of Khrushchev's conclusions from the vantage point of today. More than thirty years have passed since the Twentieth Congress and we have gained enormous experience – some positive, some negative. Now we can see what was most important – the great feat Khrushchev accomplished at that dramatic moment. There has been no return to mass repressions, although dissidents continued to be unjustly convicted; nor has it been possible to create a cult of personality, despite all the efforts of Brezhnev's lackeys, who penned nine volumes of his 'works', which were forgotten the day after his death.

With our new political experience, we can see all the failings in Khrushchev's analysis and conclusions. He condemned tyranny, but retained authoritarian power. He renounced the cult of personality, but to a considerable extent preserved the system which had conceived it. As for the lament about Stalin's personality and his tyrannical character, this is no more than infantile political thinking. How can one explain the cruelties of Nero or Caligula, Hitler or Mussolini simply in terms of their personalities?

Of course, despotism needs a despot. The question to ask is why despotism arises, carrying the despot to power, and why the people, or at least the majority, bow before the despot in spite of his obvious cruelty. It must be acknowledged that Khrushchev, having rejected the monstrous excesses of the Stalinist regime, showed in his speech at the Twentieth Party Congress that he was still captivated by many of Stalin's concepts of socialism.

Khrushchev's secret speech resounded like a thunderclap throughout the USSR and the world. The Soviet public were not prepared for such disclosures about Stalin. I remember that when the speech was read out to workers at our journal, *Kommunist*, the majority reacted unfavourably and many expressed doubts. Stalin was still too vitally associated with victory in a formidable war. The achievements of the initial period of revival of the national economy were attributed to him and, of course, the whole ideological life of the country was identified with his name.

Turmoil ensued. The most hot-headed started to demand that deStalinization went further, but this met with the toughest opposition from the party and state apparatus. All Moscow heard the news that a party organization at an academic institute had been disbanded because of demands that all those guilty of the mass repressions be prosecuted. It was said that this action was undertaken on M. Suslov's instructions and indicated the limitations that the party leadership had placed on the criticism of Stalinism. We should not forget that such outspoken supporters of Stalin as Molotov, Malenkov, Kaganovich and others were still in the leadership.

But it was no longer in their power to hold back the flood, especially as the secret speech soon stopped being secret. There are good grounds to assume that it was Khrushchev who made sure of that. I have no doubt that the initiative to disclose the content of the speech to representatives of Communist and workers' parties present at the Twentieth Party Congress came from him personally.

The first to learn of Khrushchev's speech were the heads of the delegations of the Communist Parties attending the congress – B. Bierut, V. Chervenkov, M. Rakosi, W. Ulbricht, M. Torez, P. Togliatti, D. Ibarruri and J. Koplenig.

At the end of February 1956 Josip Broz Tito already had the speech at his disposal, and he read it to members of the executive League of Communists of Yugoslavia.

On 14 March Togliatti, reporting to his party's Central Committee about the Twentieth Party Congress, criticized his own political actions in the past. On 16 March the Moscow correspondent of the *New York Times* published an article on Khrushchev's secret speech. The next day Reuters recounted its main points. From 19–21 March a milder summary of the speech was printed in *L'Humanité*, the organ of the French Communist Party. On 20 March an account of the speech appeared in the Yugoslav weekly *Kommunist*.

Copies of the speech proliferated and were soon selling on the black market in Warsaw, where one of them was brought by an American for three hundred dollars. Allen Dulles, head of the CIA, passed a copy to his brother, John Foster Dulles, the Secretary of State, who had Khrushchev's speech printed on 4 June in the *New York Times*, and on 6 June in *Le Monde*.[5]

In this way Khrushchev was the first leader in the history of Soviet rule to appeal to the international public in order to resolve the problems of intra-party struggles. He was strengthening his position in the party and in the country, relying on the support and sympathy of progressive forces in the Communist movement and even on 'bourgeois' public opinion.

The problem, however, was that Khrushchev himself had not overcome his vacillations about Stalinism. This can be traced in his memoirs. There is no doubt that his views while writing the memoirs had changed significantly from those he held when he was in power. This is not unusual. All you need do is look at the memoirs of American presidents such as Dwight Eisenhower and Jimmy Carter to see what a gap there is between what they said when they were at the top of the political pyramid and what they said after they had retired. And Khrushchev's was a special case: the leader was in disgrace, with the ambiguous title of a 'special private pensioner'.

For all Khrushchev's independence and originality, his intellectual world had not only evolved but took its final shape on the basis of Stalin's ideas. Moreover, as major theoreticians began to disappear from Stalin's circle – men such as Trotsky, Zinoviev, Bukharin and Rykov, as well as second-rank figures like Kirov, Ordzhonikidze, Stetsky and many others – Stalin became elevated in the consciousness of those around him as the only person capable of formulating theoretical and political ideas.

In the course of two volumes of his memoirs – and, strictly speaking, in all his actions as leader of the country – Khrushchev tried to rid himself of the shackles of Stalinism and escape from the captivity into which he had fallen early in life. Whatever event he remembered, whatever issue he analysed, he returned over and over again to the 'leader of all the peoples', attempting to counter his posthumous influence but often giving up in resignation.

And why only mention Khrushchev! Don't all Soviet people still live under this monstrous shadow? He has been dead for thirty-eight years. Removed from his magnificent crypt, his body now rests next to his predecessors, comrades-in-arms and successors – Sverdlov, Frunze, Kalinin, Voroshilov, Budyonny, Brezhnev, Kosygin, Andropov. By a strange irony of fate, Khrushchev is the only one who is absent. Lenin's colleagues are also absent – Bukharin, Rykov, Kamenev, Zinoviev. None of these men are discussed and written about as frequently as Stalin, especially now in the period of *glasnost*.

Ten times more is being written about Stalin than about Lenin, not to mention Khrushchev or Andropov. Can this short, narrow-browed son of an alcoholic cobbler have left such deep and perhaps indelible traces on the soul of the Soviet people? Is evil prized more highly than genius in the auction-room of history?

I have done much the same thing, as since March 1953 I have thought and written most of all about Stalin and his legacy. Even when it was forbidden, I wrote about him in Aesopian language and in oblique references to Mao Tse-tung, Hitler and Franco. It is true that in the last three years, since anti-Stalinism has revived and reached its clamorous apogee, I have virtually stopped writing about Stalin and have moved on to the subsequent eras, especially that of Brezhnev, which even today has our attempts at reform in a stranglehold.

Against my will, Khrushchev's memoirs have again pushed me back to an analysis of Stalinism. In rereading the staggering evidence of his ambivalence, we realize that we have not done with Stalin yet. Stalin is still with us, he is still within us. We have to squeeze Stalinism out of ourselves drop by drop, along with our devotion to a theory, system and practice which up to now has been falsely called socialism.

But let us return to Nikita Sergeyevich, as he more than anyone else made efforts to break out of the shell in which he was born and emerge into the light. Perhaps that is why he spoke out louder than anyone else. He spoke against Stalin. Yes, against Stalin, but was it against Stalinism? Probably not.

Of course, it is easy to be critical of Khrushchev's attitude to democracy now, when these days we have raised and formulated such significant ideas as socialist pluralism, a law-governed state and a radical reform of the political system. It would be unhistorical to demand, even from such an exceptional figure as Khrushchev, that he make a leap in consciousness and political practice the day after Stalin's cult had been overthrown. But there is another criterion which is appropriate and can be applied to analyse objectively the achievements and failures of Khrushchev's Thaw – the Leninist experience which preceded Stalin.

We did have every right in that period to expect a complete and unconditional Leninist renaissance. But this did not happen – neither in party life, nor in the area of Soviet democracy, nor in the activity of public organizations, nor in social and economic policy (although some moves were undoubtedly made in this direction).

What prevented Khrushchev, at least in theory, from pursuing this course more consistently? In practice his course was determined by the actual alignment of forces within the party leadership and the mood and views of functionaries. But in theory, alas, he remained to the end a captive of Stalinism. In his memoirs Khrushchev's hands were freed but even there, and perhaps especially there, we can see that his limitations and dogmatism are theoretically determined.

*

Of particular interest in this context is Khrushchev's discussion, in his memoirs, of the party traditions which had taken shape under Stalin and of how these traditions were reflected after his death. He says that the initiative to call the Nineteenth Congress came from Stalin personally, even though thirteen years had elapsed since the Eighteenth Congress; none of the members of the leadership dared even hint at the need to call another one. Earlier such an interval could have been explained by the war, but the war had been over for seven years before the next party congress was called.

Khrushchev recalls how one day Stalin unexpectedly told him that it was necessary to convene a congress. By that time the Central Committee had virtually stopped functioning as an effective organ of leadership. Everything was done in the name of the Central Committee, but decisions were made by Stalin alone. He did not even consult members of the Politburo, but dictated resolutions himself. For some time Stalin kept his colleagues in ignorance about the agenda for the future congress and about who would give the report. Other members of the leadership discussed this among themselves and tried to guess whether he would take it upon himself to give the progress report, but they assumed it was unlikely as he was physically weak and it would be difficult for him to spend a great deal of time at the podium. Later Stalin set a time, an agenda and named the speakers: Malenkov would give the progress report, Saburov would talk on the Five-Year Plan and Khrushchev on the Party Rules. Khrushchev testifies that he was not very happy with this commission, as it was a difficult subject to talk about, let alone to get approved under the rigid control of Beria and Malenkov. In the end his speech was considerably shortened, and the speech lasted only about an hour, to Khrushchev's indignation.[6]

Members of the leadership secretly discussed among themselves why Molotov or Mikoyan had not been entrusted with giving the progress report. As Khrushchev says, those of the pre-war leadership all saw Molotov as the future leader, the man who would replace Stalin after his death.[7]

However, at that time there could be no discussion of either Molotov or Mikoyan, as they had fallen out of favour. Even their lives were in danger. Khrushchev describes the preparations for the so-called 'elections' at the congress. According to him, all delegates were chosen by the Central Committee party apparatus, which determined how many workers, intellectuals and collective farmers there should be. In short, delegates to the congress and members of the Central Committee had been selected beforehand. 'We didn't elect people to the congress as we once used to,' Khrushchev remarks. 'Instead we were told that so-and-so must get to the congress and that someone else must be elected to the Central Committee as a member or candidate member or as a member of the auditing commission.'

Examining this practice after his retirement, Khrushchev expresses regret and even indignation: 'You can imagine what this meant. But, unfortunately, this practice, strictly speaking, remains today. The elections to the Twentieth Congress took place in this way. This is a very distorted form of democracy. These methods are incorrect and intolerable.

'I tried to find new methods and attempted to introduce amendments to the new Party Rules. But we did this very timidly. Why? Because we were products – we, the people, the leaders – we were products of the revolution. We were brought up on the example of Stalin. And for us at the time Stalin was, well, he was so great that he defied description. It was not up to us, as it were, to imagine or create, but rather to imitate.'

Therefore, Khrushchev argues, the leaders of his generation were unable psychologically to free themselves in order to search for fundamental solutions and return the party to its Leninist track of party democracy.[8]

As we can see, Khrushchev himself defined the reasons for the tenacity of authoritarianism, in which everything was done at the top by the apparatus and, in the final analysis, by the supreme leader of the party. As a sincere man he always found the strength to condemn his own actions. The three congresses which were conducted under the guiding hand of Khrushchev did not differ much in method from those held in Stalin's lifetime.

The principle of appointment by election, the accountability of leaders and the possibility of removal from office, which were proclaimed in Lenin's times, had long since been replaced by the principle of selection and placement of cadres.

Khrushchev considered the Nineteenth Party Congress an example of the total triumph of these principles. The number of candidates put forward conformed exactly to the number of seats available. Everything went automatically, without a hitch.

True, there was a minor incident at the congress, but it was a typical case. As a result of a typing error a few names, including that of General Govorov, had been overlooked, and were only remembered after the congress was over. Stalin resolved the problem by simply including the names in the Central Committee list – who could possibly disagree?

But the biggest surprise awaited Khrushchev and other leaders at the first plenum after the Nineteenth Congress. Stalin opened it himself and proposed that twenty-one people be included in the Presidium of the Central Committee. This fact itself caused surprise, as they felt that such a large number of people would not be able to handle day-to-day matters. They were even more surprised by many of the names, some of whom were quite unexpected. Some new members of the Presidium had not even been members of the Central Committee beforehand. Khrushchev later asked Malenkov and Beria who had palmed off these names on Stalin, but they denied any knowledge of it. Hence no one could guess where these names had come from.

Most unexpected of all was the composition of the Bureau of the Presidium proposed by Stalin. It included Stalin, Bulganin, Beria, Malenkov, Kaganovich, Saburov, Pervukhin, Voroshilov and Khrushchev. Khrushchev was surprised not so much by the fact that Molotov and Mikoyan were not included as by the presence of Voroshilov, whom Stalin had been treating with great suspicion over the last few years.

In all, the bureau consisted of nine people, but according to Khrushchev Stalin singled out a much narrower group which, if we include Stalin, consisted of five. Officially this was not mentioned anywhere, but it soon became apparent that Stalin most often relied on this group – Beria, Bulganin, Khrushchev and Malenkov. Sometimes Kaganovich was invited to take part, but Molotov and Mikoyan were never invited to the bureau's closed sessions and Voroshilov rarely so. Khrushchev testifies that no changes in Stalin's style occurred after the congress. As he had done from 1938 on, Stalin made all the decisions himself. Everyone bowed to his personal rule knowing that otherwise disgrace, imprisonment and execution awaited them. The sword of Damocles hung over each member of the leadership.

Strange as it may seem, in his memoirs Khrushchev describes Molotov's and Mikoyan's disgrace in detail and expresses both surprise and regret. Khrushchev's attitude to Mikoyan is understandable, as Mikoyan became his closest associate in the post-Stalin period. Molotov, however, was Khrushchev's most consistent opponent. Nevertheless, writing many years later in retirement, he condemned Stalin for what he saw as the unlawful disgrace of Molotov and for depicting Molotov almost as an agent of imperialism.

He describes how members of the 'Five' would secretly tell Molotov and Mikoyan from time to time that Stalin had called them to his Blizhnyaya dacha, where they would turn up to Stalin's displeasure. One day Stalin gave the Five a major dressing-down, particularly Malenkov, for playing these 'games' in support of the two disgraced men.

I have already discussed the patriarchal nature of absolute power, which remained intact right up to Khrushchev's death. He was never able to surmount these views even when writing about 'distorted democracy'.

Nevertheless, Khrushchev had gone a long way from his personalized criticism of Stalin at the Twentieth Congress to a struggle against the Stalinist regime. Important landmarks along the way were his meeting with Tito in 1955, the tragic events in Hungary in 1956, the June Plenum of 1957 when the Stalinists tried to overthrow Khrushchev and, finally, the Twenty-Second Party Congress, which ended with the removal of Stalin's body from the Lenin Mausoleum.

5 Tito and Kadar

I shall begin with Yugoslavia, since that was the first breakthrough from Stalinist dogmatism and great-power chauvinism to the new view of socialism. The narrowmindedness engendered by the stony isolation of Soviet society from the outside world began to give way to a new approach to the contemporary world as a whole.

In his memoirs Khrushchev begins his account by saying that a view of Yugoslavia had formed during Stalin's time and persisted for a few years after his death. It was thought that the Yugoslav economy was totally subordinate to American monopoly capital, that private banks had been re-established there and that industry was in private hands, not to mention the farming sector. Khrushchev believed in all this since, as he himself says, 'we had become so isolated and knew nothing'.

With characteristic humour Nikita Sergeyevich recalls a joke on the subject. A mullah is walking through a village and is asked where he has come from. For a laugh he replies that he has come from the other end of the village, where they are handing food out free. The people hear this and start rushing off to the other side. The mullah meets some more people and asks them where they are running to. They tell him they are going to where the food is being handed out. In the end the mullah also turns round, gathers up his robe and runs along with everyone else. Khrushchev saw this as analogous to the fairy tales that used to be told about Yugoslavia. 'We invented them ourselves and then believed them ourselves.'[1]

Khrushchev recalls Stalin's unfulfilled threats against Tito ('I need only wag my little finger and Tito will vanish'). He moved more than just a finger, but the Communist movement's entire pressure and propaganda machine could do nothing with Tito. On Khrushchev's initiative a commission consisting of party functionaries and academics was set up to study the Yugoslav issue. Their task was to analyse the political and socio-economic foundations of that country to determine whether it was socialist or capitalist. The commission included D. Shepilov, who was then noted for his progressive views. He was in charge of *Pravda* and was considered a well-educated economist (he was a member of the USSR Academy of Sciences) and subsequently had a dazzling career as a protégé of Khrushchev's, though this came to a sorry end in June 1957. But more of that later.

The Shepilov commission – as I shall call it for convenience – reached the conclusion that Yugoslavia was a country of the socialist type. In Khrushchev's view, the basis of the Soviet–Yugoslav conflict collapsed like a house of cards. Only then was it decided to establish contact with Yugoslavia and restore inter-state and inter-party relations. This approach was endorsed by representatives of the other Communist and workers' parties.

In his capacity as First Secretary of the Party Central Committee (a post to which he had only recently been elected), Khrushchev led a delegation to Yugoslavia in 1955. As soon as he arrived in Belgrade Airport he made a sensational statement apologizing to Yugoslavia and to Comrade Tito personally for the unjustified insults. Immediately afterwards, however, there was a minor incident when Tito said there was no need for an interpreter as everyone in Yugoslavia understood Russian anyway. Khrushchev was disturbed by this, as he knew that far from all Yugoslavs understood Russian. Khrushchev was concerned and even disappointed with the start of the visit, fearing that if the rapprochement went badly it might activate those forces within the USSR which had campaigned against restoring relations with Yugoslavia.

During that conversation there was one further incident. Khrushchev tried to place the blame for the mass repressions in the USSR, as well as for the mistakes in relations with Yugoslavia and all foreign Communists on Beria. This brought only ironic smiles on the part of Tito and the other Yugoslav Communists. Khrushchev was not yet able to appreciate fully Stalin's role as the initiator of those crimes. The Yugoslavs were particularly at pains to point out Stalin's personal responsibility for the break with their country. As Khrushchev stated later, 'We were not yet prepared inwardly, we had not, to put it crudely, fully rid ourselves of our dependence, as it were, our slavish dependence on Stalin, as it were.'[2]

There was one further episode that was characteristic of Khrushchev's psychology. He became acquainted with S. Vukmanović-Tempo, a member of the Yugoslav Politburo, who had initially been very critical of Khrushchev. When Khrushchev told Vukmanović that he would be the best possible candidate for the job of exacerbating relations the latter burst into laughter at such frankness. Afterwards the two men got on particularly well. Khrushchev appreciated in Vukmanović a quality which they shared – his 'coarseness', which was easily explained by the tough conditions in which the working class had struggled for victory.

Khrushchev had to agree to Tito's persistent demands for total non-interference in the internal affairs of other socialist countries and recognition of the right of each party and each people to construct socialism as it chose. Admittedly, Khrushchev immediately added the proviso that there could be no concessions on matters of Marxist-Leninist principles, theory or politics.

It was then that the Declaration was drawn up, a declaration that made the first breach not only in Khrushchev's consciousness, but also in the principles of relations between the USSR and the countries of Eastern Europe. All the members of the Soviet leadership agreed with the decision to restore relations with Yugoslavia. But as Khrushchev recounts, the letters sent out to foreign Communist Parties contained 'a sort of safety-net loophole' which meant that there might not be any real improvement in relations after all. To this could be added the continuing statements in the Soviet press that Yugoslavia could not be recognized as a fully socialist country not only because of its private farming, but in particular because of its position on international issues.

All this became known to Tito and cast a new shadow over Soviet-Yugoslav relations. Khrushchev traditionally regarded such ups and downs as the result of imperialist 'intrigue', particularly by the United States, which was endeavouring by all possible means to split the socialist countries. Most of all he blamed CIA Director Allen Dulles, whose aim was to push socialism back to the USSR's borders. Despite this, relations with Yugoslavia began to develop normally.

There was renewed tension during the Hungarian events of 1956, of which I shall speak elsewhere. For the moment I shall trace the changes in Khrushchev's view of Yugoslavia's domestic development and his gradual realization that there could be a diversity of socialist models.

That first meeting was followed by several more – in Romania, Moscow and the Crimea. In his accounts of those meetings Khrushchev states his main concerns as being above all the stance of non-aligned Yugoslavia and its refusal to join the Warsaw Pact. He says openly that the policy of non-alignment itself did not always impress the Soviet leadership, but that they were especially indignant over Yugoslavia's refusal to join the Warsaw Pact, even though it had not been directly invited to do so. As Khrushchev saw it, this was due to Yugoslavia's economic relations with the West, above all with the USA and Great Britain. What made this particularly significant was that at that time the United States was virtually prohibiting trade with the USSR and Eastern Europe, making an exception for Yugoslavia alone. Over-simplifying, Khrushchev maintained that 'imperialism never gives presents for good looks alone'. From this came the logical conclusion that Yugoslavia was helping the 'imperialist forces' to 'split up' the socialist camp. Of course, if the USA had been trading with the USSR as it was with Yugoslavia, there would, in Khrushchev's view, have been no grounds for discontent.

Wishing to get closer to Tito, Khrushchev invited him to the Crimea for a hunting holiday. He thought this was the traditional way to discuss things, to talk and get to know people better – in the best tsarist traditions of pre-Petrine Russia.

The trip to Yugoslavia in the summer of 1963, in which I happened to be involved, was particularly important, however. Khrushchev was interested in Yugoslav self-management and economic administration, especially the workers' councils. At that time the Soviet press – with official blessing, naturally – was sharply critical of those methods. With great interest Khrushchev asked the Yugoslavs all about it, visiting factories and state farms. His lively and inquisitive mind never accepted clichés, though he still maintained during his discussions with the Yugoslavs that their self-management was nothing more than a façade since the government decided the most important things – setting production plans and monitoring their fulfilment. Nonetheless, he listened to what they said about it being a socialist system in its own way and more democratic than that of the Soviet Union. Nor did the Yugoslavs' criticism of Soviet administrative practices as bureaucratic pass unnoticed. Khrushchev felt that this 'criticism' deserved some degree of attention 'because at enterprises in our country there was nothing except production conferences'.[3] He therefore believed that 'there was some grain of usefulness in these Yugoslav forms and it would thus be wrong to deny it. Although we did not state this publicly.'[4]

The one point on which Khrushchev remained totally adamant was the role of planning and commodity–money relations. He believed that a socialist state was impossible without a State Planning Committee and the central statistical and planning organizations. This was because if capitalist market relations had been abolished there must be some body to replace that elemental force, and that body was the State Planning Committee. Khrushchev considered this an absolutely essential and correct Leninist idea that had been confirmed by the USSR's entire experience. He was decidedly unimpressed by the way in which Yugoslav enterprises had access to the domestic and, in particular, the external markets. If Khrushchev is to be believed, Tito later partially admitted that his criticism was fair and believed that Yugoslavia was in difficulties precisely because of the excessive influence of market relations.

In his memoirs Khrushchev gives a more balanced assessment of the polemics at that time. He writes that one could not deny everything the Yugoslavs had achieved, that one could not limit oneself to mutual allegations and reproaches, and that nobody can lay claim to the truth and describe others' experience as opportunism or adoption of capitalism.[5] Apart from the problems of self-management, Khrushchev was preoccupied with the advanced technologies that Yugoslavia had purchased abroad, particularly in the chemical sphere. And he was especially interested in Yugoslavia's experience in developing tourism, which was then earning the country around one hundred million dollars a year. This greatly impressed Khrushchev, and he describes in detail his visits to hotels and restaurants with excellent standards of cleanliness, service and taste.

Khrushchev asked Tito how such a diverse multitude of Western tourists, often travelling in cars, was supervised, and complained that the Soviet bureaucratic apparatus created obstacles that nobody would even attempt to tackle. At the same time Khrushchev brought up the traditional problem of espionage, to which Tito sensibly replied that spies by no means always cross frontiers in cars, that they enter countries by other methods, usually in the comfort of an aircraft. Different methods must therefore be used to combat espionage, while tourists should be left in freedom.

Khrushchev was very taken with this idea. On returning home he reported on the Yugoslav experience and suggested that some thought be put into expanding the Soviet tourist industry. Quite an extensive hotel construction programme was adopted, but this went no further due to Khrushchev's fall from power. Khrushchev had dreams of large-scale tourism in the Crimea, in Siberia and in Central Asia. He even asked Tito to play host to a group of Soviet specialists who would learn how to apply the Yugoslav experience. He attached particular importance to tourism in the Caucasus. He himself adored Pitsunda – a charming small peninsula on the coast. He often spent his holidays there and it was there that his political career ended: in October 1964 he was summoned from Pitsunda to be dealt with at a meeting of the Presidium of the Central Committee . . .

Khrushchev was also preoccupied with the idea of creating more flexible structures within light industry. In Yugoslavia he had seen how quickly light industrial enterprises adapted to the changing demands of fashion, and on returning home he insistently recommended that Yugoslavia's experience be studied, that people 'use their brains' to foresee changes in consumer demand.

But there was one issue on which Tito was unable to shake Khrushchev's convictions – individual and cooperative farming. All the signs are, however, that Nikita Sergeyevich had little understanding of Yugoslavia's agricultural situation.

Tito told Khrushchev that Yugoslavia had rejected the idea of collective farms and wholesale collectivization. That alone probably irritated Khrushchev, since he never re-evaluated Stalin's policy of forced collectivization. Instead, what he remembered from the conversation was Tito's description of the setting-up of state-owned farms which, if we are to believe Khrushchev, were similar to Soviet state farms. In fact this was not quite true, but that is a separate issue. Khrushchev stressed that state-owned farms represented a socialist option which did not contradict 'our understanding of socialist construction'.[6]

Khrushchev backs this up with a reference to Lenin, though the reference is inaccurate. He maintains that when Lenin raised the issue of cooperatives he regarded state-owned farms as the highest stage in the development of agriculture and as an example for collective agriculture, producing seed stocks, breeding cattle and satisfying the needs of collective farmers.

In this respect Khrushchev even revises the experience of the Virgin Lands, where, he writes, they initially attempted to create standard collective farms which, however, proved to be an artificial form of organization for the migrants and a very expensive one as well. As a result, collective farms turned out to be unprofitable. For that reason, on Khrushchev's initiative, state farms were increased in the Virgin Lands to produce cheaper grain. Khrushchev compares the Soviet and Yugoslav experience with that of Poland, where agricultural circles or associations like primary cooperatives were being set up. Khrushchev considered this acceptable both for economic and political reasons – political, because the peasants were following the Polish workers' party, and economic, because agriculture was performing well in that country. But here too, in his assessment of Poland's experience, Khrushchev stresses the importance of state-owned farms. I shall have occasion to return to these ideas of Khrushchev's when I examine his agrarian policy.

Rounding off his reflections on Yugoslavia's experience, Khrushchev again repeats something that was for him gospel truth – that socialism means a single centralized planned economy and that this also forms the basis of agriculture. Moreover, according to Khrushchev, turning to the market, to supply-and-demand relations were 'capitalist elements'. Admittedly, learning from the bitter experience of blinkered attitudes towards what was happening in Eastern Europe, Khrushchev immediately adds the reservation that there are many possibilities for diversity in socialist construction, that it would be wrong to create any single template or model for all countries of the world and to use it as a standpoint from which to denounce as unsocialist anything that differs from it. He appeals for greater tolerance and for each country to be granted the opportunity to choose its own path depending on local historical, economic, ethnic and other conditions.

Yet despite all this he believes that the means of production must belong to the people, as must the banks – this being the most important and fundamental thing, while the state should be based on the dictatorship of the proletariat. This, in his view, is the foundation of the Marxist understanding of the transition period from capitalism to socialism.[7]

We see the difficulty with which Khrushchev surmounted his own notions of socialism, notions formed under the influence of Stalinist thinking. For both political and emotional reasons he was constantly drawn towards the idea of diversity and pluralism, but a dogmatic belief in the superiority of the state system survived unshaken.

*

Nothing came as a greater shock to Khrushchev's consciousness, or caused greater doubts and even deformations in his anti-Stalinism and his search for an effective socialist model, than what happened in Hungary in 1956. Those events may have been the cause of many of the mistakes in his new domestic and foreign policies, and there is no doubt that they triggered his monstrous outbursts against that part of the Soviet intelligentsia that welcomed the ideas put forward at the Twentieth Party Congress.

I visited Hungary several times during that period. In the 1960s I returned as a member of a party delegation led by Andropov, which also included the secretaries of the Moscow and Leningrad party organizations, Yegorichev and Tolstikov. During that trip we met many Hungarian party and state leaders and we were received by Janos Kadar. It was interesting to watch the encounter between him and Andropov. As Soviet ambassador to Hungary, Andropov had played a special role during the tragic events of 1956. I had learned of this in particular from the accounts of people who had worked with him in the embassy.

As far back as 1956 Andropov showed himself to be a man of rare insight and political intuition. Some months before the armed clashes in the streets of Budapest he had informed Khrushchev and the entire Soviet leadership of the possibility of an uprising. Andropov had proposed facilitating a natural and smooth replacement of the whole Hungarian government, which had discredited itself along with Rakosi by repressing Rajk, Kadar and other well-known Hungarians and by making major mistakes in domestic policy. He expressed doubts over whether Rakosi's successors, Geroe and later Imre Nagy, were capable of handling the situation. The former was clearly drawn towards the authoritarian methods of the past, while the latter, in Andropov's view, was indulgent towards the feelings of the mob and even towards those who wished to reinstate Hungary's pre-revolutionary regime and withdraw from the Warsaw Pact.

Khrushchev responded by sending Mikoyan and Suslov to Hungary to investigate the situation. The Hungarian leaders told them, however, that 'the Soviet ambassador is agitated' without the least reason and that they were capable of handling the situation. That was the first mistake not only by the Hungarian leadership, but by the Soviet leadership as well. The second was even more dramatic. At the very height of events in Hungary it was decided to withdraw the troops from Budapest – they were mainly concentrated in the airport and surrounding areas. The city was thereby handed over to mob rule. I do not believe that this was a deliberate provocation; most likely the Soviet leadership was responding to a suggestion by the Hungarians, reckoning that in such a situation they themselves could cope with the rebel forces. As far as I know, Andropov objected to this decision too. It is quite possible that if the Soviet troops had not been withdrawn from Budapest the terrible bloodshed could have been avoided, since it was after that withdrawal that the anti-government forces succeeded in seizing weapons (including artillery), in winning over many officers and soldiers and in forming organized detachments for an uprising.

Incidentally, during our trip to Hungary we were taken to Mount Gallert, where the holiday cottages for visiting VIPs were located. It was in one of them that Rakosi's 'abdication' took place. A member of the Hungarian Central Committee allocated us a small room decorated in rococo style. He showed us the spot in which Rakosi had sat in a small armchair, with Mikoyan on a little couch with a curved back upholstered in a bright flowery fabric. 'It was here,' laughed a Hungarian friend accompanying us, 'that Mikoyan pronounced his historic words in his thick accent: "Write your own voluntary resignation!" ' I don't know whether this is how it actually happened, but that is the version the Hungarians tell.

I happened to be present at a meeting between Andropov and Kadar. As a conversation between two leaders it was somewhat unusual. One could sense in the atmosphere a profound personal liking and at the same time a sharp tension and even embarrassment. There was too much between the two men: recollections of tense days of conflict when an agitated mob besieged the embassy with Andropov inside; the first few days after Kadar came to power, when, according to the Hungarians, Andropov followed him everywhere like a shadow and was present at almost every meeting of the Hungarian leadership; Kadar's release from prison with Andropov's assistance, and much much more.

I myself had had several previous meetings with Kadar – of an unofficial nature, of course. We had twice met on holiday in Miskhor in the Crimea – he in a state holiday cottage and I in an ordinary sanatorium, but both in the same complex. Kadar was still fairly young then and he liked to join us for a game of volleyball or chess. He was an avid player, always trying his hardest to win, and would be childishly despondent if he lost. We often competed over a chessboard, he winning some games and I others. I remember a phone call from a comrade in the Central Committee in Moscow who worked in the area of Soviet–Hungarian relations. He said: 'What are you beating Comrade Kadar for? He's suffering. Quit showing off and ruining our relations with Hungary.' I remembered this quip during a meeting in Budapest and risked telling Kadar about it. He laughed long and hard.

That was not, of course, the main concern of our delegation during the visit to Hungary. We visited many enterprises and cooperatives, and what particularly interested us – besides, naturally, the change in people's attitudes eight years after the 1956 drama – was the economic reform being introduced at the time. The Hungarians had sought and found their own solutions – in methods of party leadership and in developing commodity–money relations and market relations in both industry and agriculture. Incidentally, despite what many of us in the Soviet Union believed, the Hungarians had never set up collective farms. From the very start their cooperatives had been closer to the Leninist blueprint and had been based on the genuine interests of the peasants. It was not surprising, therefore, that they turned out to be far more productive than Soviet collective farms. Nor was it surprising that during the events of 1956 the Hungarian peasant class was virtually the backbone of loyalty to the government. Even among the workers there was a section of mainly young people who were drawn into the anti-Soviet movement, whereas the peasants refused to give the rebels any assistance whatsoever, material or moral.

Most of all, however, our discussions with the Hungarians revolved around the events of 1956 and the lessons to be learned from them. I heard more about those events on a later visit as part of a delegation led by Khrushchev to the Seventh Congress of the Hungarian Socialist Workers' Party. I was struck by how democratic that congress was. The speeches were unlike anything I had seen at our own congresses; there was no bragging and the delegates took part in debating policies and decisions, criticized various aspects of the laws passed and put forward their own proposals.

What Janos Kadar had to say was particularly interesting – not only in his main report, which contained a great deal that was new, but in particular in his closing remarks. He had not written them down. He came to the rostrum with one or two pages of text and delivered a speech that lasted at least an hour. In it, he mentioned every issue of any significance that had been raised at the congress. He agreed with most of the observations and explained that the leadership intended to act on them. He also raised new issues arising from the proposals that had been made. His manner was free, unconstrained, extraordinarily democratic and friendly, without a trace of ambition or conceit – just like a comrade amongst comrades.

His style contrasted sharply even with that of Khrushchev himself, not to mention Tito, Gomulka and other Eastern European figures whom I was able to hear and observe. There was another aspect of Kadar's style that stuck in my mind: a kind of tiredness, or perhaps bitterness or aloofness – it's difficult to put into words the expression on his face and the tone of his speech.

Was this the result of what he had gone through in prison, or of his rather unusual accession to power at a difficult period in Hungarian history? Was it an inner quality of Kadar's, an expression of his character, his modesty and lack of pretension? Did it reflect his tremendous feeling of personal responsibility? I cannot say, but I found that aspect of Kadar's style particularly attractive.

One might compare it to the impression created by two good singers with opposing styles. One admires his own voice, the other longs to convey his feelings to the listener. The latter was characteristic of Kadar, and placed him above many political songsters of that period.

Both during that congress and elsewhere I heard Khrushchev speaking about Kadar and, in particular, about the events of 1956.

*

The shock that Khrushchev felt during those events in Hungary could be compared to his experience of the arrest of Beria and the Cuban Missile Crisis which was to follow. For this reason they hold a prominent place in his memoirs.

What had happened in Budapest was ruthless carnage, to use Khrushchev's words. He thought the principal culprits were youths who had set up armed detachments and seized artillery and other weapons, while the working class and the peasantry – whom Khrushchev called the collective farm peasants – took no part. The rebels demanded the withdrawal of Soviet troops. To Khrushchev those demands were illegitimate since they ran counter to the norms established by the Warsaw Pact. And although the Hungarian parliament met several times the demands had no legal force in Khrushchev's eyes. He was especially outraged when the mob began hunting down party functionaries and particularly 'Cheka' officials. Khrushchev always involuntarily applied Soviet terminology when referring to events both in Hungary and in all the other Eastern European countries. This was quite typical: as a frank and sincere man he considered it unnecessary to make any pretences. It was not only a terminological aberration on his part – it was a subconscious belief that socialist forms were basically identical everywhere.

What was Khrushchev's attitude to the threat posed by events in

Hungary? He recounts how Hungarian émigrés were returning home via Vienna and doing all they could to stir up civil war, to overthrow the revolutionary government, to stage riots and turn Hungary in the direction of capitalism. Khrushchev was convinced that this was precisely what the West was aiming at. 'But this is not surprising,' he observes, 'since our aim is to support the progressive movement and the transition from capitalism to socialism of the working class, the working peasantry and the working intelligentsia, while the foes of socialism pursue the opposite aim – to eliminate the socialist order where it is weakest in order to force back the working class . . . and to reinforce capitalist elements and capitalism.'[8]

It was during those events that Khrushchev's so-called 'internationalist aid' policy was first put to the test. As Khrushchev emphasized many times, the Soviet Union pursued no national aims, only international aims of fraternal proletarian internationalism. For this reason special significance was attached to consulting with and securing the consent of the other socialist countries, especially China. Khrushchev asked Mao Tse-tung to send some authoritative figure to discuss the matter. On the face of it, this preferential treatment of China seems illogical, since China was not a member of the Warsaw Pact. But this did not even occur to Khrushchev, who considered it a matter of rendering 'internationalist aid' rather than a Warsaw Pact operation. Thus, it seems, the view of the great Chinese Communist Party was especially important.

At Khrushchev's request Liu Shao-chi, who was respected in the Soviet Union as one of the most authoritative Chinese leaders, flew to Moscow. By a strange irony of fate the meeting was held in Stalin's former holiday cottage and his spirit hovered in the air. They sat up all night, weighing the pros and cons of using armed force in Hungary. Both sides kept changing their mind: first Liu Shao-chi would argue that they should wait in case the Hungarian working class managed to sort out the situation itself, and when the Soviet leaders agreed Liu Shao-chi himself would suggest taking immediate and decisive action. Liu Shao-chi telephoned Mao Tse-tung many times – like Stalin, Mao worked at night, and Khrushchev used to call him a 'night owl'. Nonetheless, the all-night meeting ended with a decision not to use armed force.

On returning home, Khrushchev was too preoccupied with the issue to sleep. He realized it was an historic moment at which a clear choice had to be made. Both options were dangerous, but he was particularly worried by the prospect of a counter-revolutionary victory and 'NATO penetration into the camp of socialist countries', which would put Yugoslavia, Czechoslovakia and Romania in a difficult situation.[9]

The next morning the Presidium of the Central Committee

assembled and Khrushchev reported on his meeting with the Chinese delegation. He said that a decision had been taken at the Soviet–Chinese talks not to use armed force, but voiced his own misgivings. There was a lengthy debate in the Presidium, ending in a different decision – to use troops for 'assistance to the working class of Hungary'. Khrushchev called for Marshal Konev, who was then in command of the Warsaw Pact troops, and asked him, 'How long will it take to restore order in Hungary and smash the counter-revolutionary forces?' Konev thought for a moment and replied, 'Approximately three days.' All the members of the leadership then concluded that 'this business must be brought to an end, and as fast as possible'. Konev would be told when to act later.

Khrushchev hurried to inform Liu Shao-chi of the Presidium's decision, but since Liu Shao-chi and his colleagues were about to fly home from Vnukovo aerodrome the entire Presidium had to meet him there to report the Soviet decision. Liu replied that he was unable at that moment to confer with Mao, but that he thought Mao would agree and that they would be informed of the Chinese point of view immediately after his return to Peking. 'Consider us in agreement,' said Liu Shao-chi to the members of the Soviet leadership.[10]

Then began a round of coordination meetings and consultations with the Eastern European socialist leaders. One of those meetings was between Khrushchev, Molotov and Malenkov on the Soviet side, and Gomulka and Cyrankiewicz representing Poland. Interestingly enough, like a true master of the art of politics, Khrushchev took along to that meeting the most conservative Soviet officials so that he could rely on their firm support. It was agreed that a meeting would be convened in Bucharest that same day, involving delegations from Czechoslovakia, Bulgaria and Romania as well. Nobody was in any doubt about the need for military intervention. Moreover, the Romanian and Bulgarian representatives wanted their own troops to take part – a suggestion that was turned down by Khrushchev. He explained that there were troops in Hungary under the Potsdam Agreement and that they were perfectly adequate to suppress the counter-revolution headed by Imre Nagy. Khrushchev even went on to crack a joke of sorts: the Romanians are thirsty for battle now, he said, because they had taken part in crushing the revolution led by Bela Kun in 1919.

A jolly chap – allowing himself to draw an analogy that cast a dark shadow over the Soviet Union's entire military operation! Only Khrushchev could have done that.

The most difficult talks were expected in Yugoslavia. Khrushchev flew there at night in atrocious weather: a hurricane was raging in the mountains with flashes of lightning. It was the worst flight of his whole life, even including those he made during the war. The plane was to land on the small island of Brioni without the necessary equipment for a blind landing, and it lost contact with ground control. Malenkov was least happy in the plane. Despite his involvement in sentencing thousands of people to death he was a weak man and suffered from travel sickness even in a car.

On arrival in Brioni the delegation was greeted by Tito. In spite of the doubts caused by strained relations during the Hungarian events, he gave Khrushchev a fine welcome. He even kissed him in the Russian manner, although in the past, it seemed, he had not been too keen on the Soviet habit of kissing men.

Khrushchev had prepared himself for a harsh attack by Tito, but was pleasantly surprised: Tito was in favour of the immediate use of troops to rout the Hungarian counter-revolution. He merely asked: 'When is the Soviet troop action planned to take place?' Cunning as ever, Khrushchev said it would happen in the near future, but the exact date had not been decided. It transpired that he had told none of the Eastern European leaders the date, though before leaving he had instructed Marshal Konev to prepare for immediate action and to end the whole thing in three days.

Khrushchev told Tito of his apprehension at being in Brioni while the war was going on in Egypt. He thought an aircraft might drop a bomb, whether accidentally or not, thereby destroying both Tito and the people's government in Yugoslavia. Tito was similarly alarmed by the situation and in particular by the fate of Nasser. They sat through the entire night discussing various international and other problems – Khrushchev's second night virtually without sleep. When he got back to Moscow the members of the Presidium were already waiting at the airport and they all went straight to the Kremlin.

It was most noteworthy that in his memoirs it is precisely in the context of Hungary that Khrushchev returns again and again to the methods of class struggle in the international arena. He examines the issue first from one, then from another angle as if weighing it up anew on the scales of ideology and history. He wanted to convince himself over and over again that the decision taken in 1956 had been the only correct one. Yet the arguments he deployed to justify that decision went no further than the boundaries of traditional Stalinist preconceptions. It would have been understandable if he had spoken of the balance of force in Europe possibly being disrupted by Hungary's withdrawal from the Warsaw Pact, but it was hard to accept his generalized ideas about 'internationalist duty' and the inevitability of the use of military methods by both the capitalist and socialist sides.

Our enemies act in the same way against us, Khrushchev observes, exploiting our every omission in order to set us back and reinforce the capitalist influence. And anyway there's a struggle under way – who will get the upper hand? Will it be the working class or the bourgeoisie who wins? And this, he goes on, is why Communists and Marxists are confident that the world will be ruled by the working man and realize that victory will not come about of itself but must be won through struggle. This is why peaceful coexistence of different state systems is possible, whereas peaceful coexistence in ideology would be treason on the part of the Marxist-Leninist party. In this connection he recalls something he once said about America – 'we shall bury the enemies of revolution.' Khrushchev rejects the way this was interpreted in the American press as meaning that the Soviet people wanted to bury the American people. During press conferences in the United States he frequently explained his position as being that the American working class itself would bury the bourgeoisie and that this was a domestic matter for each country.

And now the surprising thing: from these general ideological sentiments Khrushchev makes a direct leap to the events in Hungary. 'And so that is how we, as it were, decided what our troops ought to do . . . and we moved those troops in.'[11]

Marshal Konev kept his promise: it did indeed take him three days. During my stay in Budapest eight years later I saw hundreds of buildings bearing traces of bullets, shrapnel and even shells. Most controversial and dubious was the action taken against Imre Nagy. During the suppression of the rebellion he took refuge in the Yugoslav embassy. The new Hungarian government demanded that he be handed over for trial. The Yugoslavs resisted, but eventually were obliged to hand Nagy over. They took him to his flat, where he was immediately arrested. Janos Kadar telephoned Khrushchev and asked him to remove Nagy as his presence in Budapest was a nuisance. He was flown to Bucharest in Romania and soon afterwards executed. But who gave the order for this? Khrushchev does not tell us, though one may guess that it could not have been done without Khrushchev's consent.

The secret execution of Imre Nagy was the last act of the Hungarian drama. Niccolò Machiavelli wrote of the need for a cruel ruler. If someone lays claim to your place as leader or ruler, for instance, you must inevitably get rid of him. Yet Nagy's murder was not even dictated by such cruel political necessity, it was superfluous barbarity in typical Stalinist style. There was no political expediency in it; nobody could have made Imre Nagy into a figurehead for the struggle against Kadar and the Soviet presence. Khrushchev had the opportunity to treat him in the same way as Rakosi by sending him into permanent exile in a remote Russian town. Why, then, did he not do so?

Here we begin to understand an important feature of Khrushchev's character. He was a kind man in normal human relationships, but in politics he did not recognize kindness, especially when it seemed to him that 'class interests' had been infringed. Still smouldering in his heart were the ashes of the Stalin he himself had cast down. He executed Nagy as a lesson to all other leaders in socialist countries, thinking as he did so of Gomulka and Kadar, and also perhaps of Tito and Mao. In his eyes political expediency was superior to morality. Humanity came second to security.

Perhaps without knowing it Khrushchev was thereby firing on potential reformers in Budapest, in Prague and in the Soviet Union. He set a bad example for his successors: Brezhnev was guided by it when he ordered troops into Czechoslovakia and 'internationalist aid' to Afghanistan.

Khrushchev was invited to Budapest by Kadar. He had known him only slightly before, but from their discussions had realized that Kadar was the man to lead the country out of a state of crisis and guarantee normal and prosperous development. In a speech at a rally before a wide audience Khrushchev was at pains to stress that the events in Hungary had resulted from the abuse of power by Stalin. Abuses had been committed in both the Soviet Union and Hungary as well as in other countries. He immediately added, however, that it was the result of Stalin's morbid nature, as mentioned by Lenin in his last Testament. After the rally, at Khrushchev's suggestion, he and Kadar came down from the rostrum and went into the crowd. This was a bold move by Khrushchev and was appreciated as such by the public and journalists, including the foreign press.

There in Hungary and subsequently in his memoirs Khrushchev explained time and time again his reasons for taking military action. His main argument was that the West supported the Hungarian émigré community and was exporting counter-revolution. This required intervention. But in principle, he emphasized, without exportation of counter-revolution there can be no exportation of revolution.

He was particularly at pains to reject any analogy between 1956 and 1848. In 1956, he would emphasize, it was a question of suppressing counter-revolution, whereas in 1848 Nicholas I had suppressed revolution and restored the Austrian monarchy to power, which was a disgrace for Russia. For this reason, as he saw it, the Soviet mission was a progressive one, whereas Nicholas I's intervention had been reactionary.[12]

It has to be said that during this meeting with Kadar there was a significant exchange of views on the Soviet troop presence in Hungary. Khrushchev asked Kadar whether the troops had to stay there, mentioning that other members of the Soviet leadership felt they should possibly be withdrawn. Kadar looked at Khrushchev and said: 'Comrade Khrushchev, decide for yourself. I shall say only one thing – that there is absolutely no talk in Hungary at the moment about the presence of your troops, absolutely no negative attitudes as a result of their presence on Hungarian territory. Only one thing concerns Hungarians – that Rakosi should not return.'[13] Khrushchev was pleased with this answer and once more stressed his liking for Kadar and his friendliness and trust towards the Soviet Union.

Yet Khrushchev never ceased worrying about how to justify the Soviet troop presence in Eastern Europe. He had no doubts over their deployment in East Germany, since this stemmed from treaties signed with the West after the Allied victory. As for Poland, which was building up a strong army of its own, he looked into the matter but failed to reach any conclusion.

At the same time Khrushchev stressed that it was not really a matter of troops at all, because it was not fear of Soviet military intervention that was uppermost in people's minds in those countries. In his view, 'one cannot create paradise or drive people into paradise' through fear. Other peoples too would follow the socialist path; if it was not an easy one, it was the correct path.

He was also worried that the presence of Soviet troops in the socialist countries was costing the Soviet people twice what it would cost to keep them on Soviet territory. Khrushchev was pondering the possibility of pulling the troops out of Poland and Hungary – a decision which, as we know, was never taken during his period of office.[14] In later years the so-called 'Brezhnev Doctrine' was to appear, providing a justification not only for the presence of Soviet troops in the various Eastern European countries, but for joint military intervention by the Warsaw Pact in the affairs of an individual country when a threat to their common security arose. This was the stated reason for sending troops to Czechoslovakia in 1968. It is clear that this doctrine was a major step backwards from Khrushchev's position, although he too always wavered over the permissibility of so-called 'internationalist aid' by means of armed force.

The events in Hungary triggered an explosion of feelings that had been building up within the Soviet leadership. The Stalinists, who had compiled a long list of grievances over Khrushchev's innovations in domestic and foreign policy, decided to move into the attack and remove him as party leader in one fell swoop. This was at the meeting of the Central Committee Presidium on 18 June 1957. It was an unprecedented meeting that went on for three days with two sides locked in combat – Khrushchev and the minority that supported him, and Molotov, Malenkov and Kaganovich, who led the majority. That majority decided to remove Khrushchev from the post of First Secretary of the Central Committee, but they had miscalculated their strength. Khrushchev enjoyed the support of a considerable section of the Central Committee – by then he had managed to appoint many new members to it – and most importantly, he enjoyed the support of the army under Marshal Zhukov, an active anti-Stalinist, and of the KGB under A. Serov, who was a close ally of Khrushchev's. With the help of those organizations, Khrushchev was able to convene a Central Committee plenum within a few days and for the first time in many decades it played the role of a deciding body. After a heated debate Molotov, Malenkov, Kaganovich and the 'affiliated' D. Shepilov were declared an 'anti-party group' and expelled from the leadership. Khrushchev had won one of the biggest victories of his political career.

He did not do away with his enemies in Stalinist fashion, however, as he wished to begin a new tradition in this respect as well.

It was not until 4 July that the plenum statement and a brief report on the proceedings were published. The plenum decisions mentioned the 'anti-party group of Malenkov, Kaganovich and Molotov' but concealed the fact that Voroshilov, Bulganin and others were also involved. Both Voroshilov and Bulganin remained in their posts. Molotov, Malenkov, Kaganovich and the 'affiliated Shepilov' were removed from the Presidium and the Central Committee. Saburov lost his position as member of the Central Committee Presidium, while Pervukhin became merely a candidate member of the Presidium. The plenum increased the size of the Presidium to fifteen members, including recent candidate members L. I. Brezhnev, Ye. A. Furtseva, F. R. Kozlov, N. M. Shvernik and G. K. Zhukov. A. L. Aristov, N. I. Belyayev and O. V. Kuusinen also became Presidium members.

None of Khrushchev's enemies were expelled from the party at that time; they were all given positions outside Moscow. Molotov was dispatched as Soviet ambassador to Mongolia, Kaganovich became director of the Ural mining and dressing combine in the town of Asbest, and Malenkov became director of the Ust-Kamenogorsk hydroelectric power station on the Irtysh River. Shepilov was given a professorial chair in Central Asia.[15]

The political drama within the Soviet leadership together with the events in Hungary demonstrated to Khrushchev the powerful underground forces he had brought to the surface by his report on Stalin at the Twentieth Congress. This was probably the reason for his attempts to manoeuvre around the problem of deStalinization which were typical of the following years right up to the Twenty-Second Party Congress in 1961, when the anti-Stalinist wave peaked once again.

Even then I was to observe how that manoeuvring affected human lives. Once in 1957 the editor-in-chief of the journal *Kommunist*, A. Rumyantsev – a kind man with unusually liberal convictions for that time – made an unexpected request of me. In his capacity as deputy of the Supreme Soviet he had received a letter from a prison camp from

Erik Yudin, a former philosophy lecturer at a university in Siberia, asking Rumyantsev to help free him.

He had been sentenced under the infamous Article 58-10 for anti-Soviet propaganda and agitation. His 'crime' consisted in having spoken critically of Soviet action in Hungary in 1956 and having insisted on the right of the socialist countries to organize their affairs in their own way. By way of evidence of this 'crime' the prosecutors had produced a letter written by Yudin to his sister in which he expressed his views. It had been intercepted and had formed the basis of a six-year prison sentence.

Rumyantsev was an extroardinary individual with an extraordinary life. He was a man of profound sophistication, kindness and even sentimentality who, strange to tell, had been first noticed by Stalin during the famous debate on the economic problems of socialism. As I now understand it, that debate arose from disputes within the Politburo initiated by Voznesensky, chairman of the State Planning Committee who was subsequently executed. His view, even back in those days, was that there should be a transition to a freer economy from the totally militarized system created during the war, under which orders were given and non-implementation was punished by imprisonment or execution.

Stalin had convened a conference of economists from around the country, including Rumyantsev, who came from Kharkov. On the surface it seemed a fairly abstract debate: did the law of value function under socialism? But the essence of the issue was whether the government should, at its own discretion and whim, command everything – resources, prices and people, the proportions in the economy, the standard and way of living, etc. – or whether there were objective limits imposed by economic efficiency. It was then that Rumyantsev came up with his compromise solution: the law of value remains, but functions 'in altered form'. They could thus have their cake and eat it: economic laws had to be taken into account, but politics remained dominant over economics.

Stalin liked Rumyantsev's speech and, of course, pretended the idea was his own when he promulgated it in his book *The Economic Problems of Socialism in the USSR* (which was probably written with the help of people like Rumyantsev). Rumyantsev was appointed head of the Science Department of the Central Committee and from there he moved to *Kommunist*.

He was a very good man. The fact that such people had survived the Stalinist era prompted me to the simple thought that virtually nothing fundamental changes in human nature. There are good people and bad people, but most are a mixture of both. Rousseau was wrong in believing that the system shapes the man; the system can only deform him by extracting the better or worse qualities from his nature. This is why our people have always been better than our system – always.

To return to Yudin, I was shocked by his letter to Rumyantsev, as Khrushchev had frequently stated that there were no political prisoners in the USSR. Besides, I fully shared Yudin's views. I remember taking the letter home with me, getting out a bottle of vodka and, switching on the songs of Okudzhava, weeping over this new round of cruelty.

We managed to obtain Yudin's release, but he returned a broken man. By a strange coincidence he was much later appointed editor of my book. We met in his house and I listened with anguished compassion as he sang mournful prison songs. Soon afterwards Erik died. He died as a very young man who had failed to withstand the cruel tribulations brought down upon him by the Thaw and the fluctuations in the political climate.

What particularly outraged me then was Khrushchev's lying. In fact it was after the events in Hungary that 'seditionaries' who went beyond the permitted boundaries of criticism began to be imprisoned. Painful though this realization may be, it was then also that the monstrous practice of sending particularly stubborn critics and freedom-fighters to psychiatric hospitals began. Indeed, this gratuitous deceit is one of the most unpleasant features of Russian political culture. In their handling of political opponents Soviet leaders considered deception normal and even essential, convinced as they were that the other side was doing the same.

Later I learned that under Khrushchev many hundreds of people had suffered for so-called political crimes, that is, for voicing disagreement with his policies. Brezhnev developed this practice on a massive scale and with even greater deceit, but it must be acknowledged that it began under Khrushchev.

6 Hoxha and Tito again

For a long time afterwards I remembered my visit to Albania, where I acquired my first experience of real political struggle. It was soon after the 1960 conference of the Communist and workers' parties. We were already aware that Enver Hoxha and his closest associate, Mehmet Shehu, took a negative view of our party's latest congress and virtually rejected the ideas contained in the Statement. We therefore had a difficult trip ahead of us, one that required particularly thorough preparation. Speeches had been drafted in advance to be read out at the congress and, if the opportunity were granted, at a mass rally in Tirana.

One morning Tolkunov popped into my office (unlike other deputy heads he did not stand on ceremony) and said that Andropov was waiting for us. We found him in a state of extreme irritation; he had just seen the materials we had prepared and was disgusted.

'You've been pottering about for almost half a year to produce material that is fit only for the rubbish bin,' said Yu.V. without any preliminaries. Clearly he had not yet calmed down after the rocketing he had given some other staff members just before we arrived. 'You'll have to put things right urgently,' he said, more to Tolkunov than to me. He did not yet know what I was capable of and naturally relied more on his deputy.

'Don't worry,' said Tolkunov, 'Fedor will get to work and rewrite it quickly.'

'It needn't be quick. We still have at least ten days before we have to send off the materials. The main thing is that it be done properly, that all the nuances are right. This is an unusual trip and the atmosphere will be difficult,' said Yu.V., peering at me through his spectacles.

Then, in a few clear and concise sentences, he outlined the situation and the approximate direction the speeches should take.

'All the rest,' he concluded, 'is up to your imagination.'

It is easy to talk of imagination, I said to myself as I sat down at my desk. These speeches had been written by specialists, but I knew neither Albania, its Communist Party nor the situation there. I read through the speeches and was surprised most of all by the language in which they were couched. Apart from that, they contained virtually nothing about the recently-ended conference, whereas it was obvious to me that we should spell out and publicize our position somehow.

Then I had a brainwave: I decided to dictate the whole speech anew as if I had to deliver it myself, and then smooth out the edges and knock it into a more acceptable form. I summoned a typist and began dictating. Until then I had had little experience of dictation. I had written my thesis by hand, but I wrote fairly quickly, every day completing the twelve to fifteen pages of text that I had set myself. On two or three occasions I had tried dictating leading articles for the journal. At first I was embarrassed by the presence of another person during my pangs of creativity, especially during the pauses when something got stuck inside me and refused to come out.

Strange as it may seem, however, my first real attempt was extremely successful – I dictated about twenty pages. That same day I edited the text and the next morning took it to Yu.V., who was more surprised than pleased. He read it closely and even leafed through it a second time.

'You must have had it ready-made, doing it at this speed.'

'No, I had nothing ready-made, I simply dictated it to a typist,' I declared, not without a certain feeling of pride like a star pupil.

'Well, it's a bit better than before, I think, but you realize it still needs some work.'

He then phoned Tolkunov (as I later learned from the latter) and said: 'You take a look at the speech. Fedor has done something to improve it, but it's still a long way from completion.'

I left somewhat discouraged, not because I considered the text a masterpiece – I was well aware that an official speech cannot and should not be a masterpiece. I was asked to finalize the text, but what did that mean? I wanted some clear indications of what was suitable and what wasn't, which paragraphs to remove, what ideas to add, what to edit and how. That was always the way things were done at the journal, where none of us could tolerate observations and wishes of a general nature; that simply played no part in our discussions.

I was as yet unaware that documents were prepared in precisely the opposite manner. Tasks were normally set in the most general form, such as write a speech on a specific event, write a TASS statement, write a newspaper editorial or slam our enemies for this or that. The research and writing were up to the author – let him rack his brains and we'll see what he produces.

There was something else I didn't know: the entire process was highly complex, recurrent and horribly agonizing for all concerned. In part this style was due to the principle of collective preparation and scrutiny of documents; in large measure it was because the client himself had not yet thought through the actual content of the document and was happy to begin by describing its overall aim and global conception (to use an expression that was to catch on later).

Where Yu.V. was concerned, however, things were even more complicated (yet perhaps in some ways simpler). I very quickly realized that whatever kind of text one produced he would always rewrite it from start to finish in his own hand, trying out each word for size. All he required was good prime material containing a complete set of the necessary components, both subject-matter and phraseology. After that he would invite a few people into his office, seat us at an extended table, take off his jacket, sit down at the head of the table and take a pen in his hand. He would read the document aloud, assessing each word as he went along and inviting us to take part in the editing, or more precisely in the rewriting of the text. This was done collectively and rather chaotically, like an auction. Everyone could suggest his own word, a new phrase or idea. Yu.V. would accept or reject these suggestions. Whether it was a strategic document which would decide the country's policy or the most insignificant organizational issue, Yu.V. was equally pedantic in his approach, trying to weigh everything up and missing nothing.

There was one further reason, however, which I understood only later. Yu.V. loved intellectual political work. He simply enjoyed being personally involved in writing speeches, directing the growth process of political thinking and expression. Apart from that, those 'round-the-table sessions' were good fun, though nothing more than the traditional tea was served, with biscuits or sandwiches after nine in the evening. By the end of these evening vigils the exhausted 'aristocrats of the spirit' (as Yu.V. called us) were often digressing onto other subjects, reciting jokes and snatches of poetry and drawing caricatures. Yu.V. permitted all this, but only up to a point. When it became a nuisance to him he would shout 'Back to work!' and point to the text that he had rewritten in clear, large, rounded letters.

My first lesson came in preparing for the Albanian trip. I realized that I was dealing with a man of acute and tenacious intellect, who towered above those around him not only in his infinitely responsible attitude towards work, but in a sort of inborn intuitive sense of the weight and significance of political words and deeds. Despite having taught myself since boyhood to be critical of any authority, here I was conquered and even entranced. I did, in fact, have a tendency to adore masculine intellect and charm. As a student I had deeply admired the composer Aleksey Kozlovsky, and I genuinely adored Belyakov when we had worked on the textbook on the fundamentals of Marxism-Leninism. Now life had brought me face to face with a personality of a different stature. He knew and could do that which I, in all my presumption, had never hoped to know or be capable of even in the future. He was a man born to take decisions and bear responsibility for them. Being responsive to others he very quickly noticed my attitude towards him and, I have to say, reciprocated the feeling.

But now our evening sessions over the documents were behind us and we were flying to Tirana in a small government aircraft. Inside, the plane was fitted out like a drawing-room with just a few armchairs and a large settee around a table and some velvet footstools in Empire style.

There were half a dozen of us – members of the delegation and accompanying officials: Ivan Korshun, a modest young lad who specialized in Albania, Sergei Kolesnikov, head of the service sector and me, the speechwriter or 'scribbler', as the real apparatus staff contemptuously called us behind our backs. We all killed time as best we could during the seven-hour flight. I read through the speeches, Kolesnikov looked through the list of presents to be handed out, Yu.V. spent most of the flight reading some documents and quietly chatting with Pospelov, the head of the delegation.

Petr Nikolayevich Pospelov was a short man and looked even smaller standing beside Yu.V., who was very tall. Yet in everything one could sense his importance as head of the delegation and as an official who stood a whole rung higher. For a man of his height he had an unusually strong voice – a baritone-bass, slightly muffled and not even entirely clear when making a speech, but very expressive when singing Volga songs, as I was to learn during that trip. He did not know exactly what to expect at the congress in Albania and was most preoccupied with slotting a few fresh quotes into his speech. Reading through the speech he was to deliver he quickly indicated to me a place for which a suitable quote should be found. I suggested one immediately and wrote it on a scrap of paper.

'Are you sure this quotation really is correct?' he asked me suspiciously.

'Absolutely sure, Petr Nikolayevich.'

'Perhaps you might even indicate the source?' he continued with a touch of irony.

'Yes I can,' I replied, and told him not only which volume of Lenin it was from, but the page number as well.

When we arrived at the embassy in Tirana one of the first things Pospelov did was to check that source to teach this cocky lad a lesson. How surprised he was to find I was right. This sent him into an extraordinary rapture, he put on a big smile, spread his hands in surprise and even ran around the ambassador's office.

'Well, Fedor Mikhaylovich,' he said, 'I know Lenin quite well myself. I have studied him all my life and was head of the Marx-Engels-

Lenin Institute. But to be able to select the required quote like that, from memory! I've never seen anything like it!'

I felt very awkward. I regretted not having admitted earlier the chance nature of my success. Just prior to the Albanian trip I had submitted my book for publication and discovered that the reference for that very quotation was inaccurate. The editor and I spent two tiring days finding the passage and after that I was able to repeat the quotation in my sleep.

Meanwhile, I was observing Pospelov closely, his immobile face, his stony eyes and his odd way of pronouncing the most banal words with great importance. How had it happened that he, one of the authors of *Iosif Vissarionovich Stalin: A Short Biography* had played a central role in preparing the famous Central Committee resolution 'On overcoming the cult of the individual and its consequences' of 30 June 1956? And was it not he who wrote into that resolution an assessment of Stalin as an outstanding theoretician who had led the routing of the opposition and the victory of socialism? In conversation with us he would frequently repeat: 'a bit more on the successes', 'don't forget continuity', 'not too hard on the failings' and the sacramental 'Marxism-Leninism teaches . . .' But what does experience teach? Experience . . . well, experience confirms. What else can it possibly do?

The atmosphere at the congress of the Albanian Party of Labour was, as Yu.V. put it, wretched. Its leaders had firmly set out to break with us. Enver Hoxha's report was worse than could have been expected. It contained barely concealed criticism of all that our party had been doing for the past few years. True, while pronouncing what to us were insulting words Hoxha – a stately and handsome man of military bearing – could not maintain a sharp tone of voice and even shed a few tears. But that didn't stop him finishing his speech. And, of course, almost every paragraph he spoke was interrupted by applause, which sometimes developed into a tumultuous ovation with chanting.

It was then that the first incident occurred. During one particularly blatant dig at the Twentieth Congress our delegation abstained from applauding. We were sitting in one of the side boxes in the hall and were visible to all the delegates. They noticed that we were not clapping while the entire audience was drumming out the words: 'Enver Hoxha! Enver Hoxha!' They all jumped up from their seats and began shouting the name of their leader even louder and clapping even more furiously, glancing in our direction. Some of them began banging the folding seats of their chairs.

What a sight Yu.V. was at that moment. The delegates were, I think, greatly impressed by that large figure sitting immobile and upright in his armchair, his deep blue eyes clearly visible through his spectacles. Glancing down into the hall I saw individual groups, mainly of military men, who were barely participating in the frenzy. They were clapping purely as a formality and looking around in embarrassment, glancing at Yu.V. and all of us. Gradually the storm subsided and everyone took their seats. The speaker took a sip of water – one could even hear the gurgle as he drank it from the glass – and continued his speech.

I was shocked to the core by the fury that had shone in the eyes of hundreds of people in that hall. To think that only the day before, or a few weeks ago, they had demonstrated and, I am certain, felt love or at least gratitude towards our country and our people! How could it all have changed so quickly? Did it really need only a wave of the conductor's baton to turn what was pure and white yesterday into something unclean and black today? Where did such power over human souls come from? Was it really just fear for one's own skin, a fear of becoming an outsider, of falling off the political bandwagon? Surely not. In that hall were people who had faced Fascist bullets and survived prisons and torture chambers, people whose feelings of friendship towards us were inseparably intertwined with the concept of independence for their motherland and its future. What magic power wields! What currents flow through people when they join together in a crowd – hands off our god!

Those gods were not easy to understand either. They didn't like some of our decisions; those decisions affected the situation in their party and country. But they must have realized that isolation from the Soviet Union and other neighbouring countries would be ruinous for Albania, that it would be pointless and even ridiculous to fight against the vast majority of Communist and workers' parties. It was no more than a pose. Can one really sacrifice the interests of one's country for the sake of a pose, however fine it might seem to the country's leaders?

In the interval I went outside for a breath of fresh air. I looked round and noticed an Albanian following me. I sat down on a bench and he sat down on the one opposite. I unfolded a newspaper and he took out his. I then got up and sat on the next bench. He, like a robot, did the same. I stood up once more and sat down beside him.

'Well, friend,' I said, 'what does your paper say?'

'No understand Russian,' he said, shaking his head and hands.

'Have you no understand Russian for long?' I asked.

'Long time, very long time,' he said with a smile.

'And I no understand Albanian. And there's probably no point in me studying it now. It's hardly going to be of any use in the near future.'

The Albanian continued nodding his head, either in agreement or because he really did not understand what I was hinting at.

I returned to the foyer, where the leaders and foreign guests were strolling around during the interval. Suddenly I heard the familiar loud and imperious tones of Yu.V., a voice that was already so dear to me.

Looking Enver Hoxha straight in the eye he was rapping out, 'Comrade Enver Hoxha!' – pronouncing it particularly assertively, drawing out the 'o'. 'On behalf of the Communist Parties of the socialist countries I resolutely protest against your arbitrary actions. You have driven the representative of the Greek Communist Party from this congress without the least motive or justification. We completely reject as nonsensical and groundless your allegations against him and his entire party. We demand that things be immediately put to rights and that the Greek representative be readmitted to the congress.'

The hubbub in the foyer stopped instantly, and Hoxha, pale and agitated, began shouting: 'We reject diktat! We are afraid of nobody! He is an agent of Karamanlis and other Greek monarcho-fascists. We shall permit nobody to issue commands at our congress!'

Yu.V. then straightened up to his full height and said, 'We retain the right to draw all the necessary conclusions from this incident which is without parallel in the history of relations between the fraternal parties.'

The congress continued, but we already felt as if we were in a besieged fortress. Somebody asked, 'Might they not try to throw us out of the congress tomorrow as well?' Somebody else joked, 'No. They're more likely to put a bomb in the embassy or hide one in our aircraft.' Yu.V. firmly put a stop to this talk and demanded that everyone be as attentive and cool as possible. There were to be no superfluous words or gestures that might serve as a pretext for provocation.

On the last day of the congress and after it had finished we were given the opportunity to see something of Tirana and its surroundings, accompanied, of course, by an Albanian security official. We walked along the Adriatic shore and recalled Khrushchev's idea that the Albanians should set up a holiday area there for representatives of all the socialist countries. Proud Enver Hoxha had been deeply offended by that suggestion: he dreamed of transforming Albania into a highly-developed industrial power, not of attracting capital into the country by such a humiliating – as he saw it – means as tourism.

I brought back from that trip a photograph showing Pospelov, Andropov and me. Yu.V. was in a long black overcoat and black suit. I remember my clumsy joke on seeing him like that – 'Oh, Yury Vladimirovich! You look just like a pastor in that suit!' I regretted my tactlessness terribly, but Yu.V.'s restraint was astonishing. He said nothing at all, but threw me a look making it clear that he had taken great offence.

I don't know how to explain it, but in all those years he never once cautioned me, not once. His polite, welcoming tone of voice contrasted sharply with the style of other leaders. It seems, however, that this was a privilege reserved only for Yu.V.'s advisers. He had not had the opportunity to have a full education and was in fact always learning on the job. This may explain his somewhat exaggerated respect for the erudition of those he called 'aristocrats of the spirit'. He cherished those elements of knowledge and culture that we were able to bring to the work. As for the specialists and other sector staff, they would often get short shrift from him. He simply could not tolerate bad organization, unreliability or clumsiness and reacted to them harshly.

We returned from Tirana in the same little aircraft. To wind down, however, we decided to stop over in Hungary. There I sensed particularly strongly how much Hungary meant to Yu.V. and what he meant to the Hungarian leaders. Only a few years had passed since the tragedy of 1956, when Yu.V. had played an exceptional role for an ambassador in finding a constructive solution to a most acute problem. (I shall speak of this later when discussing a special visit to Hungary by a delegation led by Yu.V., of which I was a member.) I saw the warmth and sincerity with which the Hungarian leaders greeted Yu.V.; he said something to them in Hungarian and I saw the delight with which they responded to the sound of their own language coming from his lips.

In the evening the Soviet representatives gathered around a table and relaxed after the prolonged tension of Albania. Pospelov began singing in his unexpectedly powerful bass voice, coping brilliantly with the complex roulades of Volga songs. Yu.V., as a former Volga sailor, sang along in a strong, pure and rich baritone.

The flight from Budapest was a long one and there was nothing to do. Petr Nikolayevich suggested a game of dominoes. They were one player short and sat me down as number four, although I hated the game and had hardly ever played.

By that time, however, I had already learned the rather important fact that dominoes was then considered just as obligatory a ritual as wearing a dark suit in winter and a light one in summer.

Not long before the Albanian trip I was on holiday with my wife in Varna on the beautiful Black Sea coast of Bulgaria. We were part of a small group which included the well-known and prominent industrialist Lesechko. He was a big man, very dignified in appearance. By training he was a chemist, I think, but he had an excellent understanding of many economic issues. During our visits to Bulgarian factories he would usually take over from the director to show us round and would give an interesting and knowledgeable account of the enterprise, its capabilities and problems, just as if he had built it and managed it himself.

He had two weaknesses, however – dominoes and fishing. On our very first sunny morning by the shore of that warm seductive sea Lesechko sat down at a table under an awning with two other members of our group and insisted that I join them as they needed a fourth person for a game of dominoes. I politely refused, explaining that I intended to do some underwater fishing, showing him the mask, snorkel and spear I had bought specially for the trip. 'Forget that!' he said peremptorily. 'Making an intellectual out of yourself – you'd think you're the only one who went to university.' (He pronounced 'intellectual' with the contemptuous intonation fashionable at that time.) But I still didn't join them – after all, they weren't my bosses.

My reputation in Lesechko's eyes was finally ruined by our fishing trip. It was early in the morning on a lake in poor weather. There was a very strong wind and two-foot waves were rocking the boat. I was with a friend in one boat, and Lesechko and a sailor in another. The trick was to try and make the boat stable or it would be a waste of time casting. We had a weight – a large stone on a rope – which we intended to throw into the water. But at that moment Lesechko's boat approached and he said to my friend: 'Give me the stone.' I intervened – whether it was the storm or our previous skirmishes that had put me in a buoyant frame of mind I don't know. 'Don't take our stone, old man,' I said, 'you have a sailor who can hold the boat still.' 'Give me that stone, I said,' repeated the great fisherman, red in the face and finally losing his temper. He leaned over the side, grabbed the stone in his mighty paws and dragged it into his boat.

Those little jokes were to cost me dearly. Lesechko grassed on me to the First in the presence of Yu.V. during some reception. He claimed I had been running after some Italian woman on holiday, although I had actually spent the holiday with my wife and the Italian was as ugly as sin anyway. Yu.V. said nothing to me about it, but conveyed it all to Tolkunov, who with his usual smile had a friendly word in my ear. And all that just because I had refused to play dominoes!

What tremendous weight denunciations carry within the apparatus! On thinking about the reasons for this I have often wondered whether it is a characteristic of the Russian political animal. I have identified two weaknesses in many of our leaders, including men of great intelligence and shrewdness. The first is a love of gross flattery. This is probably something that all leaders of all periods have loved, but ours in the 1960s for some reason preferred direct, unconcealed and patently exaggerated flattery – flattery on a cult scale, so to speak. The second weakness was an incurable proclivity to listen to denunciations. They wanted to know something very personal, intimate and secret about others and attached more importance to this than to their public statements and actions. You could write a dozen books defending the political line, but if someone told your boss of a single phrase uttered around a table with friends, a phrase that hurt the boss's pride, it would change his whole attitude to you, and everything you had done for him personally would be totally forgotten. That phrase might have been distorted or taken out of context, its meaning altered as it passed along the denunciation ladder, yet it would become deeply etched in his consciousness. Perhaps this is a purely physiological phenomenon: a nasty remark, especially if it is to the point, affects the nervous system so strongly that one refuses to accept any refutations. It is probably no coincidence that messengers of bad news used to be put to death, though they were guilty of nothing. In my time quiet whisperings have ended many a political career.

Learning from this bitter experience I didn't push my luck, but sat down obediently to play dominoes at Pospelov's invitation. On one condition, however – that the winner drink a glass of brandy. We had a crate of brandy with us which had been intended for receptions in Albania. The receptions never took place and the brandy remained intact. My condition had the effect of a boomerang, however. I had some incredible beginner's luck, winning game after game. Although Yu.V. did not approve of booze he, along with the others, was amused watching me. In the end I got such a skinful that I literally fell into the arms of my astonished relatives on landing in Moscow.

That trip to Albania brought me very close to Yu.V. – something which caused acute jealousy on the part of certain other members of the department. Suyetukhin was particularly indignant: 'These scribblers,' he would say disparagingly of us, 'what do they know about real life?'

Throughout the trip I had been foolish enough to make Suyetukhin the butt of what seemed to me harmless jokes. His surname was amazingly suited to him. ('Suyetukhin' comes from the word 'fussy'.) He was endlessly jumping about, trying to get himself noticed by the bosses, asking for instructions on the smallest matter and craving one thing only – to bask in a glow of approval from his superiors. And I, of course, missed no opportunity to expose these qualities, to the dislike of both Suyetukhin and Yu.V. himself.

Suyetukhin and certain other well-wishers approached Yu.V. to denounce me, but without result. To this day I do not know the reason for that astonishing privilege – many told me that he simply had a personal liking for me.

*

Though not yet closely acquainted with Khrushchev, I had often watched and listened to him at close quarters. His trips to the European socialist countries were mainly official ones, full of pomp and ceremony, which made it impossible to gain a clear view of and assess the actual problems under discussion. And those problems were frequently acute and large-scale.

It was during a trip to Bulgaria that I got to know the First personally.

I now find it hard to imagine the excitement I felt as a young man of academic leanings who had unexpectedly found himself on the political Olympus. But I remember well that I hardly slept all night before the delegation set off. I tried to get some sleep during the flight, but in vain – there was strong turbulence over the mountains, especially just before landing in Sofia.

The plane was one of the first Tupolev high-speed jets and was still in need of much improvement. Built to hold around 150–200 passengers, it was crammed full. Apart from the security men, there were journalists and a large group of party and state workers attached to the delegation. The aides and consultants were seated in the second compartment, so that we could see if not actually hear what was going on in the first compartment, where the delegation was seated. Now and again they would request documents from us or else they would summon somebody who would then scuttle off to the first compartment with files of documents in his arms just in case they were needed. I thought this fuss a little artificial and even laughable, since the speeches and documents had been prepared in advance, read through many times and officially endorsed. At other times a semblance of activity would come from the second compartment, from aides or other accompanying officials who dared to intrude into the first compartment. All this prevented me from dozing off and I was afraid that if I didn't catch some sleep I would not be up to completing or editing impromptu press statements, should the need arise. For such was my modest function, though one to which the First himself attached great importance. He loved to digress from the text during his speeches and did so without the least attention to form, anxious to convey his main idea to the audience by any possible means, and therefore repeatedly coming back to it, which made life pretty difficult for the editors.

I was familiar with his style even before the Bulgarian trip, and knew that I needed a clear head and sharp pencil at all times. In addition, we were frequently handed typed passages that he had dictated to a secretary for his next speech. Processing those dictations was particularly difficult: one had to preserve the meaning, but this meant first of all finding it, then clearly extracting it from a great pile of secondary verbiage, polishing it up and often simply rewriting the whole thing anew, but in such a way that the author could easily recognize his own thoughts and expressions, which was something by which he set great store and, indeed, the very reason for his dictating them. Usually I would redictate the whole thing from scratch, going through the text in advance to underline the most important passages.

You can understand, therefore, my excitement during that first trip. Here my work was not to pass through the filter of Yu.V., a familiar filter that guaranteed everything was spot on. I was to assume personal responsibility for the final version of the text. My texts would then be read through by the First's aides, but they tended to rely on others for literacy and style.

The plane landed and for the first time I tasted the atmosphere of a foreign trip by the top leadership: huge crowds of people holding flowers and rapturously waving little flags; loud cries of 'Hurray' and greetings; the cortege of black cars – of which there were at least twenty-five or thirty – making its way through that crowd; the bright summer sunshine. It was all extremely festive and colourful. I travelled, I think, in the fourth car with one of the First's aides and noticed a strange reaction from the public to my modest person. As soon as they saw me the cries and applause flared up with particular force. I turned perplexed to the comrade accompanying us, who explained that they were mistaking me for one of their own, a Bulgarian. I mention this because that evening a misunderstanding of a similar nature occurred, though on that occasion not on the part of the Bulgarians.

During a dinner hosted by the Bulgarian leaders in honour of the delegation, we consultants and aides were placed at the same table as our leaders, but along the opposite side. By chance I ended up directly opposite the First. Eventually he stood up, as usual, to pronounce a toast to Soviet–Bulgarian friendship and – also as usual – digressed from the toast and began reminiscing. We heard a story that he had already told at the reception after the 1960 Communist Parties' conference about how Stalin died, about how Beria was taken away, about the morals of the Stalinist leadership, about 1937 and numerous other political events. He spoke for at least two hours and I sat frozen and spellbound, listening to this confession pronounced not in an accusatory tone, but in one of sorrow and suffering. I was unable to take my eyes off him and he, noticing such unusual attentiveness, addressed me personally more and more frequently, gesticulating, explaining, persuading and going ever deeper into the memories troubling him. Everyone else sat in silence, patiently awaiting the end of his speech. And probably each was thinking his own thoughts. But I was shaken by Khrushchev's revelations, the strong passions on the political Olympus, the torturous experiences that are the lot of those at the top. 'Closer to the tsar, closer to death,' is what I was thinking at that moment. 'How that closeness turns a man inside out . . . such is the price of power.'

I do not remember how the evening ended, but I do remember lying awake for a long time, going through in my agitated mind page after page of that dark confession of a man who was both a participant and a victim of past events. In the morning I was unexpectedly summoned by the First's aide. It transpired that Khrushchev wished to be introduced to the 'interesting young Bulgarian' who had listened so attentively to him. How great was his surprise to learn who I was and where I worked!

He asked me two or three formal questions, shook my hand at length and laughed over his mistake. During subsequent meetings in Bulgaria, and in particular in the Yevstenograd Tsar Boris Palace in Varna, he nodded to me and, smiling happily, shook his head as if to say, 'What a fool I was.'

He was a simple man, courteous in his dealings with the 'intellectual servants'. He singled out and valued the speechwriters in particular, sensing that he lacked the education and culture to finish off and prepare his own speeches for the press. Many people exploited this weakness of his for their own purposes, and this became particularly common under Khrushchev's successors, when speechwriters stooped to begging payment for their services, and substantial payment at that – academic titles, prizewinners' badges, high-level posts. Yu.V. taught us modesty, to serve the interests of the state with honesty and selflessness. And those who remained faithful to the morality he instilled in us never chased after prizes or titles, these being won more by sleight of hand than by outstanding achievements in science or journalism.

In fact the First often delivered his speeches without any preparation whatsoever. Sometimes they were confused, particularly if he was greatly excited or worked up over something, During that trip to Bulgaria I heard what was clearly an impromptu speech in the miners' club. Returning from a tour down the mine and without even removing his helmet and overalls he mounted the rostrum and delivered a speech lasting around forty minutes. Nothing hindered him and nobody was hurrying him, and he gave an exceptionally neat speech with simple but concise ideas in clear grammatical form. It went down excellently with the audience and presented no difficulty at all for the editors who had to prepare it for the press.

I noticed the same thing in some of our other political leaders. Riveted to a piece of paper, they would read out a text written by somebody else in a boring and often dismal voice, yet on finding themselves in an unusual situation that required improvization, they would suddenly shake off all constraints and deliver a good, clear, literate speech. Even then I realized how agonizing the received tradition of speech-reading was, how much it impoverished the individual and reduced even an outstanding person to the level of a simple extra. After all, to read out a text written by somebody else, one that has not passed through your own mind and soul, really is intolerable. You constantly feel alienated from that text, artificially connected to it; you realize that for some reason it is necessary and that it would be dangerous to abandon the tradition, but you constantly feel awkward and hostile, whether towards that alien text or towards yourself. I met very few politicians who could deliver a speech written by someone else properly, without rapping it out like a soldier or droning on like a priest. Usually those speakers had written out the entire text in their own hand.

However, none of this presented any problem to the First. He was profoundly self-confident, unconstrained and even mischievous. When he started speaking nobody, including himself, knew how he would end.

Partly this was in his nature, but partly he exploited it for his political games. He could appear indignant and use words which in written form would definitely have caused a storm of outrage from his audience, partner or opponent. But he would get away with it, since people put it down to emotion. Sometimes it seemed that he was working himself up into such a rage that his speech was flowing on uncontrollably, yet he would gradually calm down and, finding his bearings, return to his subject, keenly following with his small, mischievous, jolly eyes the expressions on the faces of his audience. 'What an actor,' I thought as I watched these transformations. 'He's the man Oleg Yefremov needs in the Sovremennik Theatre to complete the company.'

During the rally in Dmitrov Square in Sofia Khrushchev digressed from his text more than once. I was sitting on a chair on the stage behind him, attempting to note down the new passages in the appropriate places. Suddenly his wife, Nina Petrovna, a woman with a wonderful kind peasant face, said to me: 'He doesn't realize that people are standing in the heat of the sun and he's making a mistake in extending his speech. It was too long to start with.'

It was the first time I had heard her criticize her husband and I thought to myself that he probably frequently consults her and perhaps even tries out his speeches on her. I later learned that this was indeed the case. His wife had worked for a long time as head of a party office and had a good grasp of lecturing work.

An amusing episode occurred during a reception for the delegation in the Soviet embassy. No sooner had the First entered the large reception hall than he stopped dead in his tracks. The hall was set out with tables that were literally groaning under an abundance of food and drink. In the middle of each table was a gigantic sturgeon two to three metres in length, garnished with prawns, vegetables and goodness knows what else. It was there that the First played out a scene for which, I think, he had prepared long ago. 'Do you think we have already achieved Communism? Who gave the instructions? Who finances you?' he lashed out at the ambassador who stood paralysed with fear. The ambassador began muttering something about extra resources allocated by the Council of Ministers for the reception and the food being flown in fresh, but the First didn't listen to a word. He turned to Todor Zhivkov, who nodded his head in agreement. But there was nothing to be done, and after that small hitch everyone got down to carving and scoffing those incredible fish.

In passing, I can't help mentioning that I could never understand why Khrushchev insisted on pronouncing the word 'Communism' with a soft 's'. As far as his guttural 'g' was concerned, there was probably nothing he could do about it, though I don't rule out the possibility of this also being a pretence. As for his pronunciation of 'Communism', I am 100 per cent sure it was deliberate, that he was creating a kind of standard which all the initiated were to follow like augurs. One by one the members of his entourage, including graduates from university and the Moscow International Relations Institute, adopted a similar pronunciation. This slang opened doors, as it were, into a narrow circle of people closely interconnected not only by what they did but by a common level of culture.

During our stay in Varna we were accommodated in the Yevstenograd Tsar Boris Palace in luxury I had never before experienced: there was a swimming pool in the middle of a huge room, for instance. To be honest, it gave me an odd feeling – why was all this necessary for the new leaders with their simple origins? In the case of that palace it was probably a desire to preserve a setting of historical value. But in other cases and in other countries there could be no such explanation. There was a kind of inexplicable longing among people who had grown up in poor families – more often peasant than workers' families – for luxury, and not modern but archaic luxury at that.

What was the reason for this preference amongst normal, poorly educated, country folk? It is hard to say where they could ever have seen such banquettes or causettes, but Empire style became firmly established in political affairs and long barred the way to modern decor. One of the first breakthroughs, I think, was the Palace of Congresses inside the Kremlin, built in a style which – less luxuriant and more economical, using glass, concrete, plastic and synthetic carpets – gradually supplanted the palatial decor that had crept into socialist life from who knows where.

I was shocked by all this, but I was not typical. I was young and in any case had come from a poor academic background in which even a decent writing desk was considered a great rarity. In the Institute of State and Law of the USSR Academy of Sciences I had worked at a small desk in the reading room. And at home for a long time my family and I had lived in shared flats and little rented rooms. Perhaps that was why I was embarrassed at receiving even the simplest of services afforded me by virtue of my post. When I was driven by a chauffeur I constantly felt like an exploiter of others' labour and tried somehow to compensate for the driver's services by telling him interesting stories on the way.

But in the palaces in which we stayed abroad, in the splendid chambers allocated to me not because of my rank, but as a servant of the court, as it were, I felt I was appropriating something that wasn't mine and that had come my way by mistake, and that at any moment I might be caught out.

*

I felt this particularly strongly in Yugoslavia in 1963. Yu.V. was a member of the delegation led by the First and I was 'attached', though quite closely. So closely, in fact, that I usually stayed in the same quarters as them and ate with them. But one could only call them quarters as a joke – they were royal palaces occupied, according to tradition, by Josip Broz Tito.

I had been in Yugoslavia the year before with a group of other journalists. We had travelled to every republic in the country, both the more developed ones – Serbia, Croatia and Slovenia – and the less developed ones – Montenegro, Bosnia, Herzegovina and Macedonia. It was the first country on the Adriatic that I had visited and my admiration knew no bounds.

In the course of that trip we visited over a dozen enterprises, state farms, scientific and medical establishments and creative unions. I was greatly impressed by Yugoslavia's economic reforms, particularly the decentralization, the departure from rigid planning, the concentration by enterprises on the country's domestic market and the freedom of access to foreign markets. I also liked the workers' councils, though I could see that in many ways they were a mere formality. The food shops were stocked much like those in the West and their industrial products even then were approaching world standards. I also liked the fact that the Yugoslavs had not copied our cruel and ineffective policy of collectivization. In the cultural sphere the dominant movement was modernism – a striving towards everything new and up-to-date. In short, it was probably the best period in the country's history and I thought it my duty to write the truth about Yugoslavia. On returning to Moscow I drafted a long article for *Kommunist*. It had already been typeset and prepared for printing when something unexpected happened.

One of my friends on the journal (we used to play volleyball and table tennis together) happened to find himself in a lift with Andropov and in that brief space of time managed to inform him that I had written a 'seditious' piece about Yugoslavia. Andropov demanded to see the article and even took the trouble to read it in hospital, where he was having a quick check-up. That was the only occasion in my life that I got a dressing-down from Yu.V. He wrote me a note several pages long in his usual large, precise and clear handwriting. In it he asked me not to publish the article in its existing form, given the nature of relations with

Yugoslavia at that time and the attitude the Communist Parties' Conference in 1960 had taken towards the policies of the Yugoslav League of Communists. He did not actually question what I had written, merely pointing out that it would be politically inexpedient to publish it. As this note is of great importance for an understanding of Andropov's views I quote it with some abbreviations.

Dear Fedor Mikhaylovich,

I have read your article. In the present circumstances I think that any article on Yugoslavia should answer at least two questions. First, what is happening at present in Yugoslavia, that is, how is the construction of socialism proceeding here? And second, it must explain our policy towards that country and party, *based without fail* on what we have said and written about them (the country and party) at the Twenty-First and Twenty-Second Party Congresses, in the 1960 Statement and at the BCP Congress (in the speech by N. S. Khrushchev) etc.

If your article provides a number of answers to the first question it falls down on the second. It is essential for you to explain (to show or perhaps suggest) to the reader (directly or indirectly) that our assessment of the revisionist policies of the LCY leadership are not *being revised*, but remain in force and have been fully confirmed by events themselves. It is no less important to show that in taking steps to improve relations with Yugoslavia we are consistently implementing the policy of our Central Committee since 1955 and that these steps are fully consistent and in keeping with the well-known clause in the Statement and other documents.

Naturally it is not a question of writing the entire piece in the form of political digressions (not specifically). But all arguments should at least lead to this, proceed from this and tie up the loose ends. Otherwise you (and all of us along with you) will be caught out on your phrase 'all those who are not keen to improve relations with Yugoslavia'. You must protect your flanks.

On page three, for instance, you cite some figures taken from the reference materials presented to us in abundance by the Yugoslav comrades and draw the following conclusion: 'The above figures indicate fairly rapid economic development over the past few years and a fairly sharp reduction in production growth rates in 1960 and the current year.' And that is all you say. Do you disagree with this? Then further on, quoting Todorović, you seen to continue on the subject of their 'successes'. If you, together with Todorović and the 'reference materials' now set out to prove that 'the Yugoslav economy has grown quite rapidly over the past few years' the reader is entitled to ask: 'Excuse me, but according to the Statement

Yugoslavia's socialist gains have been jeopardized,' at the Twenty-First Congress it was stated that Yugoslavia 'is not advancing but staggering towards socialism', at the Bulgarian Congress (in the speech by the head of our delegation) it was stated that the LCY's revisionist policy has led to 'failures in economic development'. Not to mention the fact that a certain Ponomaryov, along with Andropov and Konstantinov, has quoted those very same figures (unless I am mistaken) in that very journal and on the basis of them proved as clear as two and two make four that the Yugoslav economy has been falling drastically behind in the past few years. And now in that very same journal your article is proving (or at least indicating) the opposite without the least attempt to recall or explain what was said before. I find this unacceptable.

On page four you write that '1950 was a year when, for a number of reasons (especially due to the breaking of economic ties between Yugoslavia and the other socialist countries), the Yugoslav economy was in a grave state. Evidently it was in order to save the economy from stagnation that the idea (?!) of restructuring production management was conceived.'

You go on to describe how the Yugoslavs scrapped central planning, cleared the way towards uncontrollable market relations and caused the spread of parochial self-interest – in short, how they carried out policies that the Communist press (including *Kommunist*) has frequently qualified as nothing short of revisionism. Yet now, as if having forgotten all this, you write: 'Evidently it was in order to save the economy from stagnation that the idea of restructuring (?!) production management was conceived.' Well there's a case of whitewashing if ever I saw one! Indeed this is precisely what Yugoslavia has been claiming ever since 1949 in response to our accusations of revisionism. They used exactly the same logic contained in your article: the socialist countries 'blockaded' Yugoslavia and we – the Yugoslavs – were forced into 'reforms' in order to survive.

I shall not continue analysing your article from this angle, but I can assure you that if necessary I could go on citing examples at length. On page ten, for instance, you say: 'Due to mass bankruptcy amongst small peasants the villages have a labour surplus which the cities are not yet in a position to use fully.' Then you write that Belović spoke about this calmly and you ask the rhetorical question of whether the problem of rural overpopulation is not being resolved at too great a cost.

Yet everyone knows that on this issue the LCY leadership has pursued an anti-Leninist policy of bankrupting the poor peasantry, and that this approach is quite alien to Lenin's idea of agricultural cooperatives based *first and foremost* on the interests of the peasant masses and *in particular* on those of the poorer peasants. We told the Yugoslavs this directly quite recently and now, all of a sudden, here we are asking coy questions.

I could, to repeat myself, continue analysing such examples, but I think it is clear from what I have said that the article would not be useful in its present form. It may give rise to a false understanding within our party or amongst the fraternal parties, it may sow illusions within the LCY and provide a pretext for sudden attacks on the policy of our Central Committee – a policy of reinforcing relations with the LCY on a Marxist-Leninist foundation.

Clearly any article on Yugoslavia today must serve the task of reinforcing relations with that country and must accord with the policy of developing friendship with the Yugoslav people. Clearly it would be stupid and wrong to criticize the policies of the LCY today the way we did two or three years ago. But these are matters of tactics and tactics must, after all, be intelligently subordinated in our main objective of upholding Yugoslavia and the LCY not *in general* but on a Marxist-Leninist foundation. This has always been my understanding of everything said on this matter by N. S. Khrushchev and this is the only way he looks at the matter.

We are not flirting with the Yugoslav leadership, but indicating their mistakes to them directly and in an honest Leninist manner. And we have put them on the right tracks: J. B. Tito himself now acknowledges what Nikita Sergeyevich told him back in 1956. Naturally I do not think it would be useful for our friendship to 'rub their faces' in their self-criticism. But for me it is undeniable that to ignore now what we have written in these last few years and pretend that the LCY leadership is infallible would hardly be useful either. That's all I have to say.

Yu. Andropov.

What had driven Andropov to write such a brusque rebuke? My description of the living experience of self-management in enterprises, with all its peculiarities, achievements and difficulties? Decentralization, the workers' councils, cultural pluralism? Naturally I took Yu.V.'s instructions into account, asked for the article to be returned by the journal and put it on the shelf – for ever.

I did not agree with him, but I assumed that unlike us young advisers from scientific or journalistic backgrounds, Yu.V. understood politics as the art of the possible. He knew not only what had to be done, but how to do it in given circumstances. In other words, he perhaps more than anyone else in the leadership sensed and appreciated the rigid political barriers in the path of changes now overdue.

Nikita Khrushchev in 1935 when he was First Secretary of the Moscow City and Regional Party Committees.

rushchev and lin, 1 May 1932.

During the first visit to Peking, 1954. Sitting (left to right): Mikoyan, Furtseva, Khrushche Bulganin and Molotov. The woman standing is Ya. S. Nasriddinova.

Mao Tse-tung, Khrushchev and Mikoyan.

Khrushchev and Bulganin in India with Nehru and other Indian leaders, 1955.

Khrushchev and Hoxha (right) in Albania, 1959.

Khrushchev and his wife, Nina Petrovna, at the Twentieth Century–Fox studios in Hollywood with film stars Louis Jourdan, Shirley Maclaine, Maurice Chevalier and Frank Sinatra.

Khrushchev meeting President de Gaulle at the Paris summit, 1960.

(From left): Burlatsky, Pospelov and Andropov during the Soviet delegation's visit to Albania in 1961. Pospelov suggested a drive to the outskirts of Tirana to get away from the embassy, which was bugged, so that they could openly discuss the dramatic events that had taken place.

Khrushchev's first meeting with John F. Kennedy at the Vienna summit, 1961. Although outwardly friendly, neither leader understood the other and they parted with feelings of disappointment and caution.

On the phone to outer
space, talking to the first
woman cosmonaut,
Valentina Tereshkova;
with Brezhnev by his side,
1963. The achievements in
space stoked
Khrushchev's certainty
that the Soviet Union
would outstrip the United
States by 1981.

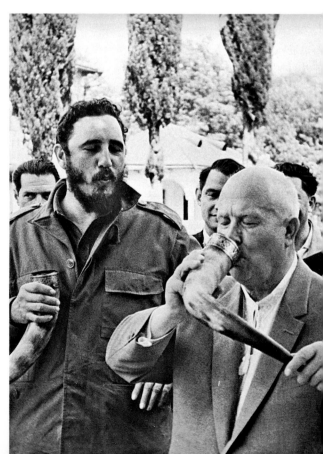

With Fidel Castro in the
Caucasus, drinking wine
from traditional Georgian
horns, 1962. This was not
long before the Cuban
missile crisis, although no
mention of deploying
missiles in Cuba was made
during Castro's visit.

hrushchev on his arrival in Belgrade, 1963, greeted by Tito. In traditional Russian style
y embraced and kissed, although Tito was not fond of this ritual.

hrushchev, in the attire of an honorary miner, speaking to miners in Yugoslavia in 1963,
Tito watches. Khrushchev rarely spoke without prepared notes, but on this occasion he
ve one of his best impromptu speeches, vividly describing his own experiences in the mines.

Khrushchev with Antonin Novotny in Prague, 1964. Khrushchev felt at the peak of power but this was his last trip abroad before his fall.

His political acumen had been noted by people who had worked with him in the embassy in Hungary in 1956, when he had predicted that an explosion was imminent and had suggested effective measures to prevent it. This, incidentally, is the reason Andropov was appointed a department head in the Central Committee after the Hungarian events. But 1956 also left him with a kind of 'Hungarian complex': he was always very cautious and even suspicious of events in the socialist countries that did not fit the Soviet model.

While in Yugoslavia the Khrushchev delegation visited an enterprise in Belgrade, where they were introduced to the Yugoslav system of self-management. We were told in detail about administrative practices, competitive recruitment to posts, the functions of the workers' councils, the difficulties and friction that arose in their relationship with the enterprise management, and – even more of a problem – their inability, due to incompetence, to exert any substantial influence on production affairs and processes.

Then it was the First's turn to speak. He made a sensational statement that subsequently appeared in all the Yugoslav newspapers and bourgeois press, though it was never, it seems, published in the USSR. What he said was this: 'I found the Yugoslavs' experience of self-management interesting. Each country chooses its own way in accordance with its traditions and culture. There is nothing wrong with workers' councils, but we in our country are taking a different path, expanding the rights of trade unions and labour collectives.' The statement was greeted with a storm of applause, especially on the part of the Yugoslav leaders who were present.

I glanced at Yu.V. to see his reaction. He continued taking notes conscientiously, looking down at his notepad. I never did find out whether the First had cleared this statement with him or whether it was an impromptu remark, and given my experience with the article on Yugoslavia, I felt it would be embarrassing to bring the subject up with Yu.V.

Brioni – an island turned entirely into a residence for President Tito – was a most beautiful place. We had hot summer weather and the whole delegation, including us accompanying officials, bathed in the sea each day and then, sitting on the shore together with the Yugoslav leaders, sipped Coca-Cola and Schweppes, which Yugoslavia was importing from the West even then, or simply drank tea out of a samovar specially supplied by our attentive hosts.

Finding myself at the same table as Edvard Kardelj, I struck up a conversation about the recently published book *Socialism and War*. I asked him if he really believed that wars between the socialist countries were possible, and when he confirmed this I asked, 'Between which socialist countries do you think war most likely?' He replied that there might be a serious military confrontation, if not war, between the Soviet

Union and China. And he quoted Engels, who had warned that the influence of great-power chauvinism and nationalism had to be taken into account. 'And how long might it be until such a war?' Kardelj replied that it was difficult to give a date, but we would witness it within ten years.

At the time everyone was very concerned about the Chinese problem. It had caused me a great deal of work, writing articles and even books on China. Nonetheless I had never held such a pessimistic view and tried to put my arguments to Kardelj.

Several years later, when Kardelj visited Moscow, I reminded him at a reception in the Yugoslav embassy of our conversation in Brioni. He barely remembered it, but maintained that he was right about everything. (It was a time of tension in Soviet–Chinese relations during the Cultural Revolution). Yet I still tried to convince him that there would be no war.

Almost a quarter of a century has passed since that argument in Brioni and fortunately it is we who were right. I say 'we' because I told Yu.V. of my conversation with Kardelj. He fell silent and thought for a long time, then said, 'Kardelj is wrong. I don't think things will go as far as war. We shall never start such a war, and China is too weak to risk such a gamble. And anyway, they have no serious grounds for war.'

Andropov, who was subsequently regarded as an extremist on the Chinese issue, did not believe in the possibility of a serious conflict with China, though he rejected their policy of pushing the USSR into conflict with the United States. But let us return to the Yugoslav trip.

Marshal Tito's residence in Brioni was a relatively small three-storey rectangular white building with a flat roof reminiscent of Greek architecture. On a small terrace paved with marble stood a statue of a naked woman in an erotic pose. During the talks between our delegation and the Yugoslavs Tito at one point came out onto the terrace where we were standing. Approaching the figure, he affectionately patted her in a delicate place and the statue slowly and invitingly began to turn. 'Pretty, isn't she?' he asked us. And then he told us how he had had his eye on Brioni as a future residence even when fighting with the partisans nearby. I was surprised to hear what the supreme commander-in-chief of the People's Liberation Army had been thinking about during the war. My features must have been registering this surprise, but Tito misinterpreted it and said: 'Yes, young man. I did not doubt our victory for a minute, nor that I would become the country's leader.'

Lying that night in my luxurious bed on the mezzanine of the lodge (a hunting lodge, I think, in which the 'accompanying officials' were accommodated), I tossed and turned for a long time, chewing over that sentence. Did this mean that predestination really existed?

When I later wrote my book on Mao Tse-tung one of my intentions was to answer that question. Tito's life, however, was probably a far more interesting and astonishing example, providing rich food for thought about the role of the individual in history.

Who seeks whom? Does man seek history, or does history seek the man? This elementary but unanswered question inevitably arises when one thinks about people who have made, or at least thought they were making, political history in our century. The sense of predestination that these people themselves experienced and, therefore, so successfully instilled in those around them is particularly striking. Was this the mystique of personality or the mystique of power? Or was it mass hypnosis?

I have found no answer though I have met many people, including outstanding modern leaders. The ancients had a straightforward answer: one needs good fortune, but one also needs valour to exploit the opportunity created by fortune, rise above the crowd and leave one's mark on history. But what about us? What is our answer?

Was Lenin's existence really a matter of chance? Can one really imagine that anybody could have replaced him as leader of the Revolution and founder of the state? Could anybody else have chosen the day of the uprising? – the 24th was too early, the 26th was too late, and consequently the 25th was the only day the small Bolshevik Party could have led the seizure of power.

Say what you will, but the historical progress requires individuals with great political will-power and the ability to cast a spell on the masses. Then and only then is success ensured.

There was an amusing incident in Brioni. We were in the ground-floor hall when suddenly a worried-looking Yu.V. came down the stairs. 'A mistake, comrades. A big mistake! Who here is responsible for the press apart from you, Fedor?' he asked me. I named a foreign ministry official and told him that on the Yugoslav side the person in charge was the former ambassador to the USSR. 'Get them all here quickly,' said Yu.V.

When everyone had assembled he asked whether the report on the talks had been dispatched, and if so, how it had listed the participants on the Soviet side. The Yugoslav ambassador said that the report had been filed and that the names had been listed in accordance with those who had actually taken part.

'Did you mention Khrushchev's son among the participants?' asked Yu.V. On receiving an affirmative reply he asked for the report to be corrected. But it was too late – it had been sent by telegraph and would inevitably end up in the Yugoslav and other foreign newspapers. 'Hold up that report before it reaches the Soviet Union at all costs so that any mention of Khrushchev's son and his aide can be removed,' ordered

Yu.V. 'The First has given me the firmest instructions on this account. He came out of the talks twice to repeat it to me.'

The foreign ministry representative said that he had already passed the report on to the TASS correspondent and that it had named not only the members of the delegation but the two individuals in question, since they had sat at the negotiating table.

'That was a mistake. A gross mistake, impermissible for a foreign ministry official. They are not members of the delegation,' exclaimed Yu.V. 'Find the TASS representative immediately and correct it!'

And so they began searching for the TASS correspondent. Brioni island was a very small place and one could cycle round it in half an hour. But although intelligence officers of both countries were sent to find the reporter it was more than an hour before he was brought before the boss. He was covered in straw, having being dragged out of a haystack where he had been asleep. To this day I remember that correspondent: immensely tall, his face flushed with drink, his clothes dishevelled, he stood swaying from side to side in front of our superiors, unable to understand what was going on.

'Have you sent the telegram on the talks?' asked Yu.V. harshly.

'I sh-sent it as required. I sent it immediately I received it from him,' said the correspondent, pointing to the foreign ministry official, who recoiled in horror.

'And what text did you transmit?'

'I transmitted the text I was given.'

'What were the names of the Soviet participants?' asked Yu.V.

'Just like it was. The entire delegation.'

'And the two last names?'

'The two last names? I struck them off. They're not members of the delegation.'

How relieved everyone was to hear this! The cold and pompous protocol writer from the foreign ministry was, I could see, ready to kiss the correspondent's drunken mug.

Yu.V. also sighed with relief, smiled and said: 'Fine, go back to sleep and make sure it doesn't happen again!'

'But what happened?' the correspondent asked me when we had moved away.

'Nothing special,' I answered. 'You've just missed a rare opportunity to lose your party card.'

The correspondent shuddered a little, despite the state he was in, but after I had explained everything to him he relaxed and even cheered up, admiring his own intuition.

Nothing was trivial for Yu.V. Any work he did had to be perfect, rounded off and as brilliant as possible. He could not tolerate anything that was half-finished, he detested carelessness and organically could not bear any form of irresponsibility. In such cases he could be merciless. If someone was unable to do something, he would understand, but if the man didn't even try Yu.V. would never forgive him. And it has to be said that everyone around him really did try hard, as a matter of conscience rather than out of fear. The parish takes after the priest, as they say. With rare exceptions Yu.V. gathered around himself a 'parish' capable of meeting the high standards he required.

There was one other curious point that caught my attention. The Yugoslav leaders invited us to a nightclub, where there was music and the youngest among us danced with a beautiful young woman – the wife of the elderly Yugoslav ambassador to the Soviet Union. One of the Yugoslavs began to make fun of the ambassador, who quipped: 'Back home in Montenegro we say that it is better to eat a young chicken with a friend than to gnaw at an old hen alone.' After that there was to be a striptease. Yu.V. immediately got up and said he was leaving as he had work to do. The Yugoslavs tried to persuade him to stay, but he was quite adamant, though he did allow us to stay if we wished. Well, I stayed and watched a striptease for the first time in my life, performed, incidentally, not by a Yugoslav but by an Austrian – rather plump, fair-skinned, big-eyed, in fact a very attractive woman.

For a first experience it was, naturally, a very tasty treat. When I met Yu.V. the next morning I tried to tell him about it, but he firmly changed the subject. He was, on the whole, a puritan, even by the strict standards then prevalent in party circles. He drank virtually nothing and nobody ever heard him pay a compliment to women (at least, not at work). He couldn't stand films with erotic scenes, though of course he did not impose his tastes on anybody else. Everyone knew that they had to behave properly in his presence and not embark on risqué conversations while he was listening. I myself saw how difficult it was for him sometimes in the presence of the First, who loved to knock back a glass or two of brandy. The First also adored telling lewd jokes and hearing them from others, and he loved to use spicy, unprintable words. I often saw Yu.V. flinching on such occasions, but as an experienced diplomat he remained calm and concealed his feelings.

As for the First, he would seize any opportunity to have a good laugh. The wart beside Khrushchev's nose – the mark of a chosen destiny, according to Chinese belief – seemed permanently aquiver with a desire to laugh and to make others laugh. I remember on the way back from Brioni island we had lunch in the mess-room of Tito's yacht *Taleb*. Sailing in that motorized yacht across the almost flat mirror of the Adriatic Sea put the First in a festive mood. He joked all the way through lunch and was always the first to break into laughter, unable to hold back. To his right sat Tito in a snowy-white admiral's uniform, chuckling along politely. We were served oranges for dessert.

Engrossed in his latest anecdote, the First didn't even notice the elegant little knife that had been placed beside him and began peeling the orange with his hands, at the same time continuing his riqué story. The juice from his crushed orange spurted in all directions and a few drops, unfortunately, landed on the President's uniform. What was he to do? The uniform was in a mess, but he couldn't offend Khrushchev. Almost imperceptibly Tito pulled a handkerchief out of his top pocket and began gently wiping his snowy-white jacket . . .

In fact there was a large element of childishness in Khrushchev. During our after-lunch strolls in the park, for instance, I saw him hold to his breast a little receiver given to him somewhere in America, I think. They say that the Soviet radio and television bosses were then broadcasting his favourite country melodies specially for him. And during the talks with Tito, when the latter was eloquently describing the concept and results of the economic reform, the First would occasionally pull out of his jacket pocket a small clock in a metal box in the form of a camera. He would hold it under the table in order not to give the impression of rushing Tito. He would glance at it and hide it away, then take it out once again, admiring it and putting it back. He wasn't interested in what time it showed; he was simply fascinated by his unusual toy, which he had obviously just been given as a present.

I saw Khrushchev in rapturous amazement over modern technology more than once. Some soldiers told me how delighted he had been with some new military toys . . .

Yu. V. was quite different. Ever since his youth, when he had been a sailor, he had been used to handling technology and gave it the attention it deserved. He absorbed huge quantities of information on technical and military progress and constantly kept track of new inventions, especially foreign ones. As far as technical toys were concerned, he was completely indifferent. Everyone in the department knew that he and his family were astonishingly modest – none of his children drove about in Fords or Mercedes, nor did they chase after foreign tape-recorders, televisions or jeans. To many of our entourage this puritanism seemed excessive, but everyone treated him with profound respect. We knew that the First had given the members of his family three Fords received as a gift from the US President – and that hurt our feelings, particularly since at that time it was very rare for a party worker to have a private car. On hearing people comment on these luxuries, I remember thinking: 'Truly children are sent as vengeance against political leaders.' At the time I could not have known how prophetic those words were to be . . .

If the Albanian trip had shown how dangerous any display of intolerance and ambition was among the leaders of other countries, the visit to Yugoslavia demonstrated the opposite – how much could be achieved with a breadth of approach and an understanding of the diversity of historical conditions, human nature and individual human destinies. 'Culture is tolerance,' someone once said. That person was absolutely right, as long as moral principles are not sacrificed, of course, since they form the basis of one's personality and of the society to which one belongs.

7 A Reformer

At the beginning of 1960 I was transferred for a fairly long time to a group working on the draft Party Programme. Boris Nikolayevich Ponomaryov, head of the Central Committee international department, was in charge.

I had met Ponomaryov before for various reasons, but not often. I now had the opportunity of seeing him almost every day for more than a year. In his group everyone took part in discussions, editing and other work. Ponomaryov was highly respected: he had been a member of the Comintern, head of Sovinformbureau of the Council of Ministers, a deputy and later head of the international department and also head of the authors' collective on the textbook on the history of the Communist Party of the Soviet Union. He spoke slowly, weighing up every word, and he was very thorough in reading texts, writing his comments in large letters in the margins. He liked to go on walks with us on the outskirts of our residence, 'Sosny', which was the finest spot I knew near Moscow. Sosny was situated in the grounds of a unique pine wood and was a sanitorium. It had a wing – a small two-storey house with balconies and terraces – in which we were housed. While walking with us in the woods along the Moskva river he used to tell us interesting stories about his years in the Comintern. He had the fondest memories of this period.

The most colourful figure in our team was Yelizar Ilyich Kuskov, who worked as a consultant in another department. He looked like a typical peasant from pre-revolutionary days with his massive, almost square face, a large fleshy nose, a hare-lip and large, sparsely placed teeth. Despite his appearance and the fact that he had never completed his education he became the centre of our organizational and intellectual life, and well deserved this honour. He had natural wisdom – slow but thorough, sharp but cunning and endlessly sympathetic and encouraging. He was like a rough diamond; not polished by civilization but civilized by his very nature. I have never known any man to be so kind and responsive. None of us had such a subtle feel for political language, and none of us had such a store of amusing and dirty country jingles as Yelizar. And, of course, he liked his drink. This weakness took him to the grave before his time. For some reason I could not go to his funeral and I blame myself for it to this day, because despite the fact that we were different in temperament and education we were the very closest of friends and had formed, against the rules, a bridge between two departments which were to some extent in competition with each other.

Yelizar was in charge of headquarters, controlling everything to do with the preparation of documents and the endless travelling of members of the group between Moscow and Sosny in the new black Volga cars. He planned meetings, liaised with the head of the group, and on occasion had access to fairly high officials. Belyakov, who is already familiar to the reader, also worked in the group. He performed his usual function of speaking long and eloquently. My friendship with Belyakov had cooled and my feelings now became focussed on Yelizar, who fascinated me precisely because he did not at all fit in with my notions of what a theoretician and propagandist, or for that matter a thinker and writer should be like. I realized you did not have to be a graduate or a postgraduate or a doctor of sciences to be a profound thinker and a good writer; indeed, natural wit and intuition count for more. We had no dearth of scholars there, but their value was only relative.

I was commissioned to work on the section on the state. My task was to lay the grounds for a transition from a state based on the dictatorship of the proletariat to an all-people's state and from this to make the necessary deductions about developing party and Soviet democracy. This task was not particularly difficult as the textbook *The Fundamentals of Marxism-Leninism* had already come out, in which all the necessary arguments had been made. I also had at my disposal the memorandum which had been prepared under O. V. Kuusinen. Moreover Yelizar, cunning fox that he was, had transferred me to another section concerning the development of socialist countries and later included me in the general editing of the whole international section. In the section on the socialist camp I had to put forward our position as enshrined in the memorandum and at the same time avoid any formulation which the other countries could take as being a diktat from the 'elder brother'.

Here I clashed with a person whose views were quite different from mine. Vladimir Vladimirovich Krasilshchikov* was at that time deputy head of our department. I had first met him about ten years ago in the company of some senior research assistants and journalists. We had sat at different ends of the table, extremely bored, until he threw

* Not his real name.

out a quotation from Ilf and Petrov's book *The Golden Calf*. I parried by also quoting from the book and so we began a game which kept us going for the rest of the evening, moving from book to book, hugely enjoying ourselves and ignoring protests from the others. When I met Krasilshchikov many years later in the department and then at Sosny we easily established our former good relations.

However, it was not long before I realized that Krasilshchikov was one of that rare breed who combine a profound and natural intellect with double-dyed conservatism and unshakeable stubbornness. He loved Stalin deeply and sincerely and particularly prized the role Stalin had played in forming the socialist camp. In the first draft of the section on the socialist system two-thirds of the text was given over to a criticism of the League of Communists of Yugoslavia, which had recently brought out its own programme. The remaining one-third was written in such a clumsy and hopeless manner that it was totally unusable.

Finding myself in a difficult situation I approached Yelizar, who said: 'Don't pay any attention to what he's scribbled; just write your bit and we'll work it out later.' I did a draft and went off to see Krasilshchikov in an attempt – to use Yelizar's favourite term – to 'marry' our two texts. Krasilshchikov became so enraged that he was almost in a state of shock. He fought for every line and defended every comma as if it were the Gospel. I didn't know what to do, so I went off again to Yelizar who, grabbing a bottle of vodka, decided to reconcile the two sides. But that didn't work. Krasilshchikov rudely refused to drink with us, although he had dutifully drunk with everyone on equal terms before, and winding himself up into a frenzy demanded in a thunderous voice that we leave his room. The worldly-wise Yelizar spread out his hands in resignation and said ironically: 'We're not understood here, Fedor, let's go somewhere else.' Krasilshchikov left the next morning and never appeared in our team again. It was the only incident of this sort although we were all under great stress: the materials had to be repeatedly rewritten and re-edited, while instructions coming from above were often unclear, reflecting the confused and hidden struggle taking place on the controversial issue of how the Soviet Union should develop.

Krasilshchikov played an important role in the events in Czechoslovakia in 1968. Working at the embassy there, he insisted more than anyone else that Soviet troops should be sent to Czechoslovakia 'to smash the revisionists'. By a strange coincidence Suyetukhin, a specialist on economic management, was also dealing with the problems in Czechoslovakia, although he knew neither the language nor the country. The two of them teamed up to send the same information to the leadership and argued against a political resolution to the problem.

The most exotic figure who came to Sosny was Aleksandr Ivanovich Sobolev, whom I have already mentioned. He had moved from the journal *Kommunist* to work on the international journal *Problemy mira i sotsializma* ('Problems of the World and Socialism') in Prague. Sobolev had an amazingly sharp but destructive mind and felt no compunction about pulling apart a text and finding contradictions, inaccuracies and vaguenesses, but he found it very difficult to be constructive. Each time he attempted to blow the house down, arguing that the text had to be completely rewritten.

'Completely?' Yelizar would say, not without spite. 'Taking what line?'

'That is what we should be seriously discussing,' Sobolev would reply.

Generally Sobolev had the habits of a princeling to whom everything is permitted. He would run naked around the house in the rain, he tried to break into the typists' bedroom at night (uninvited), he would walk out of meetings without saying a word. As for the draft Programme, he left marks and notes all over it. Ponomaryov's weakness for him was inexplicable, but he firmly believed that he had exceptional theoretical talents and demanded that we listen to him. Kuskov did not like Sobolev's visits because the leadership would be left with the feeling that our work was still raw, that it had been put together haphazardly and that discipline would have to be tightened up. Fortunately for us Sobolev would disappear for long periods, leaving havoc and disillusionment behind.

The antithesis of Sobolev was Academician Pyotr Nikolayevich Fedoseyev. He was often invited to the general discussion before we handed in our text to the head of our working group. He created a sense of stability, although he would try to simplify virtually every text, straightening it out and making it conform with already accepted documents, removing rough edges or any formulation which strayed to one side or overstepped accepted boundaries. He was very alert to such things and it was hard to slip anything through his net.

Fedoseyev would sometimes bring two or three philosophers along with him to offer suggestions in their professional area. One of the philosophers was an Armenian by nationality, married to a Russian, who drove us mad by insisting that we include something on the development of national relations by encouraging marriages between different nationalities. This seemed to him to be the main way of uniting or even blending nations. He would persistently, even doggedly push through these ideas and thoroughly annoyed everyone around the editorial desk, even the moderate and serene Fedoseyev. On one occasion Fedoseyev asked me to take away a number of pages, edit them and bring them back to the general meeting. Instead of correcting the text, which I found totally unsuitable, I decided to have some fun and taking the author's sacred formula that 'the best means of bringing nations together was through marriage', I added, 'and other forms of sexual relations between representatives of different nations'. When this was read out loud to the group it provoked great mirth and Fedoseyev, in spite of heated protests, pitilessly threw out the whole text.

I am recounting these details to show that the atmosphere was relaxed and generally very creative. It did not occur to anyone to accuse others of deviations or 'isms', which had been the practice until quite recently in theoretical discussions. But our main concern, of course, was the content of the Party Programme, its new ideas, conclusions and formulations.

One of the centrepieces of the draft Party Programme was the question of peaceful coexistence, friendly relations and cooperation with all states and peoples. It was supposed to reflect our new strategy, worked out by the socialist countries in their mutual relations with the West – the trend towards a long period of peaceful competition in the course of which the advantages of socialism would be demonstrated. This would set an example for workers' and democratic movements around the world. The other concern was the new situation that had been created by the development of thermonuclear weapons: the new nature of war and its catastrophic consequences for all peoples and states, peace as the only alternative to mutual destruction, an end to the Cold War and confrontation, and a radical improvement in the international climate.

This approach provoked strong resistance from scientific circles, whose representatives thought that this contradicted the directives on world revolution. In the memorandum which advocates of this position drafted, as well as in articles, they juggled with quotations from Lenin, written during the years of revolution and civil war, totally ignoring his absolutely clear instructions and ideas in the twenties when the USSR had entered a period of peaceful construction and began to establish diplomatic, economic and other relations with capitalist states.

Strangely enough a whole historical era had to pass before these Leninist ideas in their pure form, without extraneous elements, were developed and applied to the present day and appeared in keynote party documents.

There was much discussion about how a transition to socialism would take place in capitalist countries; or more accurately, whether a peaceful non-violent transition through parliamentary means was possible. As is known, this question had been posed by Lenin and in our day it was first set out in a broad and well-argued way in the keynote document of the British Communist Party, 'Britain's Path to

Socialism'. Stalin had participated during its editing phase, at the British Communist Party's request. Afterwards the issue was discussed in documents of the French, Italian and many other Western European parties. In this form it entered into our party's documents because, naturally, on this question we had to be directed first and foremost by the views of the Communist Parties in the capitalist countries.

And, of course, in drafting the Party Programme much space was given over to ensuring that the cult of personality and its negative consequences would not be repeated. In particular, the process of renewing Soviet legislation – all the codes and basic laws as well as the drafting of the new USSR constitution – had already begun. This remained a pressing matter for a number of Communist Parties in the socialist countries, and for some it was not only pressing but extremely touchy. In China, Albania and some other countries any criticism of the cult of personality was seen as a direct attack against their own parties and countries and even as an attempt to criticize the authority and role of certain leaders. Among our own theoretical cadres and political figures this matter provoked many quarrels, often extremely bitter ones. For this reason we listened to a variety of opposing views during our work in drafting the Party Programme. In the end the view that triumphed was the one Andropov had expressed many times in private. He said that there was no issue that could break up the Communist movement to the same extent as the issue of Stalin. He therefore advised that we restrict ourselves to short formulae taken almost word for word from the well-known resolution 'On overcoming the cult of personality and its consequences' adopted in 1956. After a long tug-of-war it was this position that triumphed.

One practical conclusion, going from past experience, was that the replacement of cadres ought to be more consistent. This point provoked the most arguments. The idea of the rotation of cadres, which had come directly from Khrushchev, underwent a series of changes. No less than ten versions were worked out in order to find an adequate formula. The First wanted to create guarantees against the extreme concentration of power in the hands of one person, against leaders who would not give up their posts or cadres who had grown old. This did not provoke much controversy as far as primary organizations were concerned, but there were fundamental disagreements over rotation in the top echelons. For all Khrushchev's authority, stubbornness and persistence, he had to yield on this issue.

The principle that the top leadership could remain in power for no more than two terms was enshrined in the initial draft. This provoked stormy protests from the younger leaders, who felt it was highly unjust that members of the older generation who had managed to hang on to their posts for so long were now trying to restrict the chances and the active participation of their successors. In the second draft two terms were replaced by three, but even this was rejected in the end. In the final text the whole plan to create a new procedure for the replacement of cadres became unrecognizable. What remained concerned almost without exception the lower structures and soon turned out to be useless in practice. It is hard to say why it was such a failure. Whether the most sensible and acceptable forms for the rotation of cadres had not been found or whether interested parties resisted it, the fact remains that Lenin's important directive against the extreme concentration of power in the hands of one person failed to be incorporated in this, the keynote document.

The most heated arguments focussed on the proposal in the Programme to include data about the country's economic development and the course of economic competition in the world arena. A. Zasyadko, a top economic planner, came to put forward this proposal. As far as I remember, members of the working group – those who were economists and those, like me, who weren't – were resolutely against it. The report Zasyadko gave seemed superficial and unscientific to our boss and to us. The calculations comparing the pace of our economic development with that of the United States were complete fabrications – pure wishful thinking.

Zasyadko himself brought the heated discussion to an end. He opened the first page of a typed manuscript of about eighty pages bound in blue, in which the words 'to be included in the Programme' were inscribed along with the familiar signature of the First. Thus, despite the view of the vast majority of the participants – and not only within the framework of the working group but on a political level as well –statistical calculations of how we would catch up and overtake the United States in the 1980s were included in the Party Programme. Enthusiasm was running high, but as we used to say in the apparatus, you need ammunition as well as ambition.

True, the hope that there would be an acceleration of our economic development was connected with economic and administrative reform, although this did not take place. Moreover, at that time even prominent economic experts could not really have foreseen that the scientific and technical revolution would develop so rapidly.

One must try to imagine the spirit of the times. Although hardly anyone believed Zasyadko's figures, enthusiasm and optimism were running high. These feelings were not without foundation; we were convinced that the Programme to be adopted would herald major structural transformations, otherwise what was the point of adopting a new Party Programme?

In fact the idea was to find forms, means, methods and a mechanism to attain a new industrial level and catch up with the more industrially developed countries which had moved on; in that way we would radically improve agriculture, ensure the supply of foodstuffs and high-quality goods for the population and set a standard of living worthy of our long-suffering people.

By then it had become clear to some of our thoughtful theoreticians that it would not be possible to attain this by simply increasing quantitative changes – more gas, steel, coal, oil, electric power, cars, clothes. This development did not promise qualitative changes and doomed the country to fall progressively further behind in the field of new technology. What was needed was to change the structure of production and administration.

Unfortunately the First was surrounded by advisers who reduced to nothing many sensible and long-overdue changes or replaced them with pure organizational decisions, which were often ill-considered and untested.

Thus, the system of new economic relations was not defined. Everything was done hurriedly, there was great resistance from the economic personnel in the apparatus who did not understand the purpose of these changes or the breaking-up of traditions and were concerned about how these changes would affect their own lives. The situation was even worse in the state administration and the structure of the party leadership.

When we spoke of the First's weaknesses we would say, 'He's got used to walking in his worn-out slippers'. That was his reputation even while he was in the Ukraine and later when he came to Moscow: that he preferred to work with an apparatus which had been handed down to him from his predecessors and rarely replaced those around him. He was, therefore, often dependent on them for information, proposals and advice. Although Khrushchev was impatient for change to the point of bursting, he was often a victim of his uncultured background and especially of the incompetence and prejudices of his entourage. The notorious press group which formed around him had a strong influence on decision-making and often pushed him from one extreme to another, exploiting his emotional, hot-headed character. Andropov understood this perfectly well. He had no desire to join the press group or to get any of his co-workers into it. He had his own access to the First and preferred to hand the documents we prepared directly to him or to other members of the top leadership.

The final stage of work on the Party Programme took place while the Twenty-Second Party Congress was in session. The draft had been discussed in party organizations, in the press and at the congress itself, and we were required to make no less than twenty corrections of a fundamental or editorial nature. Unfortunately no account was taken of a number of letters requesting that data on the economic competition between the two world systems be removed from the Programme.

Khrushchev could not be persuaded to change his position. Nonetheless, the Party Programme was greeted enthusiastically by the whole party and the people, who hoped and confidently believed that in a short historical period there would be major achievements in the economic and social development of the country and that living standards would rapidly increase.

*

I worked for a year and a half on the draft Party Programme. While we were busy on the final stages at the Sosny sanitorium in Nikolina Gora another group, situated in Gorky's former dacha on the other side of the Moskva river, was working on the party's progress report. However, not long before the Twenty-Second Party Congress we received instructions to prepare an independent report on the draft Party Programme. It had originally been decided not to have an independent report, but to include the Programme in the progress report. Then another directive was handed down, although by then there was not much time left before the congress and the group had to work feverishly to prepare the draft of this new report. A considerable part of the group worked on it, but at the final stage it was left to two people, Yelizar and me. We were told to liven up the text, give it a more conversational style and brighten up the theoretical presentation with a few political and literary digressions. I remember Yelizar and I sitting through the hot summer days in the summerhouse near our residence, vying with each other while dictating to our shorthand typist.

All those at the congress – the whole party and the people – witnessed the buffoonery that followed. At first Khrushchev read the four-hour-long progress report and then, after an interval, he again got up on the rostrum and spent another three hours reading the report on the draft Party Programme.

I think it was under Khrushchev that the curious tradition was laid down of evaluating a leader's authority by the number of words he uttered. This had not been possible under Lenin as not only he but other members of the leadership gave reports, made comments, wrote articles and often books. Stalin seldom spoke, but when he did it was full of import, conforming to Boris Godunov's remark: 'The tsar's voice should only be heard to proclaim a great festivity or a national disaster.'

Khrushchev loved to talk, in fact to gab. I went to many of his meetings with foreign leaders at which he did not let anyone else get a word in. There would be reminiscences, jokes, political comments, descriptions of different public figures – often penetrating and acute – and anecdotes – at times quite vulgar. All this created what we now refer to as his 'image' – that of a man who was spontaneous, lively and irrepressible; a person who did not use his words very seriously or responsibly. Almost thirty years have passed and I still hear the clumsy joke he made in the United States: 'We only have one quarrel – it is on the question of land. Who will bury whom?' In China they still remember when, flying into a rage at a meeting with a Chinese official, Khrushchev shouted that he would send 'the coffin with Stalin's body straight to Peking . . .'

At Khrushchev's initiative and under great pressure a major step was taken in criticizing Stalinism and exposing and condemning Stalin's cult of personality at the Twenty-Second Party Congress in 1961. As is well-known, Khrushchev pushed through a decision in the Presidium that every member of the leadership should speak on the issue – even Suslov was forced to do so. The analysis of the Stalinist regime moved forward in a number of directions.

First of all, the part played by the group which clung to Stalin after Lenin's death was fully disclosed – this included Molotov, Kaganovich, Voroshilov, Mikoyan and later Malenkov, Beria and others. Thus, the mechanism of intra-party struggle was revealed. As factions and associations in the party had been formally forbidden, secret groups struggling for power and influence had arisen. Those who had joined Stalin's group, which was supported by the new party bureaucracy, could not but succeed. Khrushchev recounted how members of this group resisted the revelations of the cult of personality at the Twentieth Congress, how they had also opposed the rehabilitation of innocent people who had been condemned and executed, and how they had tried to establish neo-Stalinism by organizing a palace coup.

Khrushchev said that the rehabilitation of Tukhachevsky, Yakir and Uborevich had been discussed at the Presidium. He had questioned Molotov, Kaganovich and Voroshilov: 'Are you in favour of rehabilitating them?'

'Yes, we are,' they had answered.

'But you had them executed,' Khrushchev said indignantly. 'Were you acting according to conscience then or now?'[1]

They didn't answer.

The Twenty-Second Party Congress decided to remove Stalin's body from the Mausoleum and to immortalize the memory of prominent party and state figures who had become victims of repressions during the cult of personality.

Finally, the question of dissenting views within the party and how to respond to them was raised for the first time by Khrushchev, although he put the question timidly and unclearly. In his concluding remarks he said: 'Is it possible to have differing views within the party at different periods of its activity, especially when there has been a turning point? Yes, it is. How are we to respond to those who express their own views when they differ from other's? In such cases we do not advocate repression but the use of Leninist methods of persuasion and explanation.'[2]

Once again he referred to Lenin's approach to Zinovyev and Kamenev after their well-known statement against the armed uprising in October 1917. Khrushchev stressed that in the years following Lenin's death Leninist norms of party life had been crudely distorted by Stalin's cult of personality. The limits that Stalin had placed on intra-party and Soviet democracy had become the norm. He had crudely trampled on the Leninist principle of collective leadership, had permitted arbitrary rule and the abuse of power.

The very fact that the question of dissent within the party had been raised represented a major step forward in party life in the post-Stalin period. But one cannot ignore the weaknesses of Khrushchev's approach to this question. In essence he reduced the question to one of responding tolerantly, loyally and mildly to people who expressed different opinions at different times. In the final analysis, however, such people should submit to the view of the majority and correct their views under the influence of criticism. This was, in effect, no different from the way the question had been posed during the struggle against the Trotskyists and later against Kamenev, Zinovyev and Bukharin. It was precisely in that period that it had become the practice for 'deviationists' to succumb to self-denunciation and condemn their own views. This was seen as the main precondition for them to retain any of their posts, as well as to remain in the party. And in the end, even before the savage outburst of criminal repressions, the 'deviationists' got down on their knees one after the other, bowed low, denounced their mistakes and promised to mend their ways. Almost everyone behaved in this way. Even Bukharin, under the cruel pressure of intra-party criticism and punishment, repeatedly came out with repentant statements.

It seems that Khrushchev simply could not tolerate the idea that the minority might prove to be right and the majority would have to recognize its errors. It certainly never entered his head that there could be a clash of opinions, proposals and alternatives where vital questions of domestic and foreign policy were concerned. Thus, even though it was at Khrushchev's initiative that a heavy blow was inflicted on the tyrannical regime and the mass repressions linked with it, the ideological basis of the authoritarian regime remained essentially untouched.

Khrushchev considered it natural and normal that a small group of leaders, headed by the Party First Secretary, should hold a monopoly on deciding all questions to do with the life and development of the whole of society. He and they, in the end, decided how to distribute financial resources, in what direction to develop collective farms, state farms, plants and factories, to whom and how to award prizes in literature, the applied arts, the theatre and science. Khrushchev did not even reflect on why this right belonged to him personally and to another ten people in his entourage whom he had picked himself. Was it by virtue of the natural qualities of the leaders themselves, or by some mandate – and if so, from whom: the party or the people? And what effect did such a regime have on the life of the people? In the minds of Khrushchev and of a whole generation of leaders the traditional model of a patriarchal peasant homestead was preserved. The patriarch was the elder either of a family or of a clan, who was elected by no one. By virtue of some natural law he had the right to decide the fate of every member of the family or clan, motivated by certain common interests. It seems that this model of authoritarian-patriarchal political culture was not overturned by Khrushchev. Indeed, he was its most democratic and perhaps most independent-thinking representative.

Paternalism, the right to interfere in any matter or relationship, the infallibility of the patriarch, intolerance of dissenting views – this was the typical age-old notion of power in Russia.

The problem of creating safeguards against a regime of personal power came up against an insurmountable obstacle – the limited political culture of Khrushchev himself and the generation of leaders of that time. In this respect the events that followed the June 1957 Plenum are revealing. As I have already mentioned, a prominent role was played by Marshal Zhukov in smashing the Stalinists. It was said at the time that during a Presidium session Zhukov came out against these people directly with the historic statement: 'The army is against this decision, and not one tank will move without my orders.' This statement eventually cost him his career.

Soon after the June Plenum Khrushchev succeeded in relieving Zhukov of his post as member of the Presidium and Minister of Defence. This was done in the traditional spirit of those times, when the Marshal was abroad. He was given no opportunity to explain himself, just as no explanation was given to the party and the people of why the most outstanding commander of the Great Patriotic War had been expelled from the political arena. And once again he had been expelled for the traditional reason: fear of a strong man.

Khrushchev always preferred to associate with flatterers than with those who genuinely supported his reforms. That is why he surrounded himself with such men as N. Podgorny, who looked starry-eyed at him and was willing to carry out any assignment. That is also why he was not impressed by independent and strong-minded people. Khrushchev was too self-confident to rely on others. This was one reason for his downfall. Those people who deep down did not share his reformist views and thought them incompetent and even eccentric got rid of him at the first convenient moment, and he had no allies to fall back on.

True, there was a time when he mixed with more refined cadres in the party apparatus, such as D. Shepilov, whom he promoted to Secretary of the Central Committee and Minister of Foreign Affairs. However, Shepilov's behaviour at the 1957 Plenum put Khrushchev off 'intellectuals' for good.

*

I first met M. A. Suslov in 1963. Andropov used to tell us at the department of Suslov's comments on the materials we were preparing. These comments were consistent so that I very quickly formed a clear picture of Mikhail Andreyevich Suslov. We would be writing a document on the possibility of a peaceful transition to socialism in other countries and he would point out that it was also necessary to mention an armed uprising; or we would say that there was no fatalistic inevitability of a world war and he would note that we also had to mention that there was no fatalistic inevitability of peace. If we stressed the importance of democracy he would recommend that we mentioned discipline; if we noted errors in the period of the cult of personality he would advise us to point out that such a period did not exist, in so far as the party had always been based on Leninist principles; if we hinted that not everything was wonderful during collectivization he would say that we should mention the historical importance of this great turning point. On the whole he was a guardian of the all-round approach so as not, as it were, to throw the baby out with the bathwater, even if the baby was covered in the dirt of Stalinism.

Our group was particularly amused by his remarks on whether to write 'Marxism-Leninism and proletarian internationalism' or 'Marxism-Leninism – proletarian internationalism'. Every time we put in an 'and' Mikhail Andreyevich would neatly cross out the 'and' in his thin handwriting and put in a dash, because after all you could not set one in opposition to the other: Marxism-Leninism *is* proletarian internationalism. Our department was fairly stubborn about this and we continued to put in the unacceptable 'and', while the other international department had wholly accepted Mikhail Andreyevich's formula and obediently put in a dash whenever necessary. Suslov did not like Andropov and was afraid of him, suspecting that he was angling for his post in the Politburo. On the other hand he befriended the head of the other international department, although he also kept him at a safe distance, opposing his entry into the top leadership; he was always to remain a candidate member of the Politburo.

I first met Suslov during negotiations with the Chinese delegation in 1963. As an adviser in these negotiations I had the opportunity of getting to know the leaders of the Chinese Communist Party quite well.

The aristocratic Chou En-lai and the lively, relaxed and entertaining Deng Xiao-ping impressed me most of all. (I later wrote an article on Deng Xiao-ping called 'Interregnum' in *Novy mir*, no. 4, 1982, and a biography which has still not been published.)

During these negotiations, which took place in the House of Receptions on Lenin Hills, Suslov, who was heading our delegation, made use of an interval to invite the other Soviet leaders and advisers to a meeting. He told us that we had to prepare a document urgently, that very day, expressing the Soviet Communist Party's position in the quarrel with the Chinese leaders. He sketched out the type of problems that should be mentioned: the cult of personality, peace and peaceful coexistence and forms of transition to socialism. This was to be called an 'Open Letter'.

What caught my attention was the expression on Mikhail Andreyevich's face when he said, 'We must inflict a blow on them suddenly while they're unprepared'; his face was suffused by a delighted, quiet laugh. We worked the whole night on the document which was approved and published immediately. The document was fine and only one thing was doubtful – whether it had been necessary to do this before the negotiations had even ended. I later realized that this was Suslov's personal style, whereas Khrushchev was always more inclined towards open, impulsive and rather ill-considered moves.

The relationship between these two leaders always remained a mystery to us. It is hard to say why Khrushchev tolerated Suslov in the leadership for such a long time after he had removed many of his other opponents – either he wanted to retain some continuity with the Stalinist leadership or he felt a strange respect for Mikhail Andreyevich's imaginary expertise in Marxism-Leninism. But Khrushchev did not like him. I was present at one session when Khrushchev attacked Suslov in a sharp, even offensive way. 'They're writing in the West that the old Stalinist and dogmatist Suslov is sitting behind my back just waiting to push me out. What do you have to say, Mikhail Andreyevich, are they writing the truth?' Suslov sat, his thin, ascetic, sickly and yellowish face lowered, without moving or uttering a word or raising his eyes.

At the February 1964 Party Central Committee Plenum Khrushchev made Suslov give a speech on Stalin's cult of personality. The instructions were passed on to me and Belyakov. We had to prepare the speech in one night. Belyakov and I remained in the office for twelve hours without a break. At first we tried to dictate to the shorthand typists but it didn't work out, because we did not know how to write for Suslov. His position was well-known: it was cautious, dispassionate, seemingly all-embracing, balanced, without extremes or bright colours. On the other hand, Khrushchev's instructions were

unambiguous: Suslov had to condemn the cult of personality resolutely. We spent half the night trying to get something together. Then
we sent the shorthand typists home and did it ourselves. Belyakov took
a pen and I dictated with encouragement from him: 'That's it! That's it!
Let it flow. Come on now!'

By morning the speech was ready, neatly typed out in three copies,
and we set off to see Mikhail Andreyevich. He seated us at a long table,
he himself sat in the chairman's seat with Belyakov closer to him and me
further away. He began to read aloud, stressing his o's like Maxim
Gorky and saying, 'Yes, that's fine. This too. Yes, well put.' At one spot
he stopped and said, 'We should strengthen it here with a quotation
from Lenin . . . a short one.' Dazed by the sleepless night, I assured
him we would find a quotation, a good one, that quotations were no
problem for us. He looked at me for the first time with a quick, sharp
glance and said, 'I'll find it myself now.' He rushed off in a sprightly
way to a corner of his office and took down one of those boxes you find in
libraries, put it on the table and with his long thin fingers very quickly
began to flick through his cards of quotations. He pulled one out,
looked at it but that wouldn't do; he got another out and read it, but that
wasn't right either. Then he pulled one out and said with satisfaction,
'This is the one.' He read it aloud and it really was a good quotation. At
that moment I made the biggest mistake of my life; obviously the
sleepless night had taken its toll. I could not restrain myself and giggled
at the picture of the country's most prominent ideologue fingering his
quotations as if they were beads, like a monk with his rosary in days
of old. I must assume that my face at the time did not have a party look
about it because Mikhail Andreyevich glanced at me for the second time
and his small grey eyes flashed. Then he lowered them again and looked
at the catalogue. I thought to myself at that moment, 'You'll cop it,
Fedya! Sooner or later you'll cop it!' True enough, I did cop it from him
– but that was under the regime that followed. He was directly involved
in the reprisals against me for an article I had written when I was
working on *Pravda*. But I will describe that episode later.

Suslov finished reading the text, thanked us and shook our hands. At
the plenum he read his report in that version; he read it expressively and
deservedly received the First's full approval. But he never forgave us
for being the vehicles through which this ideological violence had been
committed against him. He was constrained to say things against Stalin
which he did not think or believe.

Suslov played a sinister role in distorting Khrushchev's relationship
with the intelligentsia. For a long time Khrushchev regarded him as the
major authority in ideology. Feeling his weakness and even helpless-
ness on theoretical matters, Khrushchev often sought Suslov's advice
whenever the discussion was about science, literature or the fine arts. In

addition, Suslov relied on his team of young leaders who had come out of the Komsomol – A. Shelepin, V. Semichastny, Khrushchev's aide V. Lebedev and Khrushchev's son-in-law A. Adzhubey. Adzhubey was a good editor of the papers *Komsomolskaya pravda* and later *Izvestiya*, but the group of young 'supreme leaders', led by Shelepin, managed to involve him in their struggles against the liberal intelligentsia, as well as in their struggles within the party.

Khrushchev himself felt drawn to the liberal intelligentsia because of their criticism of Stalinism. The heated events around Solzhenitsyn's short story 'One Day in the Life of Ivan Denisovich' are revealing. I remember Andropov gave me the story to read after it had already been submitted for publication in *Novy mir*.

I was asked my opinion of it and, of course, vigorously supported its publication. The story was a skilful substantiation of Khrushchev's secret speech. I was told that the only person who supported its publication right from the start was Khrushchev. Thanks to his steadfast and uncompromising position, 'One Day in the Life of Ivan Denisovich' was published in *Novy mir* and the effect was akin to the explosion of an ideological bomb.

Serious battles over the story developed after its publication. At the insistence of the progressive section of the literary intelligentsia, particularly Aleksandr Tvardovsky, editor-in-chief of *Novy mir*, the story was submitted for the Lenin Prize. It was then that the pressure from the 'Komsomol group' began to tell on Khrushchev. In a recent article S. Pavlov, former secretary of the Komsomol Central Committee, describes these events with unsurpassed naivety and it is clear that to this day he is proud of the struggle he waged against the liberal intelligentsia at that time.

S. Pavlov recounts how as First Secretary of the Komsomol he was included in the committee for the Lenin Prizes. He says the very idea of awarding a prize for a book which described details of camp life 'seemed absurd'. He said much the same at a session of the Lenin Prize committee. After this he was rung up by Semichastny, who by that time had become chairman of the KGB. Semichastny told him, 'It will be more difficult tomorrow; Solzhenitsyn's supporters are getting ready to attack. I will bring you his file from those years.'

And I expect he did. Although positive reviews had been published in *Pravda* and *Izvestiya* by that time, Solzhenitsyn's name was removed from the list of entrants. Pavlov writes: 'Khrushchev understood and accepted this and I don't think he was upset . . .'[3]

Khrushchev's relations with the intelligentsia were also affected by his hastiness and desire to interfere in all matters. He was often the toy of not disinterested advisers as well as hidden opponents who were preparing for his fall. I remember very clearly that Khrushchev's visit to the art exhibition at the Manezh was provoked by a specially prepared memorandum. In it little was said about art, but it quoted the genuine or imaginary views of writers and artists about Khrushchev; that he was 'Ivan the Fool on a throne', 'a maize-lover' and a 'babbler'. At the end of his tether, Khrushchev set off for the Manezh to have it out with the artists. Similar methods were used by Khrushchev's secret opponents to poison his mind against Boris Pasternak; in the same way they managed to remove A. Nesmeyanov from the post of President of the Academy of Sciences to please Lysenko and led him into quarrels with many representatives of literature, art and science.

I was only at some of Khrushchev's meetings with cultural figures, so I will allow myself to quote from their accounts. I will begin with Mikhail Romm, the well-known film director who made the film *Everyday Fascism*. He told me a great deal about his meetings with Khrushchev (as well as with Stalin), as he had suggested I write a script about Mao Tse-tung. Here is his account of his meeting with Khrushchev:

Before December 1962 I did not personally have the opportunity of seeing or hearing N. S. Khrushchev. I must say that until then I was one of Khrushchev's fans. I was even called a 'Khrushchevite'. I had been very inspired by his speech at the Twentieth Congress and I liked his human qualities. I tried to forgive him everything. In the world of culture things were going well, we were breathing freely, there was progress in art, and from time to time we would say to each other about Khrushchev, 'True, he's no beauty; but he's a sweetie, a real sweetie.'

It continued like this until his famous visit to the Manezh in December 1962, where I was told that Khrushchev stamped his feet, raged against leftist art and at culture generally and at the young poets.

In December 1962 I received an invitation to a reception at the House of Receptions on Lenin Hills.

When I arrived there was a line of cars and people. I went into the government cloakroom, then to a first-floor suite of rooms hung with paintings, some orthodox, others not so orthodox. There was a throng of people – about three hundred or maybe even more. Everyone was there: filmmakers, poets, writers, painters, sculptors, journalists, people from outside Moscow – in fact, the whole artistic intelligentsia. A buzz of people, everyone waiting and wondering what was in store.

Through the doors which led to the main room – the reception room – one could see the tables were laid: white tablecloths, dishes and delicious food. Good Lord! It appears we're going to have a banquet! What is this? An attempt to soften us up? What's all this food for?

In the midst of all the din, greetings and questioning glances the leadership arrived. The crowd surged towards Khrushchev, the cameras whirred.

At the dinner Khrushchev stood up and said that we had been invited here to have a talk, but so that the conversation would be more cordial and open we should first have a bite to eat. Let us have a bite and then we'll talk.

We ate and drank for about an hour. At last they served coffee and ice-cream. Khrushchev got up, everyone stood up after him and with a shuffling and scraping of chairs surged into the other room.

After an interval everyone streamed back into the hall. The tables had been removed and I found myself in a different seat. I remember a few of the speeches. In one I was called a provocateur, a political illiterate and a slanderer; at the same time the poet Shchipachov was also attacked. Another speech boiled down to the statement that camp wardens were wonderful Communists . . .

Khrushchev's comments were biting, especially when Erenburg, Yevtushenko and Shchipachov spoke, and they all spoke very well.

This is when I seemed to see a new Khrushchev. At first he had behaved as the good and kindly boss of a large enterprise, hospitably urging us to eat and drink and 'We'll all have a good, hearty talk'.

He spoke so charmingly – all roly-poly and well-shaven. Even his movements were rounded, and his first remarks had been kindly. But gradually he got more and more excitable and Ernst Neizvestny was the first person he lashed out against. It was terribly difficult for him. I was amazed at the painstaking way he talked about art when he knew nothing about it, absolutely nothing. He tried to define what is 'beautiful' and what is not, what the people understood and what they couldn't. For a long time he searched for words that would describe more clearly and insultingly what Ernst Neizvestny's art was like. Finally he hit on it and delighted, said, 'This is what your art is like. Say a man goes to the lavatory and climbs into the toilet bowl and gazes from within, from inside the toilet bowl at what is above him when someone is sitting on the toilet seat. He looks at that part of the body from below, from the toilet bowl. That's what your art is like. That's your position, comrade Neizvestny, inside the toilet bowl.'

He said this to the laughter and approval of the older generation of the creative intelligentsia – artists, sculptors and even some writers. He also had the following to say: 'Here's a letter with signatures. It's a petition, by the way, about these young leftists, these artists. It says, let them work, them and others, and there will be peaceful coexistence in our art. This, comrades, is a crude political mistake. Peaceful coexistence is possible, but not in ideology.'

Ehrenburg jumped up:

'But that was a joke! Nikita Sergeyevich, the letter . . . it was just a humorous way of saying it. It wasn't intended to be offensive.'

'No, comrade Erenburg, it's not a joke. There will be no peaceful coexistence in ideology. There will not, comrades! And I warn everyone who signed the letter. And that's that!'

And that was the way the meeting at Lenin Hills came to an end. Everyone went home feeling well-fed but alarmed and confused, wondering what would happen next. Things went badly after that; the screws were turned and letters and exposés appeared in the papers. The debacle had started. It was hard times for the guilty. And I had quite a hard time of it.[4]

Another account comes from Andrey Voznesensky, one of the main heroes of those meetings with Khrushchev. He writes:

The poets who became known in the sixties probably wrote their best works in the seventies and eighties. Their poems revealed the pain of shattered illusions. Dividing up generations in poetry is mechanistic. In those years I wrote about the generations as 'horizontal' in age and 'vertical' in conscience and talent. These words about a 'vertical' generation were distorted and quoted by informers to get Khrushchev into a rage at that ill-starred meeting with the intelligentsia at the Kremlin. He called me onto the rostrum.

The blue-domed Sverdlov Hall was filled with the ceremonial dress and the white nylon shirts customary then. There were mainly officials there and a cautious sprinkling of the creative intelligentsia.

The speakers at the rostrum had their backs to the table where the Presidium sat. At this raised table were Khrushchev, Brezhnev, Suslov, Kozlov and Ilyichev. These men's portraits, ten metres high, always decorated the streets on official holidays and were carried on processions.

All our hopes were pinned on Khrushchev; I wanted to unburden my soul to him about the state of literature; I thought he would understand everything.

But hardly had I started to speak, feeling rather nervous, when someone behind my back began interrupting. I continued speaking. Behind my back I heard the microphone roar: 'Comrade Voznesensky!' I asked not to be interrupted. Again the roar: 'Mr Voznesensky – get out of our country!'

From the initial confusion and then the triumphant faces in the hall I sensed that something terrible was happening behind my back. I turned. A few metres away the distorted, malicious face of

Khrushchev was shouting. The head of state jumped up, shaking his fists in the air. 'Mr Voznesensky! Out! Comrade Shelepin will issue you with a passport.' A quite monstrous flood of words followed.
What was this for? Had he gone off his head? I was sure this was the end for me. Only the habit of remaining alert during public appearances enabled me to retain possession of my faculties.
For a long time I could not comprehend how one person could combine the best hopes of the sixties and all those powerful changes with such an obstructive old way of thinking, such philistine tyranny.[5]

That's the way it was . . . you can't rewrite history.

Khrushchev's lack of culture and education were most evident in his relationship with people in the arts; it was an organic part of the patriarchal model of power. This miner of peasant stock thought he was the living embodiment of the people and that therefore his perceptions were the criterion by which to judge art, which is created for the people and belongs to the people. Added to this, his behaviour was unbridled and uncouth, the kind of crude authoritarianism so accurately depicted by Bulgakov in *The Heart of a Dog*. How backward this sort of authoritarian is compared with, say, Lorenzo the Great or other leaders of Florence and Rome, to whom arbitrary rule was not alien, but who had a profound understanding, knowledge and love of art.

*

The negative influence of Khrushchev's advisers was painfully evident not only in cultural matters but in the sphere of state administration as well. Many urgently needed changes were replaced by purely organizational decisions, which were often untested and ill-considered. This was the case, for example, with the decision to continue the departmental and bureaucratic form of administering the economy. Departments were replaced by hastily and carelessly formed *sovnarkhozes.**

Thus, the system of new economic relations was never defined. Everything was done in haste, against strong resistance from many workers in the economic apparatus, who did not understand the reason for these changes or the breaking-up of traditions, or the changes in their way of life, as they were often forced to leave their comfortable offices in Moscow and set off for the back of beyond. The changes which took place in state administration and the structure of the party leadership caused even more problems.

---

* Councils of national economy, set up in 1957 in an attempt to decentralize the economy by transferring power to local authorities.

In his memoirs Khrushchev condemns Stalin for his autocratic ways and for making individual decisions without the advice of members of the Politburo or the Bureau of the Central Committee Presidium. He contrasts this with the Leninist method of collective leadership. Furthermore, Khrushchev declared the practice of preselecting delegates to party congresses and higher party organs a 'distorted' form of democracy.[6] As we know Khrushchev tried to include the principle of the rotation of cadres in the Party Rules, but was unsuccessful. He never wondered, however, why a small group of leaders who were nominated or in some form or other elected within the party itself had the right to rule the state and the whole people.[7]

This was typical of the authoritarian tradition that had taken shape under Stalin. The General Secretary of the Central Committee of the Communist Party of the Soviet Union was virtually the head of state. In the thirties, when Stalin established his cult and dealt mercilessly with real and imaginary opponents, he did not hold any state posts. Nevertheless, all his orders were implemented by the security organs, the People's Commissariat of Internal Affairs, the army, the Soviet of People's Commissars and all other departments. Khrushchev does not even raise the issue of a mandate from the people being necessary – even as a formality. Like Stalin, he was convinced that such a mandate had been given once and for all in October 1917 when the party had taken power into its own hands. It followed naturally that it ruled the country through its representatives.

Moreover, like Stalin, Khrushchev proceeded from the notion of the absolute nature of power. To the party leaders alone belonged the right to adopt economic plans, to regulate the standard of living, to define the nature of education and the work of cultural establishments and to implement foreign policy. Not once in the two volumes of his memoirs does Khrushchev question this axiom.

In the West the notion of the division of power and the setting up of checks and balances to prevent excessive concentration of power in the hands of one organ, let alone one person, took shape over several centuries. In the eighteenth century Montesquieu laid the foundations for the idea of the division between legislative, executive and judicial powers. The experience of the nineteenth century led not only to the formation of state institutions with an inbuilt balance, but a multi-party system where parties controlled each other.

This went hand in hand with the development of the liberal tradition, which originated from the first Bills of Rights adopted more than two hundred years ago by England, France and the United States. This tradition laid the basis for the autonomy of the individual within the state; his natural civil and political rights could not be removed. These traditions were virtually absent in Russia. Under Stalin the country returned in many ways to the mechanism of power that had existed under Ivan the Terrible and Peter I: autocracy, or rather one-man rule, was underpinned simply and directly by the merciless machine of repression.

Khrushchev rejected this machine and condemned autocracy, but he preserved authoritarian rule. He became the first Soviet leader with undisputed power who did not resort to mass repressions. But he never dwelt on the separation of powers or the distribution of functions between the party and state, let alone on the idea that political power has no right to encroach upon the social, economic, civil and political rights of individuals.

Khrushchev accepted another Stalinist tradition whose roots go back deep into Russian history – the uniting of secular and spiritual power. This explains his vigorous and unceremonious interference in the areas of science, literature, film and the fine arts.

Even when tyrannical or authoritarian regimes reigned supreme in the West they interfered only in exceptional cases in the area of science, literature and the theatre. Can one imagine, say, Alexander of Macedon 'correcting' Aristotle's conclusions in *Politics* about the proper forms of state power – monarchy, aristocracy and democracy? Or Louis XIV reprimanding Voltaire for making his Candide an immoral person? Or Elizabeth I – a fairly stern monarch – instructing Shakespeare on how to evaluate the historical role of her ancestors, the former kings of England? Only the Church, and even then not often, interfered in science, literature, philosophy and art, and only when it saw that they were directly encroaching upon its sacred writings.

We discover from Khrushchev's memoirs that he had never read Pasternak and had never even heard his name until the all too well-known scandal over the publication of *Doctor Zhivago*. He himself says that he did not understand art, particularly modern trends: this is his explanation for his mistake at the Manezh over Ernst Neizvestny and other artists.

Khrushchev's main problem, as we saw it, was that while being an extremely courageous and active political figure, he lacked the courage, education and knowledge to become a political thinker too. Generally, very few figures possess this second type of courage. The talent to reconsider one's views, acknowledge mistakes and find new answers and solutions is very rare among scholars, let alone leaders.

*

Thus, Khrushchev did not overcome his blind faith in the state, or more accurately, state socialism. Like Stalin, Khrushchev was convinced that the state, centralism, the issuing of a plan, orders and instructions from above constituted socialism's main advantage over capitalism and was the main stimulus to the country's development. He was no less a statist than Stalin and incomparably more so than Marx or Lenin.

Let us remember that Marx advocated the withering away of the state and thought that its first act – the expropriation of property from the capitalists – would be its final one, which would herald the beginning of the gradual elimination of all state institutions. To a large extent Lenin believed in the state, particularly when he became the head of the first Soviet government. Although before the Revolution he had argued against a permanent army, during the course of the civil war he and Trotsky created one of the most powerful armies in the world, which until 1927 comprised 586,000 men.[8] Lenin also created a fairly powerful party and state apparatus, although he continued to declare that the state would wither away in the future.

I do not think we need discuss to what degree Stalin aggravated this tendency. He took it as far as the deification of the state and state interests, before which everyone had to prostrate themselves; they were simply small cogs in the state machine. In 1948, three years after the war, the Soviet army had 2,874,000 men, and by Stalin's death the number was more than five million.[9]

Khrushchev actively opposed the militarization of the state. On his initiative the army was reduced to 2,423,000 people.[10] But he did not encroach upon the fundamentals of state socialism.

Even his most drastic reforms – the setting up of *sovnarkhozes* and the elimination of many ministries and departments – were superficial. The intention was to make administration more rational and bring it closer to its objects – the enterprises, collective and state farms and scientific establishments. These reforms, however, did not infringe on the principle of state socialism. They did not affect the essence of production relations, nor did they claim to offer new working conditions for the producers – the worker, the peasant and the intelligentsia – to enable them to use their initiative, independence and choice or provide a direct link to the consumer. This would have liberated the economy, weakening and later entirely removing the stranglehold of state supervision. We can see this particularly clearly in Khrushchev's agrarian policy, an area in which he considered himself to be a competent specialist. But here Khrushchev behaved even more like a 'statist' than Stalin.

Not long before Stalin's death a letter criticizing Khrushchev's idea of agro-cities was being read out at party organizations. He was then an enthusiastic proponent of turning collective farms into state farms, that is, of finalizing their inclusion in the state system. He believed that the experience of factory labour should be transferred more consistently to the countryside. He thought that this would achieve greater specialization of production, a higher level of professionalism and the use of modern equipment. Simultaneously this would open up the possibility of socially restructuring the everyday life of the countryside on urban principles.

Strangely enough, it was Stalin who initially criticized this idea. I don't think that he was protesting against the principle of incorporating collective farms into the state system, which had virtually been done during the period of full collectivization. As is well-known, the land had been entirely handed over to the state – that is, taken from the peasants and assigned to the collective farms. No one in the collective farms had the right to demand that the land or his share of the equipment and livestock be returned. The notion of so-called 'indivisible assets' was introduced and later on collective farm workers became totally tied to collective farms by the internal passport system. They were simply denied passports and could not leave their village.

Furthermore, there was at the time a widespread notion of two forms of property: the cooperative (the lowest form) which was doomed to change gradually into state property (the highest form); that is, collective farms would become state farms.

Stalin, however, considered it premature to turn collective farms into state farms. He realized that if this happened state farms, and that meant the state budget, would have to take on the colossal burden of paying the wages of toilers in the countryside, whereas there was no such obligation towards collective farmers. No state resources went towards paying for the labour of those living in the villages, which accounted for 40 per cent of the population. As for Khrushchev, he probably hoped that the broadening of state control would rescue collective farmers from poverty, destitution and hunger.

In his memoirs Khrushchev describes with heart-rending pain the terrible conditions in which peasants lived in the post-war period in the Ukrainian Republic, which was under his charge.

Khrushchev says he repeatedly referred the matter to Stalin in 1946 and in subsequent years. In 1946 there was a drought and agriculture was badly hit in the Ukraine. According to Khrushchev the harvest was very bad, but the centre set a plan that required an enormous and unreal supply of grain and other products. State procurement officials picked the collective farms and farmers clean. Khrushchev recalls the desperate letters from collective farm chairmen. One of them wrote: '. . . so, comrade Khrushchev, we have totally fulfilled the plan for state grain procurement. We have given our all. We have nothing left. We are certain that the state and the party will not forget us and will come to our assistance . . .'

'When I read this,' Khrushchev recalls, 'I felt that he thought it depended on me. I was then Chairman of the Soviet of People's

Commissars and First Secretary of the Ukraine. But I myself had to ask and beg to get something of what we needed . . .'[11]

Khrushchev says that he appealed to Stalin and other members of the Politburo repeatedly, but without success.

'Stalin reacted very harshly. He considered that everyone lived prosperously. Shevchenko said, "From the Moldavians to the Finns everyone is silent, everyone is prospering" – as if he were writing about this period. Only he was writing about the times of Nicholas I and these were the times of Stalin I.'[12] According to Khrushchev, Stalin then said that a special plenum on agriculture should be convened, although this never happened. It was then that Khrushchev proposed his idea of agro-cities, which he thought would save the peasantry.

The results were paradoxical. Khrushchev had the best of intentions: to rescue the peasant from hunger, ensure a minimum level of well-being and a steady wage in the state farm. But the means to it were counter-productive. Past and subsequent experience has shown that you cannot model a peasant on a factory worker. Further enslavement of the peasant could only lead to a decline in agricultural productivity. But Stalin, according to Khrushchev, again acted as the supreme judge and condemned the excesses and Khrushchev's idea of agro-cities, although he would not lift a finger to rescue the peasant from hunger or agriculture from ruin.

After Stalin's death a party plenum on agricultural matters was convened on Khrushchev's initiative. It was, indeed, an historic plenum. On the one hand taxes on agricultural produce were drastically reduced, especially for private plots; on the other hand state purchasing prices were increased. Later machine and tractor depots were handed over to collective farms, though admittedly for a high price. And at last, a major step was taken towards weakening the tutelage of local and central organs of power over collective and state farms.

Nevertheless, the idea of turning collective farms into state farms continued to nag Khrushchev. Everything points to the fact that he was certain that individual management, particularly on private plots, and collective management were both less efficient than state farms. He thought that state enterprises in the countryside could work just as well as those in the towns. As we have seen, this idea played no small role in the resolution to open up the Virgin Lands. Soviet economists have not yet objectively evaluated who was right in the disputes over ways to improve agriculture in that period: Khrushchev, who advocated opening up the Virgin Lands, or Molotov and others who proposed that these same resources be put towards production in the black earth and non-black earth regions. Of course, the use of the Virgin Lands for a time took the sting out of the grain problem; but no one has analysed the potential of the alternative programme.

It is interesting to note that Khrushchev's personal acquaintance with the experience of American farmers did not make him stop and think, but only strengthened his belief in the superiority of collective and state forms. But from his visit to America he brought back many productive technological methods.

There is no doubt that one of these was the introduction of maize as cattle fodder, despite the excesses that occurred when this idea was put into practice. In America he saw how poultry farming, egg production and the slaughtering of cattle had been industrialized and how agricultural production was combined with the processing of produce. Blinded by his conception of state socialism, Khrushchev wanted Western technology to be used in a centralized economy. How many speeches were made about maize, square pocket planting, fertilizers, chemicalization and irrigated areas! But the dogma that the state should manage the agrarian sector not only remained unshakable but was strengthened.

This tied in with an even more monstrously hasty decision in the sixties that prohibited the keeping of cattle on individual plots, which led to constant shortages of meat and milk products from which we have not recovered to this day. It seemed logical to Khrushchev (despite all the facts) that it was more advantageous to rear cattle on large-scale farms than on individual peasant plots. Life was sacrificed on the altar of doctrine, while the doctrine was borrowed from none other than Stalin.

The same thing can be said of Khrushchev's views on the role of the state in the industrial sector. Even in his declining years in his memoirs Khrushchev continued to criticize Bukharin and other 'rightists' for their attempt to introduce 'cotton-dress industrialization' and to preserve a multi-layered economy and cooperatives. Meanwhile Lenin, in his article 'On Cooperatives', had made this significant declaration: we are reconsidering our entire view of socialism. After Stalin this had become even more crucial. In order to return to Lenin and overcome the political and economic system of Stalinism it was necessary to place the ordinary working person at the centre of domestic policy. It was also necessary to take into consideration the experience of some fourteen socialist countries and to evaluate realistically competition with the capitalist world in the era of the technological revolution. But Khrushchev, meanwhile, continued to cherish completely utopian plans of 'catching up with and overtaking America' in the context of state socialism and worried most of all about the 'principles of Communism'. Principles are needed, and as Lenin said, people need ideals, but sensible ones . . .

As a realistic politician Khrushchev was scared to rock the boat; such freedom would inevitably go hand in hand with emotional excesses, destructive outbursts and uncivilized polemics. But as has been known from the most ancient times, in politics there is no such phenomenon as the absolutely positive or the absolutely negative. It is always necessary to choose the resolutions which will give the most productive results. And can there be any doubt about whether to reveal or conceal problems when contrasting two methods? *Glasnost* is a sword which heals the wounds it inflicts. This was said by Lenin.

Whatever happened during the cult of personality – whether planes and trains crashed or national conflicts erupted – everything remained silent as the grave. In fighting against his supporters in literature, science and the press, Khrushchev did not allow *glasnost* to develop. But *glasnost* is the mirror of the people and the people are not scared in so far as 'there's no point in blaming the mirror . . .' Indeed, one has to change the face of society so as not to complain about the mirror.

At the Twenty-Second Congress Khrushchev was already lagging behind public expectation. He continued to think that the place of Stalin in the history of our country remained the most important subject of controversy. But that was wrong. This had been the main target of the Twentieth Party Congress. In effect Khrushchev had given a straight answer then, even if with some reservations. The main target of the Twenty-Second Congress was a different one, that of the system of administration that had developed in the Stalinist era.

Seneca said that a bad mistake often acquires the importance of a crime. Stalin's obvious crimes had already been revealed and exposed. But all those mistakes that had entered so deeply into the Soviet system of administration continued to live and hinder the country from moving forward in Khrushchev's times. Few people even then openly defended the repressions of 1937. But there were many who shared Stalin's mistaken ideas and Khrushchev, alas, was one of them. That is why no scientific criticism was made then of Stalin's conceptions, which justified state socialism and the totalitarian control over society and the individual.

Under the influence of Stalinist views the Soviet experience from the thirties to the fifties became the standard by which socialism was to be judged. Everything that did not resemble this model, for example, in the countries of Eastern Europe, was seen as a deviation from socialism. Moreover, whenever these countries – Yugoslavia, Hungary, Poland – brought out a new and efficient way of developing their societies those surrounding Khrushchev would assume the pose of 'defenders of purity' and declare, 'This is not socialism. It contradicts fundamental principles.' Deviating towards capitalism was the least serious accusation. Being 'an enemy of the people' was the worst.

Khrushchev must take his share of the blame for our suspicious attitude, during the course of twenty years, to the Yugoslav and Hungarian reforms and to the discussions of socialism in Czechoslovakia and other Eastern European countries.

8 Eisenhower and Kennedy

It was only a few months after Stalin's death that we began receiving signals from the political Olympus indicating a new approach to foreign policy. In 1953 the Korean War was brought to an end at the Soviet Union's initiative. Two years later a peace treaty was signed with Austria. We heard rumours that members of the top leadership were proposing substantial changes in relations with the West.

The oddest report we received was after the arrest and execution of Beria. A secret Central Committee letter claimed that it was Beria who, as a provocation, had made a number of radical proposals aimed at international detente. These proposals allegedly included the unification and neutralization of Germany, in other words, the elimination of the German Democratic Republic in payment for peaceful coexistence and possibly also for Western economic aid. This was one of many proposals made by Beria in a kind of feverish agitation to the Presidium, probably in an attempt to change his image as Stalin's most malicious and zealous heir. Nobody was taken in by this posturing, however, even before Beria was arrested. But the fact that on that occasion he had to play, albeit with marked cards, in favour of international detente was significant. Both the intelligentsia and the party apparatus were becoming increasingly dissatisfied with the Cold War and were coming to realize that the atom bomb posed a totally new threat.

Who was it who prepared the material that went into Khrushchev's main speech at the Twentieth Party Congress? The name D. Shepilov has been mentioned: he also helped to prepare the secret speech on foreign policy. Unfortunately, in June 1957 that gifted theoretician showed himself to be an unscrupulous intriguer ready to defect to any side as long as he remained in the winning team. For the sake of justice, it must be said that even in his very first speeches G. M. Malenkov was making conciliatory noises in the direction of the capitalist countries: he spoke of our desire for improved relations and economic cooperation.

The Twentieth Congress saw the first major attempt to breach the iron curtain of the Cold War. Up until then both we and the Americans, as well as the Eastern and Western Europeans, had, in effect, acted on the assumption that armed conflict was inevitable, or at any rate that military confrontation and rivalry were insurmountable. Each side had a totally false picture of its opponent's aims. Stalin, and with him Khrushchev, was convinced that imperialism was set on destroying our system at all costs – on returning the countries of Eastern Europe to the capitalist fold at the very least, with the final objective of restoring capitalism in the Soviet Union. The West, in turn, was convinced that the Soviet Union and the Warsaw Pact were preparing to attack Western Europe and would, at a suitable moment, stretch out the hand of 'fraternal internationalist aid' to the Communists in those countries. Both Marxists and non-Marxists regarded the division of the world into two hostile camps as elementary and the two views fed off one another.

But then, at the Twentieth Party Congress, Khrushchev made the first attempt to smash this stereotype. He declared that world war was not fatally inevitable. He put forward the principle of peaceful coexistence as a basis for East–West relations. And from this he bridged the gap to the still viable concept of solidarity and fraternity between the socialist countries, and all peoples fighting for the victory of socialism in the modern world, with the idea of a peaceful parliamentary transition to the new society in the West.

One cannot say the idea was entirely new: back at the Nineteenth Party Congress Stalin had addressed a brief speech to the Communist and workers' movement. He proposed that the Communist Parties hold high the banner of bourgeois democracy and bourgeois freedoms that had allegedly been thrown overboard by imperialism. As we know, it was on Stalin's initiative that the concept of a peaceful parliamentary transition was written into the keynote document of the British Communists, 'Britain's Path to Socialism'.

Nevertheless, Khrushchev's statement at the Twentieth Congress caused a sensation. It may have made less of an impact on Western political leaders, who place more faith in real practical steps than in verbal statements, but in the USSR, particularly amongst party workers and humanitarian scholars, it seemed like a time bomb.

At the same time, the speeches at the Twentieth Congress were notable in that they preserved a range of stereotypes from the Stalinist era – above all, that the ideological struggle was inevitable, a struggle which would not only help to preserve the socialist system in those countries where it had triumphed, but also further the victory of socialism on a global scale. And bound up with this was a rather vague interpretation of the methods of supporting the liberation movement. This was later widely used as a justification for interfering in the affairs of various countries in the form of 'internationalist aid'. The Twentieth Congress failed to explain when and on what terms such aid could be given. It was left entirely to the discretion of the leaders and to their assessment of a given situation. There was, in fact, one fundamental restriction that was declared at that congress, and particularly in the 1960 Statement of the Communist Workers' Parties: the impermissibility of 'exporting revolution' or of 'exporting counter-revolution'. But as soon as 'exportation of counter-revolution' was established or assumed, 'exportation of revolution' inevitably followed, and this meant not only political assistance and arms deliveries, but where necessary military assistance as well.

I remember the bitter struggle that flared up in the journal *Kommunist* – where I was working at the time – over the correct interpretation of the principles of peaceful coexistence and peaceful transition to socialism. The vast majority of academics and party functionaries was hostile towards these concepts, and it was an uphill struggle to publish any article attacking the orthodox view.

Responsibility for ideological guidance still lay in the hands of M. Suslov and P. Pospelov – deeply conservative men who knew no other Marxism than what they had learned from Stalin's works. The appointment of A. Ilyichev as Ideology Secretary of the Central Committee changed little, partly because Suslov still had a decisive influence on theoretical matters, and partly because Ilyichev himself trailed far behind Khrushchev's innovations in political theory.

Thus, the ideology and policy of power confrontation between the two systems remained. The Cold War perhaps no longer existed in quite the same form as in Stalin's time, but the Thaw taking place in the country's domestic policies had not yet arrived.

It is true that the Soviet style of diplomacy began to change decisively. Stalin, as is well known, disliked and feared travelling abroad. The only trip outside the Socialist bloc he made as the country's leader was to Teheran, and it was probably that experience that put him off taking risks once and for all. Not only did he never visit Western Europe, he did not even tour the countries of Eastern Europe. In all likelihood the main reason for this was spy mania, his fear of becoming the victim of a terrorist attack. This aside, however, it was also an organic part of the Iron Curtain psychology: if the country was to be isolated from the outside world then the supreme leader should not set a bad example to the other leaders, and especially not to ordinary citizens. The one exception was the Potsdam meeting. Stalin took part in it because he had no other option and because it was to be the climax of his triumph in the Second World War.

Khrushchev, by contrast, not only liked but adored travelling abroad. Not for nothing did his colleagues complain in whispers about him constantly 'knocking about' abroad and around the Soviet Union itself instead of staying in Moscow. There was hardly a month in which

153

he did not go abroad, particularly after 1960. He went to Poland, East Germany, Czechoslovakia, Hungary, Romania and Yugoslavia many times. He visited China several times and the United States twice, as well as India, Austria, France and Britain. In short, he travelled a considerable part of the world in a total of about forty foreign trips.

That was the first step towards opening up our society. The West had the opportunity of seeing a Soviet leader in the flesh and there were many Westerners who breathed a sigh of relief. The 'Communist devil' turned out to be not so terrible after all. Khrushchev readily gave interviews, he was constantly in contact with journalists, he talked openly with a great deal of humour, he told jokes and reacted straightforwardly to pointed questions. The figure of Stalin – dark and monumental like a tombstone – which to Westerners had epitomized the Communist regime had been replaced by the living, unconstrained, mischievous, crafty and rather simple figure of Khrushchev.

Before moving on to foreign policy developments, I ought to say that it was precisely in this area that Khrushchev's adherence to the stereotypes learned from Stalin was strongest. In part this was because during the Stalinist period Khrushchev had played virtually no part in deciding or discussing international matters. He had simply been briefed – and even then only after the event, not on all the issues and certainly not on every aspect of each issue.

In his memoirs Khrushchev himself recalls that people were supposed to know only what was 'their due'. Khrushchev had never shown any inquisitiveness over foreign policy secrets, which were regarded as the preserve of Stalin, Molotov and possibly Beria, but certainly not of all members of the leadership. He knew very little about the pact with Hitler, the causes of the war with Finland, the secret protocol on the Baltic states and Western Ukraine, and the Korean War.

Similarly, he had been kept in the dark about the development of Soviet nuclear and ballistic weapons, about the level of sophistication of weapons prompted by the rivalry with America and the possibility of a nuclear war. He had blindly accepted at face value any explanation he was given, and in the course of the entire 'glorious decade' barely reviewed any of Stalin's major foreign policy moves. The withdrawal of our troops from Austria and the ending of the Korean War were, perhaps, the exceptions to this rule, but even those decisions had been reaching fruition while Stalin was still alive.

This, then, explains the great enthusiasm with which Khrushchev grasped the reins of foreign policy on reaching the pinnacle of power. Initially his role was insignificant, as foreign policy was handled by Molotov, who was regarded as the top authority in the field. In the two-year period from 1953 to 1955 the Soviet Union launched several

154

important initiatives aimed at reconciliation with the West. It is hard to say what role Khrushchev played in this, but there is no doubt that he was involved in the decision-taking. In their subsequent arguments Khrushchev accused Molotov of delaying the treaty with Austria and opposing the restoration of relations between the Soviet Union and Yugoslavia. From this one may deduce that Khrushchev had sought a revision of East–West relations from the very outset.

★

Khrushchev's meeting with President Eisenhower in Geneva in 1955 began a period of intensive contacts with Western leaders. The discussion between the two men centred on Germany. Although no agreement was reached, both sides tacitly accepted the reality of the existence of two Germanies. Neither the United States nor the countries of Western and Eastern Europe had an interest in reunification, as that would have meant the restoration of a powerful Germany with an unpredictable future policy.

In 1956 Khrushchev visited Britain with Bulganin. His first major opportunity to become acquainted with the West, however, was in 1959 when he took a large delegation to the United States at the invitation of Eisenhower. That trip made an enormous impression on Khrushchev. Above all, he was struck by America's technological and economic achievements and was particularly interested in private farming. Strangely, however, he devoted more attention to farm management methods than to production relations. It was there that he became obsessed by maize. He learned a great deal about seed stock efficiency and was introduced to high-productivity cattle. He visited slaughter-houses and food-processing factories. On returning to the Soviet Union he began to champion all the methods he had seen. Yet he remained a convinced advocate of the collective and even state farm system, considering it potentially far more productive by virtue of its industrial nature.

In 1960 one of the most important summit meetings was held – between Khrushchev and Eisenhower in Paris. To this day that meeting remains the subject of improbable assumptions and doubtful conjecture. There was supposed to be a discussion of the German problem, diplomatic recognition of the German Democratic Republic being something to which Khrushchev attached major importance. This was also important as it would be a pledge of European stability based on a recognition of the status quo. Soviet–American relations and the limitation of the arms race were also to be discussed.

As far as I know, there were major arguments within the Soviet leadership over the preparations for the summit. Khrushchev himself was racked with doubt. The Soviet Union was still far from nuclear and missile parity with our United States, though our programme was going ahead at full speed. Suspending that programme might have meant consolidating American superiority for a long time to come. If during the Cuban Missile Crisis two years later it was acknowledged that the Americans had seventeen times more nuclear warheads than the USSR, at the time of the Paris summit the ratio was even higher. Nobody could seriously expect the Americans to agree to disproportionate arms limitation and especially not to a reduction in their nuclear missiles, bringing them closer to the Soviet level.

There were also doubts surrounding the Americans stance on East Germany. All the signs were that the United States was not willing to grant diplomatic recognition, nor to confirm the frontier between it and Poland. For Khrushchev arms limitation was closely linked to the stabilization of the situation in Europe. They formed a single complex of issues from which no one element could be extracted alone.

Most of all, however, Khrushchev was uncertain about the position of Mao Tse-tung. Mao was resolutely opposed to Soviet–American rapprochement. He was convinced that this would be detrimental to Chinese interests and would confirm the positions of the USSR and the USA as the two powers that 'command the entire world'. In addition, China had embarked on its own nuclear programme.

The Soviet Union had initially helped Mao in developing an atomic bomb, in particular by building a heavy water plant. But to the best of my knowledge, this aid ceased in 1956, to the disappointment and intense annoyance of Mao Tse-tung. This was probably one of the reasons for Mao's opposition to Khrushchev and his policies. Khrushchev himself, in the meantime, could hardly disregard the views of his great ally, and at every stage in relations with the United States and Western Europe he constantly glanced over his shoulder to check the expression on the face of the Chinese sphinx.

In spite of all this a whole package of important proposals, plans and agreements had been put together on the eve of Khrushchev's meeting with Eisenhower. I was involved in the discussion of some of those documents and to this day I remain convinced that if they had been accepted, either wholly or in part, both the Berlin crisis and the Cuban Missile Crisis, as well as the subsequent terrifying twist in the arms spiral, could have been avoided.

Khrushchev's hesitation played a fateful role. The tiniest thing could have tipped the scales in the other direction; and that thing was the American U2 reconnaissance flight over the Soviet Union not long before the Paris summit. The aircraft was shot down by a Soviet missile and the American pilot – Captain Powers – was taken prisoner.

It is hard to say exactly how this incident influenced Khrushchev's thinking. He may have been genuinely outraged over the Americans' perfidy in continuing their reconnaissance flights over the USSR despite the warmer relations and the forthcoming meeting. But I am more inclined to believe that Khrushchev's outburst was a pretence, since both before and after that incident he regarded secret activities by the USA and even the USSR, along with perfidy and blackmail, as inevitable elements of the relationship. I know that just before flying to Paris Khrushchev called a meeting of the Presidium in the airport and proposed scrapping all the proposals and documents that had been prepared, on the grounds that it was a bad time for an agreement in every respect.

The enormous amount of work put into drawing up the Soviet position by diplomats, party workers, the military and other services was reduced to nought. Soviet–American relations were set back by the stroke of the pen. I do not believe that Khrushchev's feelings were the main factor in that decision. Most likely he had reached the conclusion that we stood to lose more than we gained from agreements at that time. Like a sword of Damocles the dark shadow of China loomed over the entire process of improving relations with the West. Nor could Khrushchev ignore the unabating pressure from Ulbricht who, for understandable reasons, wanted to make diplomatic recognition of East Germany the main precondition for a breakthrough in Soviet–American relations.

And so, on arriving in Paris, Khrushchev began play-acting. He demanded formal apologies from Eisenhower and when the latter refused to give them the meeting was called off.

When I think about this episode I am most troubled by the thought that politics is a graveyard of lost opportunities. I am convinced that slow but consistent progress along the path of curbing the nuclear arms race could have begun thirty years ago. In the end, as all the subsequent events showed, this was the central issue. Yet both sides, each for its own reasons, failed to realize this: the Americans, because they knew they had a massive superiority in nuclear weapons and falsely believed this would continue for ever; the Soviet leaders, because of their permanent inferiority complex as a result of the Americans' superiority. As a great power that had played a crucial role in smashing Fascism and with a huge army and infinite resources, the Soviet Union could not come to terms with the idea of American superiority. An historic chance to stop the arms race was missed.

Psychological factors were also at play. Eisenhower, a calm and reasonable man, could not understand Khrushchev's outburst. What was in fact caused by an inferiority complex appeared to him defiant and aggressive, a desire to humble America, particularly in the eyes of its NATO allies. The Americans underestimated the importance of the German issue for the Soviet Union. Both then and later the fact that the

United States was so late in recognizing East Germany and the status quo in Europe played a fateful role. They had to do so in the end, so why not back at the start of the 1960s? With its nuclear superiority the United States could have portrayed such a step as a magnanimous act of good will and thereby laid the foundations of a psychological and political breakthrough in relations with the Soviet Union.

*

Khrushchev's annoyance over the Americans' lack of flexibility was especially evident during his trip to New York in the autumn of 1960 to take part in the UN General Assembly session. It was made even stronger by the fact that the African states failed to support the Soviet position on Congo. Nor did the UN respond to the idea of setting up a 'trio' to perform the function of Secretary-General or to Khrushchev's criticism of Dag Hammarskjold. Finally, UN members thought his proposal to transfer UN headquarters to a European country extremely odd. It was then that an incident occurred which to this day makes many in the West smile and even sneer.

During a speech by the British Prime Minister, Harold Macmillan, Khrushchev took off his shoe and started banging it on the table in front of him. An American friend, Professor Jim Blight, told me how ordinary Americans reacted to this, taking his father, a farmer, as an example. Jim asked him if he knew who Khrushchev was and he replied: 'I remember him well: he was the one who banged his shoe in the United Nations, and even gave our farmers lessons on how to plant maize.'

Khrushchev gives quite a different account of the incident and the reasons for his behaviour in his memoirs. He says that he was terribly exasperated by the members of the Spanish delegation sitting directly in front of him. He even remembered one of the delegates – a thin, elderly, balding man with grey hair, a wrinkled face and a pointed nose. His face, as Khrushchev put it, was not flat but stretched forwards. Khrushchev took a terrible dislike to this man, not personally but because he represented Franco's Spain.

Looking at this Spanish delegate Khrushchev recalled that prior to his departure for the States he had met the General Secretary of the Central Committee of the Spanish Communist Party, Dolores Ibarruri, at a reception in Moscow. She had made the following request: 'It would be nice if you could find a moment, either in a reply or in your speech, to denounce Franco's regime in Spain.' Khrushchev was looking at the Spanish delegate and wondering how he could do this without it looking too crude. And in his speech he did indeed level some very sharp criticism against Franco, describing his regime as reactionary and ruthless in the tone usually adopted by the Soviet press.

158

It was during the reply speech by the Spanish delegate, according to Khrushchev, that the entire Soviet delegation began shouting and causing a commotion, while he himself took off his shoe and started banging it as loudly as possible on the desk.

There are certain discrepancies in the accounts of this episode. Western representatives maintain that Khrushchev's unparliamentary gesture was made during Macmillan's speech, not the Spaniard's. But this is not the point. The main thing was that Khrushchev saw nothing unusual in such a gesture, because representatives of the working class were by no means obliged to employ the same methods of diplomacy as representatives of the bourgeoisie. And it was in that spirit that he reacted to Nehru's characteristically tactful observation that such behaviour was wrong. 'Nehru and his policies are one thing,' Khrushchev argued. 'He's a neutralist and is therefore taking up a stance between the socialist and capitalist countries. But class proletarian diplomacy is quite a different matter.'[1]

I have subsequently heard a further explanation from Khrushchev's son, Sergey Nikitovich. During meetings we had with Professor Blight at the end of 1988 in the restaurant of the House of Soviet Writers, he told us that Khrushchev thought that in America, with its noisy and crude manners, where one could boo any singer or politician, such forms of protest were quite normal . . .

I myself was not in America during that visit by Khrushchev, but I did discuss his UN speech and that strange gesture with other advisers, and no matter how we tried we could not find any explanation or justification for it. More and more one had an impression of Khrushchev as a progressive but not entirely balanced figure who had yet to gain experience of dealing with world leaders. Indeed, in general, the work of our republican and regional secretaries and their virtual isolation from the outside world was really the very worst kind of diplomatic education.

It was Stalin, in fact, who began a practice which was later developed and firmly established during the Khrushchev and Brezhnev periods – that of assigning to diplomatic work leaders of republican or regional party organizations who, as a rule, had put a foot wrong somewhere. Some of them naturally mastered their new profession, especially if they were given training in the Ministry of Foreign Affairs. But the majority continued to employ the methods they were used to. In the socialist countries and the so-called countries of socialist orientation this did a great deal of harm, since the local leaders heeded their opinions on domestic policy matters, and those opinions were based on notions of the Soviet model of socialism and Stalinist stereotypes. In relations with the Western countries those diplomats were frequently simplistic and primitive in their attitudes, not to mention their breaches of diplomatic conventions. Khrushchev, then, was a fairly typical representative of this 'party diplomacy', as opposed to the real Soviet diplomatic service.

Generally speaking, the Americans, as a rich and powerful nation, never fully appreciated the feelings of others. I am not thinking of the smaller countries, for even the leaders of a great power like the USSR were extremely sensitive to any sign of superiority on the part of the Americans. Khrushchev was no exception: indeed it was he, in particular, who was responsible for our ambitions not only as a great power but as a superpower, in direct imitation of the American style of leadership.

In this respect his feelings before setting off for the US were highly indicative. During the preparations for that visit I often heard Khrushchev's aides remark on his great concern over the protocol to be followed at the meetings. At that time Khrushchev was chairman of the Council of Ministers but not of the Supreme Soviet; in other words, he was the head of the government but not head of state. Consequently, the protocol might be of a lower level than if he were visiting America as chairman of the USSR Supreme Soviet Presidium.

Khrushchev began negotiating with the American Administration via diplomatic channels, insisting that he be regarded both as party and state leader. Without beating about the bush, he made it clear that the reception he was to be given should be identical to that to be given to Eisenhower in Moscow. This might seem a secondary issue of little importance, but for Khrushchev it had a kind of symbolic significance – not only for him personally, but as a symbol of US recognition of political parity with the USSR.

In his memoirs Khrushchev observes that if one were to pick at straws then his pretensions had been somewhat exaggerated, but still he wished to rule out any possible discrimination, especially as he suspected the Americans were tempted to put the Soviet leader 'in his place'. In the end, however, the Americans accepted the proposed protocol. One can just imagine Khrushchev's childlike delight on hearing this.

At a rally in Vladivostok on 6 October 1959 after his visit to the United States he had the following to say: 'As I stood in the aerodrome near Washington before departing from America, the salute of nations was given in honour of our motherland, just as during the welcoming ceremony. I was delighted to hear our national anthem and the twenty-one cannon salvos. After the first volley I thought, "That's in honour of Karl Marx, the second – Friedrich Engels, the third – Vladimir Ilyich Lenin, the fourth His Majesty the working class, the toiling people! . . . And so on, one volley after another in honour of our motherland and her people. Not bad, comrades, not bad!'[2]

This sense of inferiority was evident in many other remarks by Khrushchev. He recalled that at the end of the war when Soviet rule had finally found its feet, the bourgeois world had been obliged to enter into contact with it. Those contacts, however, were 'unstable and shaky', and whenever it had any opportunity to take a stab at or humiliate the Soviet Union the bourgeois world did so. Hence Khrushchev's concern that Camp David would turn out to be precisely the kind of second-rate, insignificant and little-known place to which the President would invite him for a few days in order to humiliate him. Later, once Khrushchev had been to Camp David and seen how prestigious the meeting was, he observed, 'I now feel a little ridiculous and ashamed.'

The same inferiority complex troubled him in relation to the talks with the US President. Strange as it may seem, most of what he knew about America came from Maxim Gorky's book *The Yellow Devil*, which had been written in a completely different era and, as is well known, with wounded personal feelings.

Khrushchev was also worried about the prospect of a tête-à-tête with Eisenhower without either Gromyko or his other advisers at his side. He anticipated arguments and the discussion of complex issues, and was most concerned about how to put up a reasoned and dignified defence of the Soviet position 'without humiliating myself or going too far'. He himself said that he had suffered from this inferiority complex since Stalin's time. Stalin missed no opportunity to convince his colleagues that they were 'good-for-nothings', that they would be incapable of standing up to imperialism as worthy representatives of the motherland, that 'the imperialists would trample all over us'. Such were the feelings of the great peasant's son as he prepared to meet the famous general and president of a great country. Eisenhower probably suspected none of this, as he was preparing to welcome the Soviet leader with all pomp and ceremony. And that welcome really did surpass all Khrushchev's expectations.[3]

*

John F. Kennedy's victory over Richard Nixon in the next presidential election met with Khrushchev's full approval. The Soviet leaders and public opinion in the country had always been more sympathetic towards the Democrats than the Republicans. This was a tradition that stretched back to the time of Franklin Roosevelt, who was not only the first to grant diplomatic recognition to the Soviet Union in 1933, but was also the more reliable ally in the great 'trio' during the Second World War. In addition, it was known that blacks and other low-paid sections of society usually voted for the Democrats, and this was seen as a positive factor from the point of view of the traditional 'class approach' to assessing events abroad. And finally, Khrushchev found

Kennedy more attractive as a person than Nixon, especially after what became scathingly known as the 'kitchen debate' with the latter.

From the very start, Khrushchev rated Kennedy higher than Eisenhower. While he appreciated Eisenhower's great military services during the Second World War, he took a sceptical view of his politics. John F. Kennedy, on the other hand, was a young, energetic and outstanding new president who inspired Khrushchev with hopes of a radical improvement in Soviet-American relations. One cannot exclude the fact that Khrushchev, with his extensive experience of politics and life in general, thought he would be able to exert greater influence and pressure on Kennedy than on the experienced 'political wolf'. Khrushchev, therefore, willingly accepted Kennedy's proposal that they meet in Vienna, a meeting which took place in June 1961.

Khrushchev went to Vienna with quite different feelings from those with which he went to Camp David. Not only had he gained confidence, he had even become somewhat self-opinionated. If before his meeting with Eisenhower he had been concerned not to lose face, before meeting Kennedy he was more preoccupied with how to put the young president 'in his place' and secure the concessions he wanted from him.

On reading the stenographic record of those talks between the Soviet and American leaders, I was greatly surprised by the amount of attention devoted to ideological matters – capitalism, socialism, the principles of relations, etc. As far as practical issues were concerned, Khrushchev and Kennedy were unable to agree on a single point. This was partly because Kennedy treated the meeting as an opportunity to get to know Khrushchev and, perhaps, to warn him; and probably also partly because Khrushchev had set unrealistic objectives which he considered attainable. Once again, he was most of all concerned with the German question. He wanted the US and the other Western countries to grant East Germany diplomatic recognition and to legitimize the division of Germany into two states. He said he wanted the Western powers to get out of West Berlin and even returned to the idea of having three Secretary-Generals in the UN.

Kennedy did not agree to any of these demands. And as far as I am aware, there was no serious discussion of any specific aspects of Soviet–American relations.

The two leaders left that meeting with mixed feelings. Kennedy now knew that in Khrushchev he had an intelligent and sensible colleague. But he was quite unclear what the real motivation and objectives behind Soviet foreign policy were. Khrushchev, on his return to Moscow, admitted that Kennedy had made a far better impression on him than Eisenhower as someone who was capable of looking at relations with the Soviet Union in a new way. There was no doubt that the young president inspired respect in him, but he seemed 'too refined', or in other words, not capable of taking firm decisions in critical situations. To understand this attitude better (I learned of it from the advisers who accompanied him to Vienna), one must remember that it was in a struggle against the 'party intellectuals' that Khrushchev himself had come to power. People like Kamenev, Zinovyev and Bukharin un-questionably lost out in Khrushchev's eyes precisely because they were 'debaters' and 'ideologists' rather than down-to-earth practical politicians. It seems to me that Khrushchev's notions of intra-party struggles influenced his judgement of the American President.

It was a serious error, as Khrushchev was to realize during the Berlin crisis and the Cuban Missile Crisis, particularly the latter.

*

In 1963 I accompanied a party delegation led by Khrushchev and including Andropov to the seventh congress of the Socialist Unity Party of Germany. My first impressions of Berlin were strange ones. Even as we drove through the city I saw Germans in military uniform looking astonishingly like the old uniforms familiar from war films. The city itself looked quite gloomy and deserted, almost as if under siege. I was particularly struck by Pankow, the residence in which our top party and state leaders were accommodated. All roads to that residence were blocked with barriers manned by a special guard.

I cannot resist mentioning one or two amusing incidents of an everyday nature. The Germans had not been given an exact list of the officials accompanying the delegation, or else they had been told to expect fewer than were actually coming. The residence they provided was too small for all of us, which is why, for the first and last time in my life, I had to sleep in the same bed as another man. His name was Yelizar Ilyich Kuskov.

After a solid meal we went to our room. In it stood a fairly broad bed with two pillows and two blankets. They were feather blankets and rather short – enough to cover your legs or chest but not both at the same time. I'll never know how tall people managed to sleep under such blankets. No sooner had we gone to bed than my friend struck up a snore of exceptional volume and extraordinary musical variety. I nudged him gently. He woke up, apologized and then turned over and began snoring worse than before. I put up with this until four in the morning, when I went to another room and shared a bed with another man . . . But I digress.

At that time the tension of the Berlin crisis had not yet subsided. We were taken to the Brandenburg Gate and shown the wall, patrolled on opposite sides by Soviet and American troops. It was the first time I had seen it, and what a sinister picture it was. In no other socialist country was there such a sensation of being in a fortress under siege.

In my view the Berlin crisis was an overture to the Cuban Missile Crisis and in a way prompted Khrushchev to deploy Soviet missiles on Cuba. Khrushchev could not understand why the United States and its NATO allies were so stubborn in refusing to grant East Germany diplomatic recognition and to consolidate the post-war boundaries in general. In his eyes this was not only an example of the Americans' traditional strongarm policy, but also an underestimation of Soviet might. In the meantime, the Soviet Union had conducted a series of nuclear weapons tests, including tests on a powerful hydrogen bomb, as Khrushchev so proudly announced at the Twenty-Second Party Congress.

Khrushchev was infuriated by the Americans' total lack of reaction to the radical changes in the correlation of nuclear-missile forces, and their continuing to behave as if the Soviet Union was still trailing far behind.

It has to be said that the United States really did underestimate the new situation. They were intoxicated by the figures proving their numerical superiority in nuclear warheads, missiles and other delivery systems. They failed to realize that the Soviet Union had accumulated huge stocks for a devastating retaliatory strike and that the whole concept of American superiority had largely lost its meaning. Does it really matter how many times one side can destroy the other? It is enough to acquire the capability of doing so once only. The Soviet Union acquired that capability in the early sixties. This was a new factor in the correlation of strategic forces and it dictated a new policy. But the Americans were in no hurry to acknowledge that anything had changed. Khrushchev thought that some powerful demonstration of Soviet might was needed. The Americans had to be put in the same position as the Soviet Union. Berlin was the first trial of strength, but it failed to produce the desired result. Then the idea arose of deploying Soviet missiles with nuclear warheads on Cuba, in the underbelly of the United States.

The Berlin crisis and the wall dividing the city were, and still are, the subject of numerous indignant commentaries and explanations. This makes it all the more important to turn to the primary source, that is, to what Khrushchev thought, said and did during that crisis.

Khrushchev believed that the stabilization of the situation in Europe and secure recognition of the German Democratic Republic were crucial for the political climate not only in Europe but worldwide. It was in Germany that the greatest NATO and Warsaw Pact armed forces were concentrated. Berlin was therefore a kind of barometer of the international climate.

It is well known how much effort Khrushchev put into achieving a peace treaty with the two Germanies. He saw this as a major guarantee against an armed conflict. He was hoping to legitimize the state of affairs that had come about in Europe on the basis of the Potsdam agreements, to bring the military confrontation to an end and to legalize the existence of two German states – one socialist, one capitalist. From the very start he was willing to make West Berlin into a free city with special status, but only on the condition that a peace treaty be concluded.

In addition, Khrushchev was under great pressure from Walter Ulbricht, who was worried both about East Germany's political prospects and its economic problems. He complained that people from West Berlin were purchasing huge quantities of food in East Berlin, where it cost less. Then, of course, there was the problem of emigration. On the one hand, the brain drain, the outflow of intellectuals and qualified workers, and on the other, the feeling that East Germany's social and political structure was unstable. It was Ulbricht who first thought of building a wall in Berlin and firmly fixing the boundary between the two parts of the city.

As for Khrushchev, he had not only this on his mind, but also the U2 reconnaissance flights over Czechoslovakia and the other countries of Eastern Europe. This was giving rise to incidents: Soviet fighter planes were frequently forcing down aircraft that had crossed the frontiers of East Germany or Czechoslovakia without permission. The result of all this was a decision to close West Berlin to all means of transport except aircraft, as nothing could be done about this. And so the Berlin crisis began.

Dealing with the tricky question of the Berlin Wall in his memoirs, Khrushchev dwells in particular on the freedom to choose one's place of residence. He was disturbed by the argument used by Western officials and press that it was the socialist countries that were compelled to prohibit their citizens from visiting other states. This, they said, was not a question of people choosing where to live, but of being forced to live in those states. In short, 'they are forced to live in a paradise which they cannot leave' since the borders are guarded by troops. Khrushchev's reply to this was that it really was a failing, but only a temporary one. It was connected with material capabilities. If those capabilities had been better in the socialist countries it would have been easier to solve the problem. And interestingly, he saw the main advantage of socialism as what he called 'socialism's moral capabilities'.

From his point of view, of course, the dictatorship of the working class could not grant absolute freedom, but neither did the capitalist countries. The mass of the people, however – the majority even, according to Khrushchev – regards the problem of freedom or non-freedom in relation to how many basic essentials – potatoes, meat, shoes and other material goods – one can buy for a rouble or a dollar. And unfortunately, noted Khrushchev, neither East Germany nor any other socialist country was yet able to compete on this basis.

At this point Khrushchev turns on the hypocrites and dogmatists: 'Some of our smart-Alec Communists will say that this belittles our capabilities and so on. But let's take a sober look at things, as it were, because if we had greater material capabilities and satisfied these material requirements to a greater extent people would undoubtedly be happy with what they have and would not be crossing the border in such large numbers.'

Khrushchev talks about his dream of transforming East Germany into a window on the Western world, an outpost attracting the working people of the capitalist countries both ethically and politically as well as by its material achievements. 'Unfortunately,' he observes, 'we have not yet accumulated such capabilities; unfortunately, all we can give is promises. But it will happen, of that I am sure, though probably not soon.'[4]

So typically candid! Khrushchev's honesty generally won out over his cunning, though, of course, he was often cunning as well. And yet he always strove for sincerity and truth.

Being a realist, Khrushchev never thought that the Berlin crisis was fraught with the danger of an armed conflict. He was convinced that the West would swallow the pill. He was not very moved by the demonstrative actions of President Kennedy, nor by the fact that Kennedy dispatched additional troops to West Berlin or that Clay – a Second World War general – was appointed commander, or even by the fact that American tanks were moved right up to the wall itself and stood face to face with Soviet tanks for a while. Khrushchev had appointed Marshal Konev commander and Konev was ostentatiously present at the Twenty-Second Party Congress which was being held in Moscow at that moment. As Khrushchev stated: 'We were confident that there would be no armed conflict. How could we not have been, since the commander we had appointed was in Moscow at the Party Congress.'[5] The Americans drove bulldozers up to the border, followed by tanks and then jeeps carrying GIs. The Soviet tank crews calmly waited for the bulldozers to approach, before turning round and moving towards the Americans. It so happened that the American jeeps overtook the bulldozers and crossed the border. The Soviet commanders exercised restraint and let them through, but when the Americans saw they were surrounded by Soviet troops with Soviet tanks emerging from the side streets they turned round and went back to West Berlin.

Here again Khrushchev demonstrated his good sense. On hearing about this tank stand-off from Marshal Konev he proposed withdrawing our tanks and was confident that the Americans would do the same. He even predicted that no later than twenty minutes after the withdrawal of Soviet tanks the Americans would follow suit. During the Twenty-Second Congress Konev came to Khrushchev to report that exactly twenty minutes after the Soviet tanks had departed the American tanks did indeed turn around and head back into West Berlin. This, in Khrushchev's view, meant de facto recognition of the borders and the new order, after which border control was placed in the hands of East German officials. To the end of his days Khrushchev considered that to be a great victory – a victory without a single shot. The German Democratic Republic was now able to control its own territory and borders, which helped to stabilize the situation inside the country and created normal conditions for state administration.

It is interesting to note how much the East's view of the Berlin crisis differed from that in the West. It was a time at which Soviet objectives were totally misunderstood by the Americans and Western Europeans. All kinds of assumptions were made: that it was a trial of armed strength, a change in the military balance in Europe and even a provocation that might set off a nuclear war. The real objective lay on the surface and was repeated by Khrushchev several times: to reinforce East Germany's position as a sovereign state and to stabilize the situation in Europe.

9 The Cuban Missile Crisis

It was 27 October 1962, the day that Robert Kennedy later described as 'Black Saturday'. That morning I met Belyakov outside the house on Kutuzovsky Avenue where we were living. Cars had been sent for the two of us with instructions to bring us to work urgently.

'Have you sent your family off to the country, Fedor?' Belyakov asked unexpectedly.

'No. Why should I want to do that?'

'Because there may be a sudden nuclear strike against Moscow,' said Belyakov. 'The bow-string is stretched to the limit and the arrow may fly at any moment.'

To be honest I did not believe him at the time, although I realized that the situation was extremely serious. Five days earlier in a speech on American television, President Kennedy had demanded the removal of Soviet missile installations from Cuba and declared a marine blockade of the island, diplomatically describing it as a 'quarantine'. Since then hardly anyone in the Kremlin or the White House had gone to bed at a normal time. Both capitals were gripped with a nuclear fever which threatened to spill over into a nuclear exchange.

Incidentally, many years later (in 1987) during a conference on the Cuban Missile Crisis in Harvard University, I learned from Robert McNamara, Mac Bundy and Ted Sorensen – all former members of the US administration – that the President had instructed the families of White House staff to leave Washington or at least to be near a telephone. In America, as in Moscow, many were in fear of a sudden nuclear attack.

Working in a department which, amongst other things, was responsible for maintaining contact between the Soviet Communist Party and the Cuban leadership, I soon became involved in preparing documents connected with the Cuban Missile Crisis. Once it was over I was instructed to work on the text of Khrushchev's speech to the Supreme Soviet, which was to give a detailed explanation of the Soviet position during the crisis, the causes of what had happened, the Soviet–American talks and the final agreement.

168

Access to information and involvement in discussions, mainly with Andropov and his advisers, but also with Khrushchev's aides, enabled me to form a judgement on that most dramatic event in post-war history. Before discussing the Cuban Missile Crisis itself, however, there are certain events of the Cold War period that must be recalled. Otherwise it will be impossible to understand the origins of the crisis and especially the psychological backdrop against which it unfolded, or to understand how Khrushchev could decide to send missiles with nuclear warheads to Cuba and then withdraw them.

It is an interesting fact that both of those decisions were denounced by the Chinese leadership of the time: the first as adventurism, the second as capitulation. In reality, the Cuban epic was a fairly logical outcome of the development of Soviet–American relations during the Thaw. Like a flash of lightning it highlighted the absolute senselessnes of the thermonuclear rivalry that had preceded it, the full danger of the old policy, and demonstrated irrefutably that a change was needed in relations between the two nuclear giants.

I have already spoken of the political and psychological link between the Berlin crisis and the Cuban Missile Crisis. Now a few words on events in Cuba itself.

Only three years before the crisis a revolutionary government headed by Fidel Castro Rus had taken over in Cuba. And although the US administration had little sympathy for his predecessor – the dictator Batista – it was hostile towards the Cuban revolutionaries' victory from the very start. The Americans may have been alarmed by the new government's demand that they abandon the Guantanamo base and by the attempts to blockade it. It may be that the American leadership paid too much attention to Cuban émigrés who had organized a strong anti-Castro lobby in Florida. It may have been Castro's speeches in which, from the very outset, he set out his aim of demolishing America's domination of the island. It is hard to say what the reason was. But one way or another, virtually the day after Castro's victory Washington embarked on a policy of bitter confrontation with his government.

In 1960 the Americans stopped buying Cuban sugar, thereby placing the country on the brink of economic disaster, and on 2 January 1961 the USA completely broke off diplomatic relations with Cuba.

At that time Castro was neither a Communist nor a Marxist. It was the Americans themselves who pushed him in the direction of the Soviet Union. He needed economic and political support and help with weapons, and he found all three in Moscow.

In February 1961 Mikoyan visited Cuba, and in May of the same year diplomatic relations were established between Cuba and the USSR.

In the meantime, the United States continued to escalate its misguided policy. In April 1961 the Americans supported a raid by

Cuban émigrés against Cuba. There was a fierce battle between the landing force and Castro's soldiers on the south coast near Playa Largo and Playa Jiron in Cochinos Bay (the Bay of Pigs). The fighting lasted seventy-two hours. In the end the assault was not only foiled, but a considerable number of the émigrés were taken prisoner. The Cubans seized a large quantity of weapons bearing American markings. Nobody doubted that the operation had the full backing of the US administration.

In his memoir about the Cuban Missile Crisis, *Thirteen Days*, Robert Kennedy notes that John F. Kennedy was very hesitant about supporting the anti-Castro operation that had been planned before he came to power. According to Khrushchev's memoirs Kennedy admitted he had taken the wrong decision. Nevertheless, the Bay of Pigs defeat strained anti-Cuban feelings in America to the limit.

Calls were made in Congress and in the press for a direct invasion of Cuba. The Cuban leaders took a series of important military measures in case of a further attack. At the same time Cuban–Soviet relations began to develop rapidly, helped along by significant changes in Cuba itself. Castro was elected First Secretary of the National Leadership of the United Revolutionary Organizations. The Soviet Union decided to give Cuba economic aid, mainly by purchasing Cuban sugar.

In August 1962 an agreement was signed on arms deliveries to Cuba. Cuba was preparing for self-defence in the event of a new invasion by counter-revolutionaries, direct military action by various Central American states or US intervention.

To digress for a moment, I will recount an extremely interesting dialogue that took place at a conference on the Cuban crisis in January 1989 in Moscow between Risquet, a member of the Politburo of the Cuban Party Central Committee, and former US minister Robert McNamara. Risquet said that the Cuban leadership was absolutely convinced that there would be a repeat intervention against Cuba, supported in some form by the United States. This explains Castro's untiring efforts not only to create and equip a strong army, but also to set up a people's militia. McNamara for his part solemnly declared that the Kennedy administration never had any plans to attack Cuba. True, Kennedy was very worried that Castro might deploy partisan movements in Central and South America.

This was a vivid example of how each side completely misunderstood the other. Risquet also stated that although the Cubans were confident they could defeat any invasion by foreign aggressors, they were nonetheless counting on Soviet help. But the Cubans never asked the Soviet Union to deploy nuclear missiles on the island; they were well aware of the tremendous risk such deployment would entail for the Cuban people.

*

The idea of deploying the missiles came from Khrushchev himself. I edited a letter to Fidel Castro dictated by Khrushchev after the Cuban crisis was over. It was a very personal letter, in which Khrushchev openly and sincerely described how he had hit upon the idea of putting missiles in Cuba. It had happened in Bulgaria, most likely in Varna.

Khrushchev and R. Malinovsky, who was then the Soviet Defence Minister, were strolling along the Black Sea coast. Malinovsky pointed out to sea and said that on the other shore in Turkey there was an American nuclear missile base. In a matter of six or seven minutes missiles launched from that base could devastate major centres in the Ukraine and southern Russia such as Kiev, Kharkov, Chernigov and Krasnodar, not to mention Sevastopol – an important naval base.

Khrushchev asked Malinovsky why the Soviet Union should not have the right to do the same as America. Why, for example, should it not deploy missiles in Cuba? America had surrounded the USSR with bases and was holding it between its claws, whereas the Soviet Union's missiles and atom bombs were deployed only on Soviet territory. This was a double inequality of forces: inequality in quantity and in delivery times.

That, then, is how he conceived of the operation, discussing it first with Malinovsky and then with a somewhat broader group of leaders before finally obtaining the consent of the Presidium of the Central Committee.

Less clear was whether it would be possible to deploy the missile installations in Cuba and put them on combat readiness in secret. It was a small island, observed from all sides by American reconnaissance aircraft, and what's more, it was full of American agents. It was unclear whether the Cuban leadership would agree to the Soviet proposal. To decide both of these issues a delegation including Marshal Biryuzov, Alekseyev, the future ambassador to Cuba, and a number of other Soviet military and political figures was sent to Cuba. They thought it would be difficult to explain everything to Castro, but the Cuban reaction surpassed Khrushchev's expectations.

Castro discussed the issue with the entire Cuban leadership and a unanimous decision was taken to agree to the deployment of nuclear missiles. Their main motive for this was not to defend Cuba, but to reinforce the defensive might of the whole socialist camp.

As for whether the deployment could be carried out in secret, a Soviet commission made up of authoritative military specialists concluded that it could be – a mistake that cost Khrushchev very dearly. On the basis of that commission's conclusion, he and the other Soviet leaders took the decision to deploy the weapons in Cuba. One can hardly, of course, place the entire responsibility for that incompetent conclusion on the commission alone. It was obvious to every sensible politician or adviser in Moscow that it would be virtually impossible to conceal the approach of several dozen Soviet ships, not to mention the transportation and installation of bulky missiles on a small island. Nevertheless, Khrushchev with his characteristic ability to get carried away and his tendency to take risks, began the operation.

At the 1989 conference in Moscow Risquet said that at some later stage (probably after the Americans had detected the missiles) Fidel Castro suggested to Khrushchev that he make public their agreement on the creation of a Soviet military base in Cuba. The arguments in favour of such a decision seemed quite sensible, particularly in view of the fact that the Americans themselves had such bases around the Soviet Union and even retained their base in Cuba itself.

However, the proposal was not accepted by Khrushchev. He probably did not believe that he would succeed in openly concluding such an agreement with Cuba. It was, of course, a matter of concerning the sovereignty of two powers – the USSR and Cuba, yet it would never have been accepted by the USA, the countries of Latin America, the United Nations or Western Europe. One way or another, from start to finish Khrushchev believed that the only possibility was to deploy the missiles in deepest secrecy.

What were Khrushchev's objectives? He himself stubbornly insisted that there was only one explanation: to reinforce Cuba's defence capability and to guarantee its protection against invasion, whether direct or indirect, by the United States. He had hinted at this even before the missiles were deployed in a speech on 10 July 1960, when he declared that the United States should not forget that it was no longer as far from the Soviet Union as in the past. He said that the Soviet Union might, if necessary, help the Cubans to repulse armed counter-revolutionary forces using missiles. And two days later in another speech he declared that the Monroe Doctrine was long since defunct.

It is true that in the course of the following year, 1961, Khrushchev several times stated that the Soviet Union did not have nor would have a military base in Cuba. At the same time, he twice protested to Kennedy over interference in Cuba's affairs.

In his memoirs Khrushchev maintains that the idea of deploying the missiles first came to him during his trip to Bulgaria in May 1962. He thought the Americans would never come to terms with the Castro regime. They were afraid that Cuba would become an example to other countries in Latin America (as indeed the Soviets hoped), and they were willing to take extreme measures. This, according to Khrushchev, was why he decided to deploy the missiles.

He realized that first of all there would have to be talks with Castro to explain his strategy and obtain the consent of the Cuban government. Khrushchev reckoned that if he managed to install the missiles the Americans would think twice before taking any military action against Cuba. He realized that America could destroy some of the missile installations, but even if a dozen of them survived this would be sufficient for a retaliatory strike. This would place America in a difficult situation since US businessmen and industrial centres would be under threat of destruction. In his memoirs he even mentions his intended targets: New York, Chicago and other industrial cities. As for Washington, it wasn't worth talking about since it was only a small village. 'America was perhaps never in such danger of being destroyed as at that moment,' observed Khrushchev.[1]

*

Thus, both during and immediately after the Cuban Missile Crisis, as well as in his memoirs, Khrushchev insisted that his only aim in deploying missiles in Cuba was to protect the country against an American invasion. This was stated more than once by Khrushchev's son, Sergey Nikitovich, during the 1989 conference on the Cuban Missile Crisis in Moscow.

I would venture to question this explanation. I had access to information during the crisis and later made a thorough analysis of the documents, and I have reached a different conclusion. The deployment of missiles in Cuba had at least two purposes.

One of these – to defend Cuba – was justly and persistently stated by Khrushchev. Admittedly, that contention may be called into question as the Cubans themselves did not request such protection. On the contrary, they were certain that they were consenting to the deployment not in their own interests, but to strengthen the defences of the USSR and the other socialist countries. To the Cubans, as to everyone else, it was clear that the creation of a nuclear missile base on an island only ninety miles from the American mainland would greatly *increase* the risk of an invasion.

In taking such a risk Khrushchev had, I believe, one further aim in mind – that of altering the strategic balance of force between the USSR and the USA, of giving the United States a feel of what Soviet people had been experiencing during the long years of the Cold War surrounded by American bases on all sides, of demonstrating Soviet might and creating the conditions if not for military then at least political parity. Naturally the idea of a nuclear first strike against the United States never even entered Khrushchev's head: not only would that have been absolutely at odds with his political objectives and his character, but he fully realized that with its retaliatory strike the United

States would devastate the Soviet Union and destroy more than half of the country's population.

It is my belief that Khrushchev's intentions were quite different – to secure new conditions for negotiations with the United States and bring about the possibility of an equitable compromise. By these means he sought to obtain what he had wanted from 1960 to 1962, that is, recognition of East Germany, consolidation of the new status of West Berlin and the post-war borders, as well as serious changes in Soviet–American relations on the basis of detente and the limitation of the arms race.

Khrushchev's thinking was on exactly the same lines as the Americans'. Throughout the entire post-war period and even today many Americans believe that the only way to talk to the Soviet Union is from a position of strength, that the Russians understand no other language. Khrushchev thought the same about the Americans. He thought they were too strong and too self-confident; negotiating with them on equal terms was impossible without first demonstrating one's strength. Both objectives – the defence of Cuba and the alteration of the strategic balance – probably merged into one in his mind: America had to be shown that the position of the USSR and its allies had changed fundamentally.

Why do I find this interpretation of Khrushchev's behaviour so obvious? Let me reiterate that the psychological impetus for putting missiles in Cuba came from a walk on the shore of the Black Sea and a reference to American missiles in Turkey. Later, it was this very issue that was to round off the compromises achieved between Khrushchev and Kennedy. And one more thing: Khrushchev wanted the missiles to be installed at any cost, even after they had been detected. This would have been irrational unless he were hoping to demonstrate Soviet might be deploying missiles targeted on the United States.

Finally there was the secrecy. This secrecy was extremely dangerous for the Cubans. They understood the mentality of the American leaders and public opinion better than Khrushchev, and were clearly aware of the outburst of indignation that would result if the missiles were deployed secretly. To the American mind any deal, even the most sinister and unfair, seemed acceptable if it were passed openly and in accordance with international norms.

Between the end of July and mid-September the Soviet Union dispatched approximately one hundred ships to Cuba. Most of them were carrying weapons. According to American estimates the delivery consisted of forty-two medium-range ballistic missile installations, twelve intermediate ballistic missile installations, forty-two IL-128 fighter-bombers, 144 surface-to-air anti-aircraft installations, plus other types of missiles and missile patrol boats. In addition – as was established quite recently – approximately 40,000 Soviet troops and officers were sent to Cuba.

Naturally this armada of weapons and armed forces could not pass unnoticed by the Americans. Hopes of keeping the whole thing secret, up to and including installation of the missiles, proved to be a gross miscalculation on the part of Khrushchev's advisers and Khrushchev himself. On 16 October the Americans obtained proof of the deployment of Soviet missiles and warheads in Cuba. The information came from a U-2 reconnaissance aircraft, but even before that American intelligence had learned from US agents in Cuba that Soviet missiles were being transported around the island under escort by Soviet troops and officers wearing Cuban military uniforms or in civvies. That same day the information was passed on to President Kennedy.

There is no doubt that the initiative to deploy the missiles in Cuba came from Khrushchev personally. It may have been prompted by Malinovsky to some extent, but this changes nothing in substance. Fidel Castro had not asked Khrushchev for such assistance for the Cuban Revolution, although once the missiles had arrived in Cuba and were being rapidly installed with the completion of the programme in sight, the Cubans, just like Khrushchev, got carried away with the idea. One has to understand here the feelings of a small nation like Cuba faced with a powerful nation like the United States.

The Cubans constantly felt – every day and every hour – that they were living under a sword of Damocles wielded by the United States. They did not know when or how, but they were convinced that their great neighbour would eventually strike a fatal blow. And then, for the first time, they were given the opportunity of shaking a fist at that neighbour, of proving that he too was vulnerable and of giving him a taste of what they were experiencing with the threat of destruction hanging over Castro's regime.

The temptation proved too great, and the Cubans yielded to it. In addition, they hoped that by placing the Americans in the sights of Soviet missiles they could win major concessions.

What were Khrushchev's fears? No American politican or analyst nowadays believes in the possibility of a first nuclear strike by the USSR. And I now think that hardly anyone believed in it during those tense times either, although of course there was the odd hothead, especially among the generals, who argued that Khrushchev intended to unleash a nuclear war. This was absolute nonsense. Moreover, I am certain that Khrushchev not only had no thoughts of war, but never even imagined that deploying missiles in Cuba might increase the risk of war. He firmly believed – blindly and mistakenly – that he could not only deliver the nuclear missiles, but also install them in secret. This he saw as a normal retaliatory measure quite commensurate with what the

Americans had done in deploying their missiles and aircraft with atomic bombs in Turkey, Italy and other areas near the Soviet Union. To him it was a political game in the traditional Cold War spirit, a tug of war with the advantage passing to the Soviet side on this occasion.

Khrushchev reckoned that if he could deploy the missiles and target them on American cities it would be possible to begin negotiations with the United States on more or less equal terms. He could then seek a guarantee of non-aggression against Cuba, towards which the Soviet Union now had obligations as an ally. He could also seek recognition of East Germany and the post-war status quo in Europe. Effective negotiations could then begin on limiting and eventually ending the nuclear arms race. In short, it would be possible to bring about genuine East–West detente based on the principle of peaceful coexistence.

No small role in Khrushchev's thinking was played by ideological stereotypes: capitalism versus socialism, black versus white, who would get the upper hand? With this kind of approach any methods are acceptable. If the imperialists, those oppressors and exploiters of the working class, are at liberty to employ cruel methods, then the Communists, the protectors of the people, the heralds of mankind's great future, are entitled to do the same. He had learned this ideology from Stalin and to the end of his days remained convinced of it. He kept faith with the delusions of his youth. The idea of removing ideology from international relations could never have occurred to Khrushchev, nor to any of his colleagues. Only a quarter of a century later was it to become an organic element of the new thinking.

A few words should be said about our feelings – the feelings of the advisers, aides and consultants who to a greater or lesser extent were involved in those tragic events. We were not, of course, privy to the decision-taking and nobody ever asked our opinions, either on deploying the missiles in Cuba or on the way out of the crisis. That process was in the hands of a narrow group of leaders – above all, members of the Presidium of the Central Committee, the Central Committee secretaries, the Ministers of Foreign Affairs and Defence and heads of the state security bodies. But I am certain that even they had little say. To all intents and purposes, Khrushchev was already an authoritarian leader by that time. And although his fate depended in some degree on the opinions and wishes of the other members of the leadership I do not think that anybody could seriously have opposed one of Khrushchev's decisions.

During the Harvard University conference on the Cuban Missile Crisis in 1987 I happened to see an American television play on this very subject. In fact, our conference began with a video showing of my play, *The Burden of Decision (Black Saturday)*, which had been staged at a Soviet theatre. In it I tried to give a genuine and sympathetic portrayal of John F. Kennedy, Robert Kennedy and the members of the National Security Council executive – McNamara, Sorensen, Bundy and others – during that critical period.

I have to say that I was much impressed by the American actor who played Khrushchev in the American television play. Not only did he manage to look just like Khrushchev and adopt his mannerisms, but he also put across his tremendous feeling of responsibility and the sense of danger of a nuclear crisis. I was delighted to hear that the performance by the Soviet actor Andrey Mironov as Kennedy in my play had also gone down very well among the members of the Kennedy administration, as had my attempt to capture the essence of events in the White House during the crisis.

But there was one thing that I found implausible and even ridiculous – the way in which Khrushchev's relationship with the other Soviet leaders was portrayed. For instance, there is a scene in which Suslov interrogates Khrushchev in accusatory tones about his intentions and strongly opposes any compromise decision. This does not in the least reflect the relationships within the Presidium during that period. It is even less accurate as a portrayal of Suslov, a double-dealing, two-faced man who never said anything directly but always acted surreptitiously and cautiously, afraid of slipping up. It was those very qualities that enabled him to sit out more than twenty-five years as a Central Committee secretary, surviving both Stalin and Khrushchev and dying only one year earlier than Brezhnev.

Naturally Khrushchev consulted with his closest associates, but in the same way as, for example, a general consults with middle-ranking officers. They had less of an influence on him than the information that was coming in, and he endeavoured to obtain this information from the most varied sources – both via the embassy in the USA and, in particular, via the secret service. This may have been the key factor determining the decisions he took, the nature of his correspondence with Kennedy and the terms of a possible compromise.

I would like to recount a conversation I had with one of Khrushchev's aides at that time (I will not name him, since he is still pursuing his diplomatic career). The conversation took place immediately after John F. Kennedy's famous speech on 22 October 1962 on the imposition of a marine blockade around Cuba.

'At least it's now become perfectly obvious that this is a military gamble,' said my friend. 'I never believed that we could deploy our missiles in Cuba secretly. It was an illusion implanted in Khrushchev's mind by Marshal Biryuzov. Even less could one have supposed that the Americans would swallow the pill and tolerate a missile base ninety miles from their border. Now we have to think about how to get out of there fast without losing our dignity.'

I was thinking much the same thing myself, but unlike my friends I did not believe, even in those tense times, that nuclear war was a reality. I knew quite definitely that Khrushchev would not start such a war under any circumstances. And I was also absolutely convinced that Kennedy would not take the fateful decision to launch a first strike either. Neither side had the slightest reason to risk destroying half of its population in a nuclear exchange with other consequences one could not even begin to imagine.

Even then many scientists were saying that if such a quantity of atomic and hydrogen bombs were to be exploded simultaneously there could be an unpredictable global cataclysm. The atmosphere might become detached from the earth, for instance, or the earth might stray from its orbit, or else the entire surface of the planet could be contaminated and all life on it would perish.

With my academic background and tendency towards abstract thinking, I probably fell into the delusion of placing too much faith in the rational foundations of history and human life. War was irrational and therefore impossible. It was only later, having witnessed the escalation of the Cuban Missile Crisis and of the Vietnam and Afghan wars, and the insane stockpiling of many thousands of totally unnecessary nuclear warheads, that I began to feel that history and especially politics are governed not only by reason, but by chance as well. But at that time, I repeat, I did not feel the whole tragic depth of what was happening. Only subsequently, thinking back to those times, did I experience a genuine shock, which is what prompted me twenty years later to write a play about the incident.

Thus, among us advisers, many including me thought that our dear Nikita had overdone it and that, although his motives were pure, the plan had turned into a dangerous gamble.

I recall clearly, however, how my feelings began gradually to change once the crisis was over. There were two factors at work. Firstly, the outcome of that sorry affair was unexpected and in many respects a positive one. We managed to obtain from the United States a guarantee of non-aggression against Cuba as well as an agreement to dismantle the American base in Turkey. But more important still, we achieved a tremendous psychological breakthrough in the consciousness of the American leadership. Like Khrushchev, Kennedy had been profoundly shaken by feeling the breath of nuclear war. Both of them realized that nuclear rivalry could not be regarded as a game of strongarm politics. The stakes were death, but now it meant death not for one person or even one nation, but for the whole of mankind. The fear that both leaders experienced was extremely beneficial. That great warning by the ancients – Remember death! – had taken on a new apocalyptic aspect – Remember the Day of Judgement of all mankind!

The deep sigh of relief breathed by Kennedy, Khrushchev and the advisers involved in the incident was a guarantee that things would never again be the same in relations between the two great powers, just as a spring storm with its thunder and lightning heralds the sunny sky that follows.

The second thing that caused me to reassess the Cuban Missile Crisis was the criticism of our actions by the Chinese leadership. It was they who came out with the well-considered and rather venomous phrase about Soviet policy during the crisis being a tactical gamble and a strategic capitulation.

I was instructed to prepare Khrushchev's speech for the Supreme Soviet meeting after the crisis ended. I had at my disposal a great deal of information and documents of whose existence I had previously been unaware. Khrushchev, as usual, dictated in advance several parts of the speech and these were passed on to us. The dictated passages focussed on a response to the Chinese, from which it was clear that their criticism had cut him to the quick. He was indignant, insulted and irritated. Their reaction to what had happened seemed to him a particularly base attempt to gain political capital from events that had almost led to a nuclear disaster. Particularly dangerous in his view was Mao Tse-tung's renewed endeavours to bring the USSR and the USA together in a fatal clash while himself standing on the sidelines like a monkey on a hill watching the tigers fight, as the Chinese saying goes.

Although I too was indignant over the Chinese attacks, in preparing that speech I, like the others involved with it, had to tone down Khrushchev's criticism of the Chinese position. It was that position that helped me in my own reassessment of the crisis. I began to doubt whether one could describe Khrushchev's deployment of the missiles purely as a military gamble. The outcome had been a positive one in terms of USSR–US, East–West relations. Any hopes of pitting the great powers against each other in a nuclear conflict had evaporated once and for all. So perhaps things were not quite so straightforward.

Even then, of course, as someone who had been primarily educated by the standards of European culture, I found the petty and quite improper tricks that had accompanied the missile deployment quite alien: the deceitful assurances by Khrushchev himself and the other Soviet leaders that we had no plans to deploy missiles in Cuba, which were particularly senseless once the whole world knew that the missiles were there; Khrushchev's fanatical drive to continue the installation while dragging out the correspondence with Kennedy, probably so that having managed to install the missiles he would have a better negotiating position.

Yet I clearly remember that as I worked on that Supreme Soviet speech, I was already starting to reassess everything that had happened, realizing that it was impossible to find any straightforward definition, whether gamble, mistake, miscalculation or bluff. I began to realize that the Cuban Missile Crisis was the final act of the entire Cold War drama. Behind it, as in Shakespeare's play, lay the shadow of Hamlet and the gloomy shadows of those who had begun that war – Churchill, Truman and Stalin. But the happy conclusion of the Cuban scene was proof that those shadows had begun to recede into history.

The new figures – both Khrushchev and Kennedy – had shown themselves to be real world leaders and had demonstrated genuine greatness in finding a way out of the nuclear stalemate without either side losing face.

I watched Khrushchev speaking at the Supreme Soviet session where he first informed the Soviet people of the Cuban Missile Crisis. His face truly shone with happiness. It was not the face of a man who was suffering pangs of conscience or a feeling of guilt because of the sharp criticism from our former ally. No, it was the face of a victor and a peacemaker. Obviously he, just like Kennedy, clearly realized the historic role they had both played during that single moment in human history, when the ancient prophecies of the apocalypse became a reality. It was the face of a man who had saved the world. And everyone in the hall greeted Khrushchev with enormous sincerity precisely as a great peacemaker. At that moment hardly anyone was wondering why Khrushchev had deployed the missiles. But everyone was profoundly grateful that he had agreed to withdraw them. Perhaps only Khrushchev was capable of doing both with equal resolve.

*

Khrushchev's correspondence with Kennedy gives a particularly vivid portrayal of his feelings and psychological evolution during the crisis. We can see the letters gradually changing in tone. If at first he appeared provocative and even aggressive, by the end a feeling of gigantic responsibility for the destiny of his people and the whole of mankind, a desire to prevent a nuclear disaster at any cost, become more and more dominant. As a point of interest, Khrushchev's letters are of a far more personal nature than Kennedy's. This was because Khrushchev dictated his letters himself; although they were later edited this was done in such a way as to preserve not only the basic ideas, but also Khrushchev's mood, style and turns of phrase – something he valued greatly.

Although Khrushchev frequently had to be cunning, considering this an inevitable element of the political game, he was nevertheless, as I have already mentioned, deeply sincere and frank by nature. This is perhaps particularly striking when one reads his letters to Kennedy. I would like to quote a few passages. Here's what he wrote on 26 October, not long after Kennedy's famous speech on the blockade:

Our objective was and is to help Cuba, and nobody can dispute the humanity of our motivation, which is aimed at enabling Cuba to exist peacefully and develop as its people wish . . . You say you are disturbed by Cuba, that it is ninety miles by sea from the shores of the United States, yet Turkey is right beside us and our border guards glance at one another as they patrol. Do you believe you can demand security for your country and the removal of weapons that you call offensive while not granting us that same right? After all, you have deployed missiles of destructive weaponry that you call offensive literally under our noses. How then are we to square the recognition of our equal military capabilities with such unequal relations between our great states? There's no way it can be squared.[2]

That was the letter that so astonished John Kennedy and his advisers. They had received two letters that day. In the first Khrushchev said he agreed to withdraw the missiles from Cuba if the US would pledge not to attack the country. And in the second there was an additional demand – that American weapons of the same type be withdrawn from Turkey.

To this day there is great controversy over how two such different letters could have been sent on one and the same day. To me, however, the explanation seems quite simple. Khrushchev had received additional information from Soviet officials working in the United States that suggested it was possible to win further concessions from the United States, an opportunity that he immediately – and successfully – exploited.

Khrushchev's feelings were particularly vividly conveyed in his letter of 28 October 1962, which formed the basis of the final settlement:

I have a deep understanding of your alarm and that of the United States of America over the fact that the weapons you call offensive are menacing weapons. We, too, realize what kind of weapons they are.

In order to put a rapid end to a conflict that is jeopardizing the world, in order to give confidence to all peoples that thirst for peace, in order to reassure the American people who, I am sure, want peace as much as do the people of the Soviet Union, our government, in addition to instructions given earlier to cease further work on the construction sites for the deployment of the weapons, has issued a new order on the dismantling of the weapons that you call offensive, their packaging and return to the Soviet Union.

We must now be careful and take no steps that do not contribute to the defence of the states involved in the conflict, but can only cause irritation and even act as a provocation for a fatal step. We must therefore be sober-minded and sensible and refrain from taking such steps . . . We are convinced that reason will triumph, that war will not be unleashed and that there will be peace and security for the peoples.

This statement by Khrushchev and his entire style and tone can only be seen as a manifestation of genuine courage comparable, in its sobriety and rationality, with his speech at the Twentieth Party Congress, a triumph over shortsighted calculations in the tug of war with the United States. It was an important lesson for Khrushchev himself. It was an essential lesson for John F. Kennedy. It was a lesson for all future leaders of the two powers and for the whole of mankind.

In his memoirs Khrushchev expresses satisfaction and at the same time real surprise that he, a representative of the working class, and Kennedy, a representative of the capitalists, had not only managed to come to an agreement but had experienced similar feelings over the threat of war and the danger of extremism. In actual fact, the problem was far deeper. The differences between Khrushchev and Kennedy could not be reduced merely to this, nor to the 'opposition of two social systems'. It was the difference between two political cultures – the liberal-elitist (Kennedy) and the authoritarian-patriarchal (Khrushchev). Moreover, it was the difference between two historical and cultural civilizations – the American and the Russian.

The traditions of America are individualism, liberalism, non-interference by the state, supremacy of the law over government and of freedom over equality. Russia's traditions are those of collectivism, patriarchy, state control, elevation of government above the law and of equality above freedom. One way or another, all these features were reflected in the characters of Kennedy and Khrushchev, and lay at the root of their mutual incomprehension and even repulsion. And onto this were superimposed stereotyped notions (revolutionary for Khrushchev, liberal-progressive for Kennedy) of the outside world.

Finally, unlike most Westerners the majority of Russians are emotional rather than rational. This is why we have produced the great literature of Tolstoy and Dostoyevsky but no great philosophers. Russians are greatly inclined to improvisation; they find it hard to plan their lives a week or even a day ahead. History's greatest paradox is that it was the Russians who were first to begin planning the life of society as a whole (and it's no coincidence, by the way, that not a single five-year economic plan has ever been fulfilled). People in the West have very often been wrong in their predictions of the Soviet leadership's behaviour because they place themselves in their position with no understanding of the peculiarities of Russian political culture.

This makes it all the more noteworthy that Khrushchev and Kennedy finally managed to understand one another in that moment of monstrous danger. This testifies to the globalization of world problems,

problems that are surmounting age-old differences between civiliza-tions. If Khrushchev and Kennedy had continued to govern their countries, who knows, it might have been possible to avoid the subsequent twenty-year-long nuclear arms race. For already it was clear that nuclear war is impossible; already the concept of arms sufficiency for mutual deterrence had been formulated; already both Russians and Americans had realized that they were simply human beings and not blind representatives of competing systems. Why Providence saw fit to remove both Kennedy and Khrushchev from the political arena remains one of history's enigmas.

As for me, I not only respected but admired John F. Kennedy even before he became a myth after his tragic death. I saw him as the ideal politician for the nuclear age, a man who combined an ability to take decisions with the intellectual qualities of an adviser. Normally these are incompatible: Aristotle could not have been an Alexander the Great, nor Seneca a Nero, Talleyrand a Napoleon or Speransky an Alexander I.

The ability to take decisions is usually found in people with a strong character who will resort to cruel measures if they consider them necessary. Usually they are imperious and, to a greater or lesser extent, authoritarian leaders. The adviser, on the other hand, is too sophisti-cated and sees too many aspects of any situation to take a decision quickly. John F. Kennedy was both at the same time. In addition – and this was a particularly important example for me – he was not afraid to surround himself with a constellation of brilliant and talented people such as McNamara, Bundy and Sorensen.

In contrast to Kennedy, Khrushchev was not drawn to talent. The members of his press group, I. Ilyichev, A. Satyukov, V. Lebedev and others, were no more than average. Andropov was one of the few exceptions amongst the Soviet leaders, but he too preferred to 'hold his advisers above water'; that is, neither drown them nor raise them very high.

10 Advisers

I was standing with L. Tolkunov on the balcony of the first floor of the House of Receptions in the Lenin Hills. This was one of the ten or so buildings constructed on Khrushchev's orders as places for official meetings and residences for prominent guests. The houses were intended for members of the Central Committee Presidium; each one was to have his own separate cottage: not very large – about two or three storeys – and not very small – with probably three or four bedrooms.

These houses had standardized furnishings: solid oak furniture of a light brown hue, large cupboards for clothes and dishes, a sitting room with an extended round table to seat ten or twelve people and the invariable red door curtains and white lace window curtains.

But the main feature of these houses was the high walls surrounding them. Strictly they were not walls so much as one enormous long wall approximately half a kilometre in length and about three or four metres high, built so that no one would even entertain the idea of getting through. Anyway, how could anyone get through when at the entrance to each house stood a sentry-box into which two, three or even four security guards were crammed?

However, the high walls did not restrict communication between the houses as there were gates which enabled members of the Presidium and their families to socialize. I witnessed Nina Petrovna Khrushcheva speaking through the gate to Podgorny's wife about some purely domestic matter, just as their ancestors used to speak through the palings somewhere in the Ukraine. In the old days this was called 'idle chatter', but such conversations here were accompanied with an air of importance in spite of the everyday nature of the subject – they were talking about jam-making or about Siberian meatballs or complaining about the staff.

The House of Receptions was at the very beginning of this row as one approaches from Kiev station and the embankment. It was several times larger than the residential cottages and had a swimming pool, a billiards room and a smoking room – in short, it was fashioned specially for official meetings. It was here that the Sino-Soviet negotiations took place in 1962. M. Suslov headed the delegation, which included B. Ponomaryov, O. V. Kuusinen and several other figures. The Chinese delegation consisted of Peng Chen, Chou En-lai, Deng Xiao-ping and Kang Shen. We were in the negotiations hall as advisers. It was usual for representatives of the intellectual personnel, including the advisers, to gather in the basement where we discussed how the negotiations were developing, put forward proposals and, chiefly, fulfilled instructions – supplying materials and information, quickly sketching out a new document and so on. Incidentally, it was here that I first felt dissatisfied with myself; it was also, I think, the first and only time during that period that I experienced the pleasure of flattery.

Andropov had told me to draft an outline for an open letter on China's position. I began without a second's hesitation dictating to the typist. However, I had not reckoned on the time, and our delegation with Suslov at its head arrived for discussions with the group of advisers before I had finished my work. Nevertheless, as I had instructions from Andropov, I took the risk of handing over the unfinished draft outline of the open letter to Suslov and other members of the Soviet delegation.

This outline had one flaw: instead of a list of the main questions it consisted of two or three initial questions worked out in detail. In other words, it was only half-done. I felt extremely annoyed when Suslov, glancing casually at the paper, put it to one side and rather precisely pointed out other questions which should have been mentioned in the open letter. Partially they coincided with what was in my paper and partially not. I had been put down in front of my friend, Belyakov, who as always had been there when I was dictating and had only nodded his head approvingly.

The proposed list included those issues which were later mentioned in the open letter: problems of peace and peaceful existence, Stalin's cult of personality, ways of going over to socialism in other countries, mutual relations between the Communist parties of the socialist countries in the new context, and several other matters.

The conference did not last long. We immediately sat down to prepare the document, working practically all night, and by morning we were ourselves surprised by what had been achieved. It came out as a rather clear and for the times extremely progressive document on all the controversial issues on which the Soviets were in disagreement with Mao Tse-tung. You could even say that it contained certain advanced ideas, especially concerning peaceful coexistence with the West and an end to the Cold War, as well as establishing guarantees against the restoration of a regime of personal power in the socialist countries. I worked on this last section and the fact that it was adopted by the leadership practically without corrections made me feel rather proud of myself. I also felt a sense of triumph as the vast majority of the apparatus staff at the time held much more cautious and restrained views on authoritarian power.

The next day after the document had been confirmed I was standing with Tolkunov on that balcony, where I began my story. He said quite simply, as if it were a matter of small importance, 'What do you say, Fedor, to the idea of setting up a group of consultants, a sub-department, if we asked you to head it?' I still remember my feelings at that moment. It was a lovely summer's day; we were in shirt-sleeves and ties and I was leaning on the wall of the balcony, my thoughts floating somewhere in the distance.

The offer was totally unexpected, but all the more pleasant for it. It was not just the promotion, as I had never really considered a career in the apparatus. It was more like the feeling of a bright student whose ability and diligence have been noticed by his teacher, and it goes without saying that I did not have Tolkunov but Andropov in mind. Besides, I very much liked the idea of gathering together a group of intellectuals and raising new, crucial matters which might have an influence on reforms in the country. I must admit that this was one of the best moments of my life. Perhaps the only other time I have experienced anything like it was twenty-seven years later when without any special effort I was elected to the Supreme Soviet and even to the chairmanship of the subcommittee on humanitarian, scientific and cultural cooperation.

We all probably have the same psychology. When you are a child you like finding a present under the Christmas tree, not because the present is important – perhaps during the year you had been given far more important things – but because it is unexpected, you had not asked for it, you had not worked on the person – be it your mother or father, your boss or the public – and there it is, having appeared out of nowhere. Several times later, under Brezhnev, I stood for election to the Academy of Sciences. It is true that due to my inherent weakness I did nothing to get elected, thinking it was perfectly obvious to everyone that I deserved it, having written more than ten books. But the 'immortals' who had written, as a rule, no more than one or two books or even no more than one or two brochures would invariably vote me down. Thus, Tolkunov's offer was all the more pleasant and, what was particularly important, Andropov and Tolkunov allowed me to form the group virtually at my own discretion. They did not turn down any of my proposed candidates; quite the contrary, they supported candidates who for those times did not at all conform to the criteria of the apparatus.

*

The first person I chose was my old friend from postgraduate days,

Georgy Shakhnazarov. He had been born into a family with deep roots in the intelligentsia. I had seen his father – a small, frail man with a large bald head and an enormous forehead, who was by profession a lawyer – and I knew his relatives – musicians and members of the other creative professions. Shakhnazarov himself had a rich literary talent and wrote poems, plays and political books. He was distinguished by his warmth and gentleness, especially when he was young, and he had an enormous yearning for self-expression. He was the first person among my friends whom I had commissioned to write an article for *Kommunist*. After that he began to work quite successfully in one of the party journals. That is why in forming my group of 'aristocrats of the spirit' I started with him.

He was one of the few people in whose moral qualities I was not disappointed. I think that at least two characteristics are required for the job of adviser – talent and decency – and there is no doubt that in all cases I was lucky with the former, as all those invited to join the group proved to be original scholars, journalists and public figures. As for the latter, alas, not all of them subsequently endured the test of time. Shakhnazarov was the exception. Although there were periods when he harboured grudges, as his career under Brezhnev did not advance smoothly, on the whole he always retained, especially with his friends, honest, kindly and pure relationships. When I had fallen on hard times he helped me to go on my first trip abroad; and under *perestroika*, when he found himself in the top echelons of party power (in the role of adviser, naturally), it was he who helped me to get back into the political arena.

It was not easy to include him in the group. By the standards of the apparatus he stood out like a peacock. Apart from anything else, he liked to dress exotically: not only did he have a brown suede jacket but a brown suede coat as well, he wore bright trousers and ties, and expressed himself without restraint. I struggled for many months to get the department of party cadres to agree to our department's proposal, and then only for a probationary period. At first Shakhnazarov was sent to the journal *Problemy mira i sotsializma* and it was only six months later that we managed to recruit him as a consultant.

Shakhnazarov brought an element of subtle judgement and elegant style to even the most trivial document which we prepared, especially when it concerned publications in the press. He had a pleasant kindly manner and – a rare quality amongst intellectuals in Russia – the ability to take into account other people's opinions. He looked at everyone, no matter who they were, with warm, velvety and devoted eyes – be it his colleagues at work, the leadership or women, to whom he gave special treatment and who gave him special treatment in return.

Another outstanding person, although perhaps not quite to the same degree, was Aleksandr Bovin. I have never met a fatter man in my life, at least not in political circles. With a massive face of an unhealthy reddish colour, whiskers and sideburns, hazel eyes which might have been beautiful except that they were bloated, an enormous chest and stomach and hardly any buttocks, this figure was at the same time imposing and comic. By the time we met Bovin had already defended two candidate dissertations in jurisprudence and in philosophical science, but out of laziness had never taken his doctorate of science, unlike Shakhnazarov, who received the rank of a corresponding member of the Academy of Sciences.

Bovin had fine minute handwriting, much too legible for an intellectual. He was a master at writing amazingly logical prose, pages and pages of it, and rounding off his thoughts. His analytical style may have been inspired by a deep knowledge of Hegel's philosophy: thesis, antithesis, synthesis. He liked to divide political actions into pluses and minuses, calculating the sum total and making a clear deduction.

I became acquainted with Bovin in unusual circumstances. I was staying in Maleyevka, the writers' house sixty kilometres from Moscow. The verandah, where I was attempting to write my doctoral dissertation, was very stuffy. My neighbour was a woman in the last stages of pregnancy and Bovin used to visit her; soon afterwards she became his wife. I don't know if this was a happy marriage because he did not call her by her first name or her surname but by her maiden name. When he first visited her at Maleyevka he would arrive in strange faded pantaloons, which reminded me of Koreyko's trousers in *The Golden Calf*; they were a brown colour and were supposed to be of the club sort. He carried a small plastic sports bag, no doubt with sandwiches for himself – I don't think he brought anything for his not very beloved wife. I still cannot tell what it was that impressed me about him when we met, but perhaps it was the casualness of his short but precise judgements which bordered on arrogance but were undoubtedly very clever. I invited him to join the group of consultants and he came without any hitches. Politically he was much more cautious than Shakhnazarov, and his reputation was untarnished.

Bovin turned out to be the most difficult person in our group. It became apparent that he could not bear any criticism of his views, even the most polite comments. Later he clashed with Shakhnazarov and got the upper hand during the Brezhnev period, but since *perestroika* he has completely lost out.*

The most prominent of all the people whom I invited into the group was Georgy Arbatov,* whom I have already mentioned. A man of uncommon talent and, it turned out later, a wonderful manager in the

---

* Aleksandr Bovin is currently a political observer on *Izvestiya*.
* Georgy Arbatov is director of the Institute of USA and Canada Studies in Moscow.

Western mould, he had somehow acquired a nasty reputation as a radical and 'heretic' before his transfer to the appartus.

I first got to know of him when I read articles, which were never published, on the sociology of crime, written jointly with another researcher for the journal *Voprosy filosofii* (*Questions of Philosophy*). He was accused of all the earthly vices and was even investigated at a party meeting. It was he who invited me to work on Kuusinen's book. And although he did not treat me with great finesse at the end, I felt it a matter of honour to show generosity and invite this talented man into our group.

When he came to us he brought with him a spirit of intellectual ferment. His thoughts never stood still; they were alive, varied and tireless. He was also tireless in organizational matters. The first thing Arbatov did, for some reason, was to start hanging his coat and raincoat in the hall outside my office. Even then Shakhnazarov joked, 'He's got his foot in the hall but watch out, Fedor, that he doesn't take over your armchair as well.' But I was careless and underestimated Arbatov's minor but very significant gesture. Subsequently it was he who replaced me as head of the group of consultants in circumstances which I shall describe later.

During our sessions with Yu. V., Arbatov would jump up and, puffing on his pipe, stride about the office spouting thoughts, phrases and turns of speech, which were not that impressive but neither were they banal. He paid no attention to the fact that we did not like smoking in the room. Even outwardly, by virtue of his impressive figure, he immediately took up too much space in our small group. The others felt the boat was cramped. It did not enter my head at the time to feel offended, let alone to suspect any intrigues. I was confident in myself and did not want to live and work in the old way.

Aleksandr Bovin was born and lived in Rostov and had retained certain Rostovian features, in some ways similar to people from Odessa, who are a bit more vulgar than is acceptable in decent company. He entered into an alliance right away with Arbatov and became his alter ego and shadow. This predetermined his success under Brezhnev when Arbatov got the job of adviser and speechwriter to that incorrigible lover of literary prizes and scholarly awards.

Several others who had worked as consultants before also joined our sub-department. Among them was the wonderful economist Oleg Bogomolov,* who had worked in Gosplan. His judgements were always sound and he was well-versed in the economic reforms of Eastern Europe. He was sociable, inclined to sensible compromise and rational; his tranquil and rather phlegmatic character and his slightly crude sense of humour brought an element of calm to our often stormy meetings.

A fascinating person, who bore a strange surname, obviously French

---

* Oleg Bogomolov is director of the Economics of the World Socialist System Institute in Moscow.

in origin, was Lev Delyusin. He was an eminent specialist on China. During the bitter skirmishes with Mao Tse-tung he constantly 'hindered' those who wanted to throw aside all restraint. Knowing China well and supporting his arguments with facts, Delyusin would cool the ardour of zealous hacks like Bovin by simply pointing out that such-and-such was not the case, that it had never happened and wasn't possible. He liked the avant-garde arts and was the first to introduce all of us to Yury Petrovich Lyubimov and the painter Yury Vasilyev. He organized our collective visit to the preview of Lyubimov's first production of Brecht's *The Good Person of Setzuan*. For the next twenty-five years our group acted collectively and individually to form a unique bridge between the party leadership and the Taganka theatre. This tradition was preserved under Brezhnev as well.

Delyusin introduced me to Bulat Okudzhava, and since then I have become a life-long fan of this wonderfully talented person. I remember that as early as 1962 at the Central Committee dacha I would play Bulat's songs on my tape-recorder at full volume, shocking the apparatus staff with my unacceptable taste. We often went with Delyusin to see Lyubimov and his troupe and became friends with Volodya Vysotsky. Many members of our group would invite Vysotsky to their homes and he would sing and tell us about himself and the theatre. Incidentally, it was at Shakhnazarov's that Vysotsky sang his song 'The Wolf Hunt'. This song describes how ruthless huntsmen, having staked out an area with red flags, slaughter wolves, while the wolves are too scared to cross the boundary set out by the flags and die helplessly under the fire. I remember that I exclaimed, 'But that's about us! What's it got to do with wolves?' By all accounts, it was precisely this exclamation that inspired Volodya's second song: 'Important people invite me to their homes to sing "The Wolf Hunt" for them.'

Delyusin and I constantly pleaded with Andropov on Lyubimov's behalf. Evidently, as a result of our appeals, Andropov became a patron of the Taganka theatre for many years, probably seeing this as a 'valve' to let off steam. As far as I know, Lyubimov often visited Andropov, not only when Andropov was in the Central Committee but later, when he was in the KGB.

A scene at the British Embassy has become imprinted on my memory. This happened much later, around 1982 or 1983, literally on the eve of Lyubimov's fateful trip abroad. Lyubimov grabbed me by the lapels and deliberately began to speak as loud as he could so that everyone around us could hear: 'Three plays of mine have been prohibited. I shall go to Yury Vladimirovich Andropov. I'll make sure that chemist is punished – he's gone too far' – the 'chemist' being the nickname of P. Demichev, the Minister of Culture at the time, with whom Lyubimov was at daggers drawn.

The powerful group of consultants who had gathered around Andropov did not, of course, intend to limit their activities to writing speeches or fulfilling different directives for Central Committee plenums or party congresses. From the very start our plans were broad, aimed at putting forward initiatives not only concerning our relations with socialist and Western countries, but in domestic policy as well. This became increasingly feasible in view of the considerable intellectual potential in the group, which numbered eleven people. Besides, we were young, strong and believed in the future. Irrespective of our individual qualities – some were more career-orientated, others more concerned with public activity – we were all impelled by a yearning to serve the cause of reconstructing society.

During one of my trips to Prague I met Gennady Gerasimov. He was a young man of rare intellect and charm, who had had several outstanding articles printed in the journal *Problemy mira i sotsializma*, where he worked, and in other publications. He did not tackle theoretical problems, but possessed a distinctive gift for foreign affairs writing and an ability to find an unusual phrase or turn of argument. He also joined our consultants' group.

I was happy during this period but, unfortunately, it did not last long. I was swimming in an environment of clever thoughts, unexpected waves of opinions, entertaining and mischievous jokes. Here's an example: Bogomolov at that time was already amusing himself with amateur filmmaking. One day he filmed our gathering at Gorky's dacha, which is on the Rublyovskoye Highway.

This is a government highway and along it were situated most of the special private dachas of members of the Central Committee Presidium. The dacha that belonged to Khrushchev was, relatively speaking, not very large; the largest belonged to Anastas Mikoyan. Standing on a rise, it was a three-storey old brick house with several separate houses for the servants. It was said that Anastas Mikoyan had had his eye on this house even before the Revolution when he used to visit the cook who worked for the owner – some prince or oil baron from Baku. Mikoyan and his children lived the sweet life there for about sixty years. Driving past this dacha, we would involuntarily glance at this 'proletarian' country estate, amazed not so much by its splendour and grandeur as by the fact that this Baku shoemaker had so early on fixed his eye on this house and grabbed it for himself.

Almost at the end of the Rublyovskoye Highway on the right-hand side was a dacha surrounded by a high wooden fence in which Aleksey Maksimovich Gorky lived during his last years and so sadly ended his days. It was a two-storey manor house with columns and a large hall in which his piano stood. His son lived in a separate building. According to his house staff, Aleksey Maksimovich was intimate with his son's wife; nevertheless, on all accounts, he loved his son dearly. There is a story that he ran from his house to the annexe in winter to see his dying son, wearing nothing but his underclothes and felt boots. It is still unknown what his son died of. Persistent rumours circulated that he was poisoned on Beria's orders. That night cost Aleksey Maksimovich his life; he caught a cold which turned into pneumonia and soon afterwards he died.

It was at this dacha that important party documents were prepared. The dacha was perched on the edge of a precipice and at the bottom, curving like a snake, flowed the soft serene Moskva river.

Bogomolov filmed all of us in different poses at this dacha and the film came out not at all badly, capturing our different characters quite accurately. Belykov would sit in state in his armchair outdoors, warming himself in the sun, and as always uttering words of wisdom. I would sit not far from him and our housekeeper, a simple and straightforward woman, would say, 'There's Belyakov – he's Stalin, and Burlatsky – he's Lenin' to everyone's general amusement.

On the whole the atmosphere among our small collective was first-rate. If we exclude two people whom we inherited from the previous apparatus, all the people in the group were original, unusually talented and hungry for change. Andropov liked this colony of free intellectuals. After many hours of endless conversation on the telephone, ticking off officials left, right and centre, he would relax listening to our chatter on all sorts of issues concerning high politics.

I myself found this company pleasant and interesting and habitually brought forward people to introduce to Yu. V. As I have never suffered from an inferiority complex I had no fear of competition. My friend Shakhnazarov frequently warned me, 'Watch out, Fedor, you're making a mistake introducing every consultant to Yu. V. and Khrushchev. Sooner or later this will cost you dearly.' I would reply, 'I want to create a new style of doing things in the apparatus – without all this jealousy, scheming and intrigue. Even if I lose out in some way, perhaps it will help to establish a new model.' 'Well, maybe,' Shakhnazarov would note ironically, 'all the same, be more on your guard with each of them and more cautious.' Shakhnazarov proved to be wiser than me, although he himself at the time underestimated that common phenomenon in which a person can be both a genius and an evil-doer at the same time.

*

No other member of the group had access to Khrushchev. Here I retained a monopoly, although this was not deliberate on my part; rather, Yu. V. was careful to protect my authority and invariably took me with him to summit meetings or sent me on my own if he was not included in the delegation. Later he began to include me in party and government delegations, such as the visits to Hungary and several other countries. In this way, despite the virtual equality of all the consultants, the distance between them and the heads of departments was retained for purely administrative reasons. This is what I could not easily get used to later when we changed places. Most of them were promoted to high posts during the Brezhnev era, while I was pushed to the periphery. My vanity would not allow me to reconcile myself to the new balance of power in our group; the group practically fell apart. But there were also other, more important political reasons. After the cataclysms which befell me under Brezhnev, my friends stopped phoning me, and I did not phone them. Such are the rules of the game on this rung of the political ladder. In difficult times it's every man for himself; in successful times it's one for all.

We were the first team of consultants in the Central Committee apparatus. Yu. V. was a pioneer in this as well. He realized before anyone else that it was necessary to make use of the intellect in the political life of a generation of leaders who could neither write, perform or devise political strategy. But they did know what methods to use to strengthen their power and preserve it. This one had to give them credit for. In this, of course, they surpassed the 'aristocrats of the spirit' many times over. We were like youngsters compared to these experts at infighting within the apparatus, while they saw us simply as an ideological service. If not us, then others could fulfil the same role.

It is true that the majority of the leadership treated speechwriters with respect, as the ability to use pen on paper was a mystery to them. But almost never did they regard the consultants as having any serious claim to an independent political role. Here the instinct of self-preservation was at work. Promotions to different posts passed over the consultancy group. It is interesting that Yu. V. was no exception to the rule. In a short space of time Andropov replaced all the leaders of the department sectors exclusively with people from the Komsomol. He believed in their devotion and commitment and their administrative talents.

An interesting exception was our 'fraternal' international department, headed by B. N. Ponomaryov. Ponomaryov, who liked academic and journalistic work but did not have the talent for it himself, treated his consultants differently. Very soon after our sub-department was formed he set up a group of consultants in his department headed by Ye. I. Kuskov. Some quite serious people joined it. It was interesting that in contrast to our department, Ponomaryov drew people from this group for promotion to prominent posts. Practically all his deputies came from his consultants' group; in particular, Belyakov, Kuskov, A.

Chernyayev and V. Zagladin* became First Deputies. Ponomaryov continued this tradition under Brezhnev as well.

Soon consultancy bodies began to appear in other departments as well. The ideological departments, such as the departments of agitation and propaganda, science and culture joined the general trend, to be followed, surprisingly enough, not only by the economic sub-units but by the cadre sub-units of the apparatus as well – the call was, 'Let's bring in the intellectuals.' Consultancy groups began to spread like mushrooms, forming a new section of functionaries who talked in a different jargon closer to the academic, journalistic and literary world than the traditional style of the apparatus. It is true that practically none of this numerous team ever 'grew up' to the level of political leader. The highest posts they attained were as members of the Central Committee and First Deputies in charge of a department. But at least the consultants formed a reserve for high posts among the scientific and cultural elite. Having worked five or six years in the apparatus, they would become directors of institutes and academicians, receiving prominent posts in the Ministry of Culture, universities and so on. It seems I was the only one who missed out on these appointments, but I had done a great deal to harm myself at practically every stage of my career, especially in the Brezhnev period.

By the way, I accidentally almost joined Brezhnev's closest entourage. This was still under Khrushchev – I think in 1963 – when Tolkunov summoned me and unexpectedly, with his habitual smile, asked me without any preamble, 'Fedor, will you take the job of aide to the chairman of the Presidium of the Supreme Soviet, L. I. Brezhnev?' Tolkunov had just returned from Africa where he had accompanied Brezhnev, and Brezhnev had asked him to find an adviser on international matters. I said immediately, without thinking, 'No, I won't.'

I had decided once and for all that I would not work as anyone's aide. Even before this there had been hints at the possibility of working with Khrushchev. During his trip to Bulgaria his aides, Lebedev and Shuysky, sounded me out on this matter. But as I had refused to be Khrushchev's aide, it did not even enter my head to be anyone else's, especially someone I knew so little of and who seemed so insignificant as the then chairman of the Supreme Soviet.

Tolkunov then asked me to recommend someone else to the post. The devil only knows what induced me to suggest Siksotov, an adviser in the Foreign Ministry.

I had got to know Siksotov not long before while working on a joint

---

* Today Chernyayev is an aide to President Gorbachev, and Zagladin an adviser to the President.

document. He had pleasantly surprised me by his talent for quickly grasping an idea and equally quickly writing up sections or even dictating them. I only realized later that his expressions were standard Foreign Ministry clichés. He had simply become a practised hand, having worked for a long time on documents in the ministry. The first time he appeared in my office – a frail, old-looking man despite the fact that he was no more than forty – he wore an odd suit with a kind of provincial checked tweed jacket and threadbare trousers. I don't know whether it was his literary talents or his humour that impressed me more, but I gave his name to Tolkunov. Siksotov did become Brezhnev's aide and remained in that post until Brezhnev's death.

He hated me all his life with the hatred of a person who strives to overcome his feeling of gratitude for service rendered. Or perhaps he could not forgive me for my jokes, which I thought were playful but which he may have considered offensive. For example, we used to fool about with his surname, Siksotov (which sounded like 'seksot', the acronym for secret security agent); in the end our colleague was forced to change his odd-sounding surname to the mundane Alekseyev. He took his pension in Gorbachev's times with all honours and under his new surname.

*

The 'powerful group' of progressive thinkers who had gathered around Yu. V. very soon aspired to working out major problems of domestic and foreign policy. Analysing the experience of Yugoslavia's economic reforms and Hungary's political reforms after 1956, we came to the conclusion that much of what had been done there could be utilized in our country, not mechanically of course but in a creative way. We studied the tumultuous processes of integration taking place in Western Europe, enviously comparing the Common Market with the slow, bureaucratic processes of economic cooperation within the framework of Comecon. We thought of bringing our country into contact with modern technology and the best achievements of world civilization and world culture. In other words, we dreamed of reforming Russia.

Of course, not all the members of our group were equally radical. Perhaps Shakhnazarov and I felt the need for reform more strongly than the others. As for Arbatov and, in particular, Bovin, they were more interested in strengthening their own positions, although there is no doubt that they also held progressive views. I had a small misunderstanding with Bovin, which spoiled our relationship for decades to come.

He had accompanied Yu. V. to the People's Democratic Republic of Korea (North Korea) and, evidently, had held some outspoken conversations with him. When they returned Yu. V. asked me to have a talk with Bovin about his hostile feelings towards the apparatus and his arrogance about top functionaries. This was the first and only time I reprimanded anyone in the consultancy group. I found a pretext to invite Bovin to come and see me and told him of Yu. V's displeasure. I thought that I did this in the most delicate and friendly way.

Nevertheless, for many years Bovin, especially when he became Brezhnev's closest colleague and speechwriter, would recall that I had come on strong and banged my fist on the table when talking to him. Quite honestly, I don't remember anything of the sort, but such rancour simply amazes me. Offended and upset, Bovin began to depend even more on Arbatov as his patron and protector. In reply to my reprimand, he let drop the remark that, on the contrary, Yu. V. had supposedly told him during their visit to Korea that he would not be against Burlatsky's taking another job, as he had a good successor in Arbatov. I turned a deaf ear to Bovin's remark, not fully appreciating how loaded it was. Although it was not very noticeable at the time, this was the first sign of a split in our consultancy group, which had just formed into a united collective.

After my departure from the apparatus, which I will describe later, my successor as head of the group of consultants was Arbatov, who later became director of an academic institute. The question arose of a new successor and both Shakhnazarov and Bovin aspired to this post.

At that time Shakhnazarov had brought out a book, *Freedom and Equality*, in which he put forward a number of original ideas, in particular on the relations between party and state, arguing for the restoration of full power to the soviets. According to Shakhnazarov, one of his ill-wishers underlined various sections of the book and sent it to Vorontsov, Suslov's adviser, who reported to his boss the 'seditious' opinions of a consultant in the Central Committee department. As a result, Bovin was appointed head of the group of consultants, while Shakhnazarov was sent off to the journal *Problemy mira i sotsializma*, from which he returned only because of a contact he made with one of the Central Committee secretaries during that person's visit to Prague.

*

Did we sense the imminent threat hanging over Khrushchev's head? Yes and no. What we sensed most strongly was that reform in our country had just begun and that history would give us a chance to carry out the reconstruction of our system in the course of several decades.

At that time we were full of enthusiasm and faith in the possibility of forming a new society not based on Stalinism. Admittedly we found Khrushchev's final moves surprising and even suspicious. His speeches against the intelligentsia simply shocked us, as our sympathies lay with Boris Pasternak, Vladimir Dudintsev, Yevgeny Yevtushenko, Bulat

Okudzhava and Yury Lyubimov. Apart from anything else, we had been friendly with many of them for a long time. As people in the political sphere we were distressed by Khrushchev's harsh utterances about the army, the navy and the top brass. It was a clear challenge. There are things which must be done, but which are better left unsaid. And we found the decision to separate *obkoms* into industrial and agricultural sectors quite inexplicable. In our discussions we studied this decision from all sides and could not understand what its point was: had Nikita Sergeyevich decided to hit out against the functionaries or was he generally considering the possibility of setting up two parties? That decision has remained a mystery to me to this day.

On the other hand, we intuitively began to feel more and more, and I particularly so, that there was a growing danger from different quarters. I clearly remember my conversation with Delyusin when we were skiing at Gorky's dacha. I said, 'Khrushchev has done everything to bring about his own downfall. He has fallen out with the party and state apparatus, the army and the KGB. Anyone bold enough could remove Khrushchev in a flash.' The person who was bold enough came out of the ranks of the Komsomol 'young Turks'. He was A. N. Shelepin, former First Secretary of the Komsomol Central Committee, whom Khrushchev had made a Party Central Committee secretary and chairman of the Commission for People's Control.

Why was the party apparatus unhappy? In the early years of Khrushchev's accession to power he had repeatedly encroached upon the privileges of party and state workers. He eliminated the system of the so-called 'Stalin package' – a sum of money given secretly to the top-ranking members of the apparatus, the press and scientific establishments, which was not taxed and from which party dues were not even deducted. The apparatus allowed Khrushchev a relatively painless victory, as this privilege really did seem ridiculous.

But then Khrushchev turned his sights on a very important privilege – the 'feeding trough' on Granovsky Street, where at different times all prominent party figures have lived. Even to this day the names of Frunze, Tukhachevsky, Kalinin and many others are engraved on this residential building. Opposite the building in the courtyard a 'canteen for medicinal catering' was situated, where good food supplies were handed out at very moderate, subsidized prices. The 'feeding trough' was a unique club for the upper ranks of the Communist Party including, without exception, all the central establishments – the Central Committee and the Council of Ministers, the ministries and departments, the army and the KGB, the press and the Academy of Sciences. Out of the small doors of this building ministers and academicians would emerge, bent down under the weight of their packages and boxes which they dragged to their black cars on their way to or from work. I was eligible for this 'feeding trough' until I was dismissed from *Pravda* in 1967, but I hardly ever went there. In the 'house on the embankment' described by Yuri Trifonov there was a branch of the 'feeding trough' which members of the family could use, and I preferred to leave this to my wife.

Khrushchev prepared a Presidium decision to close the 'feeding troughs' three times, and three times the draft proposal was set aside under different pretexts. At the bottom of the first page of one of the draft proposals was a footnote printed in small letters stating that Lenin himself had ordered these canteens to be opened so as to 'fatten up our comrades' who had suffered imprisonment, penal servitude and the ordeals of civil war. And although this had become completely meaningless by then, when all the ex-prisoners had passed into the next world – many with the help of Stalin – the argument still continued to operate. The apparatus hung on to its privileges, fearing most of all the step that might start an irreversible process.

One aspect of this struggle was an apocryphal story of a conversation between A. Kirichenko, the second secretary of the Party Central Committee, and a man with the appropriate surname of Pivovarov (Beerbrewer), who was in charge of the Central Committee Administration of Affairs. Kirichenko told him, supposedly on Khrushchev's instructions, 'Get on with it – narrow the circle and increase the benefits.' This order, uttered with a characteristic Ukrainian accent, did the rounds among the apparatchiks. And the top leadership's benefits did indeed increase – Chayka cars, as large as tanks, made their appearance, while the right to summon a car to take you from home to work was removed from middle-ranking officials. At that time I often repeated a joke, which also did the rounds of the apparatus and did me no good, that our state had not been set up by Lenin, as we all thought, but by V. Bonch-Burevich, head of the Central Committee Administration of Affairs of the Soviet of People's Commissars, who had precisely defined the table of rank and who was eligible for what – be it a salary, special rations, a flat, a dacha, a car, a special telephone and so on.

At one time Khrushchev made an attempt to stop the use of state cars. When he was in England in 1956 he found out that only the Prime Minister and one or two other ministers had special cars. It was the same in the United States. In the Soviet Union it was estimated that officially more than half a million cars were held for the use of individuals, with one or two drivers per car; not to speak of the fact that many people used state cars unofficially.

However, all Khrushchev's moves against privileges came to nothing, though the apparatus grumbled. The swift turnover in cadres aroused great dissatisfaction. Khrushchev arbitrarily replaced the majority of republican and regional First Secretaries and, it was claimed, planted his own Ukrainian friends in these posts. The final blow was his decision to divide party *obkoms* and *gorkoms** into two sections, industrial and agricultural. No one understood or accepted this new decision. How could one divide an organ of power and set off one part of the apparatus against the other? This was Khrushchev's most unpopular action.

Many people were also unhappy at the increasingly active part played by Khrushchev's son-in-law, Aleksey Adzhubey. As Khrushchev's personal representative, he visited presidents and prime ministers of different countries, and even the Pope, and conducted various behind-the-scenes negotiations which were not reported at the sessions of the Central Committee Presidium.

Khrushchev managed to fall foul of the army command with his jibes about ships being 'old crocs' and 'shooting targets'. He was fascinated by nuclear weapons and missiles as a means of deterrence and increasingly attempted to reduce the army and conventional arms.

As for the KGB, Khrushchev demoted it for the first time to an organization on a par with an ordinary ministry. His KGB chairman, Semichastny, was not even a candidate member of the Presidium and had to grit his teeth at the frequent jabs and insults to which Khrushchev subjected this formerly all-powerful organization. All this prepared the soil for the plot. We watched the growing dissatisfaction, but did not suspect the consequences.

Khrushchev's weak point was his inability to choose a reliable deputy – a Second Secretary of the Central Committee. At first this post was occupied by A. Kirichenko, whom Khrushchev brought from the Ukraine. Tall, sharp, poorly educated though not malicious, this man very quickly provoked the enmity of all the other members of the leadership, who rapidly 'overthrew' him. All of a sudden he disappeared; he had been retired on a pension. He lived in the same dacha as me when he became a pensioner and he would often humbly ask various officials to give him a lift to Moscow. Getting to know him better, I was simply amazed that such a limited person could have clambered up to so high a post.

Another mistake Khrushchev made was to invite Frol Kozlov, secretary of the Leningrad Party *gorkom*, to take the post of Second Secretary. He was known to be a stern, harsh man, who kept control of all matters tightly within his grasp. However, he died soon afterwards. Just before his death – and this story caused a sensation among the apparatus – he asked for a priest to hear his confession. It was said that he had been involved in the Leningrad Affair, which under

---

* A *gorkom* is a city party committee.

Stalin had ended with the Leningrad leaders, Kuznetsov and Popkov, being shot.

And then Brezhnev, of course, who was not the best choice for the post of Second Secretary. In one of his conversations with foreign representatives Khrushchev expressed a high opinion of two leaders – Brezhnev and Kosygin; he also praised Shelepin, who was the prime mover of the plot against him.

Most of all the apparatus was worried by Khrushchev's democratic projects, which were being conceived one after another, sometimes spontaneously but always consistently directed against the Stalinist model of power. After setting up the *sovnarkhozes* which were a serious blow against departmental bureaucracy, and his attempt to restructure the party, Khrushchev thought up an even more radical change to the political system. At the beginning of 1964 one of the deputies in charge of the Central Committee department of agitation and propaganda and I were sent off again to Gorky's dacha to prepare a draft of a new Soviet constitution. We were instructed to put together a preliminary document incorporating all the best proposals and to prepare a memorandum for Khrushchev and other members of the Presidium.

I must admit that we got somewhat carried away and prepared a memorandum on the fundamental principles of a new constitution which sharply differed from the so-called Stalin Constitution adopted in 1936. We proposed that political power should be based on the law and that there should be free elections and separation of powers. As far back as 1957 in one of my articles I had proposed the setting-up of a regularly working Soviet parliament, elections in which several candidates would stand for each seat in the soviets, and a jury system. We included these ideas in the memorandum.

One of its main proposals was to set up presidential rule and introduce direct elections by the people of the head of state. In our memorandum we said that the First Secretary of the Central Committee should be elected and that this post should not be combined with the post of chairman of the Council of Ministers. It was also proposed that each member of the Presidium should stand for top state posts and that the most important decisions should not be adopted by the party but by the organs of state power.

On the whole Khrushchev approved of our proposals. True, he did not like those sections which affected him personally. Andropov passed on to me what he said at a session of the Presidium: 'There are some lads here who propose to remove me from the post of chairman of the Council of Ministers. Well, we'll have to think about that and see if they are right.'

Unfortunately, work on the new constitution came to an abrupt end because of Khrushchev's fall. Two decades passed before the country returned to these ideas.

All this produced an undercurrent of dissatisfaction in different spheres – in the apparatus, the army and the intelligentsia. The storm was approaching, but did Khrushchev sense it? I shall describe what I observed during his last trip abroad.

This was a visit by the party and state delegation to the Prague Summit in the summer of 1964, only months before Khrushchev's fall. Our delegation was staying in Lany, an enormous estate on the outskirts of Prague which was the summer residence of the President of Czechoslovakia. Besides the palace and several villas and hunting lodges, there was a very beautiful park with lakes and a nature reserve, which had a great variety of animals. When I think of the animals I remember the unpleasant feeling I experienced observing the life-style that Khrushchev and that generation of leaders were accustomed to.

The hunting and fishing in the nature reserve were almost the highlight of the visit. The hunters stood their guns on tripods and shot point blank at the gazelles, who came out trustingly to greet each person, as they had been trained to feed from hand. Khrushchev, Gromyko, Marshal Biryuzov and other members of the Soviet delegation succeeded in this way in shooting no less than ten of these elegant animals. In the evening a sumptuous feast was arranged around a fire; Khrushchev was attired in a huntsman's cap and frock coat and elevated to the rank of an honorary huntsman.

I did not take part in the hunt because I have never liked killing animals, but with other members of the delegation and those accompanying them I did some fishing, although this is hardly the word for it. No sooner did you throw in the hook than a trout would bite. Mykhetdinova, the chairman of the Presidium of the Uzbekistan Supreme Soviet, catching yet another fish would cry out: 'Nikita Sergeyevich, look, I've caught another one; it's so large and beautiful.' Incidentally, it was already known in Brezhnev's times that she was involved in corruption and large-scale bribe-taking, but they took pity on her as one of the first Uzbek women who had renounced the yashmak. Two steps away from me Gromyko, with an extremely self-important expression and a stony face, was catching one unfortunate trout after another from the artificial lake.

'When did you put the trout in the lake?' I half-jokingly asked the Czech fisherman who was helping us with our gear. 'Yesterday or today?'

'Three days ago,' he said quite seriously. 'We haven't fed them, that's why they're so hungry.'

He casually shrugged his shoulders. I threw away the fishing rod and went for a walk. I walked as far as the next lake where Marshal Biryuzov was sitting. This was a real fishing area. He was catching carp, using maize as bait. Biryuzov was happy: in a tub next to him two very large carp were splashing about. He, of course, had no sense of foreboding that a few months later he would die in a plane crash in Yugoslavia; the plane crashed into a mountainside as it was about to land in Belgrade.

In the same way Nikita Sergeyevich felt no sense of foreboding either. I had never seen him so happy, contented and even inspired. I attended the negotiations between him and Novotny in one of the most splendid halls of the President's palace in Parnobitki. Novotny was telling Khrushchev about the proposed economic reforms in Czechoslovakia. In fact, in his conversation he developed a fairly wide programme of changes aimed at developing market and trade relations, overcoming bureaucracy and increasing the role of enterprises; in short, all those proposals which subsequently became the basis of Dubček's and Šik's much wider and more thorough programme. It seems that even then, under Novotny, the reform movement had already begun.

Khrushchev only half-listened. The negotiations had taken place after a full luncheon, which as always had been accompanied by two or three glasses of brandy. Khrushchev took out of his pocket the special watch he had been given in America with a cover over the dial, and kept opening and closing it imperceptibly under the table, not looking at the time but simply fiddling with his favourite toy.

'We too are thinking of enhancing the role of enterprises, especially in the regions,' Khrushchev said. 'We have set up *sovnarkhozes* and are thinking of handing over a part of the enterprises to public organizations and giving trade unions a greater role. So this is all very useful.'

It seemed to me that Khrushchev did not understand what Novotny was saying. He always found it alien and even unpleasant to discuss market relations; therefore, he did not react to Novotny's points about developing a market economy.

On the whole the visit went off extremely well. One detail, however, remains etched in my mind. We were in a small room in the President's palace while a report was being read to Khrushchev and the whole delegation on the treaty to be concluded between the USSR and Czechoslovakia. Khrushchev and Andropov were sitting on palatial Empire-style settees in their favourite pose – arms folded on their stomachs, fingers interlocked. Gromyko was sitting opposite in an armchair and I was somewhere on the side. Gromyko was reading the draft treaty, which was being held in front of him by one of the heads of a Foreign Ministry department. The treaty was a rather large document, which as always was mounted in a red-leather cover. A rather curious scene took place. The diplomat who was holding the treaty in front of Gromyko (as if he could not hold it himself) felt that Andrey

Andreyevich was a bit uncomfortable, so he got down on one knee to make it easier for Gromyko. This apparently was not enough, so the diplomat got down on both knees by the side of Gromyko's armchair, carefully turning over the pages of the treaty as he did so. Nobody was particularly surprised by this scene. The picture of a prominent Foreign Ministry official on his knees, mechanically turning over the pages for his boss, was like something out of the Middle Ages, and quite offensive. I took it to heart. 'Watch out, Fedya,' I said to myself, 'you will be reduced to this if you don't get out of this game in time.'

I often remembered this scene after I had decided to leave the Central Committee apparatus. It was a very strong warning. I knew the diplomat, a man who was in his own way an unusual person with a strong character, erudite and well-known for his spiteful attitude to subordinates by which he compensated for his fawning obsequiousness to superiors. He subsequently became an ambassador to one of the most important Western countries. But for me this scene was a lesson which I remembered my whole life. When my ordeals began I would repeat to myself, 'No, I will never kneel.'

As for Khrushchev, there was not a shadow of doubt in his mind that his position was stable. On the contrary, everything indicated that he was more confident of himself than ever. All his opponents had been expelled from the Presidium and those who remained were almost exclusively men he had promoted himself. His word was law and he felt all-powerful. It was the culmination of his life: the apotheosis of power and the apotheosis of blindness. Only a few months and only one step separated him from his total downfall. Truly, when the Lord decides to destroy someone he deprives him of his reason. This is what happened to Khrushchev.

The farewells in Prague and the return to Moscow were triumphant. Brezhnev was the first to embrace Nikita Sergeyevich, making a smacking sound with his lips, kissing him and affectionately putting his arms around his shoulders. Then Podgorny came up with a joyous smile on his obtuse face, followed by Suslov, grinning ambiguously, who also shook Khrushchev's hand for a long time. After him came Shelepin with a rather stony face. All the plotters had assembled. And in the best Byzantine tradition they poured balm on the man they were preparing to stab in the back.

11 Brezhnev

In October 1964 a group of us from two Central Committee international departments were staying in a dacha out of town. On Khrushchev's direct instructions we were drafting an important document on foreign policy. There was pressure on us to hurry. Several times a day secretaries from the Central Committee would check to see how much we had done. Fortifying ourselves with coffee and other 'drugs', we were agonizingly giving birth. Suddenly the telephone stopped ringing. The day passed, then another day and still not a sound. An old friend of mine said, 'Go to Moscow and find out what's happening. This silence is rather suspicious.'

I arrived at Staraya Square. I went into the office and the first thing I sensed was the suspicious silence. No one was in the corridors, as if they had been swept away with a broom. I looked into the rooms where people were sitting in twos and threes, whispering under their breaths. I bumped into Suyetukhin, who said, 'You scribblers! While you sit and write people are seizing power!' Finally I found out what was going on. The Presidium of the Central Committee had already been in session for two days. All the members of the leadership had spoken. They were criticizing Khrushchev, proposing that he step down 'at his own request'. True, there was also another rumour that someone wanted him to stay on as chairman of the Council of Ministers. Either this did not work out or the rumour was false, but at the October 1964 plenum it was decided to adopt the statement that Khrushchev was leaving 'at his own request'.

Not long ago the journal *Ogonyok* published the reminiscences of Khrushchev's son, Sergey Nikitovich, in which he writes about the plot against his father and his enforced abdication of power. These reminiscences cast additional light on many of the events of that ill-starred period. It turns out that Khrushchev received information several weeks earlier that a plot was being hatched against him, but he had taken virtually no measures to prevent his downfall. One reason, it seems, was that he had received the information from his son and had not attached enough importance to it. He behaved like all other charismatic leaders who are deeply convinced of their lucky star. Besides, he fully trusted Brezhnev and especially Shelepin and Semichastny, whom he personally had promoted to high posts. One of the main reasons for Khrushchev's passivity in this critical situation was his confidence that Mikoyan would check the information which Sergey Khrushchev had received. Sergey had been informed by V. Galyukov, one of the security guards to Ignatov, who was actively involved in the plot. But Mikoyan let Khrushchev down. Evidently he sensed that Khrushchev's goose was cooked.

Sergey describes in detail how the security guard rang his father's flat on the government line and, not finding Khrushchev in, asked Sergey to meet him secretly. By a strange coincidence this assignation took place near the house at 22 Kutuzovsky Avenue where I lived at the time. Sergey probably fixed the meeting there because Khrushchev's granddaughter Yuliya lived in the same house. Later, on Galyukov's suggestion, as he feared he was being followed, they went out of town and Galyukov passed on the important details of the coup that was being organized.

Sergey told his father and Khrushchev asked Mikoyan to deal with it. Mikoyan invited Galyukov and Sergey to his house, which was a few hundred metres from Khrushchev's in the Lenin Hills. Galyukov related everything he knew in detail, including the fact that Brezhnev, Podgorny, Shelepin and Semichastny were involved in the plot. Mikoyan's reaction was strange, to say the least.

According to Sergey, when Galyukov finished his story Mikoyan remained deep in thought. Finally he turned his head; there was a determined expression on his face and his eyes were shining. 'Well, all right. I have no doubt that you have passed on this information with good intentions and I thank you. I would just like to say that we consider Nikolay Viktorovich Podgorny, Leonid Ilyich Brezhnev, Aleksandr Nikolayevich Shelepin and the other comrades to be good Communists, who for many years have selflessly given all their energies to the good of our people and the good of the Communist Party and we continue to regard them as our colleagues in the common struggle!'

Mikoyan asked Sergey Khrushchev to draw up a detailed report of the conversation. Sergey conscientiously fulfilled this task, but missed out the words spoken above by Mikoyan as he thought they were unnecessary. Mikoyan insisted firmly that what he had said be included word for word in the report and even glanced over Sergey's shoulder to see that there were no mistakes.

When he had finished writing, Sergey handed the report to Mikoyan. Mikoyan looked attentively at the final paragraph, thought for a while about something, and then handed the papers back to Sergey, saying, 'Sign it.'

Sergey signed it. Mikoyan noted, 'Now it's all right,' then opened a wardrobe and shoved the file under a pile of shirts.[1]

Interesting details, wouldn't you say? Sergey Khrushchev, who is still very friendly with Mikoyan's son, draws no conclusions. I shall try to make them for him.

Judging from Sergey's account, Mikoyan did not show the report to Khrushchev. He only described it to him in general outline and, evidently, in reassuring tones. Therefore Khrushchev took no counter-measures. In Sergey's account there is the faintly perceptible suggestion that his father had himself renounced the fight on the grounds that he was tired. I cannot accept this version; no, Khrushchev was a fighter, a real fighter! One need only remember the Twentieth Party Congress, or June 1957, or Hungary 1956, or the Cuban Missile Crisis. Khrushchev was still in good working form. Something here doesn't quite fit.

I think Khrushchev realized that this time it was useless to fight. It had all been conducted more skilfully than in 1957. The Central Committee apparatus, the KGB and even the army, which was headed by Khrushchev's friend Malinovsky, no longer submitted to him. Even his closest colleague, Mikoyan, was scared to take up the fight in earnest. There was nothing he could do about it. He just had to put his large head, so unruly in the past, under the inevitable blow of fate.

I am sure that Khrushchev's spirit was not broken. He was only seventy years old and could have gone on longer. Moreover, psychologically he was not prepared for his downfall; on the contrary, he felt he was at the pinnacle of power. Evidently, the suddenness of the blow and the complete unity among the other members of the leadership shook him to the core. He realized that it was not only useless to fight for power, but that his reforming zeal was futile. I think most of all he was stunned by the behaviour of his closest colleagues, whom he had selected himself. This is probably the way a man feels when he finds his beloved wife, who had previously been faithful, in bed with a lover. He is struck dumb. But if in the latter case something can be done, in Khrushchev's case there was nothing to be done.

What were Mikoyan's reflections after he heard Galyukov's tale? Perhaps he remembered his youth, when by some strange circumstance he had managed to slip out of jail in Baku. He was one of the twenty-seven Baku commissars; twenty-six were shot and Mikoyan got away. Or did he remember how he had assisted Stalin in dealing with Kamenev, Zinovyev and Bukharin? Or his own speech in 1937 at one of the party conferences where he put forward the demand (following Stalin) to 'beat, beat, beat' them? Or maybe he thought of the unsuccessful attempt to remove Khrushchev in 1957 and his vacillations about which side to support?

Who knows? But it was not without reason that a saying about Mikoyan circulated among the people: from Ilyich to Ilyich (meaning from Lenin to Brezhnev) without a heart attack or paralysis. Such people, unfortunately, live long political lives. After Khrushchev's removal, Mikoyan continued to hold high posts and retired an old man laden with honours, retaining all privileges for himself and his family. It is not known if he handed the notorious report Sergey wrote about his father to Brezhnev, and when he might have done this – before the session of the Presidium of the Central Committee or during the interval when the alignment of forces would have become clear to him. Whichever way it was, his part in this matter looks extremely dubious. I think he made use of Sergey's information for his own purposes, exactly as Shelepin and Semichastny made use of the naive members of Khrushchev's family.

I fear that Sergey Khrushchev is sincerely misled when he maintains that Brezhnev was the main instigator in the plot against his father. His mistake, however, is easy to understand given that Khrushchev and his family must have felt particulaly hostile to Brezhnev, as Khrushchev had treated no one as well as him. Besides, Sergey Khrushchev evidently cannot admit to himself the extent to which he and, in particular, Adzhubey were deceived by the Komsomol 'young Turks'. They not only managed to worm their way into Sergey's confidence and, in the case of Adzhubey, give the impression of being reliable bosom friends, but they also cunningly deceived Khrushchev's relatives at the dramatic moment of the October plenum.

No, I am certain Khrushchev's overthrow was not initially organized by Brezhnev. Many think that it was Suslov. In fact, the plot was hatched by a group of young people headed by Shelepin. They used to meet in the most unexpected places, mainly in the stadium during football matches. It was there that they came to an agreement. The main role would be taken by Semichastny, the KGB chief, who had been recommended to the post by Shelepin. His job would be to paralyse Khrushchev's bodyguard. In fact, when Khrushchev was called to the session of the Presidium from Pitsunda, where he had been on holiday with Mikoyan, he was met at the airport only by Semichastny. Evidently Khrushchev understood immediately what had happened. But it was already too late.

One could say my information comes from the horse's mouth. Soon after the October plenum of the Party Central Committee Yelizar Kuskov and I were preparing a speech for P. Demichev, who at that time was a secretary of the Central Committee. He told us triumphantly how Shelepin had gathered together the former Komsomol members, including himself, and how they had worked out a plan to release Khrushchev from his duties. He made it clear that the initiative did not come from Brezhnev and that Brezhnev only became involved in the final stages. I remember clearly Demichev's agitated remark: 'We didn't know how it would end and where we would find ourselves the next day.' Andropov gave me roughly the same information, if more briefly.

What happened at the session of the Presidium of the Party Central Committee on 13 and 14 October 1964? Sergey Khrushchev gives a detailed account of this in the words of Mikoyan's relative, A. Arzumanyan. Sergey visited him on the night of 13 October. Arzumanyan was not surprised at the late visit. He was agitated by the news and also wanted to have his say.

'Anastas Ivanovich asked me to keep our conversation secret,' Arzumanyan said indecisively, 'but I want to tell you. It's very serious. There are various grievances against Nikita Sergeyevich and members of the Presidium are demanding his removal. The session has been thoroughly prepared and everyone except Mikoyan is presenting a united front. Khrushchev is being accused of a variety of sins: the unsatisfactory state of agriculture, his disrespectful attitude to members of the Presidium, his neglect of their opinions and much else. But this is not the main thing, everyone makes mistakes and Nikita Sergeyevich has made more than enough. The point is not Nikita Sergeyevich's mistakes but the line he represents and follows. If he is removed the Stalinists could come to power and nobody knows what will happen then.'

Arzumanyan said that Shelepin and Shelest were taking the most active part. Shelepin, on behalf of those present, had enumerated Khrushchev's mistakes, lumping everything together – fundamental questions and utter trivia.

'By the way,' Arzumanyan looked at Sergey, 'Shelepin said you received your degree of doctor of sciences without having to defend your dissertation. Shelepin will baulk at nothing! Even petty lies!' Arzumanyan was indignant.

'It really was a petty lie, but it upset me very much,' Sergey remarks. 'After all, Aleksandr Nikolayevich Shelepin had always shown, if not outright friendship, at least warm feelings to me. He was often the first to ring and wish me well on holidays and always showed good will and interest at my successes. In this he differed from his colleagues, who paid attention to me only as the son of their comrade and no more than that. I was, of course, flattered by the friendliness of the secretary of the Central Committee, although deep inside I felt uncomfortable and sensed that Shelepin was insincere. But I pushed this feeling aside and did not allow it to grow. And then this undisguised treachery. Indeed, any means will do . . .'

'Voronov behaved very rudely,' Arzumanyan continued. 'He did not mince his words. When Nikita Sergeyevich called the members of the Presidium his friends, he interrupted and said, "You have no friends here!" '

This retort even provoked a rebuke from Grishin. 'You are wrong,' he said. 'We are all Nikita Sergeyevich's friends.' The others spoke in a more restrained way, while Brezhnev, Podgorny and Kosygin were, on the whole, silent. Mikoyan proposed that Khrushchev be released from his duties as First Secretary of the Central Committee while retaining his post as chairman of the Council of Ministers. This, however, was rejected.

Khrushchev had already decided to resign without a fight. He rang up Mikoyan late at night and said that if they all wanted him to resign from his posts he would not object.

'I am old and tired. Let them carry on without me now. I have achieved what is most important. Our relations and the style of leadership have changed radically. Could anyone have dreamed of telling Stalin that he wasn't suitable and should resign? There would have been nothing left of us. Everything is different now. The fear has vanished and our conversations are conducted on equal terms. This is my contribution. But I will not fight.

'I have written out a statement myself asking that I be released on grounds of health. Now it is up to the plenum to make the decision official. I have said that I will submit to discipline and will fulfil all the decisions adopted by the Central Committee. I have also said that I will live wherever I am told to, in Moscow or anywhere else.'

Sergey recounts that numerous complaints were levelled against Khrushchev on questions of foreign and domestic policy. According to him, the Cuban Missile Crisis, events in Suez and relations with China were discussed. Khrushchev had replied that, judging from all that had been said, some people's memories were letting them down, as all decisions on these questions had been reached collectively by a majority of votes. The loudest complaints concerned the personal insults that Khrushchev had allegedly meted out to all members of the leadership.[2]

I was there in the balcony of the Palace of Congresses in the Kremlin during the October plenum of the Party Central Committee. All the members of the Presidium, including Khrushchev, were sitting on the podium. Brezhnev chaired the session. Suslov gave a brief report of the session of the Presidium and said that Khrushchev had applied 'to leave at his own request'. There was no discussion. During the report and throughout the plenum Khrushchev sat, his large-browed head lowered, with his hands holding his temples. He did not breath a word, but it seemed to me that there were tears in his eyes. Adzhubey leaped from his seat. He made some strange, pathetic remarks about having married Khrushchev's daughter, Raya, before Khrushchev had become First Secretary and, I think, he again repeated that stupid joke which had always tormented him: you don't need a hundred roubles, all you need is to get married like Adzhubey. The hall was indignant. The resolutions 'to release Khrushchev at his own request' and to expel Adzhubey from the Central Committee were adopted unanimously. It seemed to me that the vast majority at the plenum breathed a sigh of relief. The plenum also voted unanimously to elect Brezhnev First Secretary of the Central Committee of the Communist Party of the Soviet Union.

Outwardly this historical drama was a farce – total hypocrisy. Suslov's report gave no analysis of the positive and negative aspects of Khrushchev's ten years in power. He omitted the resolutions of the Twentieth and Twenty-Second Party Congresses, said nothing about the Party Programme, and did not define what the new course would be. The reference to Khrushchev's allegedly voluntary resignation was hypocritical, and Adzhubey's laments were hypocritical. The decision to appoint Brezhnev was hypocritical; no one at the time considered him to be a person really capable of heading this great country. I have rarely had the opportunity of seeing such an assembly of Tartuffes. Although everyone in the lobby was whispering about Shelepin and Semichastny, outwardly it appeared that they were standing on the sidelines. Although everyone knew what steps had been taken to organize the plot, outwardly it looked like the decent resignation of a tired old man.

I sat together with other members of the apparatus and, glancing around, searched in their faces for the feelings that were raging in my soul. Alas, the faces were impenetrable. Everyone accepted the events as fitting, or else they were too frightened to reveal their feelings. I remember a comment that one of the leaders of the department of agitation and propaganda threw out: 'The Ukrainian supremacy has ended. Now Russia will again take power into its own hands.' And that was all. Hardly anyone felt that a curtain had fallen on an epoch. Hardly anyone thought what the new times would be like.

*

Power came to Brezhnev like a gift from the gods. For Stalin to change the post of General Secretary, a modest post at the time, to one which made him 'boss' of the country he had to wipe out almost all the members of Lenin's Politburo (with the exception of himself, it goes without saying) and an enormous part of the party *aktiv*.* After Stalin's death Khrushchev was not first in line, as many think, but second; Malenkov was regarded as first in line at that time. Khrushchev won the

* Party activists.

battle against powerful and influential rivals, such as Molotov, who had stood at the helm of state almost since Lenin's times. Perhaps this is why the Stalin and Khrushchev eras, each in their own way, were filled with dramatic changes, major reforms, anxiety and instability.

Nothing of the sort could be said about Brezhnev. He acquired power so smoothly that it was almost as if someone had been measuring Monomakh's cap on different heads for a long time and had stopped at his. And this hat fitted him so perfectly that he wore it for eighteen years without any fear, conflict or horror. His immediate retinue desired one thing only: that he live for ever, as they were doing so well out of it. Brezhnev himself, during a meeting with members of his regiment, proud of his recently-made marshal's uniform, said, 'I've served my time and here I am.' This phrase also appropriately describes the process by which he became leader of the party and state – he served his time and reaped the reward.

In one way there is a similarity between Brezhnev's coming to power and the Stalinist and Khrushchevean model. Nobody took him to be a serious pretender to the role of leader; in fact he himself in every way possible stressed that he was devoid of such ambitions. I remember that when a speech was being prepared for his trip abroad in his capacity as chairman of the Presidium of the Supreme Soviet, he asked his speechwriters to be 'a bit more modest, more modest . . . I am not a leader, not a ruler . . .'

Brezhnev was the complete opposite of Khrushchev. Khrushchev was bold, inclined to take risks, even adventuristic, and hungry for innovation and change. It would be a mystery why Khrushchev became the patron of a person so different to him in spirit and temperament if we did not know Nikita Sergeyevich better. As an authoritarian personality who showed no inclination to share his power and influence with others, he mostly surrounded himself with people who hung on his every word, assented to him and were prepared to run any errand. He did not need colleagues, especially not rulers. He had had enough trouble after Stalin's death with Malenkov, Molotov and Kaganovich, who had tried to banish him from the political Olympus and, perhaps, drive him into obscurity. Men like Brezhnev, Podgorny, Kirichenko and Shelest were obedient executors of his will – 'lieutenants', to use Khrushchev's rather pungent but humorous name for journalists. True, when it came to the sacred question of who would get the upper hand, it was precisely these 'lieutenants' who quickly defected to the other side. For in politics there is no love, only *raison d'état*.

In actual fact, a change of leadership in this way is rare in the history of politics. Such a method is usually only effective if the previous ruler is killed. The 'peaceful plot' against Khrushchev was successful for two reasons. Firstly, he himself in his last few years of rule chopped one branch after another off the tree on which his power was based. The second reason was Shelepin.

I don't think that there was anyone Khrushchev treated with such trust or promoted so quickly up the party and state ladder as Shelepin. In a short time Shelepin moved from being an ordinary member of the Central Committee to becoming a member of the Presidium, chairman of the Committee of Party and State Control and Central Committee secretary. The saying 'Save us, Lord, from our friends and we will somehow cope with our enemies' is true indeed.

However, Shelepin badly miscalculated. He was not well versed in history, even though he had graduated from the Institute of Philosophy, Literature and History. He was certain that Brezhnev was an intermediate, temporary figure and that, having destroyed a giant like Khrushchev, it would be no problem to deal with a person who was only his faint shadow.

Brezhnev was indebted to Khrushchev for his whole career. He had graduated from the Technical College of Land Utilization and Reclamation in Kursk and only joined the party at the age of twenty-five. Only then did he begin his political career. In May 1937 Brezhnev became deputy chairman of the Dneprodzerzhinsk city soviet executive committee and a year later he was in the Dnepropetrovsk party *obkom*. It is hard to tell whether Khrushchev assisted his progress in this first stage, but his subsequent career proceeded with the vigorous support of Khrushchev, who was then First Secretary of the Ukrainian - Communist Party Central Committee and later secretary of the Central Committee of the All-Union Communist Party (Bolsheviks). When Brezhnev was made First Secretary of the Central Committee of the Moldavian Communist Party he took many of his friends from Dnepropetrovsk with him. It was here that he made friends with Konstantin Chernenko, then head of the department of agitation and propaganda of the republican Party Central Committee, who became his closest colleague.

After the Nineteenth Party Congress Brezhnev became a candidate member of the Presidium of the Central Committee, and after Stalin's death he cropped up in the main political directorate of the Soviet army and navy. The stronger Khrushchev became, the higher Brezhnev's shares rose. By the October 1964 plenum he had become Second Secretary of the Central Committee. In this way Khrushchev had personally built a pedestal for his successor.

However, Brezhnev did not retaliate against his former patron. Khrushchev had set a precedent at the June Plenum in 1957. He relates how after the defeat of the Stalinist old guard he was rung up by Kaganovich, for many years Khrushchev's patron, who asked, 'Nikita, what will happen to us?' In reply, Khrushchev put a question to him:

'And what would you have done if you had won? Driven me into obscurity or put me against a wall? I will tell you plainly: you can go . . . you know where.' And here followed a strong unprintable word. This word inaugurated a new tradition: disgraced politicians were no longer killed, but simply dismissed. Brezhnev made use of this tradition. Having dismissed Khrushchev, he sent him off to live out his life in a dacha out of town, having prudently replaced the security guards there.

We, standing so close to the helm of power, knew nothing about the plot being prepared against Khrushchev and learned very little about the real facts after he had gone. Indeed, Churchill was right when he said of the Stalinist political system that it was a fight between bulldogs under the carpet.

Soon after the plenum I had my first and, in effect, only detailed talk with Brezhnev. In February 1965 a group of consultants from various departments were given the job of preparing the report for the new First Secretary of the Central Committee to commemorate twenty years since victory in the Great Patriotic War. We had our room not far from Brezhnev's office. I was in charge of the group and so Brezhnev's aide passed on to me his request that we analyse and evaluate a parallel text which had been sent to him by Shelepin. Later Brezhnev came to our room and, shaking hands with everyone, turned to me with a question.

'Well, what's this "dissertation" he's sent?'

One must say that this 'dissertation' was a very serious matter; nothing less than a demand in the spirit of open neo-Stalinism for a complete reconsideration of all party policy under Khrushchev. We counted seventeen sharp turns of the political rudder back to previous times: to restore Stalin's 'good name' after the decisions of the Twentieth and Twenty-Second Congresses; to renounce the Party Programme, which had already been passed with several guarantees enshrined in it against the cult of personality and, in particular, for the rotation of cadres; to liquidate the *sovnarkhozes* and return to the departmental principle of leadership; to renounce the division of *obkoms* and *raykoms* into industrial and agricultural sectors; to establish severe labour discipline at the expense of democracy; to return to the party line on the world revolution and to renounce the principle of peaceful coexistence, as well as the formula on the peaceful transition to socialism in capitalist countries; to restore friendly relations with Mao Tse-tung by unequivocally accepting his attitude to the cult of personality and his common strategy for the Communist movement; to restore the previous description of the League of Communists of Yugoslavia as a 'hot-bed of revisionism and reformism' . . . and much else in the same spirit.

I began to expound our position to Brezhnev point by point. The more I explained, the more his face changed. It began to look tense and drawn until we realized, to our horror, that Leonid Ilyich had hardly understood a word. I brought my fountain of eloquence to a halt and he said with winning sincerity, 'It's hard for me to grasp all this. On the whole, to be honest, this isn't my area. My strong point is organization and psychology,' and he made vague circular motions with his fingers spread wide open.

What was most dramatic – and this became clear very soon – was that Brezhnev was entirely unprepared for the role which had suddenly fallen to him. He had become First Secretary as a result of a complex, multi-dimensional and even odd symbiosis of forces: dissatisfaction with Khrushchev's dismissive attitude to his colleagues; apprehension at the unbridled extremes of his policy and the adventurist actions which had played their part in escalating the Cuban Missile Crisis; illusions about the 'personality' nature of the conflict with China; and particularly, the irritation felt by the conservative section of the administrative apparatus at the constant instability, jolts, changes and reforms which could never be predicted.

Not the least important was the struggle between different generations of leaders: the generation of 1937, which included Brezhnev, Suslov and Kosygin, and the post-war generation, which included Shelepin, Voronov, Polyansky and Andropov. Brezhnev landed in the middle, at the crossing of these roads. Therefore, he suited everyone at this first stage. At any rate no one protested. His incompetence was a blessing; it gave wide opportunities to the apparatchiks. Only Shelepin, who thought he was cleverer than the rest, lost out. He did not advance one step in his career as not only Brezhnev, but Suslov and other leaders too, had seen through his ambitions and his authoritarian designs.

What had happened was something that can often be observed in primary party organizations when the person who is elected secretary to the party committee is not the most active, bold and competent person but the most reliable one, who will not let anyone down personally or harm anyone without good reason. But if anyone had said then that Brezhnev would remain leader for eighteen years, he would have been laughed at outright. It seemed totally incredible.

N. G. Yegorichev, then first secretary of the Moscow committee, probably expressed the general view when he remarked in conversation with one of the leaders that Leonid Ilyich was, of course, a good man, but was he really suitable to be leader of such a great country? This remark cost him dearly as, incidentally, did his open criticism of military policy – for which Brezhnev was answerable – at one of the plenums. Instead of becoming a secretary of the Central Committee, as everyone had expected, Yegorichev spent almost twenty years as ambassador to Denmark.

★

After the plenum Andropov spoke to us at the department and furnished us with some details. I clearly remember his main point: 'Now we will proceed more consistently and firmly along the path of the Twentieth Party Congress.' At this point I was amazed by his reproach, the first in many years of joint work, addressed personally to me: 'Now do you realize why *Pravda* didn't publish your article?'

The article was not strictly mine, but the editorial board's as prepared by me; it was a full-page spread entitled 'The Cult of Personality of Stalin and his Heirs'. It had been personally approved by Khrushchev, but several months had passed without it being published. Why? After the October plenum it became clear that it had been held back specially.

Andropov was mistaken and he paid for his mistake.

A bitter struggle was being waged over the course our country should take. One course, as I have already mentioned, was an unambiguous return to Stalinist methods. The other course, put forward by Andropov to the leadership, set out a full programme which was based more consistently on the resolutions of the anti-Stalinist Twentieth Party Congress than even Khrushchev's had been.

Brezhnev was in no hurry to define his position, keeping an eye on the alignment of forces within the Presidium and the Central Committee.

It is likely that Andropov's views played no small part in his transfer from the post of Central Committee secretary to head of the KGB. Different forces were at work here. In the first place, Suslov had disliked Andropov for a long time, suspecting that he had his eye on Suslov's job. In the second place, Kosygin was under the illusion that the alliance with China could be quickly restored and wanted to dismiss the department head who had been involved in the Sino-Soviet conflict. In the third place, Brezhnev wanted to put a loyal man in the KGB to protect himself from the 'joke' that Semichastny had played on Khrushchev. In the end, Brezhnev showed he was a master of compromise: he met Suslov and Kosygin half-way, but at the same time recommended that Andropov be elected a candidate member of the Politburo and, later, a full member.

Brezhnev's main trait as political leader was revealed in the first months of his rule. An extremely cautious man, who had not taken a single rash step in his rise to power, Brezhnev adopted a centrist position from the very start. He avoided the extremes, accepting neither the reform programme conceived in the spirit of the Twentieth Party Congress nor neo-Stalinism. In effect, he followed a tradition that had taken shape after Lenin's death. Not everyone is aware that Stalin also came to power as a centrist. He joined the Kamenev–Zinovyev bloc against the 'leftist' Trotsky, and then joined Molotov, Mikoyan and others against the 'rightist' Bukharin. Only at the end of the twenties –

mainly with the aim of strengthening his own personal power – did he begin to implement the leftist programme of 'revolution from above' and terror. Khrushchev, who first bared his breast in the secret speech at the Twentieth Party Congress, began to shift to the centre after the Hungarian events of 1956. Speaking at the Chinese Embassy in Moscow he called Stalin a 'great Marxist-Leninist', and went on to fall out with the intelligentsia who had fervently supported his criticism of the cult of personality. It is true, however, that he still got carried away by extreme solutions. In October 1964 he paid the full price for his inconsistency and frivolous mistakes.

Brezhnev was different. By nature, character, education and career he was a typical apparatchik of the regional level. He was not a bad executor of others' wishes, but he was by no means a leader. Therefore, he borrowed a fair amount from Stalin and a bit from Khrushchev as well.

Let us return, however, to the report that was being prepared for the twentieth anniversary of victory in the Second World War, because it was then that the historical choice which laid the foundations of the Brezhnev era was made. Shelepin's 'dissertation' was rejected, and combined forces were applied to produce another version which at least developed, albeit not very consistently, the principles, ideas and directives of Khrushchev's era. Brezhnev invited us into his office, seated the representatives of different departments on either side of his long table and requested that the text be read aloud.

Here we learned another important detail about Brezhnev's style. He did not like reading and simply could not bear writing. He usually listened to briefings, as well as to his own speeches or reports. Whereas Khrushchev often dictated certain fundamental notions to be included in his speech, Brezhnev never did.

The reading of the draft report went relatively well. But it turned out that the main battle lay ahead when, as usual, the report was to be distributed to members of the Presidium and secretaries of the Central Committee. I was instructed to describe in general terms the suggestions which were coming in and compile a short summary. The overwhelming majority of members of the leadership were in favour of stressing Stalin's positive characteristics. Some even sent long texts to be inserted which said that it was due to Stalin that the opposition had been crushed and that socialism, the realization of the Leninist plan for industrialization, collectivization and the cultural revolution had triumphed, thus creating the preconditions necessary for victory in the Great Patriotic War and the setting up of the socialist camp.

The advocates of this position insisted that the very concept of a 'cult of personality' should be removed from the text; even more so the phrase 'period of the cult of personality'. The most adamant were Suslov and

Mzhavanadze and some young leaders, including Shelepin. Others, such as Mikoyan and Ponomaryov, suggested including a formula borrowed straight from the well-known resolution 'Surmounting the cult of personality and its consequences' of 30 June 1956.

Andropov had his own view. He suggested that the report should avoid the question of Stalin completely, that his name simply should not be mentioned given the difference of opinions and the alignment of forces which had formed in the leadership. Yury Vladimirovich said that no issue at the moment could so easily lead to a split in the leadership, the administrative apparatus, the party and the people as the issue of Stalin.

In the end Brezhnev chose a version close to the one proposed by Andropov. In the report given on the twentieth anniversary of victory the name Stalin was mentioned only once.

Soon Shelepin's supporters began proclaiming from the housetops the ambitions and plans of their leader. During Shelepin's trip to Mongolia his close friend N. N. Mesyatsev, former secretary of the Central Committee of the Komsomol, began to boast in the presence of Yu. Tsedenbal that the real 'First' was Shelepin. And when he got drunk he broke into the song, 'Be Prepared For The Great Aim'.

Tsedenbal was quick to inform Moscow. Shelepin, who was cleverer than his lackeys, stopped specially in Irkutsk on his return trip and spoke at the *obkom*, where he ostentatiously praised Brezhnev. But it was too late. He had shown his hand and everyone understood his designs. A long battle, with cunning and complicated undercurrents, began between the two leaders, which ended in Brezhnev's victory. It was only then that I appreciated his phrase: 'My strong point is organization and psychology.' Yet another example to show that dogged deliberation in politics always wins over unrestrained aggression.

When Brezhnev first came to power he would start his working day in an unusual way, spending at least two hours on telephone calls to other members of the top leadership and to many of the important secretaries in the Central Committees of republics and *obkoms*. His conversations usually went something like this: 'Well, Ivan Ivanovich, we are looking at this issue and I wanted to get your opinion . . .' You can just imagine what feelings of pride would fill Ivan Ivanovich's heart at that moment. In this way Brezhnev built up his prestige. The impression was that of a balanced, calm, tactful leader, who would not take a step without first getting advice from his comrades and full approval from his colleagues.

He almost never spoke first at the sessions of the Secretariat of the Central Committee or the Presidium. He gave everyone a chance to speak if they wanted to, listened to them attentively, and if a consensus had not been reached, preferred to put the issue aside, work on it some more, submit it for approval to everyone individually and put it up for a second reading. Under him the practice of getting agreement from numerous sources, which demanded dozens of signatures on documents, blossomed luxuriously and in the end distorted or reduced to nothing the whole point of the resolutions to be adopted.

Brezhnev behaved in the opposite way when it came to selecting cadres. If he was interested in someone he would be the first to put his signature down and achieve his end. He had learned Stalin's formula that cadres decide everything. Gradually, in a quiet and almost unobtrusive way, he managed to remove more than half the secretaries of *obkoms*, a significant number of ministers and many heads of central research institutes. He had the last word in awarding Lenin and State Prizes. In general it was not production that Brezhnev preferred to be engaged in, but distribution. This he understood well and he was never too busy to ring someone on whom an award had been conferred, particularly if it was the Hero of Socialist Labour, to congratulate him and show that the decision had been his.

This was what Brezhnev-style politics consisted of. Such people are not very competent at deciding important economic, cultural or political issues, but to make up for it they know exactly whom to appoint and where to appoint him to; whom to reward for services rendered, when and how. Leonid Ilyich worked hard to place people like himself in leading posts. They were 'little Brezhnevs' – unhurried, bland, uninspired, not very concerned about work, but skilful at distributing largesse.

He was a 'weathercock leader', one who always went with the majority and made the job of leader organically connected with the distribution of largesse. It took us back to the tradition of the state before Peter the Great when in Muscovite Russia a man was awarded the post of governor not so that he would administer the province, but so that he could retain revenues for his own use.

People connected with the Twentieth Party Congress, or simply people with a bold innovative frame of mind, were not shot as they had been in the thirties. They were quietly pushed aside, barred, restricted, suppressed. Everywhere mediocrity triumphed. These cadres were neither stupid nor totally incompetent, but they were clearly without talent, devoid of principles or any fighting spirit. Gradually they filled posts in the party and state apparatus, in the economy, in science and culture. Everything turned grey and went into decline. Like master, like man.

Brezhnev had no peers in his patient acquisition of power. He did it all unnoticed, without apparent pressure. Vacant posts were needed so that his team from Dnepropetrovsk, Moldavia and Kazakhstan could be brought into the central leadership – reliable people, who would not let him down. One by one Podgorny, Voronov, Polyansky and Mikoyan disappeared from the Presidium and the Politburo. Shelest, leader of the very large Ukrainian party organization, disappeared without it being announced, and without a murmur. At the session of the Politburo which dismissed him he said only one thing – that the Ukrainian party organization would not support the decision.

When Brezhnev lightly pushed a person off the edge of his seat, there would be some straw spread out for him to fall on. When N. G. Yegorichev was released as secretary of the Moscow party organization, Leonid Ilyich rang him up and said something in this vein: 'Please forgive me, it just turned out this way . . . Do you have any problems at the moment – family, maybe?' Yegorichev, whose daughter had recently got married and was in dire straits with a husband and child and no flat, was sufficiently weak-willed to tell Brezhnev. And guess what – several days later the young family received a flat. Brezhnev did not want to arouse feelings of animosity in anyone. If he had been an art connoisseur he would probably have been impressed by half-tint pastels, devoid of bright colours. He often gave flats as presents to people in his circle. What can one say? Imagine the President of the United States allocating flats?

Thus, Brezhnev came to power with no programme of his own for developing the country. It was one of those rare cases in modern political history when a person takes power without any definite programme. But one cannot say, in Mao Tse-tung's words, that he was a blank sheet of paper on which any hieroglyph could be written. A deeply traditional and conservative man, Brezhnev most of all feared abrupt movements, sharp turns, extreme changes. Having condemned Khrushchev for voluntarism and subjectivism, the first thing he did was to erase these radical beginnings and restore that which had proved to be workable under Stalin. In the first place, he eliminated the *sovnarkhozes* and the division of party organs into industrial and agricultural sectors – a uniquely Khrushchevean form of pluralism, and one which irritated the administrative apparatus a great deal. Top functionaries who had been sent against their will to distant or not so distant parts returned to Moscow. Quietly and unobtrusively the idea of the rotation of cadres was reduced to nothing. Instead, the slogan of stability was put forward – every apparatchik's greatest dream. Brezhnev did not return to the Stalinist repressions, but he was successful in retaliating against dissenting views.

Instead of Khrushchev's eleven-year school course, which claimed to teach pupils technical skills, the previous ten-year course was restored. Peasants got back their private plots. The maize 'epic' was relegated to the past, and Lysenko with it. The campaign to open up the Virgin Lands was gradually discarded and the focus turned on the agricultural development of the central areas of the country. Members of kolhozes received a pension and were guaranteed a minimum wage. The average amount of produce due to the state was reduced, and purchases of agricultural produce at higher prices were increased.

All these agricultural measures had been planned under Khrushchev. The last burst of reform took place at the September 1965 plenum, proposed by Kosygin. The basis of these reforms had already been discussed at the beginning of December 1962 in connection with an article by Professor E. Liberman entitled 'Plan, Profit, Bonus'. These ideas were later developed by the prominent Soviet scientists V. Nemchinov, V. Novozhilov and L. Kantorovich. On the eve of the October coup, in August 1964, Khrushchev had instructed the system proposed by these men to be implemented in the Bolshevichka factory in Moscow and in Mayak in Gorky. Several days after the notorious 'voluntary' retirement of Khrushchev on a pension, this experiment was spread to many other enterprises. Inspired by the results, Kosygin gave his report at the September 1965 plenum.

Brezhnev, however, was sceptical. Without investigating the new system thoroughly, he intuitively put greater trust in methods which, in his opinion, had produced brilliant results in the period of industrialization under Stalin. Not the least factor was his jealousy of Kosygin, who had an advantage over him as one of the oldest leaders whose authority dated back to the Great Patriotic War.

In the apparatus jealousy is the bureaucrat's synonym for envy. It has a special meaning. People on the same rung of the administrative ladder vigilantly watch to see if their colleagues are moved up before them, even if it is only ever so slightly. They are hugely irritated at any public appearance by their co-workers, especially if it is in the press or on television, or at large party or public functions.

At the start of Brezhnev's leadership, at a session of representatives of the Warsaw Pact countries, an amusing episode took place when Brezhnev, for the first and only time I think, uttered something which had not been written for him beforehand. The Romanian delegation was headed not by the party leader but by the chairman of the Council of Ministers, and he proposed that the common document be signed by leaders of the state and not the party. Here Brezhnev, as if propelled by a spring, jumped up and uttered two and a half sentences, which went roughly like this: 'That's impossible! A document has to be signed by the First in a country . . . and the First is the party leader.'

At that time Brezhnev's reaction to Kosygin's speech at the September 1965 plenum was doing the rounds of the apparatus: 'What's he dreamed up? Reforms, reforms . . . who needs them? Nobody will understand them. People have to work better. That's where the whole problem lies.' Wasn't this attitude the reason why economic reforms failed?

My personal impressions of Brezhnev may be subjective, especially as I only spoke with him once, so let us look at what other people, who knew him better, thought. Aleksandr Bovin, for example, maintains that it would be hard to call Brezhnev a major political figure, although he adds, 'Brezhnev was on the whole not a bad person, sociable, firm in his commitments, cordial, a hospitable host. He liked to hunt . . . He enjoyed the pleasures of life available to him.'

But that is by the way. What one decidedly cannot agree with is the notion of 'two Brezhnevs' – the one in action before the mid-seventies and the one after, as if at the very start of his activities Brezhnev had been a supporter of economic and other reforms. A long quotation from Brezhnev's speech at the September 1965 plenum is often used to substantiate this. However, even at that time it was known outright that Brezhnev was actively opposed to Kosygin's reforms and was to blame for their failure.

It was under Brezhnev that the tradition of terrible phrase-mongering became established, so that nine volumes were required to contain 'his' collected works. He often made speeches which were good and proper, but there was never anything behind them. His speech-writers possessed an exceptional ability to distort any fruitful idea with an unobtrusive turn in the argument. This was the case, for example, in the article 'The Building of a Developed Socialist Society', which was published in 1966 in *Pravda*. It contained, in essence, a renunciation of the slogan 'the all-out construction of Communism', recognizing that so far we had only established backward forms of socialism with a tendency in the direction of scientific-technical modernization, a reconstructed administration and democratic development. What did the people from the ideological hairdressers do? They put in Brezhnev's mouth the directive that we had already constructed a developed socialist society. The same thing was stated in the preamble to the USSR Constitution. In this way everything was turned into empty propaganda. This was the case with the 'early', and even more so with the 'later' Brezhnev.

Politics stopped being politics – for politics means taking business-like decisions and not making verbose speeches about decisions. Politics is not making declarations about the food programme but providing food in the shops; not promises of Communism but real moves to provide well-being for every person.

It is true that the word 'problem' became Brezhnev's favourite word in his initial speeches. He spoke of the problems of the scientific-technical revolution and labour productivity, the problems of food, housing and so on. And all the time he called for decisions to be taken.

But for some reason, decisions were not taken. And if they were taken, they were not implemented. The Institute of Sociological Research of the USSR Academy of Sciences conducted a study on the effectiveness of decisions taken by the USSR Council of Ministers. The results were staggering: barely more than one in ten decisions were implemented.

It is also true that Brezhnev liked socializing, hunting, fast driving. It was his style to drive 140 kilometres through the 'Communist city'. The faster the bosses drove in their new Zil cars, the slower the country crawled. But to make up for it we had words, words and more words. And the people bore the brunt!

How many thousand millions in public funds and how much public enthusiasm went into the construction of BAM, the cross-country railway, which was ill-considered and ill-equipped? And what was the cost of the 'magnificent' project to divert the Siberian rivers? What about the runaway military expenditure? At that time the living standard of the people receded to a position somewhere at the bottom of the industrially developed states.

The style of Brezhnev's speeches sharply differed from Khrushchev's. Khrushchev usually gave a draft to his speechwriters, which clearly set out what he thought and wanted, even if the literary style was chaotic. He carefully watched to see how scrupulously we had fulfilled his instructions and prized such expressions and jokes as 'give it to them hot' and 'we have one quarrel with the Americans on the question of land, who will bury whom', and so on.

Brezhnev never dictated anything and did not formulate his own thoughts. The most one could expect from him were instructions to speak with greater warmth about women, youth, workers and so on. He did not like to read his speeches beforehand and preferred to hear them out loud. Usually he would gather the whole group of speechwriters and one of them would read, while the others made comments and suggested corrections. His decisions were simple: he would listen patiently to everybody and go for the majority opinion; and if someone was particularly stubborn in his objections, he would recommend that we meet him half-way and correct it.

Brezhnev's main advisor, G. Tsukanov, played a special role in the preparation of his speeches. He was a rather charming person with a wide round face, a pleasant smile and a slight Ukrainian accent. Formerly the director of a large factory in Dnepropetrovsk, he immediately took Brezhnev's fancy and remained his aide for more than a quarter of a century. A man of common sense but not erudite, who soon came under the dominating influence of Arbatov and Bovin, he remained faithful to them throughout Brezhnev's eighteen-year rule.

For a time Tsukanov was almost Brezhnev's 'alter ego'. I observed him when he was on holiday at the Central Committee sanatorium in

Gagra, when the First Secretaries of the republican and regional parties would come cap in hand with presents and openly ingratiate themselves.

However, this man's career came to a sorry end. Brezhnev had a passion for a woman in the Central Committee apparatus who was nicknamed 'French Valka'. She worked in the shorthand office and had been in a multitude of beds in the apparatus before getting into the General Secretary's. He promoted her, made her the head of some section in the general department, gave her a flat, her own car and a large salary. In his old age poor Leonid Ilyich became jealous of Tsukanov. It is not known whether there were grounds for this, but Tsukanov lost his post as chief aide, and was transferred from his office opposite Brezhnev's on the sixth floor to a pitiful room with pitiful furniture provided by the meticulous workers of the Central Committee Administration of Affairs.

Tsukanov could not stand the blow and suffered a stroke. The last act of this melodrama was transmitted on television. Not long before he died, Brezhnev took pity on him and presented him with a decoration on the occasion of his sixtieth birthday, but read the speech in a squeaky voice without looking at Tsukanov, who was shaking like a leaf. May the Lord save us, indeed, from monarchial favours and caprices!

I invited Tsukanov home once to hear his stories about Brezhnev. He came willingly but refused to speak about Brezhnev and only complained about Brezhnev's former speechwriters, who in these different times (Gorbachev was now in power) had completely stopped seeing him or even answering his calls. But French Valka survived. Brezhnev demoted her a rung down the ladder but did not reject her services, and even after his death she continued carrying papers along the same corridors.

*

Aleksandr Bovin recounted a conversation that took place in the dacha at Zavidovo during the drafting of another speech. He told Brezhnev how difficult it was for people on low incomes to get by. Brezhnev had replied, 'You don't know what life is like. Nobody lives on their wages. I remember in my youth when I was studying at the technical college we earned extra money by unloading freight trains. How did we manage? Three bags or a container would go to them and one to us. That's how everyone lives in this country.' The saying that a fish rots from the head down is quite true. Brezhnev also regarded the shadow economy as normal, as well as thieving in the service sector and bribes to bureaucrats. This almost became the general norm of life. Remember the words of Saint-Simon, who noted a long time ago that a nation, like an individual, can live in two ways – either by thieving or by producing.

Who is to blame? Brezhnev? It is too easy to say that now. Does the blame lie then with his retinue, in whose interest it was to inflate this empty rubber vessel? Yes, more so than with him, because they knew what they were doing. But the main culprit who should be brought to the judgement of history is the Brezhnev regime, which preserved poverty and degraded the consciousness of an enormous mass of people.

Does this mean that the country simply stopped developing? Of course not. People continued to work. Industrial production grew, if slowly, although two extremely dangerous features emerged. First, the headlong growth in the extraction of fuel. As much was extracted in fifteen years as had been in the history of the country. This meant the depletion of reserves belonging to future generations on the principle of 'après moi, le deluge'. Secondly, there was a steady decline of consumer goods in general production. The country continued to move along the path of extensive development.

Those were twenty years of missed opportunities. The technological revolution passed us by. It was not even noticed, while the traditional slogan of scientific-technical progress continued to be proclaimed. During that period Japan became the second industrial power in the world, South Korea followed on the heels of Japan, and Brazil became one of the new centres of industrial power. True, we gained military parity with the most advanced industrial power in the modern world. But at what a price! The price was increasing technological backwardness in all other areas of the economy, and the further destruction of agriculture. A modern service sector has still not been created and the low living standard of the people has been frozen.

The situation became more complicated as every attempt to modernize the very model of socialism was rejected. Instead, faith in organizational and bureaucratic decisions increased. As soon as any problem emerged the leadership of the country reacted unequivocally: who deals with this? We must set up a new ministry or another similar body.

Agriculture and the food problem remained the Achilles heel of our economy. Solutions were sought in traditional methods which had already proved ineffective. The policy of turning collective farms into state farms continued.

The intensive development of the chemical industry did not produce the expected results. Despite the fact that in the seventies the USSR outstripped the USA in the production of fertilizers, labour productivity in agriculture was several times lower. A quarter of the USSR workforce could not feed the country, when 3 per cent of the US population produced so much that a significant part of it was sold abroad.

There was a single reason for the economic and technological backwardness: a lack of understanding and a fear of imminent structural reforms – the transition to financial autonomy in industry, the cooperative movement in the service sector, link and family contracting in the countryside. The most frightening thing for the regime would have been to make a decision on democratization and to restrict the bureaucracy, which was Brezhnev's main buttress.

All attempts to move in the direction of reform, to exercise economic independence or independent thought, were ruthlessly nipped in the bud.

The main lesson to be learned from the Brezhnev era was the failure of the command-administrative system which had taken shape under Stalin. Not only did the state not promote progress; rather, it increasingly hampered the economic, cultural and moral development of society. There can be no return! Even if Brezhnev had decided to support the rotten structure by relapsing into Stalinist repressions, he could not have made the system effective. The technological revolution requires free labour, personal initiative, interest, creativity, continuous searching and competition. Structural reforms and *perestroika* were indisputably the logical way out of stagnation.

As a living embodiment of the illusions of state socialism, Brezhnev brought the system to a dead end. From here the only possible way out, even though it is an extremely difficult one, is to create a civil socialist society, at the centre of which will be self-governing work collectives and active individuals. Working for themselves, they will work for society. It goes without saying that the state does not become a night-watchman; instead, like shagreen leather, its functions will shrink drastically, with only those that ensure security and progress in society remaining. Theoretically, if out of one hundred ministries and departments fifteen to twenty are retained, and out of 18 million people in the administrative apparatus two-thirds transfer to the sphere of public self-government, then our state can only gain from this as, undoubtedly, will our citizens.

The second lesson to be learned is that it is not only immoral but inefficient when leaders of the country emerge not as a result of normal democratic procedures and public activities in the party and state, but by means of behind-the-scenes manoeuvres or, worse, plots and bloody purges. There has been sufficient experience to show that in such circumstances those who come to power are by no means the most able leaders or the most convinced Leninists or the most committed to the people; rather they show the resourcefulness of Ulysses – masters of group struggle, intrigue and even plain corruption. The political mafia of Rashidov, Kunayev, Shchelokov and Medunov, the Dnepropetrovsk 'tail' in the form of Tikhonov and later the 'phenomenon' of

Chernenko – all this should be a stern deterrent to political workers of whatever rank or level.

At all times among all peoples it has been thought that ruling a state demands a certain training. We don't need to go back to the ancient world, where men such as Aristotle and Seneca acted as their rulers' mentors. In our own Russia Pushkin's close friend Zhukovsky was mentor to the heir to the throne. In modern states too it is generally considered that such work requires natural talent, education, an appreciation of civil responsibility, many years of political activity, participation in public and state affairs, the art of oratory and the skills of a publicist. We need not refer to the experience of the West – they are not a law unto us, we have our own 'whiskers'. Only we grew these whiskers, then shaved them off with much effort and hard work, leaving blood on the faces not only of individuals but of the entire nation before we learned that not every *obkom* secretary, after all, was capable of governing our great state.

Since the Revolution traditions had been laid down for a new school of political leadership. Their main principle was social origins: a person did not have to be outstanding, rich or highly-educated, he only needed to be one of us, one of the people. Of course, few people then really accepted the saying that any cook can govern the state. There was not a single cook nor, for that matter, worker or peasant in the top leadership after the Revolution. The Politburo and almost all the members of the Party Central Committee in Lenin's time – the outstanding and not-so-outstanding publicists, the passionate agitators, leaders and chiefs – came from the intelligentsia or the semi-intelligentsia of the lower middle class. At that time the masses listened to them and believed in them without that sham stupid expression on their faces which we see in the image of the peasant in the well-known film *Man with a Gun*.

After Lenin's death this generation of leaders was successively removed by the Stalinist purges, which followed one after the other. They were replaced by a younger generation, strong in character but with a lower level of education and culture. This generation was also overthrown in 1936–8. The vast majority of the generation that followed had not participated in the Revolution, but to make up for it they had a certain and specific level of party education. Many people in this generation made fantastic leaps in their careers, rising in a few years from rank-and-file workers to ministers.

Brezhnev belonged to this third generation. His progress was achieved purely through the apparatus. Even the most thorough study of this period will not reveal any record of a public speech given by the future General Secretary. He skilfully remained silent, skilfully found the necessary patrons and gradually but steadily moved upwards.

Another problem lies in the fact that not one of our leaders bothered to groom a successor or successors. We won't talk about Stalin – the slightest suspicion that such a person existed was enough for him to have the potential pretender ground into dust. He openly spoke of this to his so-called colleagues: 'When I die, you'll be done for, you'll perish!' No doubt the triumphant realization immediately after Stalin's death that 'continuity in the leadership of the state has been ensured' stems from this. Stalin's children and stepchildren were amazed that after his death the sky did not fall in and the rudder of state did not drop from their feeble hands.

To be fair, one must say that even Lenin did not bother with any heir. In his political Testament he gave an assessment of each of the top leaders, which consisted mainly of critical comments. But he found nobody (and therefore cultivated nobody) who could have become leader of the party and the country after him. This tradition was continued by Khrushchev. He drew to himself only obedient executors, although, probably, it never even entered his head that Brezhnev could become his successor in the top post. It is true that Khrushchev brought in young people such as Andropov and even Shelepin, but he held them at a distance.

Generally speaking, in all countries of the modern world political leaders are subject to malignant internal erosion. The most likely reason for this is the development of 'mass' democracy on the one hand and monstrous bureaucracy on the other. This is what gives birth to a 'weathercock leader', who tries to suit both sides. For a long time we thought that we were immune from this misfortune because of our centrally planned society. Here great disappointment awaited us, precisely as regards the political leadership, which turned out to be foolish enough to take on the functions which rightfully belong to the party and the people.

This means that the very tradition of political leadership has to be reformed, so that a new Brezhnev and even more so a new Chernenko does not find his way into the leadership ranks, let alone to the top. It is now obvious that if a person cannot rule he is inevitably reduced to artificially propagating his own cult, squandering national property and participating in corruption.

The rotation of cadres is an important and resourceful solution to this problem. But to prevent weak or, even worse, corrupt leaders from staying on for five, or even worse, ten years guarantees are needed. It is essential to transfer the centre of gravity to genuine elections and to the public arena, where candidates for high posts prove their worth.

The art of ruling is the most complex of all art forms, including the martial arts and the fine arts. We began to win the war against Fascism when Voroshilov, Budyonny, Timoshenko and Kulik were replaced by Zhukov, Rokossovsky, Konev, Meretskov and Tolbukhin. It is the same with politics. *Perestroika* means transferring leadership from cadres of the Brezhnev type to talented modern rulers, able to implement radical changes and envisage long-term objectives, not to mention the public good and elementary morality. In short, we need experts at government, not apprentices or lazy consumers of prestige, power and privilege.

The most important guarantee aginst the return of the Brezhnev phenomenon is the party's policy of socialist pluralism, which it is now implementing. Its model dates back to the Leninist period. At the same time we have the opportunity to go considerably further. The exaggerated fears that *glasnost* could be taken to extremes – that, without a doubt, accompanies any healthy course – do not in any way reflect a concern for socialism, but come from our authoritarian political culture.

Conservative traditions stand in our way most of all. Russian political culture has no tolerance for pluralism of opinion and free criticism of government activity. Only after the revolution of 1905 was a small breach made. But even then, in point of fact, it was not possible to criticize the tsar, or tsarism.

After the Revolution one of the first decrees to be adopted involved measures against the 'counter-revolutionary press' of varying shades. These measures were defined as temporary, specific to the aggravation of the class war. It is no less characteristic that after the civil war Lenin returned to the previous stance of the party, which enshrined as immutable the right to free expression of opinion. Pluralism within the party, trade unions, soviets, peasant associations and, in particular, the sphere of culture became a commonplace and an important aspect of the new economic policy. This was overthrown together with the NEP at the end of the twenties. Khrushchev made some efforts to revive *glasnost*, but Brezhnev buried it again.

Pluralism also involves a guarantee of the rights of the minority. Hasn't our experience convinced us of the importance of this? Revolutionary *perestroika*, at least in its first stage, was based on the ideas, views and will not of the majority, but the minority. That has, in essence, always been the case if we are talking of the struggle of the new against the old. Athenian democracy was the most innocent and elegant of all democracies, yet out of the mouths of the majority issued the words: Socrates must drink the poison. Drink, Socrates, drink – for the majority wills it! And in the Soviet Union in the thirties didn't Stalin lean on the will of the majority? We need not mention his associates – there was no question of it being otherwise. Even Khrushchev, the mighty destroyer of the cult of personality, participated sincerely and faithfully in the slaughter which took place according to the will of the majority. The majority considered that Bukharin was wrong. So, keep

228

walking, Nikolay Ivanovich, don't look behind you, a bullet will find its mark . . .

And in more recent times we have had Brezhnev: he wasn't alone, was he? The absolute majority in the administrative apparatus idolized him, because they received rank, prizes, money, dachas, bribes. He was also supported by those sections of society who lived and still live without fear on their shady income.

How is one to safeguard the will, interests and views of the minority – the minority which seems today to be mistaken, but tomorrow may become the standard-bearers of progress? Only through the rights of the individual in party, state and other institutions of the political system – the right to think, write and speak freely, to seek the truth and find it. There is no other way.

Of course, the minority is not always right. Therefore it must know its place and take account of the will of the majority. Without this there can be no order or discipline, not in any organization or any state. Consequently, it only has the right to claim autonomy within the framework of what is generally acceptable. But this autonomy, clearly outlined by decrees, laws and political practice, could become an enormous achievement of our democracy.

In the sphere of science and culture a guarantee of the rights of the minority is commonplace, although here we have had not a little bureaucratic violence. It has not yet been wiped out of our memories how the majority persecuted the study of genetics, branded as false the theories of relativity and cybernetics, rejected jazz and even more so rock 'n' roll, destroyed abstract art and rejected sociology and political science. Now we know that a person is three times a killer if he kills thought. There are other areas closer to power and politics where it is more difficult to guarantee the autonomy of the minority in the interests of alternative solutions. The especially fine and accurate chisel of the legislator is needed to find some balance in the combination of views and interests of the majority and minority and to establish genuine socialist pluralism.

And finally, there is the danger of adulation in political life. Stalin and Brezhnev craved adulation of the most exaggerated cult-like kind, not because they believed in such eulogies but because they enjoyed humiliating the flatterer, seeing him crushed and sprawling. Some of our home-grown Fouchets and Talleyrands passed through every political regime like a knife through butter, exploiting the artless device of flattering every new leader without any sense of proportion, to say nothing of shame or conscience.

12 **Disgrace**

Let us return to the fate of the advisers in our small group of consultants.

It was early in December 1964. At nine in the evening I was still working in my spacious office, reading the latest TASS reports and other business papers. My eye was caught by a memorandum I had prepared for the Politburo, entitled 'Planning Foreign Policy in the USSR'. As I read it through I thought bitterly how these sensible ideas would perish or be twisted into their antitheses. With great anguish I thought of what had happened – not only to our plans but generally of the turn in policy which had begun after Khrushchev's fall.

Suddenly the phone rang.

'Could you come and see me?' Andropov's voice sounded distressed and hoarse over the phone. I went into his office, sat in an armchair opposite him and was struck by the unusually despondent expression on his face.

We sat a few minutes in silence. He had lowered his eyes and I studied his face, trying to gauge what had happened. Moved by some inexplicable inner impulse I suddenly said, 'Yury Vladimirovich, I've wanted to talk to you about this for quite some time.' He looked up at me in surprise. 'I've felt increasingly awkward about working in the department. You know that I've never wanted to be and probably never could have become a functionary in the apparatus. I like writing. But that's perhaps not the main thing. There's been a sharp change in domestic and foreign policy. At first it seemed that we would go further along the road of reform, the road of the Twentieth Party Congress. Now we can see that this line has been rejected. A new period is beginning and new policies demand new people. I wanted to ask you to let me leave. I have dreamed for a long time of working in a newspaper as a political observer and I think that now is the most suitable moment. Besides, this will probably also untie your hands as many people have been looking askance at me as a fanatical anti-Stalinist.'

I said this without pausing for breath. I looked at Andropov and I do not have the strength to convey the expression on his face. He looked at me with a snake-like expression for several minutes and said nothing. This mysterious look torments me to this day – what did it mean? It seemed to me then that his expression was one of shocked displeasure at my unexpected announcement. Yu.V. had, of course, not anticipated anything of the sort. Later, when I began to compare all the facts, it occurred to me that my proposal had coincided with a dramatic moment. I cannot exclude the possibility that Andropov's summons to me late in the evening, his dejected and even oppressed behaviour, meant that he had had a talk with Brezhnev, who had proposed to him then – as it later came about – that he leave the post of secretary of the Central Committee and accept the appointment of head of the KGB. This happened considerably later, but the conversation could have taken place at this time. I do not exclude the possibility that at that moment it occurred to Andropov, who was an extremely suspicious man, that I had somehow learned of his demotion and was rushing to leave the sinking ship. Perhaps this is a figment of my imagination, but it makes sense given Andropov's reaction to my proposal. He did not try to persuade me to stay on. After a pause he said slowly in a hoarse voice, 'And who do you propose to leave in your place?'

He did not call me Fedor, as he usually did, but put the question in an impersonal and indifferent, even hostile way.

'I think that Shakhnazarov or Bovin would be equally suitable, whomever you choose. They are both fully capable of heading the group. They have been working here for two years and know their job well.'

'Bovin would probably be more suitable, actually,' Andropov said, and his voice sounded ironic. 'As for your intention of becoming political observer of *Pravda*, I won't help you. You can do that yourself.'

After this talk, brief as a gunshot, I left the office in a strange state of shock. I had apparently got what I wanted, as I had long dreamed of working as a political observer, a job that I thought would enable me to appeal directly to public opinion. I really loved newspaper work and the unique opportunity of seeing one's thoughts and feelings in print the day after writing them.

But I had not anticipated such a conversation with Andropov. Almost five years of continuous service which had gone without a hitch, a close and warm association, and this is how it had ended! I could not believe it. It should have turned out differently. That is why I think I happened to be there at a most inappropriate and difficult moment in his life. He did not appreciate my act as that of a courageous person who has abandoned his political career out of principle. But that is precisely what I thought I was doing. Andropov had on many occasions told me of the leadership's opinion of me: 'Burlatsky is a talented person; he has potential.' And now – what an insult; to be cut off in this way. No, there was something else behind it, but what I still do not know.

When I try to recreate the events and feelings that led me to my dramatic decision to make a sharp break with the Central Committee apparatus I invariably see a hurricane before my eyes; a sense of things running amok, as described by Stefan Zweig, when a person seems to act not of his own free will but like a leaf in the wind.

I would even say that it was more than that, although this may seem strange and improbable. After my fateful conversation with Andropov – it had taken place late in the evening – I returned home but could not sit still in the flat. I took my son out for a walk and in a kind of feverish excitement began to move almost at a run along Kutuzovsky Avenue – that same street where Khrushchev's son had met his informant, past the house where later both Brezhnev and Andropov lived and where later still memorial plaques were placed (the second is still there).

I could not discuss my decision with Seryozha as he was then only eleven years old. But his presence was vital. I needed to feel him by my side as I myself had lost my bearings. While I was running a feeling of something sharp, unusual and even mystical took hold of me, as if I had submitted to a radiance emanating from heaven, from the universe itself. It was as if heaven were trying to influence me in a certain direction, perhaps to protect me from taking a false step; as if it was warning me against taking that step which would ruin my fate as predestined on high. I don't remember how long this feeling lasted, perhaps five or ten minutes, but it staggered me by its clarity and strength.

I returned home weak and depressed, with a strong feeling that I had made a mistake and was somehow guilty. It was still not too late to rectify the mistake. After all, only a conversation had taken place. And particularly as afterwards Andropov – admittedly not directly but through his deputy, Tolkunov – persistently requested that I remain in the department and even offered me a post as his deputy. But I, having run amok and taken the bit between my teeth, did not think of the consequences.

I lay in bed and envisaged what would happen to me in the future. My doctoral dissertation had not yet been confirmed and was rolling along and the Commission for Higher Certification, as soon as it heard that I had left, would assume that I had been expelled and would think a dozen times before conferring on me the degree of Doctor of Sciences. I had a premonition that Brezhnev personally would not forgive me for taking this step, as he had already met me and seemed fully satisfied with my first attempt to prepare a speech for him. I even conjured up scenes that later really happened when I was expelled from *Pravda* and during other ordeals. But the political frenzy I was in was stronger: the ashes of Klaas and of my mother's fanatical spirit overcame all my fears and apprehensions.

But let us return to my conversation with Andropov. It had been preceded by a number of events which had deeply affected me. The main one I have already mentioned – the circumstances that led to Khrushchev's dismissal. But Khrushchev's departure was not the issue here, as we ourselves had seen how many rash decisions he had made towards the end. I personally thought that Khrushchev should have remained in the leadership of the country, but that his power should have been limited. Perhaps he could have retained one post: either First Secretary of the Central Committee or Chairman of the Council of Ministers or at worst Chairman of the Presidium of the Supreme Soviet. In any case he stood head and shoulders above all the other members of the older generation in the leadership. As for the younger generation, men such as A. Shelepin, P. Demichev and D. Polyansky, we were scared of them in our circle, as they had come out of the Komsomol Central Committee, which at that time was notorious as a school for careerists.

We could even have resigned ourselves to Khrushchev being released from all his posts if only he had been replaced by more worthwhile leaders. I personally knew some of those who were promoted immediately to the top. One, for example, was N. N. Mesyatsev, who had taken an active part in the coup.

I was told how on the first day of the session, late in the evening, he turned up at the USSR Committee for Radio and Television Broadcasting in Pyatnitskaya Street. The janitor barred his way as it was late, about eleven o'clock. Mesyatsev pulled out a document from his pocket and showed the Central Committee decision signed by Brezhnev (although he was not yet First Secretary of the Central Committee) appointing him chairman of the broadcasting committee replacing Kharlamov, who had prudently been sent abroad earlier – to Sweden, I think. Nevertheless, the janitor refused to let him in. Then Mesyatsev gave an order to two lads from the KGB, who pushed the janitor aside. Accompanied by these lads, Mesyatsev went up in the lift to the chairman's office, where he found the person on duty. Mesyatsev asked him one question only: 'Where are the switches which turn off all broadcasts to the Soviet Union and abroad?' Confused, the man showed him how it was done. Mesyatsev remained all night guarding the switches. Evidently, the conspirators feared Khrushchev might find some means to appeal to the people on the radio.

This story was the first indication I had that Khrushchev's dismissal had not been done according to normal democratic procedures, but as a result of a plot organized beforehand. I knew Mesyatsev well, as he worked in the same department as me. A former secretary of the

Komsomol Central Committee and a close friend of Shelepin's, he was renowned for his empty Komsomol natter on any subject, even the most serious ones. Although he worked as Andropov's deputy and was responsible for matters relating to China (evidently Andropov had gone half-way in accepting Shelepin's recommendation), Andropov virtually never enlisted his services in making decisions or even discussing problems of Sino-Soviet relations. Nevertheless, he was the first nonentity who, before my very eyes, jumped several steps up the ladder. Although this was not significant in itself, it put me and my friends on our guard.

Then I had a strange talk with V. Lebedev, an aide to Khrushchev, who had been dismissed immediately after the October Central Committee plenum. Some time in November 1964 I had gone into hospital for a medical check-up; this was the hospital for higher officials in Kuntsevo, on the outskirts of Moscow. I was there for a week and met Lebedev, who was in a terrible state after the fall of his boss and his own enforced departure. I never particularly liked Lebedev, although we got on reasonably well. He was in the press group together with Shuysky, Satyukov and others, headed by L. Ilyichev, Central Committee secretary for ideology. I had been in contact with Lebedev on many occasions. He was always polite, tactful and prudent, but I had my doubts about him, as he was one of the people who had incited Khrushchev against the left intelligentsia. I remembered the memorandum he sent to the Central Committee Presidium, where he raised the question of imposing harsher censorship and sanctions against writers.

In the hospital, where I used to play chess with Lebedev out of boredom, a revealing conversation took place. Naturally, we started to discuss the results of the October plenum, Khrushchev's dismissal and Brezhnev's coming to power. I remembered I said that now we would probably see the start of an era of genuine reforms and a full return to the position of the Twentieth Party Congress. 'You're wrong, Fyodor Mikhaylovich.' Lebedev could not restrain himself. 'You will have many opportunities to see this for yourself once things really get moving. There are no grounds to justify your hopes in the new leaders; on the contrary, they will take things back to the Stalinist order.'

I did not believe this man who had just been pushed out of power, although later I was forced to reflect on this conversation.

*

The following events, one after the other, confirmed that such an about-turn was possible. Soon after returning from hospital I prepared a memorandum on a subject I had been pondering – a planned Soviet foreign policy. It stated that previously policy had been formed essentially on the basis of departmental proposals – from the Ministry of Foreign Affairs, the Ministry of Defence, Foreign Trade, the KGB and the Central Committee departments. These proposals were considered by the Presidium of the Central Committee, but were hardly ever integrated. Therefore, they often contradicted each other. Moreover, many decisions on domestic matters turned out to have an effect on our relations with the West. The persecution of Boris Pasternak and Andrey Sakharov, motivated by domestic ideological considerations, had an enormous negative influence on relations between the USSR and the United States and Western Europe.

I put forward the idea of setting up a special body, which would bring together all the proposals from different departments, as well as of research institutes and public organizations. Such a body would prepare comprehensive documents and proposals for the Presidium of the Central Committee and the government. In other words, only then would there be a genuinely planned common strategy behind our foreign policy, taking into account separate regions and separate countries. This foreign policy commission would have its own group of advisers and consultants. Personally I hoped that Yury Andropov would be made chairman and our group of consultants, together with other groups, would work under him.

Andropov supported my proposal and my memorandum was sent to the Presidium of the Central Committee. The decision that was eventually adopted was the very antithesis of what we had planned. The Presidium set up a foreign policy commission, but at the head of it they put not Andropov but Suslov – Andropov was appointed only a secretary of the commission. Our proposal to set up a working body to prepare comprehensive documents on foreign policy was rejected. Instead, a decision was taken to set up a bureau on the planning of foreign policy under the Ministry of Foreign Affairs.

This decision disappointed me enormously. I knew perfectly well that nothing positive would come of it. Foreign policy was traditionally the prerogative of the Presidium of the Central Committee and personally of the leader of the party and the country. It was obvious that the Ministry of Foreign Affairs, as an executive organ, was in no position at all to coordinate the activities of other departments, especially the more influential ones, or to prepare comprehensive documents. Indeed this bureau soon withered away; it became little more than the refuge of ambassadors who had lost their posts. The activities of the commission also soon came to a halt as, deprived of working bodies and headed, moreover, by Suslov, it could produce nothing fruitful.

But perhaps the deepest disappointment I experienced was connected with my attempt to propose a working programme for the new leadership. Remember that this was December 1964, when Andropov was getting ready to go to Poland with Brezhnev and Kosygin. With his approval, I had set out two or three pages of proposals for a working programme on domestic and foreign policy for the new leadership.

These proposals consisted of five points. They included economic reform; the democratization and reorganization of state administration; the demarcation of party and state functions so that the party would focus only on working out a programme and a common strategy, while the whole administration and operational leadership would be handed over to state and public organs; the development of economic self-administration for enterprises and regions; a sharp reduction in arms, especially of missiles and nuclear arms, an end to military confrontation and a reduction of the military budget, and the use of the defence sector for peacetime production.

I waited impatiently for Andropov's return from Poland to find out what the results of his discussions with Brezhnev and Kosygin had been. At first, however, he said nothing. I had to ask him myself, which was not the acceptable thing to do. In practice there was a rule governing relations in the apparatus, which was formulated like this: 'Never ask the head a question if you are not certain beforehand what his answer will be.' I disregarded this rule.

Andropov told me that my proposals had not received the support either of Brezhnev or of Kosygin. Kosygin spoke in favour of economic reform, but insisted on a completely different approach to foreign policy. At the time he harboured illusions that it was possible to restore friendship and an alliance with China, and in his opinion this would inevitably lead to a definite hardening of relations with the West. (Subsequently, after his trip to Vietnam, Kosygin visited China and had a long discussion with Mao Tse-tung, and on his return acknowledged his mistake. He understood that even if the Soviet Union had made very large concessions, Mao Tse-tung would not have agreed to restore our alliance as his national aims were quite different from ours.) Brezhnev, on the other hand, in his usual cautious manner said that it would be better to think about it, that we should not be hasty, and said virtually nothing in favour of any of the proposed tasks.

Side by side with the major political events that had taken place there were two minor events which also influenced my abrupt decision to give up party work.

Ilya Erenburg once remarked that history – or the makers of history, in the person of Soviet leaders – had often accomplished policy changes by making use of him and his works for their own purposes. Stalin had done this when immediately after the end of the war he made an ideological statement – 'Hitlers come and go, but the peoples remain' – as an appeal to put an end to criticism of the German nation.

Erenburg was depicted then as a nationalist extremist. The second time was when Khrushchev made use of Erenburg's novella, *The Thaw*. Similar things, although of course on a smaller scale, happened to me many times.

It so happened that exactly two days after the October plenum, that is, on 16 October 1964, I defended my doctoral dissertation. Its main aim was to give a theoretical basis to the idea of an all-people's state and, following on from this, a programme for developing democracy. In the dissertation I naturally referred repeatedly to the Twentieth and Twenty-Second Party Congresses and Khrushchev's speeches, especially to the Party Programme and those sections of it which I had written myself on problems of democracy.

Two hours before the defence was due to begin I received a phone call from Yu. Frantsev, Dean of the Academy of Social Sciences attached to the Central Committee of the Communist Party. Greatly agitated, he informed me that a group of members of the academic council of this very conservative establishment, to which I had rashly sent my dissertation, had come to him to protest against the defence, stating that its members would vote against me. Their main argument was that the dissertation sharply criticized Stalin and defended the idea of an all-people's state, and that all this would soon be reconsidered by the new party leadership. Frantsev suggested I put off the oral examination to avoid being failed. His decision, which was probably rational at that time, seemed to me a disgraceful capitulation. I still harboured illusions about the policy of the new leadership. I replied to Frantsev, 'Don't cancel it, we will give them a fright.'

When I arrived at one of the luxurious halls of the academy, where the defence was to take place, I saw the gloomy faces of the members of the academic council, many of whom I recognized as people who had been thrown out of the party apparatus under Khrushchev. Although I felt sick to the pit of my stomach, I showed no signs of weakness in my introductory and concluding comments; quite the contrary, I intensified my defence of the ideas of the Twentieth Congress, my criticism of the cult of personality and the reasons for rejecting the dictatorship of the proletariat and for developing democracy.

The members of the council were thrown into confusion. They did not know how to react to this challenge. As a result, no one criticized my dissertation. I was only asked one question on a peripheral issue about the nature of the revolution in Bulgaria. Everything seemed to be going smoothly. However, the secret vote was terrible: of the twenty-five people, seven voted against. The pass mark required two-thirds of the votes, or fifteen people. This meant that I was literally hanging on by the skin of my teeth. Frantsev put a brave face on the sorry business, announcing that the examination showed that their decision had been correct, despite the opinion of a number of members of the academic council.

Nevertheless, it was a painful blow to my vanity. I did not even want to have a party to celebrate, although this was the custom at the time. Only because members of our consultancy group insisted, a few of us, without inviting any of the examiners or members of the academic council, celebrated the event briefly at my home in a fairly gloomy mood.

The next day Andropov specially called me in and said that I should have warned him earlier that I was preparing for the defence so that the necessary measures could have been taken to ensure a smooth passage. I said that in the end it had turned out all right. Andropov did not agree, saying that the results of the defence constituted a challenge to the Central Committee apparatus and him personally, not to speak of myself. Whether this was the case or not, I experienced some bitter moments. Moreover, for me this was the first alarming signal of a new turn in policy by the party leadership.

The other episode concerned the preparation of Kosygin's speech for his trip to Vietnam at the end of 1964. It was expected that en route he would go to China and meet Mao Tse-tung. Kosygin, as I have already mentioned, reckoned that it would take him 'two hours' to smooth over the misunderstanding with the Chinese leaders. We drafted Kosygin's speeches jointly with officials from the Foreign Ministry. We were invited to discuss these speeches with Andrey Andreyevich Gromyko.

Gromyko was literally beside himself, shouting, 'Don't you realize changes have taken place? What have you shoved into this speech – peaceful coexistence with the West, the Twentieth Congress, criticism of Stalin? All this has to be rewritten again in the spirit of our new policy of a tough struggle against American imperialism, which is attempting to strangle the revolution in Vietnam. Express it in a new way, talk warmly of our unswerving friendship with the Chinese people.'

Here, I must admit, I could take no more. I had already been wound up by all the changes that had occurred. Without rising from my seat and with my teeth almost clenched, I said, 'Andrey Andreyevich, we work for the apparatus of the Central Committee of the Communist Party and are only prepared to listen to comments from our leadership, especially on such fundamental matters of policy.'

Gromyko's jaw dropped at my audacity. He had evidently never heard anything like this from his subordinates. And the whole group of consultants who had gathered there literally froze. But to give the minister his due, he restrained himself and did not reply to my attack. Instead he rang Andropov and gave vent to his indignation. Andropov passed on his remarks to me with a slight reproach.

Another clash also produced a strong impression on me. One of the first promotions Brezhnev made to the Central Committee apparatus was the appointment of his former assistant, S. Trapeznikov, as head of the science department. Soon after this I ran into Trapeznikov (I had known him before) at a reception at the Polish Embassy. He seized hold of me and spent a long time trying to convince me that Khrushchev had his own personal motives for criticizing Stalin and that Stalin, despite certain excesses, was a great Leninist and had secured the victory of socialism in the USSR. With great persistence, Trapeznikov tried to ram down my throat the significance of the collectivization of the countryside, about which he later wrote a two-volume book. 'You don't know what it was like,' Trapeznikov said. 'Look at me. When I was sent to carry out collectivization the peasants broke my hand and legs with a pitchfork. It was a real battle for socialism.'

Trapeznikov really was invalided for life: he limped and had a deformed hand. Moving away from him, I was careless enough to say to a friend, 'You wouldn't believe that this lame pup tried to convert me to the Stalinist faith.'

Well-wishers immediately conveyed my tasteless joke to Trapeznikov. He remembered it well and I paid the price for it when I found myself working under him at the Academy of Sciences.

I was also dismayed by the fact that I could not fully work out Andropov's position. I saw him getting into the same car as Shelepin many times, when they were seeing off or greeting official figures. Such a close asociation with the 'young Turks' (perhaps it was opportunistic) seemed to me a betrayal of the line of the Twentieth Congress. Yury Vladimirovich soon moved away from them when he realized that power lay on Brezhnev's side. Anticipating somewhat, he also remained on good terms with Shelepin for a long time. Running ahead, I will mention how two years later during the meetings of representatives of Communist Parties at Karlovy Vary I observed the following scene. Brezhnev was coming down the stairs followed by Shelepin, who was looking at him with eyes filled with open hostility, while Andropov was holding 'iron Shurik' (as he was called) under the elbow, clearly trying to calm his rage. Looking ahead even further I remember that the pretext for Shelepin's expulsion occurred during his visit to England when a number of documents were published relating to his activities as head of the KGB. How did these materials find their way into the English papers and who was behind it? Was it perhaps Andropov, on Brezhnev's behest? We don't know . . .

There is one more incident worth reporting. When I was elected to the party conference of the Central Committee apparatus, I gave a speech in which I described the work of our group of consultants, as well as that of consultants in other departments. In particular, I talked of the problems that were being discussed in preparation for the conference of Communist and workers' parties and problems relating to the domestic policy of individual parties. Again I spoke the truth, but the truth was not to the liking of one of the secretaries of the Central Committee, who was in charge of the conference. In his concluding remarks he said, without mentioning my name, 'Who actually determines policy – consultants or the Presidium and the secretaries of the Central Committee?' He said the same thing to Andropov, criticizing my speech and the improper role I had claimed for consultants in decision-making.

This shows the psychological climate that was affecting our group of consultants. It was no accident that I often happened to hear – both within and outside the Central Committee – about 'Burlatsky's child prodigies'. The apparatus did not like the fact that the scholarly intelligentsia was beginning to have a greater influence in drafting documents and speeches than their 'native' apparatchiks.

All this had accumulated in the two months after the October plenum and ended with my decision to leave the apparatus. My close friends, especially the consultants in our department, knew that I had left of my own free will but they were perplexed, thinking that I had made the biggest mistake of my life.

After my decision to leave I had an informal gathering for all of them at my home. The table was laden with bottles of vodka and sandwiches, which had been bought in a hurry. A strange atmosphere of caution, anxiety and perplexity reigned. I could not be completely frank about the political reasons for my action; therefore, when talking with the consultants I did not use the word 'resignation', as I had freely done with Andropov and Tolkunov. I had spoken to them in private; here there were a great deal of people and no certainty that what I said would not be conveyed to my opponents tomorrow. I gave a short speech which went something like this:

'Friends, I am leaving because I think that in these circumstances I should not remain. I don't want to and can't take responsibility for what will be done now. The country has entered a new phase and we cannot determine what this phase will be and how long it will last. But it is obvious that the ideas of the Twentieth Congress, the ideas of the reformation of Russia, have been set aside for a certain time. We do not have the means to influence the course of events now, but each of us has the right to make his choice – whether to participate or not at this turning point. I have made my choice. This doesn't mean that I am challenging anyone here to do the same thing. Politics demand patience and perhaps I am too impatient, but I think that I can influence events from the sidelines, appealing to public opinion. Possibly this is also an illusion. In any case, the decision has been made and I have burned my bridges. Some of you may achieve your ends and have a substantial influence on the broader political scene. Probably Arbatov or Shakhnazarov or Bovin will. I hope so. As for me, I'm temporarily dropping out of the game.'

A major argument arose about how to evaluate my action. Arbatov, who had already given me his opinion, remained silent. Incidentally, he had shown his usual nobility of spirit by advising me not to go to *Pravda* but to take a position in one of the institutes of the Academy of Sciences, saying that I would find it more meaningful and substantial and that it would be more tranquil there. I was in a fever of irritation and burst out, unfairly, 'If you impose your advice on me I'll name someone else and not you as my successor.' After this, Arbatov withdrew into himself during the farewell dinner at my home and, as I remember, said practically nothing.

But Shakhnazarov and Bovin got into an embittered argument. They discussed my action as well as the general principle of how advisers should behave in situations where they did not agree with the politics being put forward. Shakhnazarov, who was extremely honest and emotional, tried to prove that I had behaved correctly and would return to the apparatus on a white charger. Bovin, with his usual rough directness said, 'It's a mistake! It's a mistake that will dog Fyodor throughout his career and maybe throughout his life.'

I recalled this categorical statement many times later. Bovin, who became Brezhnev's most trusted speechwriter, clung to that office with tenacity, probably assuming that in every game you had to be the winner and justifying himself by saying that he had tried to introduce progressive ideas into Brezhnev's speeches even in the most difficult times, such as during the events in Czechoslovakia in 1968 and the tragic invasion of Afghanistan.

This Last Supper with the consultants ended on a sad note. Everyone left looking gloomy and somewhat bewildered. Each one of us had to confront a new situation in our lives and to find the moral ground on which we would stand, while thinking at the same time of our own futures.

It is strange that we hardly ever mentioned Nikita Khrushchev's fate. He had virtually dropped out of our minds, in much the same way as no one notices the queen when she is removed from the chessboard by an opponent. Does anyone in a game think where she is, whether she has been put on the table or under it, or how she feels? Such is the fate of a political figure. One day he is the focus of universal attention; his face, threatening or smiling, simple or refined, is all over the newspapers and television screens. Then the mystical moment arrives and the focus changes: there is a different face on the screens and in the papers, and what happened yesterday seems never to have existed. We, who even at that time regarded ourselves more or less as 'Khrushchevites', did not think of or remember this man who had stirred our souls during the Twentieth Party Congress. One can explain this in different ways, but it still has to be reckoned with. When a writer dies interest in him is usually redoubled, as in the case, for instance, of Pasternak or Vysotsky, but a fallen political figure goes into oblivion for a long time.

What really was the main reason for my leaving the Central Committee apparatus? When I think about it now I see a whole set of reasons rather than any single one, and they have more to do with emotions than with rational convictions. I felt a sense of protest against the political regression; yes, that weighed very heavily on my mind. I repeated dozens of times to Kuskov and Belyakov that I was leaving and they could all go to hell. I also wanted to return to doing something creative. I had always considered myself more of a scholar and writer than a politician. But to be completely honest, there was another reason, and that was my mistaken assessment of Brezhnev. Like many others I was absolutely certain that he was a temporary figure and that he would not last more than two or three years. I saw that there were more dangerous forces standing behind him – the neo-Stalinists; but I also believed it was inevitable that the reformers would return as there was no other course of development for the country. I thought, probably naively, that through the press, especially with such a liberal editor as A. Rumyantsev at *Pravda* who, incidentally, had been appointed to this post through Andropov on my recommendation, I would be better able to fight the slide into Stalinism and continue the politics of the Twentieth Party Congress. This explains the persistence with which I wrote articles in *Pravda* against totalitarian regimes, and on the need to revise the Party Programme and to reject the utopian idea of 'Communist construction' in favour of becoming part of modern technological civilization.

But I was deeply mistaken. Brezhnev's limp and lazy centrist politics proved to be surprisingly in tune with the expectations of the apparatus and a sufficiently wide stratum of the population. Brezhnev lasted eighteen years and would have lasted longer if he had lived. He suited a large number of people, if not everyone.

My mistake is all the more unforgivable as I had more than once demonstrated a strongly developed political intuition. I had a foreboding about Khrushchev's fall and not long before Mao Tse-tung's death I predicted the fall of Jiang Jing and the return of Deng Xiao-ping. Probably one sees things better from a distance. I was too deeply involved in the political kitchen to make a worthwhile assessment of the cooks. Infantilism is the most typical and dangerous disease of advisers. There is also a kind of scientism; we are inclined to believe in the logic of the political process when this process has so many group influences that the results may be entirely illogical. Besides, it is impossible to exclude the fact that history or predestination has its own ends, unknown and unfathomable to the human mind, arranging figures on the chessboard in its own way.

★

Shelepin, of course, was informed of my memorandum analysing and exposing his neo-Stalinism. The mechanism by which such information is conveyed has always been a mystery to me. Of course, in principle, it is understandable that if several people are involved in a conversation it is impossible to conceal its substance. Nevertheless, only four or five people took part in the discussion of Shelepin's 'dissertation'. I don't exclude the possibility that Brezhnev passed on the contents of the conversation to other members of the leadership and it reached Shelepin in this way. One could also assume that Brezhnev spoke of my memorandum in Shelepin's presence to make him anxious, while at the same time remaining aloof as a person who is simply passing on someone else's opinion. In any case, it took no more than a day or two before Shelepin heard of my 'insinuations'. Of course he was quick to fight back.

At a session of the Politburo he came out with a sharp attack against me, accusing me on two counts. The first was as follows: Burlatsky had divulged the 'secret of his status in the Central Committee of the Communist Party of the Soviet Union to American intelligence, having written an article in the journal *Soviet Life*, intended for the United States and other Western countries, in which he revealed where he worked in the Central Committee'. While saying this Shelepin held a copy of the journal *Soviet Life* tightly in his hands, shaking it before the eyes of members of the leadership. In fact, there was no article by me in it. That issue had an article written by Shakhnazarov, with a photo of him showing his wonderful, almost bald head and a mention of his post, but nothing about me. It was impossible to confuse us: neither his name nor his face bore the slightest resemblance to mine.

The second accusation was no better than the first. He reported that I had been 'shooting off' ideas intended for Brezhnev's speech in *Pravda*. This is what is called a blow below the belt. Nothing was more aggravating to our clients, especially to Brezhnev, than the hint that someone had attempted to get into the press beforehand with a speech, thus minimizing its worth. Leonid Ilyich was particularly touchy about such things. It is not surprising that I was dismissed immediately not only from the leadership but from preparing the report on the twentieth anniversary of victory in the Great Patriotic War.

What amazed me most was not so much that decision as the discussion that took place in response to Shelepin's obvious slanders. After Shelepin's speech, Brezhnev asked a strange question: 'Where does Burlatsky work now?' He had just signed the order transferring me at my request to *Pravda* as a political observer, and perhaps that had imprinted itself on his mind.

Shelepin, obviously not knowing about my transfer, responded, 'In Andropov's department.' The reaction that followed seems psychologically incredible to me to this day. Andropov said, 'He doesn't work in my department any more.' And that was all. Not a word in my defence. He knew for certain that these accusations were totally false, especially as Shakhnazarov's article had been submitted for his approval. He knew perfectly well that I had not yet managed to have a single article published in *Pravda*. But he said nothing.

I had served him for five years with the faithfulness of an intellectual hound who thinks he is guarding the home when in fact he is guarding his master, assisting his promotion up the political ladder. To a considerable extent his appointment as Central Committee secretary was due to the fact that he was able to take on the preparation of Khrushchev's most important speeches by relying on our assistance. Even if we assume that from his point of view I had behaved unethically in leaving his department against his will, how could he simply write off a person who had done him no harm but had simply decided to leave, and even then not as a personal affront but because he no longer believed in the work he was doing? By his answer he ostentatiously deprived me of his patronage and handed me over completely to the 'Komsomol gang' to be torn to pieces. He had even refused to provide objective testimony on my behalf.

I acquired the details of this episode from Kuskov, who had got them from Ponomaryov. The latter had related the events with great relish so that it would reach my ears. At first I could not believe it. It seemed unlikely and did not conform to my image of the person whom I had worshipped. 'So much for gratitude from the powers-that-be. That's what betrayal means. Surely you can't regret your decision to leave now?'

I moved to *Pravda*, where I was crammed into a large barn-like office. Obviously everyone knew that I had fallen out of favour. Incidentally, no one could understand my reasons for leaving. My opponents were delighted that 'Burlatsky's prodigies' had got their comeuppance. My supporters assumed and were quite convinced that I had been expelled from the apparatus against my will.

In the meantime my clash with Shelepin ended relatively well. The deputy head of the Central Committee Department of Agitation and Propaganda, an old acquaintance, invited me to see him. He made a semi-official announcement.

'I am sure you have heard the critical remarks made against you in the Politburo. We were instructed to deal with this. In the first place you were accused of publishing an article in the journal, *Soviet Life*, where you divulged your place of work. There is no evidence of this. In the second place you have been accused of 'shooting off' ideas for speeches in articles in *Pravda*. This has not been substantiated either, as you have had nothing published. The matter is closed. You can sleep soundly.'

'How can I sleep soundly?' I asked him. 'Accusations have been made and all the members of the Politburo heard them. You ought to send a note to this effect to those at the top. That will convince them that these claims were unfair.'

'What are you talking about?' my old acquaintance said, giving a broad and rather sad smile. 'What are you pushing me into? Don't you know who spoke against you? Do you want me to accuse him of lying? You've worked so many years in the apparatus and you still come out with such suggestions. The matter is closed. Be content with that. Work calmly, if you can.'

But of course I could not work calmly. I felt as if I were on the top of a volcano about to erupt. It was not just Shelepin; sooner or later someone would spill the beans to Brezhnev that I had thrown down a challenge by not wanting to become his speechwriter. Therefore, even though I was working on *Pravda* I did not feel safe. This did not stop me from writing over the next two and a half years a whole series of articles in the paper in which, directly or indirectly, I criticized the regime of personal power and advocated the democratic ideas of the Twentieth Party Congress.

I made use of allegory, which I partly borrowed from N. Dobrolyubov, the hero of my first book. Dobrolyubov wrote in the critical period of the first reforms in Russia in the 1860s and constantly resorted to indirect, oblique ways of expressing his views. The art consisted in finding a suitable subject through which you could demonstrate your position without the risk of completely submerging the point you wished your reader to understand.

One such subject was the regime of personal power in China. Our conflict with Mao Tse-tung continued and this gave me the opportunity of comparing Maoism with Stalinism. I prepared a series of articles on Mao Tse-tung's biography, which were gathered together and sent to the Politburo. Suslov, however, was strongly opposed to their publication. He possessed a surprisingly good nose for anything seditious and immediately understood that the underlying intention was to settle accounts with Stalin, using China as an example. I was only able to publish these articles in a small book, *Marxism or Maoism*, which came out after I had been expelled from *Pravda*.

Another subject, which was in many ways more accessible and could be used with greater freedom, was General Franco. In 1966 I was included in one of the first groups that went to Spain. The group consisted of Konstantin Simonov, Roman Karmen, Karen Kara-Karayev and other cultural figures. We spent twenty days travelling all over Spain. The most vivid impressions came from our meetings in Madrid. During a bullfight in the Spanish capital we were introduced to Franco. The Caudillo – a small, grey, respectable old man – sat a few rows above us. Our interpreter asked if we would pay our respects to the general and we felt it would be impossible to refuse. The general waved to us with his pale hands. I felt after this that I had the full moral right to write about Franco and Francoism.

But, of course, this was not the main point. I had decided to use Francoism to reflect on how our system had evolved after Stalin.

On my return to Moscow I published four long articles with such colourful titles as 'The Crisis of Totalitarianism' and 'The Erosion of an Authoritarian Regime'. Subsequently they came out in a small book called *Spain, the Bullfight and the Caudillo.*

In these articles I made quite unambiguous comparisons between Francoism and Stalinism, analysing the causes of the inner erosion of the regime of personal power and its deep roots. At the end of the articles I asked if it was possible to return to a cult of personality and an authoritarian regime after the death of the dictator. I concluded that there would be no return to this model in its pure form as it had been the result of unique historical circumstances and was concentrated in the unique personality of the dictator. I wrote that it was possible to slide back, but that there would be no repetition of the mass repressions and the cruellest manifestations of the totalitarian regime.

The Moscow intelligentsia, reading these articles, was amazed that the author continued to be employed by *Pravda.* My rival and opponent on the paper – another political observer, Georgy Zhukov – despite his bulk and customary immobility ran around the office screeching that the Spanish sketches were Burlatsky's swan song. Zhukov went with my Spanish articles to the ideology assistant, V. Golikov, hoping to open the leadership's eyes to the whole truth behind these articles. Golikov went to Brezhnev, but the latter could not make out what possible connection there could be between Francoist Spain and the socialist Soviet Union. So for a while nothing came of it.

Golikov had greater success with Suslov. As one of the people in the apparatus later told me, Suslov carefully read the articles, underlined the seditious passages and put question marks in the margin in red pencil. This was the first sign of disaster. Even after I had received information about the impression these articles had produced among the leadership I continued to write in the same vein. I myself find it hard to explain or understand what impelled me to continue, knowing that there was a threat hanging over my head. I can only compare it with a reckless gambler who cannot stop playing until he has lost everything.

I remember when I was on holiday in Gagra in the Caucasus I played in a volleyball team against the team from another sanitorium. I made the foolish mistake of wearing silk instead of cotton socks. Having landed on the ground after a jump, I felt an awful pain in my legs. Nevertheless, I continued playing, ignoring the discomfort for another four points. Even after I had left the volleyball court I went off to the tennis court and tried to play there. A nurse who was passing by noticed me limping and asked what had happened. Hearing my reply she took me to have an X-ray. It turned out that I had fractured a bone in my left leg. How can one explain the stupidity of continuing to play with a fracture in one leg and a severe sprain in the other?

The same sort of thing happened when I was working on *Pravda*. In the grip of a reckless and self-defeating contest with the leadership of the country, who possessed all the power and would have thought nothing of crushing me with a slight movement of an eyebrow, I continued in the same spirit.

A second episode that occurred was more humorous than dramatic. I was asked to write a short article in the journal *Novoye Vremya* for the Lenin jubilee. There was nothing special about my article. It reflected on the danger of missed opportunities and the importance of intuition in politics. As an example I referred to Lenin, who had accurately picked the date for the uprising in October 1917: 24 October was too early, 26 October was too late – it could only have been 25 October, the unique chance for the Bolsheviks to seize power.

Unexpectedly I was invited to the science department by a reviewer whom I knew, Grisha Kvasov, who was thin as a lath, smiling and obsequious.

'You have been instructed,' Grisha said, 'to write an explanation to the General Secretary about your article in *Novoye Vremya*.'

'What explanation?'

'Explain your reasons for writing the article.'

'I don't understand. What do you mean, my reasons? What reasons do you need for writing about Lenin? Tell me plainly what comments you have in mind.'

'I don't know what comments,' Grisha said with his ambiguous smile. 'I was told to get an explanation from you and that's all.'

'Who told you, Grisha, go on, you can tell me. Do you really think I believe that the General Secretary reads articles in *Novoye Vremya*? Doesn't he have anything better to do? Well, tell me in secret, who are the instructions from?'

'Who? Well don't tell anyone . . . it was Golikov. But it's a definite instruction, so sit down and write.'

'I don't intend to write anything, Grisha. And you can tell Golikov to be more precise about his comments.'

'You'd better write, Fedor, you can't get out of it.'

'Okay, Grisha, if you won't ask Golikov what specific remarks he has in mind, then I will. Tell him that Fedor refused to write an explanation and sends him to . . .' Here followed an unprintable expression.

'Watch out, Fedor, you'll go too far. I'm not going to pass on anything. If you want, ring him up yourself, but don't mention me.'

I went into the next office and rang Golikov on the government line.

'This is Burlatsky.' There was a pause and no reply. 'Are you listening?'

'Yes.'

'Well, Comrade Golikov, I'd like to know what specific comments you have on my article on Lenin.'

'Comments? The comment is simple.' Here he raised his voice to a scream. 'You are advocating Trotskyism in your article! That's my comment. It was not Lenin but Trotsky who argued that power should be seized on the 25th. Lenin insisted on the 24th.'

'Comrade Golikov, think what you're saying! That means we have been celebrating our revolution according to Trotsky – on the 25th, and not according to Lenin – on the 24th. And how did it come about that the Revolution was won on the 25th, that is, if we are to believe you, on the date suggested by Trotsky and not Lenin?'

'I don't understand a word. You're confusing me. I have received a letter of protest from a group of old Bolsheviks. So . . . write to the General Secretary of the Central Committee.'

I could stand it no longer and again sent comrade Golikov packing with a four-letter word. This was extremely rash as he later became the main instigator of the 'trial' that broke my career.

In the meantime the climate in the country was getting worse and worse. The persecution of Solzhenitsyn began. Censorship became tougher. What remained of Khrushchev's Thaw was living out its last days. The theatres were groaning under stronger ideological control. The press and its 'lieutenants' (Khrushchev's apt expression) became more right-wing and greyer before one's very eyes.

It was at this time that I befriended and grew close to Len Vyacheslavovich Karpinsky, a member of *Pravda*'s editorial board, who worked in the department of agitation and propaganda. He was the son of a famous revolutionary, who had joined the party about the same time as Lenin and had worked alongside him for many years. He had called his son Len in memory of Lenin. Len Karpinsky had come from a Komsomol background and the peak of his career had been as secretary in charge of agitation and propaganda in the Komsomol Central Committee at the beginning of the sixties. He had a bright, lively and imaginative mind, and a talent for grasping the most complex theoretical problems and presenting them, at least verbally, in an unusually attractive form. His political views developed in quite a different way from mine. Under Stalin his father had concealed what he thought and maintained an essentially conformist outlook. Initially this had an effect on his son's views.

'When the Twentieth Party Congress took place,' Len explained once, 'I was working as secretary of the Komsomol *obkom* in Gorky. We had a specific task before us – to produce a higher yield of milk in the countryside. We put all our efforts into this. At the time I thought, what's all this about Stalin? And I ignored everything that was being said about his crimes. I only realized what it meant later.'

When I met Len he had already moved to the left. His anti-Stalinist views were probably strengthened by our many discussions and quarrels about Stalinism and the fate of our country. Rather carelessly we had got into the habit of gathering at Karpinsky's flat or dacha, to which Mikhail Shatrov and many other writers, journalists and actors came. And despite the fact that the cold winds were blowing strongly, we discussed everything uninhibitedly – Stalin, the plot against Khrushchev and the new conservative era. (Looking ahead, I will mention that materials from these social gatherings later figured as evidence in the case to expel Karpinsky from the party and were used by the Party Control Committee to prepare a similar case against me.)

In the end Karpinsky and I had become such close friends that we settled in one state dacha, which had been offered to us by A. Rumyantsev, the editor-in-chief of *Pravda*. Strictly, this dacha was designated for Rumyantsev's personal use. It was a luxurious two-storey manor house in Serebryanyy Bor on the Moskva river, situated on a plot of about ten acres and surrounded by a fence. Our friends and some famous singers used to go there, and we would organize parties where music and politics and love intermingled.

Len Karpinsky had recently divorced his wife, with whom he had three children. She was a woman with a strong character, who later became a famous scholar. She was replaced in his affections by a young student from the institute of foreign languages, whom he had brought from Gorky – a pretty, sweet and affable girl. With her he also acquired her two young daughters, so he immediately became the father of five children. On the whole, in terms of impracticality, Len could have vied with Demosthenes. His elite origins had left him with somewhat lordly inclinations and a feeling that he was protected and had a guaranteed existence, which was unusual in other families.

The main theme of our endless conversations were the economic, political and cultural reforms in the country. He was captivated by Bukharin, whom he was reading at the time, and dreamed of a Leninist

249

renaissance. I was more drawn to the experience of the developed civilized Western world. It seemed terrible to me that our country in so many ways was still wearing out the clothes of the eighteenth and nineteenth centuries when many other countries had already glanced into the year 3000. Len was a much more orthodox Marxist-Leninist than those people who later trampled on his life and who believed themselves to be the successors of theoretical orthodoxy. I had been educated to a considerable degree on the Russian and Western history of social and political thought and was inclined to see all the problems of our life from the angle of modern civilization and the conditions specific to Russia.

We often thought of Khrushchev and the strange fate of reformers in Russia – Boris Godunov, or advisers such as Speransky under Alexander I or Stolypin under Nicholas II. For us they served as a stern warning against liberalism in our country, with its deeply-rooted authoritarian and patriarchal political culture.

Having come together, our alliance was so powerful that it was bound to have explosive consequences. That is in fact what happened. During one of our conversations with Yury Lyubimov, who was telling us about the Ministry of Culture's latest attempt to suppress his productions at the theatre, I suggested to Karpinsky that we jointly write an article with a critique not only of theatre politics, but generally of our censors and the methods the party leadership employed in the arts. He took up my idea and called a meeting at the newspaper office, which was attended by many prominent theatre directors. They recounted incidents which were not only monstrous but simply absurd.

A production would be rehearsed under the supervision of representatives of the USSR Ministry of Culture. Then the day would come when the Ministry had to give its official sanction to the production. Representatives of the Ministry would come to the theatre, sit down and watch the performance. If they noticed any controversial scene or 'hints' at something or other they would get up without saying a word and in single file, one after another, scurry out of the theatre. Then somewhere information would be compiled, a denunciation would be written and in the end the production, which had taken a year or two or even three to prepare, would be banned. This was the typical cri de coeur from the theatrical elite. It was then that Karpinsky and I prepared our article, which was initially entitled 'Genuine and Imaginary Sensations'.

Taking as examples Yury Lyubimov's Taganka Theatre and Oleg Yefremov's Sovremennik Theatre, we showed the full absurdity of the prevailing order. Our idea was simple in the extreme and, incidentally, has been put into practice without any difficulty in the period of perestroika. We wrote that it was necessary to hand over the running of the theatrical repertoire to the theatre, its collectives and those working in them. They themselves would make decisions about the repertoire and, moreover, it would then be done professionally, while their failures would be reflected in the press, on television and in viewers' responses. Unprofessional ministerial vigour with its bureaucratic and denunciatory zeal was not needed and was harmful not only to the arts but to proper relations between the state and the intelligentsia. The strongest part of the article, which later provoked the angriest accusations from Brezhnev's lackeys, said the following: there are two approaches to social problems – one is to conceal them, the other is to expose them. In the former case the problem is driven inwards, grows and in the final analysis leads to a crisis. In the latter, when problems are discussed publicly, a mechanism for solving them is worked out. This idea went beyond the limits of the subject and strictly speaking touched on the whole Brezhnev policy. Evidently, it touched its sorest spot.

At that time Rumyantsev was no longer editor-in-chief of *Pravda*. He had been dismissed from the management of the paper for publishing two articles about the intelligentsia, in which serious questions had been raised about developing intra-party democracy and strengthening the influence of the more educated and cultured sections of the party in all spheres of party activity. He was replaced by M. Zimyanin, who had it seems been picked by Brezhnev personally.

I remember clearly the first time he came to the office. I had known him before he became ambassador to Czechoslovakia. He was a short man with sharp features and a very distorted mouth, reminiscent of the devil Woland's grimace in Bulgakov's novel *The Master and Margarita*. His puny body jerked constantly with impatience, his hands moved continuously and his face looked like a wrinkled apple – so annoyed and irritated was he by everything that surrounded him.

'I have never been involved in newspaper matters,' Zimyanin stated with a kind of jaunty pride at his first meeting with the editorial board. 'True, when I was young I worked for six months on an area paper, but that doesn't count. However, I think I understand politics pretty well; here I have experience. And that is probably the most important thing for the editor of the nationwide party newspaper, *Pravda*.'

This coronation speech was hardly inspiring, especially as many of us knew several episodes of Zimyanin's biography. It was known that immediately after Stalin's death Beria went to Belorussia to recommend Zimyanin for the post of First Secretary of the republic in place of P. Patolichev. However, the Belorussian party organization – and I think this was the only case of its kind – decisively rejected Zimyanin as a candidate and elected Patolichev. It was then that Zimyanin entered the diplomatic service, at first in the reserves at the Ministry of Foreign Affairs and later as ambassador to Czechoslovakia.

When I worked in the Central Committee department I had the rather unpleasant task of passing on to Zimyanin some comments made by Khrushchev. I wondered whether he remembered this while I listened to the horrible words of this insignificant man, who had been 'recommended' as our editor.

It was to Zimyanin that I handed the article Karpinsky and I had written on 'Genuine and Imaginary Sensations'. He evidently read it carefully and said that the article, probably correctly, reflected the abnormal situation in the arts, but could not be published at the present time as the political wind was blowing in the opposite direction. I remember that he was impressed by some of the ideas: that the party leadership had itself created these imaginary sensations, that by banning certain cultural figures it was inflating their authority, that it was arousing passions about performances or works of literature which were not deserving of them and which would not have provoked much attention or made much of a stir in a tranquil atmosphere. But I don't think he liked the idea of radically changing the methods of the party leadership in the area of culture.

Anyway, Zimyanin did not raise any serious criticism of the article, but said that at the present time it had to be set aside. I collected the article from him and related our conversation to Karpinsky. He suggested we show the article to Boris Pankin, editor-in-chief of the youth paper *Komsomolskaya pravda*. I agreed and we went to see Pankin, who read the article while we were there. He liked it but did not make a decision on whether to publish it.

In the meantime I went to the Crimea for a holiday. The people I talked to there – mainly personnel in the party apparatus – put me in a pessimistic frame of mind. I felt how remote my views were from the mood of the functionaries. They were intoxicated by the new order that had taken shape under Brezhnev. The motto of 'stability', which fully guaranteed their positions and protected them from whatever controls there might be, delighted them. Leonid Ilyich was their god and they cursed the 'terrible' times under Khrushchev when the political boat rocked on the waves of 'subjectivism and arbitrary rule'.

While I was on holiday in the south I received an unexpected call from Kuskov. He told me that the appointment for the post of executive secretary of the journal *Problemy mira i sotsializma* would be decided urgently and suggested I go to Prague in this capacity. I refused.

Later I had reason not so much to regret this decision as to reflect often on the jokes fate plays on us. If I had agreed and a decision had been made, I would have escaped all the subsequent dramatic events which flared up over the publication of the article Karpinsky and I had written.

Len rang me in the Crimea and, in his usual somewhat limp manner, without spelling things out, said that the article would probably be published, but that it was more likely Pankin would decide against it. Exhausted by the sun and without fully reflecting on the possible consequences of such a publication, I mumbled something in reply. Evidently, Karpinsky took my not very articulate answer to signify my consent.

So there I was sitting on the shore of the Black Sea coast when I noticed some commotion among the holiday-makers. They were moving amongst each other, holding a newspaper in their hands and all but pointing their fingers at me. I went up to one of my acquaintances and asked him what was going on. He said, 'Well, you've certainly stirred up the pot. Pretty bold, but how will it end?'

I took the copy of *Komsomolskaya pravda* and read our article. It had a new title, 'On the Road to the Premiere' and had been edited a great deal, but its essence had been preserved. A few days later I returned to Moscow. My wife and I went to the dacha in Serebryannyy Bor and I set out to look for Karpinsky, sensing the worst. Karpinsky was in bed with his wife, although it was not yet seven in the evening. He came out, yawning and stretching, and with his usual haughty laugh, said, 'There's been such a furore here! They say Brezhnev himself is angry at the article. It's already been discussed by the editorial board. I said that it was your idea primarily, but that I should be punished and not you . . .'

The next day the deputy editor of the paper called me in. He said that at four o'clock there would be a meeting of the editorial board at which the article would be discussed. He assured me that there was nothing to worry about, as only some minor punishment was being envisaged. We would be given an administrative reprimand for publishing the article on the side without our editor's permission.

I still do not know whether this was a provocation or whether he himself did not know of the 'trial' that was being prepared for us. If I had suspected what was to happen at the editorial board meeting I would, of course, have tried to delay it, especially as I was still on leave and not obliged to come in. Having been misled, Karpinsky and I appeared at the meeting, at which, as I recall, fourteen people were present.

It was all very formal. After a short and sharp introduction from Zimyanin, who with his contortions and grimaces condemned our article as a major political error, he invited each person to put forward his position and express his opinion. A proper auto-da-fé ensued. One after the other the members of the editorial board got up and delivered accusatory speeches. None of the speeches quoted the article. They were couched in general terms and it sounded like a verdict was being passed. Therefore, they were all much the same.

I cannot remember now who said what. Only two people took a different position. The first was Georgy Kunitsyn, head of the paper's section on literature and the arts. He not only spoke out against the criticism but threw in a careless phrase: 'What is this – a return to 1937? I don't understand and I don't accept this and I would like to protest strongly against this trial.' The other person was Yury Voronov, the editorial staff's executive secretary. He said virtually nothing, neither for nor against, but abstained from voting. At a very tense moment in the discussion Zimyanin was unexpectedly called away to the government telephone. Karpinsky and I had no doubt that our fate was being discussed. He was absent for about an hour. He came back looking confused and, therefore, even more embittered.

'It has been proposed,' he said, and his eyes flashed with hostility, either at the authors of the article or at those who had placed this heavy burden of decision on him, 'it has been proposed that the question of releasing Burlatsky and Karpinsky from their posts be put before the Central Committee of the Communist Party.'

I felt as if I had been struck by lightning. I don't know how I remained seated. I can honestly say that it had never entered my head that they would retaliate in this way. I loved my work as a political observer and felt really happy for the first time, taking a childlike pleasure in every article. To be deprived of a forum at that moment seemed to me like death itself. In a moment of weakness I said that although I did not really understand what the accusation consisted of, as practically the whole editorial board had spoken out against our publication I was asking to be given the opportunity of remaining at my job on *Pravda*.

I rang Aleksander Yakovlev, who then held the post of first deputy in the agitation and propaganda department of the Central Committee. He immediately picked up the other phone in his room – the special government telephone – and spoke to someone, saying that Karpinsky and I should not be punished so harshly. He spoke loudly so that I could hear his words, but the response he received was apparently negative. I still do not know to whom he spoke, but it was most probably an aide to either Brezhnev or Suslov.

Karpinsky behaved in a more relaxed way. He had for some time felt oppressed by his work on the paper. In particular, he did not want to be in charge of the agitation and propaganda section and not long before had been transferred at his request to head the cultural section, whose functions were unclear. Perhaps because of this, or for some other reason, he spoke out quite sharply and critically at the accusations directed at us. However, the editorial board's decision, dictated from above, was categorical. Karpinsky and I wrote out a joint explanation, as well as separate ones which we had agreed upon. Because I valued my work on *Pravda*, Karpinsky agreed that I explain what had in effect happened regarding the publication, that it had to all intents and purposes not been submitted for my approval at the last stage. I regret to this day that I succumbed to the temptation of adding this explanation, even though it was true.

I also showed another weakness. I rang Andropov and asked him to help me stay on at the newspaper. Andropov advised me to appeal to Suslov and I understood then who had been primarily behind this action. I did write to Suslov with the same request, but it remained unanswered. A few days later – very quickly – a decision was taken by the Central Committee. And that is how a political observer, who has the status of first deputy editor of *Pravda*, and a member of the editorial board were released from their posts in connection with the publication of an article in *Komsomolskaya pravda*. Boris Pankin, who had approved the article but had been abroad when it was published, returned and stated that he knew nothing about it. Several others at the paper were punished, but Pankin subsequently was promoted on Suslov's recommendation. *Komsomolskaya pravda* published a leader condemning our article on behalf of the paper and the Komsomol Central Committee. The ripples spread wider and wider and the case became a sensation, which was written about abroad and was reported on the foreign radio stations broadcasting to the Soviet Union.

This was the first stern warning to journalists and the intelligentsia. The reprisal had been swift and severe. Other reprisals followed. A few months later Kunitsyn was expelled from *Pravda* and Voronov was sent off as a correspondent to East Germany, where he lived for almost thirteen years as if in exile.

In the meantime I was invited to see Zimyanin. Only later did I learn that he had wanted to offer me the job of correspondent in Poland. However, by this time I had fully recovered from the first shock and had told that same deputy editor who was behind the provocation to make sure we appeared at the auto-da-fé, to tell Zimyanin he could go to . . . (and an unprintable word followed). I was naive enough to add, 'We'll see what happens after the next party congress; we'll see then where you'll be and where those you've purged will be.'

Zimyanin became even more embittered. Having set out on this path he could not stop. More than ten talented journalists were dismissed from the paper over the next few years because they could not come to terms with the Brezhnev era. Among them were Yegor Yakovlev, G. Lisichkin, Yu. Chernichenko, A. Volkov and others. I went into 'exile' as a research fellow at the Academy of Sciences thanks to the fact that I had been confirmed as a doctor of philosophical sciences.

My phone stopped ringing. Previously to that everyone, or at least a great number of people, had needed me and I had tried to do everything

I could for those who asked me for help. On the whole, I was not unusual in this. Kindness is natural to the majority of Russian and other Soviet people. In the West I have often met very responsive and charitable Christians of a messianic frame of mind. Their kindness differs from the kindness of the Russians, proceeding more from a sense of duty, while ours comes from the soul. Our people are much better than our ideology or our laws or our system. This is an important guarantee of change for the better.

I used to get calls from members of the leadership of the country and endless calls from editorial boards. I had felt like a cog in the state machine, necessary for it to revolve. Suddenly, there was complete silence. Even close friends, even the consultants whom I had brought into the Central Committee stopped ringing.

Why? Did they fear the phones were tapped? Were they unable to help? Did they think I had broken the rules of the game? Arbatov once said to me, 'You shouldn't have done it. Not to mention the fact that you nearly prevented me from being appointed director of the Institute.'

In fact, Arbatov behaved better than most. He told me about a conversation he had with Brezhnev about me. It had taken place as they were driving back from one of the dachas out of town. Brezhnev was at the wheel and Arbatov was in the front seat. He told Brezhnev about me and my talents as a speechwriter. Leonid Ilyich asked kindly, 'Why not recruit him to do my speeches?' I don't know what Arbatov replied, but nobody tried to recruit me. Among Brezhnev's aides the general opinion was that 'Fedor considers this too trivial for him; he doesn't want to write speeches but prefers to cash in on his books.' Part of it was true; I did not want to write for Brezhnev. But I did participate in preparing Kosygin's speeches at the Twenty-Fifth and Twenty-Sixth Party Congresses. By doing this I dropped even further in Brezhnev's estimation and in that of his entourage.

How did Andropov react to my drama? With great caution. He feared that his long-standing enemy Suslov would make use of my 'reckless' articles against him. But in 1968 an aide of Andropov's, who had known me from our joint work in the Central Committee, proposed at the request of his boss that I write an article in *Pravda* and guaranteed that it would be published. Yury Vladimirovich set a condition, however. I had to speak out unambiguously in support of our action against Dubček and the sending of our troops into Czechoslovakia. I refused, and thus for many years lost my chance to be 'rehabilitated' or to receive any real support from Andropov. When in subsequent years I was twice removed from my posts – in 1972 and 1975 – I could no longer turn to Andropov for support.

★

I first met Andrey Dmitriyevich Sakharov sometime at the end of 1970. I cannot remember exactly when, but it must have been then because I gave him my book *Lenin, the State and Politics*, which came out at the end of that year. It was Yakov Borisovich Zeldovich's idea that we should meet. I had been friendly with Zeldovich for a number of years and we often played tennis together and visited each other. One day Zeldovich suggested I get in touch with Sakharov.

Andrey Dmitriyevich had written a pamphlet entitled 'Reflections on Progress, Peaceful Coexistence and Intellectual Freedom', which had already been published abroad, and the reason for the visit was to talk to him about it. Not long before, I had given Zeldovich a copy of a long paper called 'A Plan for Universal Peace: Utopia or Reality?' which I had given at a sociology conference in Varna in 1970. Zeldovich liked the paper, especially the section where I argued that universal peace, which was a synonym for the prevention of thermonuclear catastrophe, was a value common to all mankind – it was the supreme value that stood higher than national, class or other values of any state or nation. Zeldovich was also impressed by my appeal for cooperation between scientists from all over the world and, in particular, by my proposal that scientists from East and West should draw up a plan for universal peace, involving stage-by-stage disarmament, an end to the nuclear arms race and a transition to what I called a planned peace.

'You know,' Yakov Borisovich said to me, 'I think that some of your ideas are very similar to Andrey Dmitriyevich's. It worries me that he is surrounded by consultants who are not very competent. As he's started working on political problems it would probably be useful for him to hear your professional opinion. I could arrange for you to meet him.'

At that time I was in a difficult position: I was not allowed to go abroad and my articles were not being published. The paper mentioned above, which was published by the United Nations, did not get into the Soviet press. Nevertheless, I decided to go and see Sakharov, although I assumed that in some organizations this would go down as another black mark in my file. So, having phoned Andrey Dmitriyevich, I arrived at his small two-storey house not far from the Academy of Sciences Institute of Nuclear Problems. Andrey Dmitriyevich was at home alone; he welcomed me cordially, offered me tea and biscuits and for the next two and a half hours we talked, mainly about his ideas in the pamphlet, which Zeldovich had given me to read beforehand in a manuscript copy.

It is worth remembering that at that time Sakharov was not the person we have become used to over the past twenty years. I knew of him as the creator of the thermonuclear bomb, a prominent physicist in our country and a man who had been awarded the Hero of Socialist Labour three times. We knew very little about his public activities or his political ideas. Therefore, his pamphlet produced an even stronger impression on me. I had never read anything like it by a Soviet author. It was a manifesto that presented a truly liberal, original and unparalleled view of all aspects of the world today, an understanding that seemed to emanate from somewhere on high. When my article on a planned peace was rejected by a Moscow journal the editor, who was from the party apparatus, said that it attempted to speak 'above the fray'. If that was the case then Sakharov's pamphlet was not simply 'above the fray' but more like the words of an emissary of Providence, who was fulfilling either the will of history or God's word. Such was the tone of his pamphlet. It was impossible and even meaningless to assess it within a narrow professional framework. It was a view cast from the cosmic heights over humanity and its conflicts everywhere on the globe, which at the same time appealed in a lucid, unhysterical way to us all to come to our senses before it was too late.

Most of all I was struck by Andrey Dmitriyevich himself. His slow, halting speech, which seemed to be drawing sounds and ideas from some extremely deep well, his thin voice which seemed impossible to attribute to the man who had created the most monstrous weapon of mass destruction in history, his absolute certainty of the truth of his ideas – all this created the impression that one was in the presence of a prophet and seer, rather than a mere earthly being. In this he sharply differed from Zeldovich. My first meeting with Yakov Borisovich had also produced a strong impression on me. I felt I was communicating with a brilliantly organized machine. I had never met a man who could formulate his views in such a precise and complete form; moreover, he was very quick, as if he had prepared in advance specially worked out scientific formulae to deal with all aspects of life. Whatever the subject – domestic or foreign policy, human relationships, tennis or love – Yakov Borisovich would shoot out his formulae and they would be delineated with the precision of bricks in a building. This amazed me and I saw it as a sign of a remarkable mind.

Sakharov's method of thinking was quite the opposite. He spoke in a faltering voice as if uncertain, reflecting deep in himself. His sentences were stumbling and unpolished, but his thoughts were absolutely precise. His manner deceived me at first. I did not think it would be difficult to influence him, to persuade him to change the wording of his ideas a bit or even to express them in a different way. I soon realized that this was a hopeless endeavour. Andrey Dmitriyevich was one of those people who, once convinced of something, would stand by it to the end. He also had little concern for details and was not inclined to make small corrections which, he thought, would break the harmony of his newly constructed thoughts.

What did we talk about? We began with an issue that Andrey

Dmitriyevich had always considered especially important: the convergence of the two social systems – capitalism and socialism. He had written that these systems had played a drawn game, especially in the military sphere. They had proved their strength and it was now time to stop the military contest, which had become dangerous and pointless. By convergence he meant that both parties should use what was best in both systems. The two systems had played a 'fifty-fifty' role – he liked using this American expression – and it was now time to consider how they could enrich each other instead of fighting each other.

I put forward a slightly different view. Like others, in particular Western liberal scholars of that time, I adhered to the idea of convergence, but I considered that its advantage to us lay in using all the best achievements of modern civilization, not only in industrial development and in science and technical progress, but in the sphere of education, culture and democratic values. Therefore, I advocated the concept of a 'convergence of civilizations', rather than a 'convergence of systems'. Moreover, I had deep doubts that the West in its turn would really want to utilize our experience on equal terms, that is, to meet us half-way along the road of social development.

My arguments, however, did not impress Andrey Dmitriyevich. He even paid little heed to the idea that we were only on a par in the military sphere and not at all in industrial development or in particular in living standards. The idea of convergence was very important to him as the foundation of a logical system, in which the new needs of this process were reflected. The culmination of this system was world government. Andrey Dmitriyevich was convinced that such a government would inevitably arise no later than 1984. I remember I expressed serious doubts about the possibility of such a world government not only in this century but in the foreseeable future or even in the next century. Moreover, I felt that a world government in the context of our modern, differentiated communities would inevitably be totalitarian or even fascist. I had expressed these views in my pamphlet on planning global peace even before meeting Andrey Dmitriyevich.

However, Andrey Dmitriyevich was adamant on this issue as well. He was firmly convinced that only a world government would be able to prevent a nuclear war and resolve other problems common to mankind. He believed that the logic of history would lead mankind to this common denominator. I could not help joking and said we should bet a box of Armenian brandy against a bottle of mineral water if we lived to 1984 and could check out his hypothesis of a world government.

In 1988 Andrey Dmitriyevich and I happened to be in France at the same time and we held a joint press conference at the Soviet Embassy in Paris. The attention of the journalists was, of course, fixed on Sakharov, although I also expressed my views on a number of issues.

After the press conference I turned to Andrey Dmitriyevich and reminded him that he owed me a bottle of mineral water. He did not remember our light-hearted bet, but when I reminded him he said, 'I have no doubt about the idea – it's simply a matter of time, and time does not lend itself to accurate prediction.'

Who knows, perhaps Andrey Dmitriyevich was right. When we hear from the lips of such an important politician as François Mitterrand, the President of France, that it is possible to create a federation embracing Western and Eastern Europe Sakharov's idea of a world government no longer sounds so utopian, even though of course it is still not very likely historically.

During that conversation with Andrey Dmitriyevich we dwelt on the question of how to influence the Soviet leadership. I suggested that, first and foremost, Sakharov should form a lobby of nuclear scientists, men such as Zeldovich, Khariton, Flyorov, Aleksandrov and others. I argued that if he managed to get the support of such a group of influential scientists he would be able to talk directly to Brezhnev and other Soviet leaders. Sakharov doubted this and told me of his attempts to influence Khrushchev, in particular his proposal to put a total stop to nuclear weapons testing, which Khrushchev had rejected. He said that he had sent appeals to Brezhnev and other Soviet leaders which had gone unanswered and had only caused irritation. Andrey Dmitriyevich added with bitterness that it would be hard to unite a sufficiently influential group of scientists as they were divided amongst themselves by scientific rivalry and different political views.

I had also put forward the idea of setting up an international lobby of scientists, who could put pressure on their governments to end the arms race. Andrey Dmitriyevich listened to this proposal very attentively. I think he had thought about it before. Anyway, soon after, I learned that he had sent Brezhnev and other leaders a memorandum in which he put forward a number of important ideas to limit and halt the arms race and to resolve many other problems.

But he did not believe in the effectiveness of these methods, and he proved to be right.

'I will do it my own way,' he said. 'I think that the fate of individuals is the most important thing. Any theory, view or position is tested out on them. General concepts are only valuable in politics when they have a real influence on the human condition and human rights.'

This simple and lucid view amazed me. I tended to think of reform as being more concerned with changing the structure of political and social institutions and less with the fate of specific individuals. I realized at the time that I had met an exceptional thinker, one of the greatest liberal thinkers of our century. Nor did Andrey Dmitriyevich respond with distrust to my proposal to set up a union of scientists, mainly atomic physicists, of the USSR and USA, East and West, who would prepare plans and proposals to strengthen global peace. I was, frankly, very worried about one thing: how Andrey Dmitriyevich's past work in creating the most frightening weapon for the destruction of mankind could be reconciled with his absolutely selfless devotion to the ideals of humanity and goodness. I knew that Sakharov was the first in the world to make the hydrogen bomb, which was a hundred times more destructive than the atomic bomb. I also knew that J. Robert Oppenheimer, head of the Manhattan Project, had consciously applied the brakes on making a hydrogen bomb in the United States, as advocated by Edward Teller. I knew that Petr Leonidovich Kapitsa had even refused to take part in making the atom bomb and for a long time remained under house arrest in his dacha in Nikolina Gora. I also knew that Niels Bohr had refused to take part in making the atom bomb and made desperate efforts to prevent its use and any military contest in this area with the Soviet Union. Back in 1944 he had visited Franklin Roosevelt and Winston Churchill to persuade them to reveal the secret of the atom bomb to the Soviet Union and nip in the bud the very possibility of a nuclear contest. They rejected Bohr's project, but his stance was a moral example to all scientists.

I was itching to ask Andrey Dmitriyevich how he felt today about his part in making atomic and hydrogen weapons, but I did not dare. After our meeting I put this question to Zeldovich. He shrugged his shoulders, gave me a meaningful look and said, 'I am surprised that a person so closely connected with politics can ask such naive questions. Nuclear weapons are the result of technical progress, which nobody anywhere can stop.'

I did not continue the discussion, although it has remained for me a matter of personal choice, which each scholar has to make. In the end many physicists preferred to study the stars rather than create weapons as powerful as a thousand suns for the destruction of all living creatures on earth.

Not long before Andrey Dmitriyevich's death I read his answer to this question in the journal *Ogonyok*. I realized that prominent scientists on both sides of the ocean had been convinced that the making of atomic weapons by competing countries would act as a deterrent, despite its threatening nature. In some way they proved to be right, although I have my own view on this.

Despite my doubts, the meeting with Sakharov influenced me greatly. The persecution and vilification of Andrey Dmitriyevich, which began soon after and in which hundreds of his colleagues willingly or unwillingly participated, was one of the most disgraceful episodes of Brezhnev's regime. Sakharov's unyielding stand set an example for everyone who did not wish to be reconciled to the collapse of Khrushchev's Thaw.

Now, twenty years later, when the whole panorama of the life of this solitary fighter against tyranny spreads out before the eyes of our generation and we remember how he stood out not only against the foolishness and cruelty of power but against the servility and prejudice that gripped almost the whole of society, we see this great figure with different eyes. Whatever the internal path which led him to his insights, the greatness of his deeds has staggered everyone. Sakharov is not simply a personality but a public institution that gathers around itself all that is honest and truthful in us. His untimely death is an irreplaceable loss to the public movement, which has placed the simple norms of morality higher than politics.

I think that Goethe's words best fit Andrey Dmitriyevich: that one must strive for what is impossible in order to achieve what is possible. This is what distinguished his public activity from our professional work, which was most often based on the principle that politics is the art of the possible. In the final analysis, the ideas Sakharov defended – convergence, a world government, the direct transition to Western democracy, morality as the only criterion of politics – greatly influenced public consciousness.

*

I expect it will be of interest to the reader to know what happened to our group of consultants. Arbatov and Bovin continued to work as speechwriters under Brezhnev and even became his very closest advisers. They were voted onto the Central Committee and became deputies in the highest organs of power. The former headed a very prominent academic institute and received the tital of academician. The latter was awarded the State Prize for his part as consultant on a film about Afghanistan. They were talented and, on the whole, progressive men, who thought that as politicians they were obliged to play the role of shock-absorbers against the conservative course Brezhnev had taken.

As for me, I experienced, perhaps, some of the best years of my life. No one would publish my articles and over the next four years, from 1967–71, I was not allowed to go abroad, not even to the socialist countries. Thus, I was able to engage myself fully in what I had always dreamed of in my youth. Over the next three years I wrote several books, including *Lenin, the State and Politics*, a biography of Mao Tse-tung, the sketches on Franco and Hitler and a book on Machiavelli – in short, I continued to blow the anti-Stalinist trumpet.

About three years later I was invited by Rumyantsev, who held the post of vice-president of the USSR Academy of Sciences, to be deputy director of the new Institute of Empirical Sociological Research. We tried to set up sociology as well as political science as disciplines of study. I took temporary revenge for my defeat in *Pravda* by inviting almost all those who had been sacked from the paper by Zimyanin to work as senior research assistants. I started off, of course, with Len Karpinsky. All this was used against me two and a half years later when the Institute of Empirical Sociological Research was closed. More than 140 people were forced to leave the institute and I was the first to be sacked, on Brezhnev's direct instructions. But that is another story.

Thus, all attempts at continuing Khrushchev's anti-Stalinist line came to an end in the political atmosphere under Brezhnev. Of course, this was only one of many struggles that took place. I have described these events not because they were more significant than, say, those that developed around Aleksandr Solzhenitsyn, Bulat Okudzhava, Yevgeny Yevtushenko or Andrey Voznesensky. No, they are interesting in so far as they took place within the political elite, of which much less was and is known.

Subsequently, the lives of the participants in these events took different directions. After yet another organized campaign against me at the Institute of the State and Law of the USSR Academy of Sciences for trying to set up political science as a discipline, I went to work at the Institute of Social Sciences attached to the Party Central Committee, thanks to the patronage of B. Ponomaryov and, in particular, his deputy V. Zagladin. This saved me from being expelled from the party, which was being planned by the Party Control Committee. I worked there for thirteen years awaiting better days.

The whole time I was tormented by the strange thought that Brezhnev would outlive us all. On the eve of his death I had an article published in *Novoye vremya* with the expressive title 'Interregnum', again making use of material from China. Although the similarity was transparent, I put across the view that troubled times, an interregnum, awaited us until such time as a genuine leader and, probably, a reformer came to power in the country.

I gave an analysis of the state-bureaucratic socialist system and its vices and tried to substantiate the necessity and inevitability of structural reforms, the formation of a pluralist economy and a pluralist political system. I spoke with great admiration of Deng Xiao-ping as the first socialist reformer. This was on the eve of Yury Andropov's accession to power. When he became General Secretary he remembered me and offered to give me back my job as political observer. The spark of kindness towards me, which had burned back in the sixties, had never been extinguished from his heart.

So one day early in the morning I was asked urgently to ring M. Zimyanin, who had remained ideology secretary in the Central Committee. I rang and heard his secretary speak a few words before

Zimyanin literally grabbed the receiver. In his usual shrill and sharp voice he asked, 'Can you come to the Central Committee now?'

I answered fairly calmly and collectedly, 'Yes, I suppose I can.'

'Come, then.'

Zimyanin, still the same fidgety person, met me without his jacket, wearing a green synthetic cardigan buttoned from top to bottom.

'There is an instruction,' he said, pointing up to the ceiling, 'to give you back your post as political observer. How do you feel about it?'

'I have moved away from journalistic work,' I said calmly. 'Where do you suggest I go? To *Pravda*?'

'No, I very much ask you not to insist on that. If you returned to *Pravda* that would mean that *Pravda* was apologizing to you and that is impossible. You must realize that. I ask you not to bring up the question of *Pravda*.'

Then I asked Zimyanin to create a similar post on *Literaturnaya gazeta* (there had not been one there before) and to give me the same rights and powers that I used to have at *Pravda*. Also I asked if I could hold down my other post as head of the faculty of philosophy, as I did not want to break with academic work. Zimyanin immediately agreed and a few days later everything had been resolved. It seemed that justice had triumphed, but it had taken fifteen years . . .

By this time Khrushchev had already died, and there was no one I could tell how I had suffered for being faithful to what had been best in his politics and how I had taken my small revenge. Soon afterwards Yury Andropov died and Chernenko came to power.

*

I would like to add some concluding remarks about Andropov as a political leader. Earlier in the book I tried to give a sketch of him based almost exclusively on the time I worked with him in the Central Committee apparatus. This was during Khrushchev's Thaw when people like Andropov showed their best colours. It was an era that not only permitted but encouraged this. I have also tried to convey my feelings as a young man full of enthusiasm. Having become infatuated in turn by Belyakov and Kuskov, it is no wonder that I was especially drawn to Andropov, who was the most outstanding figure in my field of vision. Perhaps it was the admiration of one who considered himself to be no more than a political adviser for someone who already appeared to be one of the country's leaders.

What was particularly impressive about him was his talent for making quick, operational and accurate decisions.

But today I have the chance to look at him anew, taking into account his subsequent actions. His career still needs to be thoroughly researched, of course. We do not yet have access to that period of more than fifteen years when Andropov headed the KGB. We know very little about the part he played in Czechoslovakia in 1968 or the decision to send troops to Afghanistan, or the military and intelligence operations that were carried out there. We know hardly anything about his attitude to dissidents, to Sakharov's exile or Solzhenitsyn's persecution. Nevertheless, I shall still try to give a general assessment of this man who was destined, if only for a short period, to become the fifth leader of the Soviet Union.

Andropov belonged to Khrushchev's or, one could say, Brezhnev's generation of Soviet leaders. I should point out that I had very little personal contact with Andropov after my dramatic departure from his department early in 1965; only a number of personal meetings and a few fleeting conversations. I remember two meetings best of all. The first was accidental and occurred in the Party Central Committee building when I was preparing material for the speech Kosygin was to give at the Twenty-Sixth Party Congress in 1981. I had been recruited several times to draft his speeches and this meeting, as far as I remember, was connected with Andropov's comments on Kosygin's speech. Andropov did not seem to be in the best physical form; he was agitated and spoke quickly and nervously, which was not at all like he had been in the past. One thing he said struck me. Turning around he said quite unexpectedly, 'You know, I worry every time Leonid Ilyich travels through the streets of Moscow!'

I could not restrain myself and threw a surprised, even flabbergasted look at him. He suddenly wagged his finger at me and said, 'That's your sort. You've never understood what it means to feel responsible for every matter you are entrusted with.'

His words about Brezhnev rang in my ears for a long time. I could not believe that he was really worried about the security of this weak, old leader. I still cannot understand what impelled him to say this and why to me. For me it was a sign that Yury Vladimirovich had changed. Did he really identify himself so closely with his role as protector of the head of state? Had it become a habit to demonstrate his devotion to Brezhnev? Whatever the reason this was a different Andropov, though even in his younger days he was known for his respectful attitude to the leadership. I had noticed this many times. Although he used to put up patiently with the jokes we consultants freely made on a wide range of topics, as soon as we mentioned Khrushchev or the other leaders barriers would shoot up. But to reveal his inner anxiety for the 'Gen-Sec' in a private conversation when there was practically no reason for it is something I could not comprehend.

The other meeting was connected with the drafting of his article for the journal *Kommunist*. On becoming General Secretary of the party, Yury Vladimirovich decided to make his first and, in some respects, keynote statement. I was one of the people recruited to prepare the materials for this article. Its main points were the need to overcome the backwardness in technology and the standard of living, to strengthen order and discipline in the economy and to fight corruption and irresponsibility. The first draft contained a number of important ideas about developing the cooperative movement in towns and in the countryside and introducing democratic forms of leadership in state enterprises – in short, it tended towards the Leninist ideals of the NEP period. However, the article fell into the hands of *Kommunist*'s ideologists, who changed the thrust of it. The main emphasis was placed on state power, state control and discipline, although in places it retained elements of a wider dialectical view on the processes of economic and social development in the country.

What was Andropov's programme as leader of the party and state? To what extent was it a new programme and his own? It is difficult to give a clear answer because his serious illness did not really allow him to define his aims, plans and directives. Most of all he was anxious to clean up the Augean stables of society: the shadow economy, bribery, the bureaucracy of the state apparatus and the everyday violation of order and discipline. But none of this could take the place of a programme of political change. The idea of deep structural reform was already in the air and, moreover, Andropov was well acquainted with reform from Khrushchev's Thaw. But it is hardly likely that he was prepared for a sharp turn towards a new way of thinking.

What can we say was especially characteristic of this leader, given the fragmented information we have regarding his position during the critical period from 1960–80?

In my opinion his strongest point was his businesslike character, which augmented his astute perception of the political side of every problem. A businesslike character is fairly rare among Russians and particularly among Soviet leaders. As Russia never had any significant experience of capitalist development it tended to cultivate two types of leaders: ideological or military. The ideologists were distinguished by their predilection for verbosity, and propaganda often became a substitute for politics. This was true for the majority of Lenin's Politburo. It is no wonder that Lenin rated organizational talent so highly when he discovered it in, for example, Sverdlov or Stalin. Khrushchev, as I have already noted, had an extraordinary tendency to hold forth on ideological matters.

This characteristic was totally absent in Andropov. If necessary he could give a clear and brilliant speech, but he did this extremely rarely. He valued practical decisions above all and scrupulously checked that everything had been done according to plan. He skilfully selected those with executive talents and repeatedly checked their efficiency.

Organizational talent was probably the most admirable feature of this leader of our country.

The ability to penetrate deep into the heart of any political problem was second nature to him. He thought only in political categories. Whether the issue was collective farms, enterprises, party organizations or any event in Eastern Europe or the West, his assessment was always political; that is, he appraised matters from the point of view of state policy and the impact any event or decision would have on its interests.

Casting a glance over Andropov's record during the Brezhnev period I am forced to remember weaknesses which I observed during the Khrushchev years. He belonged to the generation of wartime Soviet leaders. I think this determined his world outlook and particularly his attitude to Eastern Europe, China, the West and developing countries. This generation thought in the following terms: we have won the bloodiest of wars and sacrificed an enormous number of victims on the altar of victory; hence we are obliged to retain and increase everything that we gained thereby. Above all, this applied to Eastern Europe. As far as I remember Andropov, like Khrushchev and even Stalin, regarded these countries as gains resulting from the Second World War and what had been gained at such a high cost was the socialist camp. They were our allies and our buttress and defined our place and the place of socialism in the world.

This approach goes back to Lenin's interpretation of world revolution. Lenin considered the October Revolution to be the proletariat's first volley against the bastions of capitalism. For a long time afterwards he believed that the revolution would break out in other countries at any time. Only at the beginning of the twenties did Lenin begin to re-evaluate the situation and decide on the transition from War Communism to NEP within the country and a policy of peaceful coexistence outside it. In Stalinist ideology the idea of world revolution and breaking off countries and peoples piece by piece from the capitalist camp combined with traditional Russian imperialist thinking. Stalin did not distinguish between the state interests of Soviet Russia and the interests of world socialism. Khrushchev, who to a large extent discarded the Stalinist method of dealing with the socialist countries and the West, nevertheless retained his loyalty to the main ideological principle that the socialist camp was our world and the capitalist camp was not – although some day it too would be 'ours'.

Of course, Andropov's view of the process of world development was more comprehensive than Khrushchev's, but in essence he shared the same approach. This can be seen in Andropov's attitude to Hungary in 1956, to Czechoslovakia in 1968 and, in particular, to the sending of troops to Afghanistan. The ideology of two opposing camps, the class war over spheres of influence between the USSR and the USA, the inadmissibility of retreating from positions that had been gained in different regions of the world, the use of any methods, including military ones, in the interests of defending the revolution abroad and our state interests (these were usually intertwined) – such was the range of Andropov's political thinking. He seemed to be moving towards a view of the world based on common human values, but he never crossed the boundaries set way back at the beginning of our revolution.

Such a view can easily be called 'imperialist' if we admit it also applied to Western countries, particularly the United States. It was a fairly typical phenomenon of the Cold War, which was not eliminated either in Khrushchev's or Brezhnev's times, despite Camp David, the warmer spell after the Cuban Missile Crisis and the results of the Helsinki Conference in 1975. West and East remained on different sides of the barricades and the leaders, both there and here, remained captive to similar notions.

When I recall accompanying Andropov on visits to Yugoslavia and Hungary I am overwhelmed by contradictory feelings. On the one hand, I observed Andropov's enormous interest in reforms in Yugoslavia and particularly in Hungary. I remember that during the visit to Hungary he painstakingly wrote down everything we were told about changes in the economy, in the planning bodies, in enterprises, the freer formation of prices, genuine cooperatives in the Hungarian countryside, the democratic methods of party work and so on. I had the impression that he considered this experience extremely important and useful to us. When he came to power I thought he would implement reforms on the Hungarian model. On the other hand, I observed that whatever the circumstances the most important thing for him was Eastern Europe's loyalty to its obligations under the Warsaw Pact. In all circumstances our allies' obligations were of primary importance, while domestic changes were considered to be connected with these obligations and to a certain extent derived from them.

It is particularly difficult for me to reconcile my understanding of Andropov with the facts that have become generally known today of his direct involvement in the decision to send troops to Afghanistan. Two points seemed strange to me: the fundamentally mistaken attitude that Soviet troops could be used abroad when there were no serious grounds for believing that the defence of our country was at stake; and the totally unrealistic appraisal of the situation in Afghanistan. I expect Andropov would have found it difficult to argue against Brezhnev's position when the sending of troops had undoubtedly already received the support of Gromyko and Ustinov. But how could Andropov, with his enormous political experience, including the grim experience of participating in events in Hungary in 1956 and his wide knowledge of the very complicated problems of national revolutions in developing countries

– how could he have so mistakenly assessed the situation in Afghanistan? One can only assume that the views and personality of this exceptional man were eroded over the long years of Brezhnev's regime.

Andropov did not yield to the spreading influence of corruption which embraced almost all levels of the political structure in Brezhnev's times. On the contrary – and this became known after he came to power – he gathered information and files on all the abuses committed by the party and state apparatus. He did not seek personal rewards, although in his later years he received the title of Hero of Socialist Labour and the rank of general in the army. However, constrained by ideas of 'preventive', 'precautionary' actions to avert social, political and national conflicts, he undoubtedly carried out repressions against dissidents and many outstanding cultural figures who were expelled from the country. It is true that Yury Lyubimov right up to the end of his days as director of the Taganka Theatre saw Andropov as his last hope, the only person capable of responding to his productions in an objective and sympathetic way. Lyubimov told me that himself, although I cannot say that it did him any good. Most likely it didn't.

But as far as foreign policy was concerned, especially relations with Eastern Europe and the developing countries, Andropov changed for the worse under Brezhnev. This is only comprehensible if we remember his painful experience in Yugoslavia and Hungary.

I have often been asked whether Andropov, if he had lived longer, would have become a reformer and proclaimed the new thinking. It is hard to say, but it is obvious from his past, his way of thinking and his system of values that he was ill-prepared for such a role.

*

At the April 1985 plenum Mikhail Sergeyevich Gorbachev became General Secretary of the Central Committee of the Communist Party of the Soviet Union. A new era began. We were happy to have lived to see this moment and immediately got down to work, trying to build a bridge from Khrushchev's Thaw to the new and inspiring prospects of structural, economic and political reform.

Interestingly, four members of our consultancy group have been elected people's deputies – Shakhnazarov, Bogomolov, Arbatov and myself, and three have become heads of sub-committees in the USSR Supreme Soviet.* Gennady Gerasimov headed the press department of the Ministry of Foreign Affairs from 1986–90 and is famous through-

---

* In addition, Shakhnazarov is an aide to the President, and Arbatov and Bogomolov are members of the Consultative Council to Boris Yeltsin, Chairman of the Supreme Soviet of the Russian Federation.

out the world. I have been elected a member of the Supreme Soviet and head of the sub-committee on humanitarian, scientific and cultural cooperation within the framework of the Committee for International Affairs.

Was this accidental or a recompense for our ordeals during the Brezhnev period? It is hard to say. But whether or not this is the case, justice has triumphed and it has happened in our lifetime – a rare thing indeed. Evidently there is some logic after all to the political process. Different policies call for suitable people to implement them. It is no accident that I was called in the period of Khrushchev when I was so young, naive and inexperienced, although full of anti-Stalinist passion; and it is no accident that I was pushed aside, suppressed and 'put in my place' in the Brezhnev years; and it is no accident that I have been brought back under Gorbachev. Everything in the right season. Time is something which works for us or against us. You need patience and faith to be certain that your time has not yet passed.

Arbatov once told the poet Boris Slutsky (perhaps with bitterness), 'Fedor will never return to serious politics.' He did not believe then that there would be new times, absorbed as he was in serving and striving to bring common sense to Brezhnev's speeches and actions. Besides, Arbatov has always been distinguished for his kindliness and humanitarianism. He helped people when he could. And, of course, Arbatov is a real professional. I think that in this he is not inferior to Kissinger, whose career has probably always stood as the summit of his desires. Therefore, although he had to stand as a candidate twice in different constituencies, in the end he was elected a people's deputy. Perhaps he has overcome the biggest obstacle in what has been, on the whole, a very successful political career.

The Brezhnev period was a difficult ordeal for our group, as well as for other groups of advisers. It was not just the very great temptation of joining a corrupt system of state theft and waste. It was even more complicated for people who could not but lead an active political life to find a niche for themselves. Who was right? Was I right in throwing down a challenge or were those people right who continued to serve the new god in the hope of absorbing the shocks of his negative influence on society and bringing an element of culture and progress to his policies? I don't know; it is a hard question to answer.

During the years I was ostracized I watched with growing irritation how the careers of many advisers advanced rapidly, how they became academicians and members of higher party and state bodies by succumbing to inevitable compromises. Today my hand does not rise to cast stones at them. Politics is a special game, not delicate or moral. The political animal frequently must face a difficult choice – whether to stand on the sidelines or make the best of difficult circumstances, not staking your whole career on one card. Therefore, let us say in the words of Jesus Christ: judge not and thou shalt not be judged. Let each person choose his own road. Time will put everything in its proper place.

I have been reproached for publishing too much in the new Gorbachev era. It is true that in four years I have had a large book, *The New Thinking*, published, my play about the Cuban Missile Crisis, *Black Saturday*, has been staged, I have written several works on *perestroika* ('Two Views from One Office', 'One Year Later' and others) and so on. It is not that I am a prolific writer or that I have a belated desire to return to a political career. It is simply the right time. Independent of the jobs I have held, the time has come to put into effect all that has accumulated in the course of twenty years.

A crisis in one's public life, or if you like, in one's career is often accompanied by domestic crisis. Human nature is such that one seeks compensation for failure, and this draws him even further into the deep. This is what happened to me.

I loved my son Sergey and my younger one, Aleksey, very much and I was spiritually tied to my wife and the whole family. Sergey had a dramatic involvement (or that's how I perceived it) at the same time as I was being persecuted and suppressed. When he had barely turned sixteen he fell in love with his schoolteacher, who was seventeen years older than him, and became virtually estranged from me and the family. My wife, a prominent physicist who loved her work more than her family, could not understand my public struggles and the deep distress I felt over Sergey's fate. The family began to fall apart and I began to lose my footing. All it needed was a slight push from the side, which came from a charming woman who helped me through this emotional anguish. Perhaps one day I will relate the typical drama of a political animal. But I will say right now that during a time of ordeal one should not seek consolation in other things. This is the wrong path to take. Consolation can only be found in oneself, in one's soul, for this is the God that our revolutionary ancestors deprived us of.

As Shakespeare noted, time is stronger than man; it pushes us this way and that, lighting up either our best or worst features. The new Gorbachev era has taken us all back to our youth, to the enthusiasm of Khrushchev's Thaw.

Epilogue: Gorbachev

There is an old saying that a man's character shapes his destiny. Nikita Khrushchev became a victim of his own character, not only of his surroundings. He was unable to overcome his hasty, impetuous, emotional disposition.

One of Khrushchev's advisers told me of a surprisingly astute remark Winston Churchill made to Khrushchev during Khrushchev's and Bulganin's visit to England in 1956. The old British lion said, 'Mr Khrushchev, you are undertaking great reforms. That's good. I would simply advise you not to be too hasty. It's not easy to jump over a precipice in two steps. You might fall in.'

I will be so bold as to add that nor can one jump over a precipice without knowing which side one wishes to land on.

In the old days they said a person gets furthest when he does not know where he is going, when his steps are winding and uneven – either he lurches sharply forward or he is abruptly forced back. Many of Khrushchev's economic and social reforms were like that.

Time has failed to disperse the numerous myths around Khrushchev both here and abroad. Having shared the fate of other reformers, Khrushchev did not win objective recognition in the consciousness of the masses. The people who at one time elevated Ivan the Terrible and condemned Boris Godunov could not, after Stalin, accept a public figure devoid of mystique, an earthly sinful creature susceptible to mistakes and errors. During the Thaw Sholokhov is supposed to have said about Stalin, 'Of course, there was a cult, but there was also a personality.' This was a hidden reproach to Khrushchev. It was a reproach to a person who, like Shakespeare's Claudius, had swiped the throne lying at his feet.

In the meantime the West considered Nikita Khrushchev to be on a par with John F. Kennedy and Pope John XXIII, and the worsening international climate at the end of the sixties was attributed to the fact that these leaders were, for different reasons, no longer in the political arena. Many books came out containing an analysis of 'Khrushchevism' as a new socialist tendency.

One might say that a prophet is without honour in his own country, but that would be inaccurate; the problem is deeper and more complicated. Perhaps Ernst Neizvestny, the sculptor with whom Khrushchev conducted his 'cavalry-charge polemics' at the Manezh, came closer than anyone else in his evaluation of Khrushchev. The sculpture he made for Khrushchev's gravestone – a bronze head on the background of a white and black marble slab – ingeniously symbolizes the contradictions of the Thaw and its main hero.

Now, almost a quarter of a century later, when we compare the periods before and after October 1964, we can see Khrushchev's strengths and weaknesses better. His main achievement was to destroy Stalin's cult of personality. This has proved to be irreversible, despite the stealthy attempts to put the pedestal back in its place. They have not succeeded, which means the plough dug in sufficiently deeply and the ploughman did not toil in vain. The courageous decision to rehabilitate many Communists and non-party members who had been repressed and executed in the period of the cult of personality has restored justice, truth and honour to the party and the state. A powerful blow was inflicted against the arrogance of super-centrism and bureaucracy, even though it was not always effective or appropriate.

Under Khrushchev the foundations were laid for changes in agricultural development: purchase prices were raised, the burden of taxation was sharply reduced and new technology came into use. The opening up of the Virgin Lands, for all its faults, played its part in providing food for the population. Khrushchev tried to make the countryside learn from overseas experience and this was, in effect, the first agricultural revolution. Even his obsession with maize was well-meant, albeit excessive and naive. But gigantomania in the countryside and the reduction of private plots had a harmful effect.

Khrushchev's name is associated with major achievements in science and technology, which helped to lay the foundations for strategic parity. Yury Gagarin's meeting with Khrushchev, marking our country's breakthrough into space, is an image which remains before our eyes. The policy of peaceful coexistence announced at the Twentieth Party Congress became, after the shock of the Cuban Missile Crisis, an increasingly stable platform for establishing agreements and businesslike compromises with the West. We have to go back to the Thaw to find the sources of the Helsinki Agreement, which consolidated the results of the Second World War and proclaimed new international relations, economic cooperation and the exchange of information, ideas and contacts.

It was at this time that the country set out to resolve many social problems. The standard of living of the population in the cities and countryside began to improve gradually. But the intended economic and social reforms came to nothing. The tragic events in Hungary in

273

1956 inflicted a serious blow to the hopes of the reformers. No small part was played by Nikita Sergeyevich's self-confidence and carelessness in matters of theory and political strategy. 'Khrushchevism', as a concept of renewed socialism, failed. If we use an image much loved by the First Secretary's main opponent, Mao Tse-tung, Khrushchev walked on two legs – one boldly striding into the new era, the other helplessly stuck in the mire of the past.

Why did the reforms in the sixties fail? One might answer as follows: the conservative forces got the upper hand over the reformers because the apparatus and, in fact, society as a whole was not yet ready for radical changes. This answer, however, is too general. We have to explain what it was that the conservatives exploited.

I think one of the mistakes was that the search for a concept of reform and ways to implement it was based on traditional administrative and even bureaucratic methods. Khrushchev usually gave instructions to the ministries and departments to 'work out' economic, cultural or political problems – that is, to that very administrative apparatus which was supposed to restrict its own power. After all, the apparatus had always made use of direct, indirect or ambiguous decisions to avoid being controlled.

In both socialist and capitalist countries when reforms have been more or less successful they have usually been put together by a group of specialists, mainly scientists and public figures, who work under the guidance of the leader of the country. This was the case, say, in Hungary, Yugoslavia and China. In Japan I met the professor who engineered the Japanese 'miracle'. In West Germany a plan of reform was drawn up in his time by Professor Erhard, who subsequently became Chancellor of the country.

The second mistake is summed up in the words, 'The people are silent.' Today, glasnost enables us to see clearly how little was done to provide people with information about the past, about real problems and decision-making; not to mention that the general public was excluded from the struggle for reform. How often did I hear people say at the time, 'How is Khrushchev better than Stalin? Under Stalin we had order, bureaucrats were thrown into prison and prices were lowered.' It is no coincidence that by the October 1964 plenum a near majority of the people breathed a sigh of relief and looked forward to favourable changes.

The final lesson relates to Khrushchev himself. This bold and active man with a naturally acute political mind eventually succumbed to the temptation to listen to hymns in praise of himself. 'Our Nikita Sergeyevich!' – wasn't this the beginning of the fall of this acknowledged fighter against the cult? Hangers-on drowned him in a sea of flattery and eulogy in return for high offices and the highest awards, prizes and ranks. And it is no accident that as things got worse in the country the chorus of hangers-on and flatterers sang more loudly and triumphantly of the successes of 'the glorious decade'.

Khrushchev's main problem, as I see it, is that he was never able fully to drive out of his mind the fanatical idea that the ends justify the means. The Lenin Old Guard believed that it was making a revolution which at any moment would resound throughout the world. The death of several million Whites and Reds was a small sum to pay for the radical reconstruction of the life of all humanity. The Stalinist generation believed that the triumph of Communism in our country and in another dozen or so neighbouring countries was close at hand. Hence, the deaths of ten or twenty million people was necessary and justified. The Khrushchev generation still clung to its belief in the imminent advent of perfect Communism, which was conceived of as universal happiness and peace. Defaming a group of 'insignificant intellectuals' was, therefore, no more than sweeping away debris from the great highway. For the Brezhnev generation the might of the super-state and its thermonuclear arms, capable of intervening in events anywhere in the world, justified privileges, corruption and the suppression of independent thinking. Each new leader experienced a kind of intoxication with the greatness of the task history had assigned him.

It is now becoming clear that *perestroika* offers not distant promises but real changes here and now. It is no longer possible to justify one's inability to resolve problems – whether of food supplies, shops, housing or education – by referring to the scale of impending transformations. What is taking place now is *perestroika*, and what happens later – we'll see.

The withdrawal from Afghanistan is *perestroika*. The treaty on European missiles is *perestroika*. *Glasnost*, the new electoral system, the new institutions of power – all this is *perestroika*.

Today's ends and means affect the fate of hundreds of millions of people. Therefore, each step has to be measured in its own right, not forgetting, of course, the future programme for the renewal of society. For each generation lives on earth only once, alas, and deserves to be treated as an end and not a means.

Communism sprang from the soil of the poverty and deprivation of the masses. For them it was a dream of a well-fed life, of equality in the distribution of welfare, when the rich, the exploiters and the bosses in the person of state bureaucrats would vanish. In Russia it also sprang from a fear of capitalism, hence the yearning to set up a society without a market, without money, with direct distribution – a society without a state. But the Russian tradition of faith in the tsar and in the greatness of the state soon gained the upper hand. It was then that Stalinism appeared. Society stagnated, losing all initiative for development. What is the solution to this?

The solution to this is to form a civil society with a pluralist economy and democracy. Such is the *perestroika* initiated by Gorbachev, who represents our generation, the children of the Twentieth Party Congress.

When travelling abroad I have often been asked what the differences and similarities between Khrushchev and Gorbachev are. It is not easy to answer this question, although I knew Khrushchev and have accompanied Gorbachev abroad four times, including the summits with Reagan in Geneva, Reykjavik and Washington.

What do these two men have in common? In the first place, their personal qualities – vigour, a reforming disposition and an intuitive sense of democracy. They were both born in villages: Gorbachev, moreover, in a Cossack region which still retains its yearning for the Russian tradition of communities of free men who had escaped serfdom. Furthermore, they both represent the social-democratic trend in the party, out of which emerged such figures as Bukharin, Rykov, Rudzutak and Voznesensky. This social-democratic trend never died despite the Stalinist massacres. Indeed, the party was conceived and existed for twenty years as a social-democratic organization and it was only in 1918, intoxicated by the hope of an impending world revolution, that it changed its name to Communist. Its ugly nature was revealed in War Communism under Lenin and in total state supremacy and control under Stalin.

This initial social-democratism, fortified by the expectations of the people and the demands of the economy, lived on. And it is precisely this that explains such apparently inexplicable phenomena as Khrushchev's accession to power after Stalin and Gorbachev's after Brezhnev.

But Gorbachev is very different from Khrushchev. First, in his education – he graduated from Moscow University, the most prestigious university in the country, where he studied in the Faculty of Law, which is particularly important as a political basis. Later he graduated from an agricultural institute. But the most important thing is that he represents the new post-war generation of Soviet leaders, which exhibits a new democratic political culture.

This political culture has two sources. The first is anti-Stalinism, a charge powerful enough for more than one generation. In every honest, thinking person Stalinism cannot but arouse the most fierce hostility, protest, opposition and desire to change radically such a monstrous, inhumane system.

The second is the world today. Under Stalin the country was completely isolated. It bristled against the outside world with its tanks and ideology. Khrushchev opened a window in this world and was the first person, despite the resistance of his own 'class' nature, to ponder

276

the question whether or not everything might be as wonderful as we had thought.

Gorbachev is a man who has his eyes wide open. Not a single major event, not a single significant fact in modern civilization passes him by. He has discovered the whole world and thirsts to open this world to all Soviet people. It is easier for him to do this than it was for Khrushchev, as fate exempted him from involvement in the Stalinist crimes, in the suppression of freedom in Hungary, as well as in sending troops into Czechoslovakia or in the adventurism of Afghanistan.

There is another fact which I find especially surprising. Gorbachev is the first real parliamentary leader in the whole history of Russia. Where he learned this and where this intuition originates, God only knows. He understands and loves democratic work. He has set up the first Soviet parliament and carries through all its reforms underpinned by public opinion, *glasnost* and democracy. He believes not only in reform from above, as did Khrushchev, but in reform from below, one which passes through the soul and life of every person. I hope he will be successful and that the forces of right- and left-wing extremism will not hinder him, hinder us all from embarking upon a new historical path.

Khrushchev, who knew so little of the outside world, was deeply and sincerely convinced of the superiority of our system and, moreover, of his own superiority over Western leaders. He was proud that in his youth he had tended cattle and sheep and that he had working-class roots. He felt sincere contempt for Eisenhower, Kennedy and Adenauer, who had been born into rich families. He was convinced that the worldwide victory of Communism was only a matter of time. In the same way he disliked 'intellectuals', who could be used but never given power.

Gorbachev himself represents the intelligentsia. His political language is up to the highest world standards. The concept of the pluralism of modern civilizations and the search for their mutual enrichment comes naturally to him.

Finally, we now live in a different era. Khrushchev ruled the country during the period of the first thawing of the ice of Stalinism within our country and the Cold War outside it. A society casting off the fetters of Stalinist autocracy found it difficult to understand Khrushchev's uninhibited and brash populism. Almost no one on the political Olympus and very few at its base were ready for Khrushchev's reformism.

We now live in different times. The Brezhnev era had a deeply traumatic effect on public consciousness. There is an awareness not only that we lag behind the rapidly developing outside world, but an acute sense of how disgraceful our lives were. Everyone, regardless of what rung of the social ladder he was on, could see that more often than not those who flourished were the immoral and cunning ones – whether in the service sector, production, the arts and sciences or politics.

Moreover, the ripples and then the surging waves of the technological revolution abroad have begun to reach us. It has washed over boundaries, joined countries and broken ideological stereotypes.

And now spring has arrived: a wonderful time, but a very dangerous one. Its symbol is Gorbachev and his reforms. But as de Tocqueville once said, every person who begins reforms must know that they are fraught with revolution. Our revolution has already cost us fifty million lives. Isn't that enough blood for one country? The transition from Stalin's legacy to a new society is to be found by taking the path of structural reforms, which will bring us step by step to the creation of a modern civil society with a pluralist economic, cultural and political system. Along this road may we be enlightened by what is best in our people and in all the peoples of the earth!

I hope that my book will give readers in the West a better picture of one of the most interesting episodes in the history of our country – the great decade after Stalin. It will help them understand more clearly what is taking place today and what could happen in the future.

There is no mystery to the Russian soul; that is nonsense invented by people who, finding themselves on the sidelines of European civilization, would like to produce some model of life for the whole of humanity. What is real is the history of our country which, like dozens of civilizations today, is agonizingly joining the modern technological revolution. Overcoming decades and centuries of isolation, the legacy of an authoritarian-patriarchal political culture and the vices of statism, it is gradually and spontaneously joining the world community. In some ways its history is like that of other not very developed countries. If it is possible to gain any understanding of the reality that surrounds us then we can understand and explain the Russian phenomenon too.

We will enter the modern world in our own way. We do not want to be the same as others, nor do we want to emphasize our differences. I would like to believe that this world, the world of the twenty-first century, will be propitious both for us and for all mankind.

Notes

CHAPTER THREE: A POPULIST
1. *Rasskaz o pochotnom shakhtyore* (*The Story of an Eminent Miner*), 1961, p. 9.
2. Roy Medvedev, *Khrushchev*, 1986, p. 10.
3. N. S. Khrushchev, *Vospominaniya* (*Memoirs*), ed. V. Chalidze, vol. II, p. 14. All references are to this edition.
4. *Rasskaz* . . ., p. 13.
5. *ibid.*, p. 16.
6. *ibid.*, p. 16.
7. *ibid.*, p. 24.
8. *ibid.*, p. 100.
9. Medvedev., p. 20.
10. See M. Koryakov, *Po stranitsam vospominaniy pervogo sekretarya TsK KPSS* (*Pages from the Reminiscences of the First Secretary of the Central Committee of the CPSU*), pp. 24–6.
11. Khrushchev, *Vospominaniya*, vol. I, p. 4.
12. Koryakov, p. 27.
13. Medvedev, p. 30.
14. Khrushchev, *Vospominaniya*, vol. II, pp. 7, 9.
15. Crankshaw, Edward, *Khrushchev: A Career*, London, 1966, pp. 137–8.
16. Koryakov , pp. 15, 16.

CHAPTER FOUR: STALIN
1. Here and later in this section material comes from the book, *Khrushchev o Staline* (*Khrushchev on Stalin*), New York, 1988.
2. *ibid.*
3. See N. S. Khrushchev's Report at the Twentieth Party Congress of the CPSU (the 'secret speech').
4. *ibid.*
5. See Yu. Aksyutin, *N. S. Khrushchev: Materialy k biografii* (*N. S. Khrushchev: Materials towards a Biography*), 1989, pp. 36, 37.
6. Khrushchev, *Vospominaniya*, vol. I, pp. 92ff.
7. *ibid.*, pp. 92ff.
8. *ibid.*, p. 92.

CHAPTER FIVE: TITO AND KADAR
1. Khrushchev, *Vospominaniya*, vol. II, pp. 160–1.
2. *ibid.*, p. 172.
3. *ibid.*, p. 188.

4. Khrushchev, *Vospominaniya*, vol. II, p. 88.
5. *ibid.*, p. 192.
6. *ibid.*, p. 204.
7. *ibid.*, pp. 212, 213.
8. *ibid.*, pp. 218, 219.
9. *ibid.*, p. 222.
10. *ibid.*
11. *ibid.*, pp. 230–5.
12. *ibid.*
13. *ibid.*
14. *ibid.*
15. Medvedev, p. 46.

CHAPTER SEVEN: A REFORMER
1. *Khrushchev o Staline*, p. 29.
2. *ibid.*
3. S. Pavlov, see *N. S. Khrushchev*, pp. 205–6.
4. *Ogonyok*, no. 28, 1988.
5. Aksyutin, pp. 120–2.
6. Khrushchev, *Vospominaniya*, vol. I, p. 92.
7. See Aksyutin, p. 326.
8. *ibid.*
9. *ibid.*
10. Khrushchev, *Vospominaniya*, vol. II.
11. *ibid.*
12. *ibid.*

CHAPTER EIGHT: EISENHOWER AND KENNEDY
1. Khrushchev, *Vospominaniya*, vol. I, pp. 170–1.
2. *Pravda*, 8 October 1959, 'Rasskaz o shakhtyore' ('Story of a Miner').
3. Khrushchev, *Vospominaniya*, vol. I, pp. 176–8.
4. *ibid.*, p. 159.
5. *ibid.*

CHAPTER NINE: THE CUBAN MISSILE CRISIS
1. Khrushchev, *Vospominaniya*, vol. II, p. 182.
2. Robert Kennedy, *13 Days*, pp. 121–2.

CHAPTER ELEVEN: BREZHNEV
1. Aksyutin, pp. 255–9.
2. *ibid.*, pp. 278–83.

Index